Abstracts from Loudoun County, Virginia
Guardian Accounts

Books A–H

1759–1904

Patricia B. Duncan

HERITAGE BOOKS
2012

HERITAGE BOOKS
AN IMPRINT OF HERITAGE BOOKS, INC.

Books, CDs, and more—Worldwide

For our listing of thousands of titles see our website
at
www.HeritageBooks.com

Published 2012 by
HERITAGE BOOKS, INC.
Publishing Division
100 Railroad Ave. #104
Westminster, Maryland 21157

Copyright © 2000 Patricia B. Duncan

All rights reserved. No part of this book may be reproduced or transmitted in any form or by any means, electronic or mechanical, including photocopying, recording or by any information storage and retrieval system without written permission from the author, except for the inclusion of brief quotations in a review.

International Standard Book Numbers
Paperbound: 978-1-58549-590-0
Clothbound: 978-0-7884-9345-4

GUARDIAN ACCOUNT BOOKS A-H
MAIN ENTRIES

HERYFORD, Henry 1
GRAYSON, William 1
HAGUE, John 1
WILLCOXON, Elizabeth 1
WEST, Cato and Charles 1
HURST, Elizabeth (Orphan of John) 1
MONROE, Rosey 1
CHINN, Rawleigh 1
CHINN, Christopher 1
LANE, Presley Carr 1
POLLARD, Orphans of Thomas 1
OXLEY, Evered 2
MINOR, Ann, John, Nancy and William 2
SHEID, Orphans of James 2
SCOTT, Orphans of Joseph 3
HELLEM, Mary Ann (Orphan of Meredith) 3
DONALDSON, Baley (Orphan of Bailey) 3
THORNTON, Anthony, Benjamin and William 3
CONNER, Samuel 3
REED, Catharine and Jesse (Orphans of Reuben) 3
THOMPSON, Israel, Pleasants and Sarah 3
BRADFIELD, Hannah and Rachel (Orphans of Jonathan) 4
HAWLING, Elizabeth, John and Mary (Children of John Wilcoxon) 4
SKINNER, Elijah 4
BRENT, Hugh 4
WORNELL, Thomas 4
SANDERS, Barbara, Bethany, Nancy, Patience and Parmela 4
KEVAN, Michael 5
CUNARD, Elizabeth 5
BALL, Burgess 5
NICHOLS, Lydia, Rebecca and Thomas (Orphans of Henry) 5
ROACH, Richard, Nancy, Jemima and Ruth 5
TAYLOR, Samuel 5
NEALE, Elizabeth C. (Orphan of Presley Jr.) 5
ELLIOTT, Sally C. 6
HUGHES, John (Son of Francis) 6
PERRY, Benjamin, Samuel, Elisabeth, Mary, Margaret and Amelia (Heirs of Samuel) 6
ELGIN, Sarah (Orphan of William) 6
McILHANY, Cecelia, Elizabeth, James, Louesa, Mary and Mortimer 6
CARTER, Elizabeth (Orphan of Peter) 7
KEIGHN, John 7
WRENN, William and Mary 7
POWELL, Heirs of Leven Jr. 7
DOUGLAS, Louisa 7
CRAVEN, Harriet and Lucretia 7
OSBURN, Abner, Harriet, Massey and Patience 7
POWELL, Maria A. and Sally 8
SHEPHERD, Leven 8
DAVIS, Polly 8
EVERHEART, Jacob, John, Joseph and Sally (Heirs of Jacob) 8
FISHER, Thomas D. 8
LACY, John, Robert A. and Westwood A. [LACEY] 8

SMITH, Ann	9
POTTS, Joseph L. & Mahala (Heirs of David)	9
POWELL, John Leven and Alfred	9
MEAD, Martha	9
MEAD, Joseph	9
BRADFIELD, Julian K. (Orphan of Joseph)	9
SMITH, Mary & Susannah	9
CHILTON, Charles W.	9
WALTMAN, Samuel	9
BRONAUGH, Patrick H. W.	9
FRANK, Elizabeth Ann	9
FRANK, Hannah Ann	9
FRANK, William	10
SCHOOLEY, Sarah Ann (late Sarah Ann SMITH)	10
MARLOW, Mary W. (late M. W. SMITH)	10
GREGG, Sarah Ann and Martha L. (Orphans of Samuel)	10
HALL, Mary, Delilah and William	10
HOGUE, Phebe, Elizabeth and Rachel (Children of James) [HOGE]	10
SHAW, Susan Bailey	10
GREGG, William	10
FONTAINE, Alice Virginia	11
FONTAINE, Lucy Norborne	11
McGAVACK, Mary Pleasant	11
DEAVER, Deborah, Margaret and Daniel (Children of Bazell)	11
CRAVEN, Ellen and Euphemia	11
RUSSELL, Estate of William	11
RUN, Sarah	11
THORNTON, Heirs of Charles	11
HAWLING, Heirs of William	12
HATCHER, Mary A., Emsey F., Gourley R., Amanda M., Anna V. and Ruth Anna (Children of Joseph)	12
McDANIEL, John, Nancy and Elizabeth (Orphans of James)	12
HOGE, Isaac	12
VERTS, William	12
VERTS, Henry	12
VERTS, Peter	12
BOUGHMAN, Mary Ann, John William, Charlotte, Catharine, Sarah Ann and James Andrew (Children of Ann)	12
BAUGHMAN, Charlotte E. and John W.	13
BUSSARD, Milton M.	13
BUSSARD, Perriander L.	13
SANBOWER, Julian	13
DOWDELL, Heirs of Moses	13
WIRTZ, Loucinda	13
WIRTZ, Susannah	13
WIRTZ, Mary Ann	13
EVERHEART, Sarah	13
EVERHEART, Elizabeth (Infant of J.)	13
EVERHART, Sarah J.	13
CRAIG, Nancy, Samuel & William	14
HURDLE, Pleasant	14
HURDELL, Ann Noland	14
McKNIGHT, Amy W.	14
RAWLINGS, Samuel A., Mary Virginia E. and John M. (Heirs of Stephen)	14
WIRTZ, Jacob	14
SMITH, Alexander M., Mary Ann and Maria E. (Estate of Lewis M.)	14
GOODIN, Rachel	15

HOGE, Elisha H. and Anna E.	33
CONARD, Jonathan T.	33
CONARD, Jane A.	33
LORENTZ, Laura V.	34
SCHOOLEY, Charles G.	34
GRAY, Albert W.	34
OSBURN, Lucinda	34
PLASTER, John H., James H., Michael M., William A. and Sarah Frances (Heirs of George)	34
GREGG, Gilford G.	35
COCHRAN, Sarah	35
TRUNDLE, Esther	35
SANBOWER, Samuel F. and Mary F.	35
BROWN, William	35
BURKE, Mary F., Virginia E. and Charles W.	36
VIRTZ, Margaretta, Daniel, Isaiah, Priscilla and Elizabeth C. (Children of Peter)	36
HAVENER, Mary J., Harriet E., William H. and Robert (Heirs of James)	36
DOWELL, Albert B.	36
STOUTSENBERGER, Samuel T., Ann E., Frances A., and Emanuel W.	37
BALL, Mary A., Margaret and Elizabeth	37
THOMPSON, Elizabeth	37
LITTLETON, Bushrod	38
BLEAKLY, Eliza P. and Florence L. [BLEAKLEY]	39
DOWELL, Jane A.	39
DOWELL, Conrad F.	39
NICEWARNER, Christian Thomas, John M., Harriet J. and Emily	40
FAWLEY, Martha A., Ann E., Mary J., William, George P., James M., Ellen C. and Samuel S. (Heirs of George)	40
OSBURN, Decatur, Sanford J. R., Oscar, Octavius, Emeline M. and J. T. M.	40
RICHARDS, Laney A., David F. and Sarah E. (Heirs of Thomas)	40
PIERPOINT, Francis	40
BIRDSALL, David H., Mary Etta and Rebecca Ann (Children of David)	40
STOUTSENBERGER, Albert C. and Elwina T. (Orphans of Mary and Samuel)	41
COLSTON, Nannie F., Elizabeth M. and Susan L. (Heirs of Thomas M.)	41
SHAFER, Lydia, Joseph H. and Mary Ellen (Heirs of John)	43
STRIDER, Joseph L.	43
ANSEL, Susan	43
STONEBURNER, Daniel	43
STONEBURNER, Catharine and Daniel	43
STONEBURNER, Catharine	43
STONEBURNER, Sarah	44
CORDELL, Jacob and Margaret Jane (Children of Adam)	44
CORDELL, Henrietta, John F. and Joseph H. (Children of Adam)	44
WRIGHT, Edward S. and Sarah Ann	45
DOWELL, Archibald P. and Thomas D.	45
POTTS, Thomas W. and John Lewis	45
CHINN, Samuel Walter	45
KALB, Benjamin D.	45
KALB, Silas D.	45
GIBSON, Grace N. and Ella J. (Children of Dr. William)	45
DILLON, Anne E., Joseph Abdon and Jonah W. (Children of Isaac)	47
DILLON, Annie E.	48
SMITH, William G., Henry H., Joshua and John R. (Children of Jonas)	49
KERCHEVAL, Robert H.	49
STEPHENSON, James, Lloyd, John and Josephine (Children of James)	49
HIXON, Bettie	51
CONARD, Henrietta L.	51
CONARD, Stephen H.	51

MATTHEWS, Heirs of Catharine 51
OSBURN, Louisa A. and Walter C. 51
DOWELL, Catharine 52
SMITH, Eliza Jane, Susan Sophia, Samuel George and Eve Virginia (Children of Jacob) 52
BEANS, William H. H., Victoria, Rachel A., Josephine and David (Children of Absalom) 52
BEANS, David and Josephine 53
BEANS, David H. 54
MOCK, Heirs of George W. 54
DOWELL, Charles W. 54
BOND, Eleanor C., Sarah F. and Thomas 54
COMPHER, J. H. W., Jonas Curtis, Sarah C., Ann E., Marietta & William F.
    (Heirs of William) 54
COE, Aurelius 55
McNULTY, William T. 55
MAGILL, Thomas H. M. and Annie E. T. 55
McFARLAND, Alice S., Maurice W. and William T. (Children of Jonathan F.) 56
ORAM, Enos and Lucinda Jane (Children of Henry) 56
SKINNER, Heirs of Gabriel 56
SULLIVAN, Mary F., Samuel M. and Anna Bell
    (Children of Samuel by Rubanion TILLETT) 56
WORSLEY, Elizabeth, Thomas L. and Ann Edwards 57
DOWELL, Virginia E. and Laura 57
WOOD, Joseph 57
NUTT, George Whitfield 57
ROWLES, Edmund J. 57
JEFFRIES, Mary Francis and Joseph O. (Children of B. B. and Tacey) 58
BEDINGER, George R. 58
BEDINGER, Virginia 58
CLARKE, Archie M., Elizabeth J., Mollie A. and Isaac V. (Heirs of A. H.) 58
CONARD, Joseph E. 58
MINOR, Benjamin W. 59
VIRTS, Heirs of Michael 59
FRY, Marietta C. E. C. and O. J. C. C. 59
BOND, Thomas D. 59
MOFFETT, Louisa 59
EWERS, Laura C. and James Isaac 59
OVERFIELD, Jessie 59
OVERFIELD, Richard 59
JEFFRIES, Joseph D., Ann C., Mary T., Martha J. and Hannah (Children of B. B.) 59
CRIM, John 60
RAWLINGS, Mrs. Lucinda 60
FRAZIER, Thomas J., Catharine America, William C., Mary Jane,
    Margaret and Samuel H. (Heirs of Samuel H.) 60
GREGG, Mary Virginia 61
NIXON, John E., Joel R., Hannah E. and Parelia F. 61
OVERFIELD, Marshall 62
STUCK, Jane C. and Margaret Ann 62
REDMOND, Ann 62
HOUSHOLDER, Adam M. [HOUSEHOLDER] 62
HOUGH, William H. Sr 63
BEALES, Jefferson F., Benjamin C., Margaret, Rodney D. and Norval V. 63
ORRISON, Townshend and Laney Ellen 63
ORRISON, Amanda 63
WILEY, William Decatur 63
JAMES, Florida C., Sarah C., Mary V., Robert M. and Thomas B. 63
JAMES, Mary V., Sarah C. & Cecelia 64
MANN, John W., Mary L., Joseph William, Abner W. and Franklin S. L.

(Heirs of George W.)	64
GOCHNAUER, Pembroke S., Preston B. and Charles W. (Heirs of David)	64
GOCHNAUER, Charles W.	65
NICHOLS, William	65
GEORGE, Anna Belle, Olivia and William S. (Children of Solomon)	65
WIRE, Mary Ann, Susannah F. and Martha J.	65
WRIGHT, Ella and Elizabeth	65
SHAFER, John M.	65
ARNOLD, Thomas Clayton	66
LOVE, Samuel H.	66
ARNOLD, Americus S. and Annie E.	66
TAYLOR, Samuel Townsend	66
WHITE, Rachel	66
HAMPTON, Jonah Nichols and James Franklin	66
HOLMES, Joseph F.	67
COOPER, George T. or F.	67
WASHINGTON, Sally B., Lily and Rosa (Children of Samuel E.)	67
COOPER, Sarah R.	67
NICHOLS, Maria, M. Virginia, L. Ellen, Louisa and George W. (Children of Henry H.)	67
RUST, Sallie J., Manley T., John C., Mary Ellen, James Buckannan and Margaret Virginia (Children of James W.)	68
TAYLOR, Emma D.	69
HICKMAN, George S., Luther W., Etchison H. and Margaret Susan Mary (Children of Peter)	69
LEITH, Nellie E., Susan V., Richard D., Theodore and George Ernest (Heirs of Theodore)	70
COE, Elizabeth	71
POTTERFIELD, Julius W.	71
POTTERFIELD, Silas	71
POTTERFIELD, Catharine	71
BROWN, Joseph J.	71
STOUT, George W.	71
COOPER, Benjamin and Thomas	72
COOPER, Thomas	72
COOPER, Benjamin	72
HOGE, Henrietta and Elizabeth G.	72
HOUSEHOLDER, Alice M.	72
LEITH, Louisa	72
ELGIN, Robert, Rosalie and Ida (Children of Robert E.)	72
HUMPHREY, Virginia G., Ann Eliza and Abner Edward (Children of Abner G.)	72
NEER, Nathan	72
BIRDSALL, Children of Benjamin Jr.	73
BOGER, Catharine	73
OSBURN, Walter C.	73
OSBURN, Children of T. V. B.	73
PUSEY, William N. (Child of Joshua)	73
MANN, J. W. C.	74
BROWN, Addison	74
HAMILTON, Lydia A.	74
ANDERSON, Lulah, Thomas E. & Nannie D.	75
PHILLIPS, Richard S. & Arthur W.	75
JEFFRIES, Hannah V.	75
PIGGOTT, William, Thomas, John, Bushrod, Mary J. and Isaac (Children of Burr)	75
SMITH, William B.	75
VIRTS, Henry J. J., Clara Hannah C., Rosella V., Mary L., Orra J., America Elizabeth and Annie Rachel (Children of Henry)	75
HOUGH, Elizabeth H.	76
BOGER, Ella Virginia	76

BRADEN, Cecelia L., Robert & Rodney Walter 77
SHREVE, Virginia, Francis, Mary and Daniel S. (Children of William) 77
STOCKS, William 77
STOCKS, John H. 77
SHRIVER, Emily Gertrude, Martha Ellen & Willie 78
SHRIVER, Alice R. & Annie Mariah 78
BRADEN, Florence M. 78
WHITLOCK, Henry and Mattie E. (ROBERTS) 78
ROGERS, Maria C., Ellen V., George R., Laura Lee and Charlotte R.
   (Children of Arthur L. and Charlotte) 78
HOUSEHOLDER, Kate C. & Daniel P. 78
PAXON, Lillie 79
BUSSARD, M. W. 79
HOUGH, Edgar 79
HICKS, Kimble G. Jr. 79
SCHOOLEY, Annette F. & Kate F. 79
FOSTER, F. H. 79
BEAMER, Michael T. 79
RUST, R. L. B. & M. A. E. 79
MATTHEWS, Jonathan, Rodney & Mary C., John and Jesse 79
BENTLEY, Maria W., Robert, Elizabeth P. and Ann C. (Children of R. M.) 79
PANCOAST, Alberta M., Lillias and Rosa Lee (Children of Joseph) [PANCOST] 79
HAWLING, Children of Joseph L. 80
LLOYD, Annie & Maud 80
SHOEMAKER, George, William, Sarah, Elizabeth and Mary (Children of Josiah) 80
PAXSON, Alice B. 80
FRY, Isabella 80
THOMPSON, George S., Ann Eliza and Barbara Cornelia (Children of Joseph) 80
DABNEY, R. Heath 80
BEAMER, John Samuel 80
JONES, Henrietta, John William & Arthur Lee 80
FILLER, William H. & Sarah J. 81
PIGGOTT, Ruth Hannah 81
GREGG, Phebe A. 81
HAWLING, Eugene 81
HAWLING, Cecil 81
BEAMER, Julia E. 81
CRIM, John Edward 81
HATCHER, Lindig and Lucy (Children of Rodney G.) 81
HUTCHISON, James 81
SMITH, William P., Mary J., Thomas J. and Samuel J. (Heirs of Phebe) 81
STEADMAN, Carrie H. 81
CARTER, Alice V. 81
NEER, Florence 81
BENTLEY, Nellie, Belle & Kate (Children of E. L.) 81
MOORE, Sarah A. & Mary S. 82
RUSSELL, Emily M. 82
RUSSELL, Matilda 82
VIRTS, Rosa A. 82
BROWN, Children of Albert O. 82
HILLEARY, H. C. 82
LYNN, Gertrude & Fanny 82
VANSICKLER, Rosa Bell 83
ELGIN, Ida F. (Child of Robert & Margaret) 83
STEER, James M. 83
DOUGLAS, James E. 83
RUST, Frederick G. 83

LESLIE, John B., John A. and John E. (Children of John) 84
PAXSON, Derizo C. 84
WHITE, John K., Robert A., George Anna S., & Mary Louisa 84
HUNTER, Virginia D., Mary M., John B. & Margaret E. 84
MANN, F. S. L. 84
JAMES, Fleet, Eliza, Mollie, Alice J. & Matson 84
MOORE, Nancy 85
HOLLIDAY, Rosa Lee & Anna 85
PAXSON, Anna Beall 85
BEAMER, Rachel 85
BEAMER, William Francis Augustus, George Henry Thomas, Joseph Michael Bronaugh,
    Maggie Ellen Frances, Daniel Wine Washington, Mary Alice Virginia,
    Mary Lina May and Samuel Randolph William (Children of Michael) 85
NICHOLS, George W. 86
NIXON, George 86
CHAMBLIN, Rosa & Laura 86
McFARLAND, Edgar 86
LAYCOCK, Edward & Lulu 86
COOMBS, Mrs. Sallie A. 86
COOMBS, Mrs. Sarah A. 87
LICKEY, Eugenia D. 87
JANNEY, Mary G., Robert W., Cora and John C. (Children of George W.) 87
STEER, William E. 87
PINKARD, C. F. 88
WARNER, Malinda E. & Mary E. 88
GRAHAM, James E. 88
LOVELESS, Elizabeth 88
MOORE, M. E. & C. 88
TITUS, Wilbur F. 88
SLAYMAKER, Edmund W., Archie C., Amos, Wm. J. & Mary E. 88
HEFNER, Carrie 88
HARPER, Wells A., Robert N., Charles E. and James W. (Children of Robert) 88
MANN, Joseph H. 89
WHITLOCK, Robert T. & Henry W. 89
FILLER, Sarah J. M. 89
SMALE, Emma S. & Mary M. 89
HAVENNER, William A. 89
SHRUEEY, Mrs. Sarah 89
SHUMAKER, Maggie E. 89
STOUTSENBERGER, Clara 89
BARTON, Sarah Amanda 89
WHITE, Daniel 89
JAMES, Sarah 90
GARDNER, James 90
LOVETT, Caroline 90
RUSSELL, Louisa 90
HUGHES, John 90
LOGAN, Anna 90
KEENE, Washington 90
BALDWIN, Orion 90
YELLOTT, W. R., Florence & R. E. 90
YELLOTT, Mrs. Virginia & children 90
NIXON, Mary A. 90
BYRNE, Henry M., Thomas W., Uriah E., Annie L., Virginia M., Sydnor B. & George M. 91
KEEN, Lucy 91
ROLLINS, V. G. S. & Mary 91
LAUCK, W. C. 91

Name	Page
YAKEY, Minnie Belle	91
PAXSON, Clara	91
DILLON, J. W.	91
SHUMAKER, William B., George J., Sarah, Mary and Elizabeth (Children of Josiah) [SHOEMAKER]	92
RAMSEY, Samuel T.	92
FOLEY, Miss Margaret J.	92
MILBOURNE, Orra & Blanche	92
KERCHEVAL, George E.	92
COOPER, Margaret E.	92
TAYLOR, Harriet B.	92
WRIGHT, Joseph & Beverley	92
CRAIG, John A. Jr.	92
WALKER, R. L.	92
MASON, Mary A. V. B.	92
HAMMERLY, Mary E.	93
CHAMBLIN, John R. & H. C.	93
FIELDS, Emily J. [FIELD]	93
CRAVEN, Giles T.	93
HICKMAN, G. L. Kurtz, Elnora A., Benjamin J., William S. and John E.	93
PAXSON, Fannie H., Hattie A., Wm. C. J., Charles & Louisa E.	93
ARNIS, Annie R., William H., Chista V.	93
HUTCHISON, Mary E., Franklin, Maria L. & Melville	93
HOUSE, Samuel M. J. & Mary H.	93
PETERS, Walter G., William R., Edward W. & Robert J.	93
GLASCOCK, Orra M., May, Fenton F., Lilly and Alfred	93
HOUGH, E. Stanley	93
HAWS, Ella & Oscar	93
OSBURN, Maurice	94
NIXON, J. Ellwood	94
NIXON, Parelia	94
HESSER, Martha E.	94
KING, Randolph	94
TIPPETT, Henry, Elizabeth & Sarah	94
CHICK, Edward	94
LOVE, E. Dilley	94
SNOUFFER, Ashton	94
WILEY, Edgar T.	94
WILEY, Charles H.	94
WILEY, Annie J.	94
BEATTY, Bettie Jane, Harry W. and Chester M. (Children of William)	95
MERCHANT, Leroy W.	95
MOFFETT, Mary C., John L., Charles H. and Gracie A. (Children of L. C. [Maffett])	95
DODD, Mary E., Lilly S., Robert A., Ethel A., William H., John G., Ruth V., Nora J., Ida G. and Bettie (Children of Margaret E.)	95
DODD, J. B.	95
THOMPSON, Irving P.	96
THOMPSON, J. Harry	96
BARTLETT, William	96
HOUGH, L. W. S.	96
FURR, John L.	96
SKINNER, Mary C.	96
SKINNER, Willie H.	96
RICE, J. E.	96
MILBURN, Ann E.	96
BEACH, Martha E.	96
CARTER, Eleanor H. & Robt. C.	96

HESS, Sarah Amanda	96
BOGER, John E.	96
HEATON, Cecelia D.	96
SURVICK, Nora, Carrie and Mary B. (Children of Benjamin)	96
ROLLINS, Virginia G. R. & Margaret M.	96
VIRTZ, Henry T.	97
HOUSE, Mary H.	97
RICKARD, Jesse L. & Walter C.	97
MINOR, Annie M.	97
CHICK, Charles Edward	97
McCARTY, George B.	97
SILCOTT, Mary	97
WOODS, Blanch	97
YOUNG, Susannah B.	97
PIGGOTT, Mary E. & Albert S.	97
PEYTON, Cabel Y.	98
BEVERLEY, R. A.	98
DIVINE, Arthur Fairfax and Jessie (Children of Emily)	98
BARTLETT, Ella	98
CLAPHAM, Elizabeth	98
FURR, Minor	98
PANCOAST, Lula, Carrie & Harry	98
FLING, W. F.	98
ROWLES, Mary C.	98
HUMPHREY, William D.	98
CARTER, John F.	98
CARTER, Francis M. Jr.	98
CARTER, William Maulsby	98
RAWLINGS, Corrie Lee, Emma Mary and Eva V. (Children of John M. Jr.)	99
LOVE, F. T.	99
LOVE, C. C., Edgar L., Rufus T. & Lacey R.	99
GARRETT, Thomas E. & John B.	99
CLINE, Beulah, Corrie V., A. T., Gracie J., Fannie B. & Mabel R.	99
TAVENNER, J. Wilmer	99
LACEY, Charles H.	100
DARR, Alice & Maggie	100
FOX, Manly	100
DUNBAR, Edward McVeigh	100
NICHOLS, Thomas W.	100
LUCIUS, Katie & Charles	100
HELM, Lizzie C. & Thomas M.	100
CRAVEN, Lillie B.	100
TRITTAPOE, Walter T. [TRITAPOE]	100
WRIGHT, B. Oden & Jos. E.	100
SWANK, Samuel	100
WENNER, Bessie	100
MATTINGLY, Hattie	100
RITICOR, Joseph	100
KEYS, Louisa	101
FOSTER, Margaret M.	101
DISHMAN, Edna E. & Charles E.	101
GIST, Harry S.	101
MORRIS, George H.	101
GIBSON, W. B. & W. E.	101
JACKSON, Charles H. & Hannie	101
TURNER, Lucy	101
JORDAN, Claretta, Robert, Bertha, Katie & Lizzie	101

LITTLEJOHN, Forrest C., Paul V & Horace C.	102
CHINN, Mary E.	102
DONALDSON, Robert B. & Margaret E.	102
WILLIAMS, Rebecca J.	102
TRITAPOE, William M.	102
MOORE, Thomas R.	102
LOVE, Thomas E.	102
JENKINS, Joseph R., Ruth H., Sallie & Samuel T.	102
NUTT, Daniel, James & Carrie	103
SWANN, Thomas	103
CHAMBLIN, Clara F.	103
HAMPTON, Elwood	103
BEAMER, Bessie W.	103
WARNER, Bessie	103
DONOHOE, Willie E. & Lee E.	103
LENT, Cornelius	103
CHANCELLOR, Helen E. Jr. & Wm. F.	103
CONARD, Bessie J.	103
FURR, Walter L., E. S. R. & Minnie	103
NOLAND, Philip H.	103
LITTLETON, S. Campbell	103
SANBOWER, Harry H. & Edgar H.	104
FLETCHER, B. J.	104
FENTON, Annie L.	104
PIGGOTT, Henry	104
SANBOWER, Annie G.	104
SILCOTT, Zula B. & Ella May	104
DILLON, William	104
FRY, William H.	104
ATWELL, Ruth V.	104
RAMY, Walter	104
RAMY, Louisa	104
KELLY, Elizabeth	104
PETTITT, William F.	104
INDEX	105

INTRODUCTION

The following are abstracts of the Guardian Account records of Loudoun County, Virginia. These original books were filmed by the Genealogical Society of Utah at the Loudoun County Court house, Leesburg, Virginia, beginning in February of 1952. Microfilms of these books are currently available through the Interlibrary Loan Service of The Library of Virginia, 800 East Broad Street, Richmond, Virginia 23219-8000.

Loudoun Co. Reel No. 96	Guardian Accounts A 1759-1823
Loudoun Co. Reel No. 132	Guardian Accounts B 1823-1837
Loudoun Co. Reel No. 97	Guardian Accounts C 1838-1852, D 1853-1859, and E 1859-1870
Loudoun Co. Reel No. 133	Guardian Accounts F 1869-1875, G 1875-1886, and H 1886-1904

Guardians were appointed for individuals, usually minors, who had inherited money or who were orphaned. The Guardian was to monitor and control the spending of funds in providing the necessities of the individual's lifestyle while maintaining the funds principal. In the early years, Guardians were required to periodically present the Court with an accounting of income and expenditures. In later years these presentations were requested every year. Proper receipts and vouchers were required and the Guardian was usually compensated for his troubles with a small commission.

Committees were appointed for individuals who were considered of unsound mind. As with the Guardian, the Committee was expected to provide the individual's necessities while maintaining the principal value of the estate.

A typical entry would be similar to the following:

> William T. Osburn in account with Phineas Osburn his Guardian:
> 1 Apr 1850 to John Turner for mending boots, 12 June 1850 to T. M. Osburn for store goods, 20 Jun 1850 to James Carroll for shoes, 21 Jun 1850 to Mary P. Overfield for tuition, 16 Dec 1850 to Ann E. Hope for clothes, 31 Dec 1850 to Thomas Osburn for board, 10 Mar 1851 to Jesse Thomas for tuition, 18 Jul 1851 to M. E. Peck for tuition, 3 Nov 1851 to David McIntosh for tuition, 8 Dec 1851 to Dr. Abner Osburn for medical bill, 27 Dec 1851 to Stephen Baxton for tuition, 31 Jul 1852 to E. A. Adams for clothes, 16 Nov 1852 to Dr. F. A. Davison for medical acct., 27 Nov 1852 to J. K. Fairfax for sewing, 4 Dec 1852 to A. T. Welsh for tuition, 25 Dec 1852 of hire of William and Mary
> I hereby certify that I have examined stated and settled the account of Phineas Osburn Guardian of William T. Osburn and report a balance in the hands of said Guardian of $2820.29 with [interest] thereon from 17 Mar 1853, as will be shown by the above account. The former settlement was made and returned in March 1850, and under the Code of July 1850, the Guardian was required to lay his papers before the commissioner within six months after the expiration of one year from the passage of the law of July 1850, the limit being the 31 Dec 1851, but he failed to lay his papers before the commissioner, until 3 Mar 1852, thereby forfeiting his commission on the transactions of the first year of this account, which it will be perceived I have allowed. I have stated above that the papers were laid before me on 3 Mar 1852, but my engagements have been such, under the accumulation of accounts prior to the appointment of Mr. Sinclair, that without doing injustice to others, I have been unable to close this account until now. I further report that it has been duly posted in a list at the front of the Courthouse, and also that I have examined the Guardianship bond, the penalty of which is deemed sufficient, and the security considered ample.
> 13 Feb 1854. An account of Phineas Osburn, as Guardian of William T. Osburn, having been returned to the Clerks Office of this Court one month ago, and no exceptions being filed thereto, the same was examined by the Court, found to be correct, confirmed, and ordered to be recorded.

The majority of accounts listed expenses for everyday living, which I usually did not include in the abstract. I included dates and items which I felt were of importance genealogically to give a better understanding of that individual's life. I also included all references to slaves, indexed under the heading Negro. A full name index has been included.

Abbreviations used in these abstracts:

[letter:number] - [Book: page #]	CtOD – Court order dated	RtCt – Returned to Court
Admr - Administrator	Exor – Executor	S/A – Settlement Account
Apr – Appraiser	Gdn – Guardian	Scr – Subscriber (acct reviewer)

LOUDOUN COUNTY, VIRGINIA
GUARDIAN ACCOUNTS
1759-1904

GUARDIAN ACCOUNT BOOKS A-H

HERYFORD, Henry
S/A with Chas. TYLER: beginning 7 Jan 1759; paid the midwife for coming to Negro Wench. RtCt 14 Nov 1759. [A:1]

S/A with Chas. TYLER: beginning 7 Jan 1760, paid William BERKLEY for board; income from crops. RtCt 11 Nov 1760. [A:3]

GRAYSON, William
S/A with Ben. GRAYSON: beginning 22 April 1758; paid cash in Philadelphia for a lottery, schooling and board when at Philadelphia, sundries purchased at Cedar Run, Negro's cloaths; cash rec'd from Thomas KNOX Esq. since in London, legacy from Col. GRAYSON's estate. RtCt 9 Jun 1761. [A:4]

S/A with Benjamin GRAYSON: beginning 5 May 1761; paid Thomas BROWN for his share of the crop, repaid for bringing a Negro wench to bed, balance of account settled with Mr. John ORR. William went to England and is of lawful age. RtCt 14 Jun 1763. [A:11]

HAGUE, John
S/A to Ann HAGUE (a Quaker): 14 Aug 1770 and 1771 paid to board two children (Samuel & John HAGUE) for 2 years and 10 months. RtCt 10 Sep 1771 [A:15]

WILLCOXON, Elizabeth
S/A with Gdn John Willcoxon HALLING: 1770-71 paid for cloaths, schooling & board about 2 years.; income from hire of a Negro woman and boy 20 months next Christmas. RtCt 28 Sep 1772. [A:16]

WEST, Cato and Charles
Cato vs. Charles WEST paid 1770 schooling and board each year. RtCt 29 Sep 1772. [A:16]

HURST, Elizabeth (Orphan of John)
S/A with Henry BREWER: (orphan daughter of John HURST, Jr. dec'd) paid for one year board at £6. RtCt 30 Sep 1772. [A:17]

MONROE, Rosey
S/A with Gdn John HALL: beginning 1772; general expenses; rec'd cash from James BUCKLEY. RtCt 23 Mar 1773. [A:17]

CHINN, Rawleigh
S/A with Leven POWELL: beginning 18 Mar, 1771; paid for items for Negroes Nell & Milly, income from hire of Negro Isaac & Nell, interest paid on three bonds. RtCt 15 Mar 1774. [A:18]

CHINN, Christopher
S/A with Thomas CHINN: beginning 12 Sep 1771 paid for rum and sugar for Negro woman, items for Negro boy; income from W. CUNNINGHAM books being the estates share of your uncle. RtCt 10 May 1774. [A:22]

Christopher CHINN vs. Chas. CHINN: beginning 1 Mar 1775; general expenses. RtCt 4 May 1775. [A:25]

Mr. Christopher CHINN vs. Chas. CHINN. beginning Aug 16 1779, paid Thomas BEATTY for raising a man in the District, paid Thos. BARTLETT as Gdn to Christ. CHINN, income from old tobacco note. RtCt 12 Jun 1780. [A:26]

Ch. CHINN vs. Christopher CHINN: beginning Aug. 1775; cash to my son Elijah, paid Mr. CLARK for laying 2 Negro wenches; paid my son Charles for inspecting tobacco, leaving £46.7.4. [A:34]

LANE, Presley Carr
S/A with Har. LANE: beginning 1782; paid Charles DAVIS for crying Negroes, expenses to go to Westmoreland (schooling), income from hire of Negroes Dabbors & Whitely. RtCt 12 Aug 1783. [A:44]

S/A with John ORR: beginning 1776; expenses from Warm springs, paid to settle with Mr. TRIPLETT at Leesburg; expenses attending Mr. LANE's settlement Leesburg and Newgate, paid Miss Sally LANE for you, paid crying Negroes and to examining inspectors books at Dumfries from 1770-1777, income from rent for Newgate & Sanford House, Nov 1778 copy of John WILSON deed of gift, paid board & schooling in Westmoreland, income from Negro Dabas hire deducting his inoculation & Whaley's hire, 7 Jan 1780 paid John WALKERS for arbitrators & self settling with Wm. LANE [A:48]

S/A with John ORR.: beginning 1776, 1781 paid Mr. Wm. ELLZEY, paid John ORR & co. from Jan 1776-Nov 1, 1782 (interest accounts), 1781 income from the former to the present Gdn of and in behalf of P. C. LANE as per award, leaving £48.10.7 10. RtCt 10 Nov 1782. Scrs: Wm. HUTCHISON, R. T. HOOE, Josiah WATSON. [A:56]

S/A with H. LANE: beginning Aug 1783; paid Mr. Sandford COCKERILL for boarding Negro Whitley while under inoculation for small pox, income from tobacco crop, from Mr. John ORR for rent of Sandford Houses, rec'd part of rent due at Newgate rec'd in the hands of Mr. Amos FOUCH; rec'd of Wm. Bernard SEARS in part of hire of Negro Whitley. RtCt 15 Sep 1784. [A:77]

S/A with Gdn Hardage LANE: beginning Sep 1784; income from rent at Newgate and taxes, paid part of expenses at Alexandria to sell your tobacco, income from Amos FOX for hire of Negro Dabbor. RtCt 8 Aug 1785. [A:82]

POLLARD, Orphans of Thomas
S/A with Gdn Thomas CHINN: beginning 26 Nov 1778; paid John HAZARD for taking up Negro Hannah, paid Burr HARRISON for his trouble with Flora, paid midwife for the

delivery of N. Jean & Dr. BARBER for examining Negro Lucy who was disordered (fowl disorder), paid ferrage at Lawrees, paid Mrs. CARTER for provision for your Negroes to travel on in January; paid for board, washing, mending of three children, paid Fauquier tax of Jean & children who were at the time of hiring and assessed to me before they were hired; £1782.40.7. RtCt 13 Sep 1784. [A:59]

S/A with Gdn Thomas CHINN: beginning 9 Jan 1783; paid for my trouble with Jean & children; paid James LEITH for crying your Negroes, paid William YATES for a midwife for Negro Hannah; paid 2 levies for Braxton POLLARD; leaving £23.5.1. RtCt 14 Jun 1785. [A:71]

OXLEY, Evered

S/A with Gdns John SAUNDERS & John OXLEY: they have not been able to receive any money or other things in right of the said orphans or either of them given under my hand this eighth day of August 1785. Scr: John ALEXANDER. RtCt 9 Aug 1785. [A:85]

MINOR, Ann, John, Nancy and William

S/A of Ann MINOR with Francis HARRIMON: beginning 1785; income from hire of Negro woman and boy. RtCt 12 Sep 1786. [A:95]

S/A of Ann MINOR with Gdn Saml. D. HARRYMAN: beginning 14 Sep 1786; as above. RtCt 10 Sep 1787. [A:104]

S/A of Ann MINOR with Saml. D. HARRYMAN: beginning 12 Sep 1787; income from hire of Negroes Judy and boy Adam. RtCt 14 Oct 1788. [A:109]

S/A of Ann MINOR with Saml. D. HARRIMAN: beginning 5 Oct 1788; paid 1 quarter of singing school, income from hire of Negro Judy and Adam. RtCt 12 Oct 1789. [A:120]

S/A/ of Ann MINOR with Saml. D. HARRIMAN: beginning 20 Oct 1789; income from hire of Negro woman and boy. RtCt 14 Dec 1790. [A:123]

S/A of Ann MINOR with Gdn Saml. HARRIMAN: beginning 6 Oct 1790; income from hire of Negroes Jude & Adam. RtCt 13 Dec 1791. [A:129]

S/A of Nancy MINOR with Francis MINOR: beginning 18 Dec 1782; 28 Sep 1783 income from hire of a Negro woman and boy [A:86]

S/A of Nancy MINOR with Gdn Francis MINOR: (infant) of John MINOR dec'd; beginning 1784; income from one year hire of Negro woman and boy. RtCt 9 Aug 1785. [A:87]

S/A of William MINOR with Francis MINOR: beginning 18 Dec 1782; income from hire of Negro woman. RtCt 9 Aug 1785. [A:89]

S/A of William MINOR with Franc's HERRYMAN: beginning 1785; income from hire of Negro woman. RtCt 12 Sep 1786. [A:93]

S/A of William MINOR with Gdn Saml. D. HARRYMAN: beginning 14 Sep 1786; income from the hire of one Negro woman. RtCt 10 Sep 1787. [A:102]

S/A of William MINOR with Saml. D. HARRIMAN: beginning 22 Sep 1787; income from hire of Negro Winny. RtCt 14 Oct 1788. [A:111]

S/A with Gdn Saml. D. HARRIMAN: beginning 6 Nov 1788; income from the hire of Negroes Viny, Sale & Bett. RtCt 12 Oct 1789. [A:115]

S/A of William MINOR with Gdn Saml. D. HARRIMAN: beginning 27 Oct 1789; income from hire of Negro woman and 2 girls. RtCt 11 Dec 1790. [A:124]

S/A of William MINOR with Saml. D. HARRIMAN: income from hire of Negroes Vinney, Bett & Sall. RtCt 13 Dec 1791. [A:133]

S/A of John MINOR with Francis MINOR: beginning Dec 1782; income from hire of Negro woman and girl [A:90]

S/A/ of John MINOR (infant) of John MINOR, dec'd.: beginning 1784; income from hire of Negroes Fanny, Poll & James. RtCt 9 Aug 1785. [A:91]

S/A of John MINOR with F. HARRIMON: beginning 1785; income from hire of two Negro woman & one boy; cash for a horse. RtCt 12 Sep 1786. [A:94]

S/A of John MINOR with Gdn Saml. D. HARRIMAN: beginning 14 Sep 1786; income from hire of two Negro women & one boy. RtCt Sep 1787. [A:106]

S/A of John MINOR with Gdn Saml. D. HARRIMAN: beginning 22 Sep 1787; income from hire of Negro woman, old Fanny & boy James. RtCt 14 Oct 1788. [A:113]

S/A of John MINOR with Gdn Saml. D. HARRIMAN: beginning 27 Oct 1788; income from hire of Negroes Poll, Fanny & James. RtCt 12 Oct 1789. [A:117]

S/A of John MINOR with Gdn Samuel D. HARRIMAN: beginning 27 Oct 1789; income from hire of Negroes Poll, old Fanny & boy Jim. RtCt 11 Dec 1790. [A:121]

S/A of John MINOR Gdn Saml. D. HARRIMAN: beginning 5 Oct 1790; income from hire of Negroes Fanny, Poll & Jinny. RtCt 13 Dec 1791. [A:131]

S/A of John MINOR with Gdn S. D. HARRIMAN: beginning 30 Sep 1791; income from hire of Negroes Jim, Fanney & Pall.. RtCt 10 Dec 1798. [A:148]

SHEID, Orphans of James

S/A with Guardians Thomas SANGSTER & George WINN: beginning 17 Jun 1774 ; paid cost in chancery suit, widow SHEID's dower, income from sale of the moveable estate and slaves, leaving £316.14.11.3; also nine shillings and three pence paid to William DEBELL who intermarried with one of the orphans. Scrs: Geo. SUMMERS, Chas. ESKRIDGE, Har. LANE. RtCt 10 Apr 1787. [A:98]

SCOTT, Orphans of Joseph
S/A with Guardians Robert SCOTT ???? & Saml. SCOTT dec'd: beginning 1777; paid a few expenses. RtCt Jan 1792. [A:125]

HELLEM, Mary Ann (Orphan of Meredith)
S/A with Gdn Thos. LITTLETON: (orphan of Meredith HELLEM dec'd) paid 2 years boarding and clothing at £8/year; income from hire of a Negro man. RtCt 8 Dec 1794. [A:134]

S/A with Thos. LITTLETON: income from hire of Negro man and boy [A:135]

S/A with Thos. LITTLETON: beginning 3 Dec 1798; paid 1 year schooling; income from hire of Negro man & boy and rent of land; leaving £21. Scrs: Joseph SMITH., Samuel MURRAY, Patrick CAVAN. RtCt 14 Jan 1799. [A:151]

S/A with Thos. LITTLETON: beginning 1798; income from hire of Negro Timothy; leaving £19.10.3¾. RtCt 13 Jan 1800. [A:155]

DONALDSON, Baley (Orphan of Bailey)
S/A with Gdn Thos. LITTLETON: income from the estate of S. D. HARRYMAN; income from hire of 1 Negro in 1794 and hire of Negro man & woman. RtCt 9 May 1796. [A:136]

S/A with Thomas LITTLETON: (orphan of Bailey DONALDSON) beginning 31 Dec 1798; income from hire of 2 Negro men, leaving £41 3/8. Scrs: Joseph SMITH, Samuel MURREY, Patrick CAVAN. RtCt 14 Jan 1799. [A:154]

S/A with Thomas LITTLETON: income from hire of Negro Peter, leaving £37.9½. RtCt 8 Jan 1800. [A:158]

THORNTON, Anthony, Benjamin and William
S/A of Anthony THORNTON with Gdn Samuel LOVE: beginning 1782; income from hire of Negro Lucy and rent from Broad Run land. Anthony THORNTON being of full age approved acct on 7 Jan 1797. Scrs: James NISBITT, Francis ADAMS. RtCt 9 Jan 1797. [A:138]

S/A of Benjamin B. THORNTON with Gdn Samuel LOVE: beginning 1782; paid board of old Phill for 8 years; income from hire of your & Anthony's Negroes and rents of lots in Leesburg and lands adjacent. Benjamin Berryman THORNTON being of full age approved acct on 4 Jan 1797. Scr: James NISBITT. RtCt 9 Jan 1797. [A:140]

S/A of William THORNTON with Gdn Samuel LOVE: paid Dr. WILLFORD for board, income from hire of Negroes including Sall and rents from lots in Leesburg & adjacent lands, rents from BIGGERS lot for 90-96. RtCt 9 Jan 1797. [A:143]

CONNER, Samuel
S/A with Gdn Preston HAMPTON: beginning 1785; income from Clater SMITH in part for rents he rec'd., from Stephen HUNT arrears of rent for 1786 and 1787 which Clater SMITH had not rec'd., from Stephen HUNT for rent of 1788-93, from Joseph BRADEN for rent of 1788-95, from Luke BIRD for HUNT's place 1793-95, and from Clater SMITH dec'd. of tenants. Scrs: James COLEMAN, William STANHOPE, and Johnston CLEVELAND. RtCt 9 Oct 1797. [A:145]

REED, Catharine and Jesse (Orphans of Reuben)
S/A of estate of Reuben REED with Gdn Wm. REED: paid boarding and clothing for Jesse and Catharine REED from 1793, the last S/A, income of Thos. MACKEY for rent of plantation and from hire of Negro Ned, leaving £43.19. Scrs: William LANE Jr., Chas. ESKRIDGE, Francis ADAMS. RtCt 13 Feb 1798. [A:147]

S/A with Thomas BLINCOE: (orphans of Reuben REED) beginning 1801; income from hire of Negro Ned whilst the said Negro was in Kentucky 1798-1800 and 6 years rent of the plantation belonging to the orphans 1797-1804; by amount of an order of Wm. REED vs. Benjamen BERKELEY; paid widows dower. Scrs: Johnston CLEVELAND, Chas. LEWIS, James LEWIS. RtCt 11 Jun 1804. [A:147]

THOMPSON, Israel, Pleasants and Sarah
S/A of Israel THOMPSON with Asa MOORE: beginning 6 Feb 1799; paid school in Chester County PA and Weston School for tuition; income rents from house in Leesburg; has 1 bed and furniture & silver table spoons, ?, 1 silver watch in possession of his mother to be delivered to him when of age. Appears by his father's will that when he arrives to the age of twenty one years some back lands the exact quantity not mentioned are to be divided between him and his brothers. Scrs: Chas. BENNETT and John HAMILTON. RtCt 12 Jan 1802. [A:159]

S/A of minor Israel THOMPSON with Asa MOORE: beginning 15 Sep. 1800; paid for alteration property of thy lott in Leesburg; paid to Weston School and expense getting thee home from Weston when sick, paid A. WRIGHT for the use of his mare and the loss of the eye going for thee to Weston as settled by arbitration; sundry clothing, gave thee to bear there & horses expenses to Alexandria when going to assist Wm. KENWORTHY in his school; paid for going to Baltimore with thee to precure a place for thee including the hire of two horses; paid thy mother for boarding thee; income from rent of house [A:162]

S/A of estate of Sally THOMPSON with Gdn Jas. MOORE: beginning Aug 1800; expense of taking her to Maryland to school; paid boarding and tuition at Westtown; Scrs: Josh DANIEL, John HAMILTON, Robt. BRADEN RtCt 13 Sep 1802. [A:165]

S/A of minor Israel THOMPSON with Gdn Asa MOORE: beginning Oct 1802; paid Weston School, income from rent of house and lot in Leesburg, income from Wm. KENWORTHY for they service as assistant in his school.

Scrs: Chas. BENNETT and Josh'a DANNIEL. RtCt 11 Nov 1802. [A:167]

S/A of Israel THOMPSON (minor) with Gdn Asa MOORE: beginning 22 Nov 1802; general payments. Scrs: John HAMILTON, James HAMILTON, Robert BRADEN. RtCt 10 Jun 1805. [A:173]

S/A of Pleasants THOMPSON with Abijah JANNEY: beginning 29 Aug 1800; paid John WILLIAMS for taking her to Sandy Spring school, paid her mother, paid at Westtown school. Scrs: Chas. BENNETT, James HAMILTON, Robert BRADEN. RtCt 9 Dec 1805. [A:174]

S/A of Sarah THOMPSON Jr. with Gdn James MOORE: beginning 16 Sep 1802; paid for schooling at Westtown, paid thy mother her order. RtCt 9 Dec 1805. [A:176]

BRADFIELD, Hannah and Rachel (Orphans of Jonathan)

S/A with Gdn John HEAD: beginning Feb 1802; paid travelling to Pennsylvania to Leuelend?; paid board, from rent in Pennsylvania. Scrs: Notley C. WILLIAMS, Jesse JANNEY, James HEATON. RtCt 13 Mar 1804. [A:169]

S/A of Hannah & Rachel BRADFIELD orphans of Jonathan BRADFIELD with Gdn Benj'n. BRADFIELD: beginning 1807; paid for going to Pennsylvania to rent some lots; income from two years rent in the hands of Jas. BRADFIELD. Scrs: Stacy TAYLOR, Jesse JANNEY. RtCt 11 Mar 1811. [A:218]

S/A of Rachael BRADFIELD with Benjamin BRADFIELD: CtOD 9 May 1814; beginning 1810; paid tax on two lots in Pennsylvania, income from rent for the plantation that Jonathan BRADFIELD dec'd. possessed, leaving $298.17½. Scrs: Jesse JANNEY, Jesse HIRST, Stephen WILSON, Bernard TAYLOR. RtCt 13 May 1816. [A:253]

S/A of Hannah GRIGGSBY (late Hannah L. BRADFIELD) with Gdn James BRADFIELD: income from Benj'n. BRADFIELD for rent, leaving $644.89. Scrs: James HEATON, Mahlon TAYLOR, Stacey TAYLOR. RtCt 12 Aug 1817. [A:273]

HAWLING, Elizabeth, John and Mary (Children of John Wilcoxon)

S/A of Mary HAWLING with Gdn William HAWLING: beginning 1806; income from 12 years hire of Negro Pegg, one share of money paid for building, one half share given by the widow, leaving £113.5.10½ Scrs: Aaron SANDERS, Isaac STEERE, John LITTLEJOHN, Samuel MURREY. RtCt 10 Feb 1806. [A:178]

S/A of John HAWLING with Gdn William HAWLING: beginning 1806; income from share of his fathers estate as per S/A by the commissioners in the year 1794 except Negro Peter, income from 10 years hire of Negro Peter, income from 6 years rent of plantation, paid schooling at Leesburg; boarding paid Barrett HOUGH, by money paid for building house which Wm. HAWLING has to pay the Legatees, charges for board, corn, and clothing shall be offset for the services of the ward with a relinquishment of interest. Scrs: Aaron SANDERS, Isaac STEERE, John LITTLEJOHN, Samuel MURREY. RtCt 10 Feb 1806. [A:179]

S/A of Eliz. HAWLING with Gdn William HAWLING: beginning 1806; income from 12 year hire of Negro Crab. The subscribers have adjusted and settled the acct. of Wm. HAWLING Gdn of Elizabeth HAWLING one of the children and devisee of Jno. Wilcoxon HAWLING dec'd and do report a balance of £161.10. Scrs: Aaron SANDERS, Isaac STEERE, John LITTLEJOHN, Samuel MURREY. RtCt 10 Feb 1806. [A:182]

SKINNER, Elijah

S/A with Gdn Nathaniel SKINNER: beginning Jun 9 1801; dividend of his fathers estate, income from interest on this sum nine years, paid for schooling, leaving £82.15. Scrs: Israel LACEY, John TYLER, Robt. ARMISTEAD. RtCt 10 Mar 1806. [A:184]

S/A with Gdn Nathaniel SKINNER: income from his father's estate, income from interest on this sum nine years, paid for schooling, leaving £82.15. Scrs: John TYLER, Robt. ARMISTEAD. RtCt 10 Mar 1806. [A:194]

The Kentucky land loss in TRIPLETT's bond. Interest on this sum 9 years. On a review this day of these accounts of the estate of Phinehas SKINNER dec'd. we are of opinion that the Kentucky land ought to be taken out of the acct. and also a loss of £11-14-0 in Frances TRIPLETT's bond making in all £10-16-9 this with interest 9 years making in all £16.13.3 in our opinion ought to be deducted from the sum of £82-15-5 which was the balance due on a settlement made by us on the 20th Jan 1806. We are also of opinion that one eighth part of the costs of two suits between the Admr.. of Phinehas SKINNER dec'd. with Frances TRIPLETT that is of the pltffs. cost in the suit at common law & one eight part of the deft. suit in chancery ought also to be deducted from said sum. Scrs: Israel LACEY, John TYLER, Robt. ARMISTEAD. RtCt 13 Mar 1809. [A:196]

BRENT, Hugh

S/A with Gdn Burr POWELL: beginning 14 Nov 1805; income from Wm. WOOD for hire of Negro Solomon. Inventory of estate: Negro Solomon a young man about 21 years of age. Negro Rachel a girl about 7 years of age. RtCt 12 May 1807. [A:185]

WORNELL, Thomas

S/A with Wm. GUNNELL Jr: beginning 1792; paid schooling & board, paid midwife's fee to Negro Henny, paid Apr 1792 for coffin & grave for Negro child, paid for inoculating Airy & her 2 children, paid to board Negro Henny & 3 children. Scrs: Geo. SUMMERS, Wm. STANHOPE, Will LANE. RtCt 12 May 1807. [A:186]

SANDERS, Barbara, Bethany, Nancy, Patience and Parmela

S/A of Barbara SANDERS with Gdn Presley SANDERS: CtOD 7 Jan 1808; beginning 1807; income from hire of Negro Kimmico and rent from plantations [A:191]

S/A of Patience SANDERS with Gdn Presley SANDERS: beginning 1807; income from hire of Negro Sally and rents from plantations [A:191]

S/A of Nancy SANDERS with Gdn Presley SANDERS: beginning 1807; income from hire of Negro Pegg & children and rents from plantations. [A:192]

S/A of Bethany SAUNDERS with Gdn Presley SANDERS: INCOME from hire of Negroes Simon & Billey and rents from plantations [A:192]

S/A of Permela SAUNDERS with Gdn Presley SANDERS: income from hire of Negro man Adam and rents from plantations. Scrs: William DULIN, Jno. ROSE, Isaac STEERE. RtCt 9 May 1808. [A:193]

S/A of Patience SAUNDERS with Gdn Presley SAUNDERS: beginning 26 Feb 1810; income from hire of Sally for 1808 and 1809 and sale of corn & oats. [A:223]

S/A of Nancy SAUNDERS with Gdn Presley SAUNDERS: beginning 26 Feb 181; income from sale of corn and oats. RtCt 14 Oct 1811. [A:224]

S/A of Bethany SAUNDERS with Gdn Pressley SAUNDERS: beginning 26 Feb 1810; income from hire of Negroes Simon & Bill and sale of corn & oats. [A:225]

S/A of Parmelia SAUNDERS with Gdn Presley SAUNDERS: beginning 26 Feb 1810; income from hire of Adam and sale of corn & oats. Scrs: Samuel LUCKETT, Isaac STEERE, Isaac LAROWE. RtCt 14 Oct 1811. [A:226]

Received of Presley SAUNDERS Gdn to Patience, Nancy, Bethany & Parmelia SANDERS this sum of $2329.37 being a balance due them as per an as his successor as Gdn for my four sisters. Signed 2 Mar 1810 by John SANDERS. Teste Aron SANDERS. RtCt 14 Oct 1814. [A:227]

S/A of Bethany SANDERS with Gdn John ROSE: CtOD 14 Apr 1817; beginning 26 Sep 1811; income from purchase of Negro boy George, income from hire of Negro boy Simon, one boy & girl Phebe, 10 Apr 1817 paid sundries liquor at wedding, leaving $750.79. Scrs: Jno. LITTLEJOHN, Thomas SANDERS, Saml. M. EDWARDS. RtCt 8 Dec 1817. [A:227]

KEVAN, Michael
S/A of estate of Michael KEVAN with Gdn Jas. CAVAN: There is no estate belonging to the ward that I know of. RtCt 10 May 1808. [A:194]

CUNARD, Elizabeth
S/A of Elizabeth CUNARD now Elizabeth HESS with Gdn Anthony CUNARD: paid one third of Eliz't. JACOBS & Geo. ABLE's bonds for £156.4.6 per year receipt Oct 26, 1805 one third being £52.1-6 equal to $173.58. RtCt 8 Jan 1810. [A:197]

BALL, Burgess
S/A with Guardians Leven LUCKETT & William NOLAND: CtOD 10 Apr 1810; beginning 1806; paid Geo. W. BALL for his own use; paid for Fayette BALL's tuition at Charlotte Hall; paid agent in Kentucky; paid Mildred Washington BALL balance of lottery tickets; paid Christopher COLLINS tuition of the girls; paid for sundry articles furnished Doct. PEYTON for the Bigspring farm by Benj. MCROY acting as overseer in the year 1806; income from hire different Negroes to Doct. PEYTON, viz James, Gardner, James, Netly, Hannah, from April 1806 till Nov. 1808; by John HUFF's acct. vs. Doct. PEYTON in 1808; income from hire of Negroes, viz. James, Gardner James, Milly & Hannah and from rents. RtCt 14 May 1810. [A:200]

I hereby authorize the County Court of Loudoun to appoint my brother Fayette BALL my Gdn he being chosen by me as such. 11 Nov 1816. Martha Dandridge BALL. RtCt 11 Nov 1816. [A:268]

NICHOLS, Lydia, Rebecca and Thomas (Orphans of Henry)
S/A with Guardians Mahlon TAYLOR & George TAVENER: (orphaned children of Henry NICHOLS) beginning 1807; paid Eli NICHOLS one of their wards; paid Rebecca LOVE one of their wards; income from George SHOEMAKER, James LOVE, Andrew HOSPITAL, James WATTERS for rent. Scrs: Stacy TAYLOR, James HEATON, R. BRADEN. RtCt 13 May 1811. [A:212]

ROACH, Richard, Nancy, Jemima and Ruth
S/A of Nancy, Richard, Jemima, and Ruth ROACH with Gdn George TAVENER: misc. payments. Scrs: Stacy TAYLOR, James HEATON, R. BRADEN. RtCt 13 May 1811. [A:215]

TAYLOR, Samuel
S/A of estate of with Gdn John F. SAPPINGTON: beginning 30 May 1810; misc. payments. RtCt 11 Mar 1811. [A:216]

NEALE, Elizabeth C. (Orphan of Presley Jr.)
S/A with Gdn William S. NEALE: (orphan of Presley NEALE Jr.) CtOD 13 May 1801; beginning 1 Nov 1801; expenses in removing Negro Harry from Westmoreland to Loudoun and for his expenses in going to Westmoreland in order to settle with Presley NEALE former Gdn - the whole principal of said Elizabeth C. NEALE's Estate (inherited from her father) being a Negro man and £25-6-4½ Virginia Currency. Scrs: Isaac HOUGH and William PAXSON. RtCt 8 Jul 1811. [A:220]

S/A with Gdn William S. NEALE: (now SCHOOLEY) CtOD 9 Jan 1815; beginning May 1812; paid A. H. CLARKE for his expenses in going to Westmoreland to collect money from Presley NEALE; income from hire of

Negro Harry, leaving $106.15. Scrs: John WILLIAMS and John H. McCABE. RtCt 13 Mar 1815. [A:250]

ELLIOTT, Sally C.
S/A with Gdn Richard H. HENDERSON: beginning Jun 1807; income from rents; paid fee in motion vs. J. GRIFFITH; in bond for S. C. ELLIOTT as the desire of her mother sent by Linny on going to the Springs; suit vs. David ELLIOTT. RtCt 12 Jan 1813. [A:228]

HUGHES, John (Son of Francis)
S/A with Guardians Wm. & Mary CARR: (son of Francis HUGHES) beginning 1807; division expenses in the County of Mathews wt. Lawers fees in recovering estate; income from hire of slaves belonging to your dec'd father; Oct 1810 paid costs of suit agst. H. HOUGHES of Clorter your part; income from hire of Maria, Phill, and Luckey (1811-1812). Negro Lucky killed 1813. RtCt 14 Sep. 1813. [A:231]

S/A with Wm. CARR: income from hires of Negroes allotted by said CARR; income rec'd 16 Dec 1819 of William CARR his note due to me for $35.64 due on the said 16 Dec 1819 which is in full of all demands which I have examined said CARR & Mary his wife (late Mary HUGHES) as my Gdn – in witness I have here unto my hand & seal. John HUGHES. Teste: Fleet SMITH. RtCt 10 Jan 1820. [A:294]

PERRY, Benjamin, Samuel, Elisabeth, Mary, Margaret and Amelia (Heirs of Samuel)
S/A of heirs with Gdn Sandford RAMEY: beginning 2 Jan 1811; income from rent of one farm & two Negroes the property placed in my hands belonging to the estate of Perry; income from hire of Negro Jacob 1809-1812 and hire of Negro Manuel 1810-1812. Scrs: Robt. BRADEN, John BRADEN, Chas. BENNET. RtCt 11 Jan 1814. [A:234]

S/A with Gdn Sanford RAMEY: beginning 22 Oct 1822; execution the esc'rs. of SANDERs vs. PERRYs heirs.; income from hire of Negroes Jacob & Emanuel for the year 1818 and rent of farm [A:320]

S/A with the comm'rs. Sanford RAMEY & John BRADEN: income from sale of slaves Jacob & Emanuel; paid widow's dower, $189.28 4/7 share each to Benjamin PERRY, Saml. PERRY, Elisabeth CASEY, Mary PERRY, Margaret PERRY & Amelia PERRY. It appears from this statement that Benjamin PERRY is entitled to $20.07 from Sanford RAMEY as Gdn (including Saml. PERRY's share owned by Benjamin PERRY). And also the sum of 378.57 ¼ due him from Sanford RAMEY & John BRADEN comm'rs. for the sale of Negroes as stated in the above acct. (including Saml. PERRY's share) Scrs: Robert BRADEN, Alex'r CORDELL. RtCt 12 Feb 1823. [A:321]

S/A with Gdn Benjamin PERRY: beginning 1809; $287.01 paid to widow; $94.69 each paid to Elisabeth CASEY, Mary PERRY, Margret PERRY & Amelia PERRY; 1 Jun 1817 balance due to the said Benj'n. W. PERRY & Saml. PERRY the sum of $98.64; 1815-1818 income from rent of farm and hire of Negroes Jacob & Emanuel; paid widow's third $287.01; Benj'n & Saml PERRY's share (owned by Benj'n. W. PERRY) $191.34; $95.67 each to Elizabeth CASEY, Mary PERRY, Margaret PERRY, and Amelia PERRY. RtCt 12 Feb 1823.[A:323]

S/A with Gdn Benj. W. PERRY: beginning 1809; balance due to Benj. & Saml PERRY, widow of Sam PERRY, also sisters Elizabeth CASEY, Mary PERRY, Margaret PERRY, & Amelia PERRY, income from hire of Negroes Jacob & Emanuel and rent of farm. RtCt 12 Feb 1823. [B:51]

S/A with Gdn Sand. RAMEY: beginning 22 Oct 1818; income from hire of Negroes Jacob & Emanuel.

S/A of estate with Commrs. Sandford RAMEY & Jno. BRADEN: income from sale of Negroes Jacob & Emanuel 1 Feb 1819. RtCt 12 Feb 1823. [B:53]

ELGIN, Sarah (Orphan of William)
S/A with late Gdn Francis ELGIN: (daughter of William ELGIN); beginning 1806; income from sundry bonds & notes received from Frederick E[L]GIN Exor. of Wm. ELGIN dec'd. to collect; 1807 bonds taken for the hire of slaves; cash rec'd in the state of Maryland; paid nursing & burial of Negro Aany and nursing attendance of Negro George 11 days; paid Frederic ELGIN in Kentucky for the benefit of the ward; paid Oct 1813 for supporting Henny's three youngest children, Prisy, Charles, & Joe besides their mothers services which goes in discharging of her two older children's support. Scrs: Thomas FOUCH, Kephe E. ROZZELL, Thomas MOSS. RtCt 13 Jun 1814. [A:236]

McILHANY, Cecelia, Elizabeth, James, Louesa, Mary and Mortimer
S/A of Elizabeth McILHANY (now dec'd.) with Gdn Margaret McILHANY: beginning April 1814; one fifth of the rents on McDANIELS place being allotted for dower; paid her share of the debts of James McILHANY dec'd. not settled with personal property; lawyers fees in suit against CRAVEN; expense in sending to Kentucky concerning lands & to Richmond to get the sale confirmed of the Goose Creek tract land; my dower in WILSON or HURSTS lot; income from rents; 1809 from one house sold by Maj'r BOGGESS. RtCt 14 Jun 1814. [A:239]

S/A of Mary McILHANY now DAVIS with Gdn Margaret McILHANY: CtOD 12 Apr 1814; beginning April 1806; Apr 1814 paid part of debts of James McILHANY dec'd. not settled with personal property. Scrs: Stacy TAYLOR, Abiel JENNERS, Craven OSBURN. RtCt 14 Jun 1814. [A:241]

S/A of Cecilia McILHANY with Gdn Margt. McILHANY: beginning 1809; income from 4 years rent of Henry WINEGARNER's place now HOLLINGSWORTH and half the rents on Jacob SMITH's place. RtCt 14 Jun 1814. [A:242]

S/A of Mortimer McILHANY with Gdn Margt. McILHANY: beginning 1812; 1814 paid to build a house on JACOBS lott, now OGDONs. RtCt 14 Jun 1814. [A:243]

S/A of James McILHANY with Gdn Margt. McILHANY: income from rents. RtCt 14 Jun 1814. [A:244]

S/A of Louesa McILHANY with Gdn Margaret McILHANY: income from rents. Scrs: Stacy TAYLOR, Abiel JENNERS, Craven OSBURN. RtCt 14 Jun 1814. [A:245]

CARTER, Elizabeth (Orphan of Peter)
Memo of 12 Jun 1813 of a settlement made by consent of Gdn Elam CARTER of the late Elizabeth CARTER now Elizabeth PERRY & John PERRY who married said Elizabeth in the presence of us subscribers agreeable to a rule of the county Court of Loudoun dated Ma[r]ch 1813: Jan 1812 amt. rec'd of John CARTER of Peter CARTER. RtCt 14 Jun 1813. [A:247]

S/A of Elam CARTER late Gdn to Elizabeth CARTER wife to John PERRY: 7 Jan 1813 amt. received of John CARTER Exor. of Peter CARTER dec'd. who was father of the said Elizabeth. Scrs: Johnston CLEVELAND and Chs. LEWIS. RtCt 14 Jun 1813. [A:268]

KEIGHN, John
S/A with Gdn John T. WILSON: income from rents derived from the Mead Alley tenements in Philadelphia. This is a statement of the rents of the whole of Mead Alley property of which John KEIGHN is but half owner. RtCt 14 Feb 1815. [A:248]

WRENN, William and Mary
S/A with the estate of Gdn Mary DULIN: 1813 (for original see will book); CtOD Nov 1814; income from hire of Negroes Sam & Mary; divided the remaining part of the estate of Wm. DULIN dec'd. consisting of slaves among his legatees Edward DULIN (given Negroes Moses Senr., Milly, Lewis & John and Edward to pay in cash unto Hannah SMITH $66.67 and John DULIN Gdn of Wm. & Mary WREN $66.67) and Hannah SMITH (given Negroes Thomas, Tiner & Nancy). Scrs: Aaron SAUNDERS and George SINCLAIR. RtCt 13 Mar 1815. [A:251]

S/A of Mary WREN with Gdn Jno. DULIN: beginning 24 Nov 1814; income from Wm. & Mary WREN's part of Mary DULIN's estate, due from M. DULIN their late Gdn, due from Edward DULIN-division of slaves; income from hire of Moses and from rents; 1 Jan 1819 sold Nance; leaving $111.86. RtCt 8 May 1820. [A:296]

S/A of estate of William WRENN with Gdn J. DULIN: CtOD 8 Oct 1821; paid Dr. MARLOW in division of slaves between himself and Wm. WREN; rec'd $4273.04 due from the Gdn of Wm. WREN in full amount continued; income from hire of Negroes Moses, Sam, Mary B. & Nance; sold Nance in Feb 1818 of E. DULIN in part of Wm. WRENN share of legacy from Jas. WREN to Hary DULIN; income from rent of farm and shop & tools. Scrs: Presly CORDELL, Saml. M. EDWARDS, Thomas SANDERS. RtCt 10 Jun 1822. [A:308]

S/A of estate of William WREN with Jno. DULIN: CtOD 8 Oct 1821; beginning 17 Nov 1814 when he began living with J. DULIN, paid for clothing and board, income from rent of farm and hire of Negroes Moses, Mary & Nance. Sold Nance in Feb 1818. RtCt 10 Jun 1822. [B:55]

POWELL, Heirs of Leven Jr.
S/A with Cuthbert POWELL Gdn to the children & agent of the widow the estate being yet kept together for the benefit of the whole: income from hire of Negroes, paid A. GIBSON for Mr. SINCLAIR's dower in Hopewell land, paid clerk Fauquier Records (deed) from SINCLAIR, income from hire of Negro Grace; paid tax on Broad Run land; affidavit to Tennessee relating to land suit; rents. Scr: Burr POWELL RtCt 12 Mar 1816. [A:256]

S/A of Mrs. E. S. POWELL and children with their agent Burr POWELL from the death of said L. P. Jr. to the appointment of C. POWELL as Gdn of the children: paid for Cornelius Negroes for Sandy; tuition for Sandy; blanket for Colin; income from hire of Milly, from hire of Tim and rents. RtCt 12 Mar 1816. [A:262]

S/A of widow and children with Cuthbert POWELL Gdn to the children of agent for the widow: beginning Mar 1816; paid Jno. McIVER advances he made in Ten. on land business, paid tuition of the boys. RtCt 11 Nov 1819. [A:288]

DOUGLAS, Louisa
I hereby choice of Armistead T. MASON as my Gdn & request the County Court of Loudoun to receive & take bond of him as such. Louisa DOUGLAS. Witnessed 8 Jul 1816 by Charles DOUGLAS. RtCt 8 Jul 1816. [A:268]

CRAVEN, Harriet and Lucretia
S/A of Lucretia CRAVEN, now Lucretia WHITEHURST with Gdn John H. CRAVEN: cash rec'd from George SINCLAIR her former Gdn; income of 1810 of Sarah CRAVEN for rent, leaving $562.14. Scrs: Jno. ROSE, Thomas SANDERS, Samuel EDWARDS. RtCt 12 May 1817. [A:270]

S/A of Harriet CRAVEN with Gdn John H. CRAVEN: rec'd 1811 of Sarah CRAVEN Admr of Abner CRAVEN dec'd by the hands of William DULIN & Joseph CRAVEN, leaving $550. Scrs: Jno. ROSE, Thomas SANDERS, Samuel M. EDWARDS. RtCt 12 May 1817. [A:271]

OSBURN, Abner, Harriet, Massey and Patience
S/A of Abner OSBURNE with Gdn James HEATON: CtOD 9 Mar 1818; beginning 1806; income from rents, paid

schooling, leaving $35. Scrs: L. ELLZEY, John WHITE, Samuel PURSEL. RtCt 11 May 1818. [A:278]

S/A of Harriet OSBURN with Gdn James HEATON: CtOD 9 Mar 1818; income from rent of land 1808-17 by T. LARKIN; paid schooling, board, clothing; leaving $665. Scrs: L. ELLZEY, John WHITE, Saml. PURSEL, Fras. STRIBLING. RtCt 11 May 1818. [A:279]

S/A of Massey OSBURN with Gdn James HEATON: CtOD 9 Mar 1818; 1805-1810 income from rent of land to H. OSBURNE; paid board at dancing school; leaving $283.74. Scrs: L. ELLZEY, John WHITE, Saml. PURSEL, Fras. STRIBLING. RtCt 11 May 1818. [A:280]

S/A of Patience OSBURN with Gdn James HEATON: CtOD 9 Mar 1818; income from rents of land; paid 8 yrs. Board, leaving $251.83. Scrs: L. ELLZEY, John WHITE, Saml. PURSEL. RtCt 11 May 1818. [A:281]

POWELL, Maria A. and Sally

S/A of Maria A. POWELL with Gdn Cuthbert POWELL: beginning 28 Apr 1815; paid Sally for you at Aldie; income from shares of Potomack bank stock. RtCt 9 May 1819. [A:282]

S/A of Sally POWELL with Gdn Cuthbert POWELL: beginning 28 Apr 1813; paid you by order on A. GIBSON; income from shares of Potomack bank stock. RtCt 9 May 1819. [A:283]

S/A of Maria & Sally POWELL with C. POWELL: beginning Oct 1815 ; purchase of a Negro girl at the sale in part of the legacy, income from B. POWELL for a legacy left them by L. POWELL payable from sale of Ohio land; income from note in Kentucky in which their father had an interest. RtCt 9 Mar 1819. [A:283]

SHEPHERD, Leven

S/A with Gdn John LITTLEJOHN: beginning Oct. 1815; suit agt. Perry, general expenses, leaving $9.42¾. Scr: Saml. M. EDWARDS. RtCt 10 May 1819. [A:284]

S/A of John SHEPHERD infant: beginning 25 Nov 1814; expenses, income from rents, leaving $222.75. RtCt 10 May 1819. [A:285]

DAVIS, Polly

S/A of estate of Polly DAVIS (deaf & dumb) with Gdn Jason DAVIS: beginning 13 Apr 1818; has only rec'd. $500 of the legacy but shall retain the interest on the other $300 when rec'd. Signed: Cochran VIAA, Chester Cty Wash., Marlbro Township Penn. RtCt 9 Nov. 1819. [A:287]

S/A with Gdn Jason DAVIS: beginning 8 Nov 1821; income from two years interest on $800 left her by her brother Joseph to my care. RtCt 13 Nov 1821. [A:308]

S/A with Gdn Jason DAVIS: paid 1821-22 board & clothing, interest of $48 each year on $800 left by brother Joseph DAVIS. RtCt 9 Nov 1824. [B:1]

EVERHEART, Jacob, John, Joseph and Sally (Heirs of Jacob)

S/A with Guardians Anna DEAVER late Anna EVERHEART & Basil DEAVER: beginning 1810; income from rent of mill from 1811 up to this time; deduct one third for the widow's part; $350 each due wards Jacob EVERHEART, John EVERHEART, Joseph EVERHEART & Sally EVERHEART on May 21 1819. [A:292]

S/A of John EVERHEART with the Gdn Anna DEVER late Anna EVERHEART: paid amount allowed Anna DEVER late Anna EVERHEART for schooling & clothing of said John from 21 Mar 1819 to the time he left home to learn his trade. [A:292]

S/A of estate of Joseph EVERHEART with the Gdn Anna DEVER late Anne EVERHEART: paid amount allowed Gdn for schooling boarding & clothing said ward from 21 Mar 1809 up to the time he left home to learn his trade. [A:292]

S/A of estate of Sally EVERHEART with Gdn Anna DEVER late Anna EVERHEART: paid amount allowed Gdn for schooling boarding and clothing of said ward from 21 Mar 1809 up to the time she left home. $350.91¾ due each ward and after deducting a proper allowance for the maintenance & education of each child we find that the Gdn owes Jacob EVERHEART $71.80 ¼ on the 21 May 1819, & a like sum of $71.80 ¼ to each. RtCt 13 Nov 1819. [A:292]

FISHER, Thomas D.

S/A of estate of Thomas D. FISHER with Gdn Isaac E. STEER: beginning 2 Feb 1809; paid six days attendance at Philadelphia on business of estate. Scrs: James MOORE, John WILLIAMS, Thomas PHILIPS. RtCt 10 Jan 1820. [A:295]

LACY, John, Robert A. and Westwood A. [LACEY]

S/A of Westwood A. LACY with Gdn Wm. COOKE: beginning Jul 1819; income from hire of Negroes Charles and Maddison. RtCt 12 Mar 1821. [A:303]

S/A of Robert A. LACY with Gdn Wm. COOKE: beginning Jun 1819; paid Henry PEERS for board, paid midwife for your Negro; income from hire of Lazett for 1819 and 1820. RtCt 12 Mar 1821. [A:304]

S/A of John with Gdn Wm. COOKE: beginning Jul 1819; paid Henry PEERS for board; income from hire of Negro Henly? RtCt 12 Mar 1821. [A:306]

S/A of Westwood A. LACEY with Gdn Wm. COOKE: beginning 31 Jul 1819, paid expenses at West Point, income from hire of Negroes Charles & Maddison. RtCt 12 Mar 1821. S/A of Robert A. LACEY with Gdn Wm. COOKE: beginning 12 Jun 1819; paid board, income from hire of Negro Lizette. RtCt 12 Mar 1821. [B:49]

SMITH, Ann
S/A with Charles SMITH – beginning 1818; paid board and schooling through 1823, income from hire of Negroes Silva & Delpha and rent of farm. RtCt 12 Apr 1824. [B:2]

S/A with Gdn Chas. SMITH: paid doctor bills, schooling, boarding & rents, income from hire of Negroes Silvia & Delphia, leaving $123.28. RtCt 12 Feb 1828. [B:29]

POTTS, Joseph L. & Mahala (Heirs of David)
S/A with Gdn Robert BRADEN: (estate of David POTTS) CtOD 12 May 1823; beginning 23 Dec 1815; paid board & tuition, income from rent and crops of farm, leaving $251.28. Scrs: Abiel JENNERS, Thomas PHILLIPS. RtCt 11 Oct 1824. [B:4]

POWELL, John Leven and Alfred
S/A with brother & Gdn Cuth POWELL: beginning 1 Apr 1821; paid board & tuition. RtCt 9 Mar 1824. [B:7]

S/A of John L. POWELL with Cuthbert POWELL: beginning 20 Jan 1824; from cash of his mother, paid tuition, leaving $998.76. Scrs: W. A. POWELL, Burr POWELL, A. GIBSON. RtCt 7 Apr 1826. [B:18]

S/A of Alfred POWELL with Cuthbert POWELL: beginning 20 Jan 1824; paid S. R. POWELL for board, balance of $192.89. Scrs: Wm. A. POWELL, Burr POWELL, A. GIBSON. RtCt 9 Apr 1827. [B:20]

S/A of J. L. & A. H. POWELL with Cuth. POWELL: beginning 14 Jan 1824; payments and receipts totaling $1782.32. Scrs: Wm. A. POWELL, Burr POWELL, A. GIBSON. RtCt 9 Apr 1827. [B:22]

S/A of Cuthbert POWELL Gdn to the children and agent for the widow of Leven POWELL Jr. with Burr POWELL as her agent: beginning 11 Nov 1819, payments, income from rents and sale of Turnpike stock. RtCt 11 Oct 1830. [B:109]

MEAD, Martha
S/A with Gdn Wm. MEAD: beginning 30 May 1817; income from rent of land, leaving $713.55. Scrs: Presley CORDELL, Edward SUMMERS. RtCt 15 Mar 1826. [B:11]

MEAD, Joseph
S/A with Gdn Wm. MEAD: CtOD 13 Nov 1824; beginning 30 May 1817, income from rent of land, leaving $731.10. Scrs: Presley CORDELL, Edward SUMMERS. RtCt 11 Jan 1825. [B:12]

BRADFIELD, Julian K. (Orphan of Joseph)
S/A with Gdn William BRADFIELD: (orphan child of Joseph BRADFIELD) income from government pay due Jos. BRADFIELD as a field soldier, leaving $293.44. Scrs: Edward B. GRADY, Timothy CARRINGTON, Stephen JANNEY. RtCt 8 May 1826. [B:15]

SMITH, Mary & Susannah
S/A of Mary & Susannah SMITH with Gdn Stacy TAYLOR: beginning 1824; Mary now Mary TAYLOR (of Mahlon K. TAYLOR,) income from notes, leaving $256.31. Scrs: Noah HATCHER, Valentine V. PURSELL. RtCt 14 Nov 1826. [B:16]

CHILTON, Charles W.
S/A of estate with Gdn John ROSE: CtOD 12 Feb 1827; beginning 30 Jun 1824; expenses to Washington and Bath Springs, cash paid for Negro man Martin & Ara his wife, income from hire of servants Bill, Easter, Moses, Eliza, & Mary, leaving $1146.46½. Scrs: Sand. M. EDWARDS, Enos WILDMAN, James RUST. RtCt 13 Aug 1827. [B:18]

WALTMAN, Samuel
S/A with Gdn Jacob WALTMAN: beginning 1 Sep 1827; interest in estate of late John & Emanuel WALTMAN, paid tuition and board, leaving $1030.48. RtCt 14 Jan 1828. [B:32]

S/A with Gdn Jacob WATERS: beginning Mar 1827, paid tax and tithes, income from rent of grandfather's estate, leaving $1078.65¾. RtCt 13 May 1833. [B:198]

BRONAUGH, Patrick H. W.
S/A with Gdn Francis W. LUCKETT: beginning 11 Dec 1826; paid John BOYD for board, expenses at Philadelphia, leaving $563.51¾. RtCt 12 Jan 1829. [B:33]

FRANK, Elizabeth Ann
S/A with Gdn Thomas J. MARLOW: beginning 4 Dec 1825; paid board & schooling, medical services for Negroes, income from estate of Samuel FRANK dec'd & Hannah FRANK dec'd and from rent of farm, leaving $215.55¾. RtCt 14 Apr 1828. [B:34]

S/A with Gdn Thos. J. MARLOW: beginning 2 Jan 1828; paid for boarding two Negro children, income from rent of farm, hire of three Negroes and dividend on road stock [B:103]

S/A with Gdn Thomas J. MARLOW: beginning 1 Apr 1830; paid clothes for Negro Tom, income from rent of farm and hire of servants [B:147]

S/A with Gdn Thomas J. MARLOW: beginning 7 Feb 1832; division of slaves, Mar 1834 advance to buy wedding clothes, income from hire of Negroes Tom & Bill, leaving $350.26. RtCt 9 Feb 1835. [B:261]

FRANK, Hannah Ann
S/A with Gdn T. J. MARLOW: beginning 4 Dec 1824; same expenses & income as Elizabeth FRANK, leaving $241.04¼. RtCt 14 Apr 1828. [B:36]

S/A with Gdn Thomas J. MARLOW: beginning 2 Jan 1828; same as Elizabeth FRANK's acct. [B:105]

S/A with Gdn Thomas J. MARLOW: beginning 1 Apr 1830; bought clothes for Negro Tom, income from rent of farm and hire of servants. RtCt 9 Apr 1832. [B:146]

S/A with Gdn Thomas J. MARLOW: beginning 7 Feb 1832; paid board, income from hire of Negro Jack (burial clothes paid for 31 Dec 1834), rent of farm and hire of Negro Samuel, leaving $278.20. RtCt 14 May 1838. [B:445]

FRANK, William
S/A with Gdn Thos. J. MARLOW: beginning 4 Dec 1824; paid board & tuition, same expenses & income as Elizabeth FRANK, leaving $274.26½. RtCt 14 Apr 1828. [B:38]

S/A with Gdn Thos. J. MARLOW: beginning 2 Jan 1828; same as Elizabeth FRANK's acct. RtCt 11 Oct 1830. [B:106]

S/A with Gdn Thomas J. MARLOW: beginning 1 Apr 1830; bought clothes for Negro Tom, income from rent of farm and hire of servants. RtCt 9 Apr 1832. [B:149]

S/A of estate of William FRANK dec'd with Gdn Thomas J. MARLOW: beginning 12 Mar 1832; income from sale of Negroes and rent of farm, leaving $1335.17. RtCt 14 Jul 1834. [B:233]

S/A of estate of William FRANK dec'd with Gdn Thomas J. MARLOW: beginning 1833, paid to George MARLOW in right of his wife, paid Jonas P. SCHOOLEY in right of his wife, paid George D. SMITH in right of his wife, paid Gdn of Elizabeth (now Elizabeth STONE), paid Gdn of Hannah Ann FRANK, totaling $1320. RtCt 9 Feb 1835. [B:264]

SCHOOLEY, Sarah Ann (late Sarah Ann SMITH)
S/A with Gdn Thos. J. MARLOW: beginning 19 Jul 1824; paid tuition, income from hire of Negroes Harry, Cato, girl Priscilla, Henry & Sam, income from estate of Wm. SMITH and Hannah FRANK, leaving $288.20. RtCt 14 Apr 1828. [B:39]

MARLOW, Mary W. (late M. W. SMITH)
S/A with Thomas J. MARLOW: beginning 29 Mar 1824; income from hire of Negroes Harry, Henry, Sam, boy Cato & girl Priscilla, leaving $286.74. RtCt 14 Apr 1828. [B:42]

GREGG, Sarah Ann and Martha L. (Orphans of Samuel)
S/A of Sarah Ann GREGG & Martha L. GREGG with estate of late Gdn Casper ECHHART: income from rents, leaving $511.44. RtCt 13 Apr 1828. [B:45]

S/A of Sarah Ann GREGG with Gdn David REECE: beginning 13 Mar 1830; income from estate of Samuel GREGG, sale of Negro Ellick, and rent of Western Land, leaving $683.19½. RtCt 8 Sep 1834. [B:242]

S/A of Sarah Ann GREGG with Gdn David REECE: beginning 11 Jul 1834; income from rent of land in Ohio and rent from Nathan GREGG, leaving $769.17¼. RtCt 9 May 1836. [B:302]

HALL, Mary, Delilah and William
S/A of infants Mary HALL, Delilah HALL & Wm. HALL with Gdn Walter ELGIN: beginning 14 Sep 1828; income from Thos. HALL Admr of Jonathan HALL, leaving $99.49 to Mary and $61.66 each to Delilah & Wm. RtCt 13 Apr 1828. [B:46]

HOGUE, Phebe, Elizabeth and Rachel (Children of James) [HOGE]
S/A of Phebe, Elizabeth and Rachel with Gdn Henry S. TAYLOR: paid for school books, income from bond and rent, leaving $5067.0. RtCt 9 Jun 1829. [B:48]

S/A with Phebe HOGUE, Elizabeth HOGUE, Rachel HOGUE with Gdn Henry S. TAYLOR: beginning 16 Dec 1831, income from rents and sale of timber. RtCt 11 Mar 1833. [B:192]

S/A of Phebe HOGE and Elizabeth HOGE with Gdn Henry S. TAYLOR: beginning 23 Mar 1828; income from William HOGE & Thomas HATCHER Execs of Isaac NICHOLS dec'd James RUST's deed of trust principal. S/A of Rachel HOGE with Gdn Henry S. TAYLOR: beginning 27 Aug 1829, same as above. RtCt 13 Feb 1832. [B:140]

S/A of Phebe HOGE with Gdn Henry S. TAYLOR: beginning 1833; paid Hannah Hoge, income from crops, leaving $2167.77 [B:222]

S/A of Elizabeth HOGE with Henry S. TAYLOR: beginning 13 Mar 1833; income from crops and sale of wood, leaving $1790.32. [B:222]

S/A of Rachel HOGE with Henry S. TAYLOR: beginning 16 Mar 1833, paid Hannah HOGE, income from sale of crops, wood and wool, leaving $3205.12. RtCt 10 Mar 1834. [B:223]

S/A of Phebe HOGUE with Henry S. TAYLOR: income from sale of crops, leaving $2211.14 [B:283]

S/A of Elizabeth HOGUE with Henry S. TAYLOR: income from sale of crops, amount advanced in building a house, leaving $1901.48. [B:284]

S/A of Rachel HOGUE of Henry S. TAYLOR: income from sale of crops and wood, leaving $3297.86. RtCt 12 Oct 1835. [B:285]

SHAW, Susan Bailey
S/A with Gdn Rebecca SHAW: CtOD 16 May 1827; beginning 31 Jan 1826; paid clothing and board. RtCt 13 Apr 1829. [B:64]

GREGG, William
S/A of estate of Wm. GREGG with the estate of Aaron GREGG as Gdn of his children: beginning 12 Feb 1820; five children – Resin GREGG, Rebecca GREGG, Wm. GREGG, Ruth GREGG, Mary GREGG (dec'd by 1 Aug 1820 – her share divided amongst other four and mother Margaret HARPER). RtCt 12 Aug 1828. [B:66]

FONTAINE, Alice Virginia
S/A with Gdn Wm. NOLAND: beginning 11 Jul 1828; paid board & tuition, cash from Lucy M. FONTAINE and Mary B. FONTAINE from division of slaves, income from sale of Negro boy John to T. ROACH. RtCt 8 Feb 1830. [B:69]

FONTAINE, Lucy Norborne
S/A with Gdn William NOLAND: beginning 4 Mar 1828; paid tuition & board, Negro Patty sold 26 Sep 1828. RtCt 8 Feb 1830. [B:73]

McGAVACK, Mary Pleasant
S/A with Israel McGAVACK: beginning 11 Sep 1817; interest payments. RtCt 12 Apr 1830. [B:77]

S/A of Mary Pleasant McGAVVICK with Gdn Presley CORDELL: income from Patrick McGAVVICK and Israel McGAVVICK for rent of land, paid midwife for Negro Grace, payment in full of $352.54¾ on 9 May 1831 to Nathan COCHRAN who she married. RtCt 11 Jul 1836. [B:365]

DEAVER, Deborah, Margaret and Daniel (Children of Bazell)
S/A of Deborah PARKER late Deborah DEAVER, Margaret MORGAN late Margaret DEAVER and Daniel DEAVER with Gdn Jacob EVERHEART dec'd: beginning 9 Feb 1825; paid Abraham DEAVER for expenses, income from legacy of Jacob WALTMAN Sr. RtCt 12 Apr 1830. [B:79]

CRAVEN, Ellen and Euphemia
S/A with Gdn Joseph GORE: beginning 31 Dec 1820; paid tuition, cash paid mother, income from hire of Negro Levi. RtCt 12 Apr 1830. [B:82]

RUSSELL, Estate of William
S/A with Gdn Henry RUSSELL: amt. left to children by first marriage, widow, shares to Nancy RUSSELL (became 21 on 14 Aug 1825), Mary RUSSELL (became 21 on 18 Oct 1818), Polly RUSSELL, Rachel RUSSELL, (became 21 on 13 Dec 1821), Mahlon RUSSELL (became 21 on 7 Aug 1823), James RUSSELL (became 21 on 24 Apr 1827), Emily RUSSELL. RtCt 12 Apr 1830. [B:87]

RUN, Sarah
S/A of Sarah RUN late Sarah EVERHART with Gdn Jacob EVERHEART: beginning 15 May 1820; income from rent, paid mill repairs, leaving $1269.49. RtCt 12 Apr 1830. [B:91]

THORNTON, Heirs of Charles
S/A of Sarah WATERS with Gdn Alfred BELT: beginning 5 Jul 1828; general payments leaving $61.60. RtCt 17 Jun 1830. [B:94]

S/A of Sarah WATERS with Gdn Alfred BELT: income from estate of Charles THORNTON. RtCt 14 Nov 1831. [B:138]

S/A of Sarah WATERS with Gdn Alfred BELT: beginning 11 Mar 1833; income from hire of Negro Fan and rent of farm, leaving $54.57. RtCt 9 Dec 1833. [B:214]

S/A of Sarah WATERS with Gdn Alfred BELT: beginning 28 Aug 1831; payments and interest, leaving $112.48. RtCt 12 Nov 1834. [B:251]

S/A of Sarah WATERS with Gdn Alfred BELT: beginning 4 Jul 1835; paid Walter EVANS for board, income from hire of servant Fanny and rent of farm, leaving $173.35. [B:290]

S/A of Sarah WATERS with Gdn Alfred BELT: beginning 17 Aug 1836; paid board, income from hire of Fanny, leaving $215.44. [B:372]

S/A of Sarah WATERS (now Sarah McKIMMEY) with Gdn Alfred BELT: beginning 31 Dec 1836, paid midwife for Negro Fanny and board, leaving $173.35. [B:216]

S/A of Mary THORNTON with Gdn Alfred BELT: beginning 5 Jul 1828; legacy from relative in Pennsylvania and from Amos SINCLAIR, your part of rent of land from death of Charles THORNTON after deducting legacies to Catharine JORDAN & Sarah KNOTT. Scr: W. A. POWELL [B:96]

S/A of Mary THORNTON with Gdn Alfred BELT: beginning 16 Jul 1830; income from hire of Negro girl and from legacy. [B:137]

S/A of Mary THORNTON with Gdn Alfred BELT: beginning 11 Sep 1832; paid board, income from rent and legacy from PA & Amos SINCLAIR's estate, leaving 101.73. [B:214]

S/A of Mary THORNTON with Gdn Alfred BELT: beginning 11 Sep 1833; income from hire of Negro Caroline and rent of land, leaving $8.75 2/3. RtCt 12 Nov 1834. [B:252]

S/A of Mary THORNTON with Gdn Alfred BELT: beginning 20 Sep 1834; paid board, income from hire of servant Caroline, rent of farm, and legacy from PA, leaving $227.71. RtCt 9 Nov 1835. [B:289]

S/A of Mary THORNTON with Gdn Alfred BELT: beginning 6 Dec 1835; paid for bringing her from Charlottesville, income from hire of Negro Caroline and rent of land, leaving $227.71. RtCt 14 Nov 1836. [B:373]

S/A of Mary THORNTON with Gdn Alfred BELT: beginning 12 Oct 1836; income from hire of Negro Caroline and rent of farm, leaving $227.71. [B:416]

S/A with Alfred BELT Exor of estate: beginning 10 Feb 1832; paid tuition and board, income from rents. RtCt 12 Nov 1832. [B:181]

S/A of Mary Ann THORNTON with Gdn Alfred BELT: CtOD 15 Aug 1838; paid board, income from hire of Caroline & int and rent of 29 acres extra under this will; leaving $227.71 (she having now arrived at age 21y). S/A of

John McKIMMA [McKIMMY] & Sarah his wife, late WATERS with Gdn Alfred BELT: income from hire of Negro Fanny; 26 Oct 1838 paid John McKIMMY in full. RtCt 14 Nov 1838. [C:29]

HAWLING, Heirs of William
S/A of Martha HAWLING one of the heirs of Wm. HAWLING with Gdn Wm. HAWLING (now dec'd): beginning 1 Jan 1827, income from servant Lloyd, paid boarding old man Charles, servant Eliza. RtCt 13 Sep 1830. [B:97]

HATCHER, Mary A., Emsey F., Gourley R., Amanda M., Anna V. and Ruth Anna (Children of Joseph)
S/A of Mary A. RECTOR (wife of Caleb RECTOR) late Mary A. HATCHER with Guardians Gourley REEDER & Joshua HOGUE: beginning 1824; income from rent of Fauquier farm, payment to Caleb RECTOR, income from rent of tavern lot and Ohio land, paid widow. RtCt 11 Apr 1831. [B:118]
S/A of Emsey F. GIBSON (Nelson GIBSON) late Emsey F. HATCHER with Gdn Gourley REEDER & Joshua HOGE: as above. RtCt 11 Apr 1831. [B:120]
S/A of Gourley R. HATCHER with Guardians Gourley REEDER & Joshua HOGE: as above. RtCt 11 Apr 1831. [B:123]
S/A of Amanda M. HATCHER with Guardians Gourley REEDER & Joshua HOGE: as above. RtCt 11 Apr 1831. [B:125]
S/A of Anna V. HATCHER with Guardians Gourley REEDER & Joshua HOGUE: as above. RtCt 11 Apr 1831. [B:129]
S/A of Ruth Anna GIBSON formerly HATCHER with Gdn Joshua HOGUE: beginning 1824, as above. RtCt 14 Feb 1831. [B:133]
S/A of Anna HATCHER with Gdn Gourley REEDER: beginning 1831, paid for a horse of Jonah HATCHER, income from rent of tavern and farm, sale of wood, rent from Ohio farm, and from Fauquier farm, cash paid Samuel RECTOR her husband on 17 Apr 1834, totaling $944.35. RtCt 14 Jul 1834. [B:229]
S/A of Amanda HATCHER with Gdn Gourley REEDER: beginning 8 Nov 1831; income from rent of tavern, farm, rent from Fauquier and rent from Ohio, paid H. COCKE her husband on 26 Apr 1834, leaving $588.65. RtCt 14 Jul 1834. [B:336]

McDANIEL, John, Nancy and Elizabeth (Orphans of James)
Inventory of estate of John McDANIEL, Nancy McDANIEL, and Elizabeth McDANIEL with Gdn Thomas ROGERS: beginning 1 Apr 1831; income from Archibald McDANIEL, Edward McDANIEL dec'd, and Jno. BRADEN Exor of James McDANIEL dec'd. RtCt 9 May 1831. [B:136]

S/A of John, Nancy & Eliz'a McDANIEL with Gdn Thomas ROGERS: beginning 4 Sep 1831; paid board, income from Arch'd McDANIEL Exor of Edward McDANIEL dec'd it being in part of the interest of Jas. McDANIEL dec'd in his father's estate and from Archibald McDANIEL Admr of Ann McDANIEL dec'd widow of Edward McDANIEL, totaling $2338.12. RtCt 8 Jul 1833. [B:206]
S/A of John, Nancy & Elizabeth McDANIEL with Gdn Thomas ROGERS: beginning Apr 1833; paid board & tuition, income from rent of land, cash of Arch'd McDANIEL Execs of Edward McDANIEL. [B:361]
S/A of John, Elizabeth & Nancy McDANIEL with Gdn Thomas ROGERS: CtOD 13 Feb 1838; paid board & clothing; income from rent of land, leaving $2417.92. RtCt 18 Nov 1843. [C:164]

HOGE, Isaac
S/A with Gdn Jonas JANNEY: beginning 29 Aug 1829; income from rents and book accts. RtCt 13 Feb 1832. [B:144]
S/A with Gdn Jonas JANNEY: payments and income from crops totaling $1730.89½. RtCt 12 Aug 1833. [B:209]

VERTS, William
S/A with Gdn Ebenezer GRUBB Jr: CtOD 13 Feb 1832; beginning 26 Oct 1829; paid tuition & board, income from rent of John BOOTH and Ann SANDFORD and from rent in MD. RtCt 9 Apr 1832. [B:151]

VERTS, Henry
S/A with Gdn Ebenezer GRUBB Jr: beginning 27 Oct 1829; paid tuition & board, income from rent of E. AXLINE in MD and rent of John BOOTH. RtCt 9 Apr 1832. [B:155]

VERTS, Peter
S/A with Gdn Ebenezer GRUBB Jr: beginning 15 Oct 1830; paid tuition & board, income from rents. RtCt 9 Apr 1832. [B:158]
S/A with Gdn Ebenezer GRUBB Jr: beginning 10 Nov 1832; income from rent in MD due from John VIRTS. RtCt 9 Mar 1835. [B:271]

BOUGHMAN, Mary Ann, John William, Charlotte, Catharine, Sarah Ann and James Andrew (Children of Ann)
S/A with Gdn Thomas J. MARLOW: beginning 13 Feb 1828; income from Robert BROWN the Gdn in MD, settlements of Mary Ann BOUGHMAN, John William BOUGHMAN, Charlotte Catharine BOUGHMAN, Sarah Ann BOUGHMAN (now dec'd) & James Andrew BOUGHMAN, payments also to sister Margaret for board & tuition. RtCt 9 Apr 1832. [B:161]
S/A of Mary Ann BOUGHMAN with Gdn Thomas J. MARLOW: CtOD 9 Feb 1835; 1 Jan 1832 balance due Sarah Ann BOUGHMAN dec'd., income rec'd of M. SHOVERS Execs, leaving $115.42 which has been paid

over to her she having arrived of age. RtCt 10 Feb 1841. [C:95]

S/A of James A. BOUGHMAN with Gdn Thomas J. MARLOW: beginning 1 Jan 1832; paid tuition, balance due Sarah Ann BOUGHMAN dec'd, payment rec'd from M. SHOVER Execs. Full payment on Feb. 23, 1841. RtCt 11 Mar 1841. [C:101]

BAUGHMAN, Charlotte E. and John W.

S/A of Charlotte E. BAUGHMAN with Gdn Thomas J. MARLOW: beginning 1 Jan 1832; paid sister Margaret for tuition, leaving balance of $172.17 on the 1 Apr 1840 paid to her, having arrive the age of twenty one years. Also balance due to John W. BAUGHMAN of $8.85 with int. from the 15 Nov 1838, paid off on 29 Jun 1839. RtCt 14 Jan 1845. [C:177]

BUSSARD, Milton M.

S/A with Gdn John M. WILSON: beginning 1 Apr 1830; income from rent of farm and hire of Negroes, leaving $68.95. RtCt 11 Jun 1832. [B:166]

S/A with Gdn John M. WILSON: beginning 14 Sep 1832; paid midwife for delivering Cass, income from rent of farm & house and hire of Negroes Henry & Charity, totaling $139.66¾. RtCt 13 Oct 1834. [B:248]

BUSSARD, Perriander L.

S/A with Gdn John M. WILSON: beginning 20 Feb 1830, income from rent of farm, hire of Negroes, leaving $34.83½. RtCt 11 Jun 1832. [B:168]

S/A with Gdn John M. WILSON: beginning 14 Sep 1832, paid midwife for delivering Cass, income from rent of farm and house, leaving $102.46. RtCt 13 Oct 1834. [B:245]

SANBOWER, Julian

S/A with Gdn Ferdinando F. STUCK: beginning 9 May 1831; legacy from Adam KARN Admr of M. SHOVER, leaving $275.39. RtCt 10 Sep 1832. [B:170]

S/A with Gdn F. F. STUCK: beginning 20 Jul 1832; income from Adam KARN Exor of Magdelena SHOVER from estate, leaving $319.89. RtCt 9 Jun 1834. [B:227]

S/A with Gdn F. F. STUCK: CtOD 12 Jun 1838; amt. rec'd of Geo. RICKARD under decree of the Court. Ward now of age and paid in full. RtCt 14 Nov 1838. [C:31]

DOWDELL, Heirs of Moses

S/A with Gdn James GILMORE dec'd: beginning 1827; division of Negroes Dick & Godfrey, income from rent, settlements of Isaac DOWELL, Elizabeth DOWDELL, Thomas G. DOWDELL & Mary DOWDELL (living with and supported by Charles WILLIAMS). RtCt 10 Sep 1832. [B:172]

S/A with Gdn James GILMORE dec'd: income from rents, crops, hire of Negroes and sale of Dick, settlements with Isaac DOWDELL, Elizabeth DOWDELL, Thomas G. DOWDELL & Mary DOWDELL (living with and supported by Charles WILLIAMS). RtCt 12 Nov 1832. [B:185]

S/A of Elizabeth DOWDELL with Gdn Charles WILLIAMS: beginning 28 Apr 1832; income from rent of Big Spring farm, 31 Jul 1832 from S. M. BOSS Admr of James GILMORE dec'd former Gdn, from rent of farm over the mountain. RtCt 13 Jul 1835. [B:278]

WIRTZ, Loucinda

S/A with Gdn Michael EVERHEART: beginning 27 May 1830; general payments leaving $193.04. RtCt 13 May 1833. [B:196]

S/A with Gdn Michael EVERHART: beginning 1 Jan 1833; income from rent of John WIRTZ, legacy from Jacob WIRTZ and from hire of Negro woman, leaving $102.71½. RtCt 13 Jun 1836. [B:358]

WIRTZ, Susannah

S/A with Gdn Michael EVERHEART: beginning 27 May 1830; legacy, payments, leaving $117.86¾. RtCt 13 May 1833. [B:201]

S/A with Gdn Michael EVERHART her Gdn: beginning 16 Oct 1832; income rent from Jno. WIRTZ, legacy from Jacob WIRTZ, totaling $168.32¼. RtCt 13 Jun 1836. [B:356]

WIRTZ, Mary Ann

S/A with Gdn Michael EVERHART: beginning 27 May 1830, legacy in hands of E. GRUBB, income from rents, leaving $31.54¾. RtCt 13 May 1833. [B:204]

S/A with Gdn Michael EVERHART: beginning 1 Jan 1833; income rent from John WIRTZ in MD, legacy from Jacob WIRTZ, leaving $78.39. RtCt 13 Jun 1836. [B:353]

EVERHEART, Sarah

S/A with Sarah EVERHEART: (infant of J. EVERHEART) beginning 5 Nov 1829; income from rent of farm, leaving $79.90. RtCt 9 Sep 1833. [B:210]

EVERHEART, Elizabeth (Infant of J.)

S/A with Sarah EVERHEART: (infant of J. EVERHEART) beginning 5 Nov 1829; income from rent of farm, leaving $3418¼. RtCt 9 Sep 1833. [B:212]

EVERHART, Sarah J.

S/A with Gdn Peter STUCK: beginning 3 Dec 1832; paid tuition and board, income from rent of farm, leaving $395.32 due to Gdn. Besides the rents charged in the preceding account there is a balance due from the estate of John WENNER dec'd who intermarried with the widow the mother of Sarah J. EVERHART. RtCt 12 May 1840. [C:69]

S/A with Gdn Peter STUCK: beginning Jan 1839; paid tuition, board and house repairs, leaving $285.13. RtCt 15 Apr 1848. [C:283]

Sarah WASHINGTON late EVERHART with Gdn Jacob SHAFFER: CtOD 13 Jun 1848; beginning Jun 1846;

28 Aug 1846 to Samuel E. WASHINGTON her husband, leaving $25.92 due to Gdn. RtCt 13 Aug 1849. [C:320]

CRAIG, Nancy, Samuel & William
S/A with Gdn Rebecca CRAIG: beginning 5 Nov 1833; income from land sold in Morgan Co., rent of farm, and hire of Negroes George & Charlotte, leaving $426.74. RtCt 9 Dec 1833. [B:216]

HURDLE, Pleasant
S/A with Gdn William RUSSELL: beginning 12 Nov 1830; paid Nancy HURDLE for support, income from Silas A. MARMADUKE Admr of Noland HURDLE dec'd, leaving $39.18. RtCt 10 Feb 1834. [B:218]

HURDELL, Ann Noland
S/A with Gdn William RUSSELL: beginning 12 Nov 1830, paid Nancy HURDELL for support, leaving $39.18. RtCt 10 Feb 1834. [B:220]

McKNIGHT, Amy W.
S/A with Gdn James T. BRADFIELD: beginning 24 May 1830, income from crops and interest, totaling $393.74½. RtCt 14 Apr 1834. [B:225]

S/A with Gdn James T. BRADFIELD: (now Amy W. HOWELL) beginning 1834; balance of $426.76½. Scrs: Thos. NICHOLS, Timothy TAYLOR Jr. RtCt 8 Sep 1834. [B:239]

RAWLINGS, Samuel A., Mary Virginia E. and John M. (Heirs of Stephen)
S/A with Gdn William RAWLINGS: beginning 1833; payments to Jno. M. RAWLINGS, S. A. RAWLINGS & Sarah RAWLINGS for boarding, etc. of Jno. M., Samuel A. & Mary V. E. RAWLINGS, income from rents and hire of servants. RtCt 12 May 1834. [B:227]

S/A of widow Sarah HART late Mrs. Sarah RAWLINGS with Wm. RAWLINGS Gdn of children & Admr: CtOD 8 Jan 1838; beginning 1834; in from rents and from hire of Negroes Lovey, Edward, James, Alfred, Morear, Marias & Jim; 7 Sep 1837 from J. C. WILLIAMS on Execs. vs. C. TURNER; leaving $93.30. S/A of children with Gdn William RAWLINGS: beginning 1834; paid board and tuition, ¼ part of estate from Admr. acct; leaving of Samuel A. RAWLINGS $401.34½, leaving Mary Virginia Elizabeth RAWLINGS $469.64, leaving Wm. RAWLINGS $234.11½ and leaving John M. RAWLINGS $346.63 ½ RtCt 15 Aug 1838. [C:9]

S/A of Jno. M. RAWLINGS with Gdn Wm. RAWLINGS: CtOD 13 Dec 1839; paid board & tuition, 23 Nov 1838 paid for coffin for Negro Howard, leaving $35.79 RtCt 8 Feb 1840. [C:50]

S/A of Samuel A. RAWLINGS with Gdn Wm. RAWLINGS: paid board & tuition; income from hire of Negro Jim, leaving $113.37. Scrs: A. GIBSON and Burr WEEKS. RtCt 10 Feb 1840. [C:52]

S/A of Mary V. E. RAWLINGS with Gdn Wm. RAWLINGS: CtOD 13 Dec 1839; paid board and for items for Negro girl Merrica; leaving $88.73. Scrs: A. GIBSON and Burr WEEKS. RtCt 10 Feb 1840. [C:53]

S/A of Mary V. E. RAWLINGS with Gdn William RAWLINGS: beginning 2 Jan 1841; paid board & tuition, 8 Feb 1842 interest on proceeds of sale of Negro woman Maria. S/A of Samuel A. RAWLINGS with Gdn Wm. RAWLINGS: paid board & tuition and for items for Negro James. S/A of John M. RAWLINGS with Gdn Wm. RAWLINGS: travelling expenses to Missouri; income from rent of land in 1840. Scrs: Robert F. LUCKETT and F. W. POWELL. RtCt 7 Mar 1842. [C:124]

S/A of John M. RAWLINGS with Gdn William RAWLINGS: beginning 13 Aug 1842; paid land tax, tuition and board. S/A of Samuel A. RAWLINGS with Gdn William RAWLINGS: paid board, income from hire of Negro James. S/A of Mary V. E. RAWLINGS with Gdn Wm. RAWLINGS: beginning 26 Apr 1842; paid board and tuition. RtCt 10 Sep 1844. [C:174]

S/A of Samuel A. RAWLINGS with Gdn Wm. RAWLINGS Gdn: beginning 15 Aug 1846; paid college fees at Carlisle; (says continued, but not on next page). [C:220]

S/A of John M. RAWLINGS with Gdn Wm. RAWLINGS: beginning Oct 1844; general expenses. RtCt 13 Nov 1846. [C:247]

S/A of Samuel A. RAWLINGS with Gdn Wm. RAWLINGS: beginning 1843; paid tuition and board; Sep 1845 start of college; income from hire of Negro James. RtCt 13 Nov 1846. [C:248]

S/A of Mary V. E. RAWLINGS with Gdn Wm. RAWLINGS: beginning Jul 1844; paid board and tuition. RtCt 13 Nov. 1846. [C:249]

S/A of Mary V. E. RAWLINGS with Gdn Wm. RAWLINGS: beginning Jan 1847; paid board, income from rents and hire of Negroes Edward & Levy. RtCt 15 Nov 1848. [C:294]

S/A of Samuel A. RAWLINGS with Gdn Wm. RAWLINGS: college fee at Carlisle, income from hire of James, leaving $72.80. RtCt 15 Nov 1848. [C:296]

WIRTZ, Jacob
S/A to 26 Dec 1831 with Gdn Michael EVERHART: beginning 9 Dec 1830; income from crops, leaving $40 26 Dec 1831. Scrs: John MOORE, Jacob WATERS. RtCt 14 Jul 1834. [B:232]

SMITH, Alexander M., Mary Ann and Maria E. (Estate of Lewis M.)
S/A of Alexander M. SMITH with Gdn Reuben HUTCHISON: beginning 23 Sep 1833, general payments leaving $32.86½. Scrs: J. BAYLEY, Chs. LEWIS. RtCt 8 Sep 1834. [B:240]

S/A of Mary Ann SMITH with Gdn Reuben HUTCHISON: beginning 13 Aug 1833, general payments leaving $44.32½. Scrs: J. BAYLEY, Chs. LEWIS. RtCt 8 Sep 1834. [B:241]

S/A of Maria SMITH with Gdn Reuben HUTCHISON: beginning 10 Dec 1833, general payments leaving $3.08. Scrs: J. BAYLEY, Chs. LEWIS. RtCt 8 Sep 1834. [B:241]

S/A with Gdn Alexander HUTCHISON: CtOD 9 Apr 1838; beginning Feb 1837; paid support of old Nancy Betsy & two children and medical attendance of Mary & child, rec'd cash of J. S. EDMONDS in part of Execs. vs. Wm. WRIGHT, income from hire of Negroes Washington, Bob, Ben & John and rents. S/A of Alexander M. SMITH with Gdn Alexander HUTCHISON: paid board & tuition, leaving $57.83¾. S/A of Mary Ann SMITH with Gdn Alexander HUTCHISON: paid hire to Middleburg school and tuition, leaving $21.90¼. S/A of Maria SMITH with Gdn Alexander HUTCHISON: paid hire to Middleburg School, board & tuition, leaving $65.53½. Their grandfather Reuben Alexander HUTCHISON dec'd whose Guardianship account I am now settling was appointed their Gdn, and the motion of said Alexander HUTCHISON, who was also the Exor. of Reuben HUTCHISON dec'd his father. RtCt 10 Sep 1838. [C:25]

S/A of heirs with Gdn Sampson HUTCHISON: CtOD 11 Mar 1840; beginning May 1838; paid for coffin for black child, medical for Matilda, coffins for 3 black children, fee in suit vs. R'd. JOHNSON, repairs & tax on house & lot in Aldie, and fee for defending Negro Henry; income from hire of Negroes Fenton, Jane, Matilda & 2 children, old Clair, boy Ben and woman, Malinda, Washington and Bob, Sarah, John, Lewis & Malinda. S/A of Mary Ann SMITH with Gdn Sampson HUTCHISON: paid board & tuition & music lessons; cash from Admr. of Reuben HUTCHISON dec'd, leaving $589.30¼. S/A of Maria E. SMITH with Gdn Sampson HUTCHISON: as above, leaving $1307.87½. S/A of Alexander M. SMITH with Gdn Sampson HUTCHISON: paid board & tuition; cash from the Admr. of Alexander HUTCHISON dec'd his late Gdn, leaving $1216.20¾. RtCt 17 Sep 1840. [C:83]

S/A of heirs with Gdn Sampson HUTCHISON: paid for goods stolen by Negro Henry, paid half the cost of a partition fence in Aldie, paid for coffin for Negro child, for taking up George runaway and board of three Negro children while their mother was run away, income from hire of Washington, Charles, Fenton, boy Ben, Sanford, Matilda & child, Melinda, girl Sarah, Jane, Charles & boy Henry. S/A of heirs with Gdn Sampson HUTCHISON: paid boy Henry's jail fee and for coffin of Negro child, income from rent of house & lot in Aldie, seven suits in Fauquier, paid boarding Negro children of runaway mother, income from hire of Negroes Washington, Charles, Fenton Ben, Sandford, Matilda & child, Melinda, Sarah, Jane, Charles & Henry. S/A of Mary Ann FOSTER late SMITH with Gdn Sampson HUTCHISON: paid board, leaving $1.81¼. S/A of Maria E. SMITH with Gdn Sampson HUTCHISON: paid board & tuition, leaving $1214.48¼. S/A of Alexander SMITH with Gdn Sampson HUTCHISON: general expenses, leaving $1339.08 ½. RtCt 10 May 1842. [C:145]

General S/A with Gdn Sampson HUTCHISON: CtOD 14 Aug 1844; expenses for Negroes George, Bob & Lewis, amt. of Fielder HOOPER & Robert ROSE's bond charged to Gdn. S/A of Alexander M. SMITH with Gdn Sampson HUTCHISON: income from hire of Ben, Fenton, Malinda, John, Matilda & 3 children and Frances, from rent of house in Aldie; paid the diff. between legal & ordinary fee in suit vs. E. BARRY, leaving $312.72. S/A of Maria E. SMITH with Gdn Sampson HUTCHISON: paid board and tuition, income from hire of Jane, Sarah, boy Sanford, Washington, Mary & 2 children & Charles, paid repairs to Aldie house, leaving $1194.57. S/A of Thomas R. FOSTER who intermarried with Mary Ann SMITH with Gdn Sampson HUTCHISON: income from rent of house in Aldie, leaving $114.89 due to Gdn. RtCt 14 Mar 1846. [C:215]

S/A of Mary Ann FOSTER with Gdn S. HUTCHISON: CtOD 12 Oct 1849; paid board, payments on bonds, leaving $1.81¼. S/A of Maria E. SMITH with Gdn S. HUTCHISON: paid school in Alexandria, leaving $1214.48¼ . S/A of Alexander SMITH with Gdn S. HUTCHISON: paid board and tuition, leaving $1339.08½. The slaves were divided among the three wards and those allotted to Mary Ann surrendered to her husband Thos. R. FOSTER. RtCt 17 Mar 1842. [C:130]

S/A of to Maria E. SMITH now CARTER with Gdn Sampson HUTCHISON: income from hire of Negroes Mary & child, Sarah, Washington, Lane, boy Jeff, Jane & child, Charles & girl Eliza, income from rent of house in Aldie, leaving $9.83. S/A of Alexander M. SMITH with Gdn Sampson HUTCHISON: paid for items for Negroes Malinda & Washington, leaving $8.11. S/A of Thomas R. FOSTER & wife with Sampson HUTCHISON: as above, leaving $48.33. RtCt 14 May 1850. [C:331]

GOODIN, Rachel
S/A with Gdn Chas. B. HAMILTON: beginning 6 Aug 1828; refund to Mrs. Anne GOODEN, cash rec'd for land, leaving $189.52. RtCt 8 Dec 1834. [B:254]

GOODIN, Martha
S/A with Gdn Chas. B. HAMILTON: beginning 6 Aug 1828; payment rec'd for land, leaving $199.24½. RtCt 12 Jan 1835. [B:256]

SLATES, Solomon, Eliza Ann, William and Mary
S/A William SLATES with Gdn Jacob SHAFFER: beginning 10 Dec 1832; division of land, income from Adam SLATES' estate and from Frederick SLATES' estate, leaving $485.61½. [B:258]

S/A Mary SLATES with Gdn Jacob SHAFFER: beginning 10 Dec 1832, division of land, income from Adam SLATES' estate and from Frederick SLATES' estate, leaving $485.61½. RtCt 9 Feb 1835. [B:259]

S/A Solomon SLATES with Gdn Savilla SNOW, late Savilla SLATES: beginning 10 Dec 1832; division of land, income from estates of Adam SLATES and Frederick SLATES and from rent of farm with widow entitled to 1/3, leaving $485.61½. [B:266]

S/A Eliza Ann SLATES with Gdn Savilla SNOW, late Savilla SLATES: beginning 10 Dec 1832; division of land, income from estates of Adam SLATES and Frederick SLATES and from rent of farm with widow entitled to 1/3, leaving $485.61½. RtCt 5 Feb 1835. [B:267]

S/A Eliza Ann SLATES with Gdn John SNOW and Savilla his wife: beginning 7 Sep 1835; paid tuition, income from rent of land and sale of wood, leaving $485.61½. RtCt 10 Apr 1837. [B:377]

S/A Solomon SLATES with Gdn John SNOW and Savilla his wife: beginning 3 Oct 1835; paid tuition, income from rent of land and sale of wood, leaving $485.61½. RtCt 10 Apr 1837. [B:378]

S/A William SLATES with Gdn Jacob SLATES [Shaffer?]: beginning 24 Dec 1834; paid John SNOW for board, income from rent of land, paid T. R. SAUNDERS for tuition, leaving $485.61½. RtCt 10 Apr 1837. [B:380]

S/A Mary SLATES with Gdn Jacob SHAFFER: beginning 24 Dec 1834, paid board & tuition, income from rent of land and sale of wood, leaving $485.61½. RtCt 10 Apr 1837. [B:382]

S/A of Solomon SLATES with Gdn John SNOW & Sevilla his wife: CtOD 11 Feb 1839; paid tuition, income from rent of farm, leaving $485.61½. S/A of Elizabeth Ann SLATES with Gdn John SNOW: paid tuition, leaving $485.61½. RtCt 15 Oct 1839 [C:37]

S/A of William SLATES with Gdn Jacob SHAFER: CtOD 11 Feb 1839; paid tuition, leaving $485.61½. S/A of Mary SLATES with Gdn Jacob SHAFER: paid tuition, leaving $485.61½. RtCt 15 Oct 1839. [C:43]

S/A of Eliza Ann SLATES with Gdn John SNOW & wife: paid tuition, income from rent of lot and wood, leaving $898.44½. S/A of Solomon SLATES with Gdn John SNOW & wife: as above, leaving $921.83½. S/A of Mary SLATES with Gdn Jacob SHAFER: payment of taxes and rent of lot, leaving $1032.24½. S/A of William SLATES with Gdn Jacob SHAFFER: as above, leaving $1165.87½. RtCt 9 Sep 1845 [C:201]

S/A of Eliza Ann SLATES with Gdn John SNOW and Sevilla his wife: CtOD 11 Mar 1841; paid board & tuition, leaving $485.61½. S/A of Solomon SLATES with Gdn John SNOW: paid tuition, leaving $485.61½. RtCt 10 May 1841. [C:101]

S/A of Eliza Ann SLATES and Solomon SLATES with Gdn John SNOW: beginning Nov 1845; Conrad SLATES present Gdn, income from rent of farm. RtCt 9 Feb 1847. [C255]

S/A of William SLATES with Gdn Jacob SHAFFER: CtOD 11 Mar 1841; beginning 31 Dec 1838; income from rent of land and loads of wood, leaving $485.61½. S/A of Mary SLATES with Gdn Jacob SHAFFER: beginning 31 Dec 1838; paid board & tuition, leaving $485.61½. RtCt 10 May 1841. [C:109]

S/A of Mary SLATES with Gdn Jacob SHAFFER: CtOD 13 Jun 1848; income from rent and interest, leaving $860.13. S/A of William SLATES with Gdn Jacob SHAFFER: paid him in full. RtCt 11 Sep 1848. [C:293]

RICHTER, John and Charles William (Children of George)

S/A of John RICHTER and Charles Wm. RICHTER with estate of late Gdn Henry RICHTER dec'd: beginning 31 Dec 1821; Sanford EDWARDS new Gdn. RtCt 9 Feb 1835. [B:269]

CLOWES, Elizabeth, Thomas and Mary Jane

S/A with Gdn Charles B. HAMILTON: beginning 1 Apr 1834; income from rent of land, board, leaving each with $101.03. RtCt 13 Apr 1835. [B:273]

ROLLINGS, William H., John M., Samuel A., and Mary Virginia Elizabeth

S/A of William H. ROLLINGS with Gdn William ROLLINGS: beginning 9 Apr 1835; paid James B. BISCOE for schooling. [B:275]

S/A of John M. ROLLINGS with Gdn William ROLLINGS: beginning 16 May 1834; paid Sarah ROLLINGS for schooling. RtCt 11 May 1835. [B:275]

S/A of Samuel A. ROLLINGS with Gdn William ROLLINGS: beginning 16 May 1835; paid Sarah ROLLINGS for board. [RtCt 11 May 1835. [B:276]

S/A of Mary Virginia Elizabeth ROLLINGS with Gdn William ROLLINGS: beginning 10 Apr 1835; paid Sarah ROLLINGS for board. RtCt 11 May 1835. [B:277]

S/A of Mary V. E. ROLLINGS with Gdn Wm. ROLLINGS: beginning 28 Dec 1835; paid board & tuition, leaving $102.20. [B:436]

S/A of Wm. H. ROLLINGS with Gdn Wm. ROLLINGS: beginning 28 Jan 1836; income from sale of horse, leaving $312.95. [B:437]

S/A of John M. ROLLINGS with Gdn William ROLLINGS: beginning 5 Sep 1835, tuition, leaving $153.26. [B:438]

S/A of Samuel A. ROLLINGS with Gdn Wm. ROLLINGS: beginning 5 Sep 1835; paid tuition, leaving $139.46. RtCt 7 Jan 1838. [B:438]

WHALEY, Mary

S/A with Gdn James WHALEY: beginning 1 Jan 1833; income from William WHALEY Admr of estate of Levi WHALEY, leaving $190. RtCt 13 Jul 1835. [B:277]

DANIEL, Hester, James, Mary & Hannah
S/A with Gdn Eli PEIRPOINT: beginning 1827 income from rents and interest, totaling $472.05. RtCt 9 Nov 1835. [B:286]

LOVE, Maria, Lydia, Henry and Sarah (Children of Samuel)
S/A of Maria LOVE, Lydia LOVE, Henry LOVE & Sarah LOVE with Gdn Eli PIERPOINT: CtOD 13 Apr 1835; beginning 1827; income from rent from estate of John LOVE. RtCt 9 Nov 1835 [B:288]

McGAVOCK, Estate of Henry
S/A with Gdn William RUSSELL: beginning 17 Dec 1827; wards are Pamelia, Henry & John McGAVOCK, paid board & tuition, income from rent of house, paid for items for servant girl, income from estate of James McGAVOCK, leaving $219.42½. RtCt 9 Nov 1835. [B:292]

RICKARD, Mary, William, Dewanna, John and Emily Jane (Children of George)
S/A of Geo. RICKARD with his children and wards Mary BAKER, Wm. RICKARD, Dewanna RICKARD, John RICKARD and Emily Jane RICKARD: CtOD 12 Oct 1835; money left them by grandfather Frederick COOPER. RtCt 16 Dec 1835. [B:297]

S/A of William H. RICKARD with Gdn Gideon HOUSEHOLDER: CtOD 8 Oct 1838; paid R. H. HENDERSON fee in friendly suit; leaving $258.45½ 24 Jan 1839 paid in full as ward has arrived of age. RtCt 15 Oct 1839. [C:31]

S/A of Duanna RICKARD with Gdn Gideon HOUSEHOLDER: CtOD 11 Jun 1839; (now Duanna PAXSON) amt. rec'd of Geo. RICKARD, late Gdn, leaving $2.09 ½ as will be shown by the within account out of which the clerks fee for recording this report is to be paid. RtCt 15 Oct 1839. [C:39]

WHALEY, Levi
S/A with Gdn James WHALEY: income from William WHALEY for rent of farm and from Wm. WHALEY Admr of John WHALEY dec'd. RtCt 14 Mar 1836. [B:299]

HIXSON, David
S/A of estate of James HIXSON dec'd with David HIXSON ward and son of decedent: beginning 29 Sep 1818; income from 1/7 part of amt. rec'd by dec'd of David LEE's Execs (legacy to his mother) and from interest from 29 Sep 1818 to 23 Apr 1836, totaling $618.70. RtCt 13 Jun 1836. [B:304]

ELGIN, Charles W., John G., Armistead M., Isabell, and Francis W. (Heirs of Charles)
S/A of Charles W., John G., Armistead M., Isabella, and Francis W. ELGIN with Guardians Tilghman GORE & Rowena late Rowena ELGIN (widow of Charles) his wife: beginning May 1824; paid for items for repairs, income from hire of Negroes Bob, James, Joe, Joshua, Emily and Nace, from rent of farm, and from Gustavus ELGIN's Admrs [very long acct.] RtCt 13 Jun 1836. [B:307]

S/A with Gdn T. GORE: CtOD 10 Feb 1841; beginning March 1836; subscription to Presbyterian Church, paid for rebuilding corn house, expenses to Morgantown back on business of estate. S/A of Armistead M. ELGIN with Guardians Tilghman GORE & Rowena his wife: paid board, income from rent of farm, cash of Gustavius ELGINS Admrs, income from hire of Charles FENTON, acct paid in full. S/A of Isabella ELGIN with Guardians Tilghman GORE & Rowena: paid board & tuition, income from hire of women Harriett & three children, leaving $215.75 due to Gdn. S/A of Francis W. ELGIN with Guardians Tilghman GORE & Rowena his wife: paid board servant George, income from hire of Joseph, 4 May 1839 to him when going to school in Rockville, leaving $221.12. S/A of Charles W. ELGIN with Guardians Tilghman GORE & Rowena his wife: income from rent of farm, leaving $451.02. RtCt 11 Apr 1842. [C:134]

LOVE, Nathan
S/A with Gdn Jonah NICHOLS: CtOD 11 Apr 1836; income from estate of Rebecca LOVE, paid board and schooling, leaving $907.67. RtCt 12 Sep 1836. [B:360]

S/A with Gdn Craven BROWN: CtOD 12 Oct 1841; general expenses. Scrs: Joshua OSBURN and Jonah HATCHER. RtCt 10 May 1842. [C:142]

DANIEL, Tacey Jr.
S/A with Gdn Tacey DANIEL: CtOD 13 Oct 1836; beginning 9 Feb 1832; paid board from 9 Feb 1829, income from rent of land, Wm. KING intermarried with Gdn Tacey DANIEL, no balance left. RtCt 10 Oct 1836. [B:370]

HOUGH, Ezra, John & Armistead
S/A with Gdn John WINE: CtOD 10 Aug 1835; paid board from 1 May 1824, payments from Jane HOUGH, John SCHOOLEY, Wm. H. HOUGH, Wm. STEER, leaving $116.11. RtCt 12 Dec 1836. [B:374]

DODD, William & Benjamin
S/A with Gdn Ludwell LUCKETT: CtOD 14 Feb 1837; beginning 12 Mar 1832; paid for keep of Negro girl Sarah, Negro Ann & children and Isaac, income from interest, totaling $351.98. RtCt 12 Apr 1837. [B:384]

WOOD, Mary F.
S/A with Gdn Thomas ROGERS: CtOD 9 Jan 1837; beginning 1 Nov 1835; paid Luke & Susanna GOINS for board, income from rent of house, leaving $7.79½. RtCt 14 Jun 1837. [B:387]

WOOD, Amanda
S/A with Gdn Thomas ROGERS: beginning 1 Nov 1835; paid Luke & Susanna GOINS for board, income from rent of house, leaving $2.50½. RtCt 14 Jun 1837. [B:388]

SMITH, George, Catharine and Elizabeth (Children of John)
    S/A of George SMITH with Gdn George VINCEL: beginning 1 Mar 1835; income from rent, paid M. SANBOWER for board, leaving $193.19½. [B:389]
    S/A of Catharine SMITH with Gdn George VINCEL: beginning 1 Mar 1835; income from rent, paid M. SANBOWER for board, leaving $179.90¼. [B:391]
    S/A of Elizabeth SMITH with Gdn George VINCEL: beginning 1 Mar 1835; income from rent, paid M. SANBOWER for board, intermarried with Jacob SHORT, leaving $123.68. RtCt 14 Aug 1837. [B:393]
    S/A of Catherine SMITH with George VINCEL: CtOD 13 Mar 1839; beginning 21 Sep 1837; income from rent of farm, leaving Catherine SMITH who has intermarried with John RUSSELL $170. 84¼. S/A of George SMITH with Gdn George VINCEL: beginning 21 Sep 1837; paid tuition, income from rent of farm, leaving $280.95½. RtCt 13 Apr 1841 [or 40]. [C:99]

CHAMBLIN, Norval
    S/A with Gdn Price JACOBS: income from rents and hire of slaves, totaling $1009.11¾. RtCt 11 Sep 1837. [B:396]

ROGERS, Walter Thomas
    Inventory of the estate of Walter Thomas ROGERS an infant by Gdn Francis ELGIN: income from bonds, Negro boy Townsend. RtCt 11 Sep 1837. [B:398]
    S/A with Gdn Francis ELGIN: CtOD 14 May 1839; paid board, income from hire of Negro Townsend, leaving $712.52¾. RtCt 15 Oct 1839. [C:41]
    S/A with Gdn Francis ELGIN: CtOD 11 Jun 1847; beginning 23 Sep 1846; income from hire of Negroes Townshend & Gerrard and rent of land, leaving $1694.68. RtCt 11 Aug 1847. [C:276]
    S/A with Gdn Francis ELGIN: CtOD 12 Jun 1849; paid tuition, 6 Mar 1848 paid for coffin for servant Townshend, income from hire of Jerrard, leaving $1740.28. RtCt 12 Mar 1850 [C328]
    S/A with Gdn Francis ELGIN: CtOD 16 Jun 1841; paid board and tuition, cash of S. M. BOSS and Walter ELGIN, Execs, leaving $105.88¼. RtCt 15 Dec 1841. [C:123]
    S/A with Gdn Francis ELGIN: CtOD 13 Jun 1843; paid tuition, income from hire of Negroes Gerard and Townsend and from rent, leaving $64.66½. RtCt 18 Nov 1843 .[C:160]
    S/A with Gdn Francis ELGIN: CtOD 11 Jun 1845; paid tuition, income from rent and hire of Negroes Townshend & Jared, leaving $1366.89. RtCt 9 Dec 1845. [C:205]
    S/A with Gdn Francis ELGIN: beginning 8 Sep 1851; general expenses, income from hire of Negro Gerrard; leaving $2250.11. RtCt 13 Feb 1854. [D:20]
    S/A with Gdn Francis ELGIN: beginning 1 Jul 1853; paid tuition, paid $2392. 05 ½ having attained the age of twenty one years. RtCt 14 Jun 1855. [D:106]

WALTMAN, Rachael, Margaret and Susan (Orphans of Jacob)
    S/A of Rachael CLOPPER late WALTMAN with Gdn Emanuel WALTMAN: beginning 24 Mar 1827; income from rent of farm, paid board & tuition, owing $101.46. [B:399]
    S/A of Margaret LOCKHART late WALTMAN with Gdn Emanuel WALTMAN: beginning 24 Mar 1827; income from rent of farm, leaving $35.71¼. [B:405]
    S/A of Susan WALTMAN with Gdn Emanual WALTMAN: beginning 10 Mar 1827; paid for rent of ferry and tuition, owing $30.37½. [B:409]

CASSADY, William H. (son of John H.)
    S/A with Gdn Robert MOFFETT: (son of John H. CASSADY who died in the spring of 1827) beginning 24 Oct 1827; income from rent of farm to Gdn's brother Benjamin MOFFETT and also Edw. THOMPSON, paid for tuition at Leesburg Academy and St. Mary's College, leaving $791.22; Wm. H. arrived of age in 1834. RtCt 12 Dec 1837. [B:418]

RICHARD, Emily Jane
    S/A with Gdn Gideon HOUSEHOLDER: beginning 14 Sep 1836; general expenses leaving $344.57¼. RtCt 8 Jan 1838. [B:440]

JETT, Catharine
    S/A with Gdn Peter JETT: income from rent of two pieces of land and sale of Negroes Mar 1830, leaving $1356.03. RtCt 13 Feb 1838. [B:441]

NICHOLS, Jonah, Catharine, Nancy, Mary Ann, William, Nathan, Elizabeth, Susan, John Ellwood, and Phebe Louisa (Children of Margary)
    S/A of Jonah, Catharine, Nancy, Mary Ann, William, Nathan, Elizabeth, Susan, John Ellwood and Phebe Louisa NICHOLS with Gdn Swithen NICHOLS: cash from Swithen NICHOLS Admr of Margery NICHOLS, leaving $1190.05. RtCt 9 Apr 1838. [B:443]
    S/A with Gdn Swithen NICHOLS: CtOD 12 Mar 1849; payments to Jonah NICHOLS, Jacob NICHOLS, Admr. of estate of Cath'ne NICHOLS, Nancy NICHOLS, William N. NICHOLS, and John E. NICHOLS, income from Admr. of Margery NICHOLS dec'd. RtCt 17 May 1849. [C:311]

CARR, Washington Mains
    S/A with Gdn Archibald MAINS: expenses to Dickinson College, income from rent of stable, paid for support of Allison, income from hire of Negroes Henry, Harriet, Charlotte, Giles & Caleb, leaving $1878.51¼. RtCt 15 Aug 1838. [B:451]
    S/A with Gdn Archibald MAINS: beginning 9 Jan 1834; paid tuition, repairs corn house, repairs to saw mill, and Dickson College, income from rent of stable and hire of Negroes Henry, Harriet, Charlotte, Giles & Caleb, paid

James THOMAS for support of Allison, expenses from Carlisle, paid George RHODES for exchange in land with John CARR, from John CARRS Execs. rec'd 29 Apr 1835 omitted; leaving $1878.57¾. RtCt 15 Aug 1838. [C:1]

S/A with Gdn Isaac VANDEVANTER: beginning 22 Apr 1837; paid James THOMAS for boarding servant Allison, income from rent of farm, rent of saw mill, from hire of Negroes Alfred, Caleb, Charlotte, Harriet & Giles and from Gabriel VANDEVANTER Exor. of A. MAINS dec'd. late Gdn of W. M. CARR; leaving $1030.75. RtCt 15 Aug. 1838. [C:19]

S/A with Gdn Isaac VANDEVANTER: beginning 1 Mar 1838; paid James THOMAS for board of Negro boy, income from rent of farm and saw mill and hire of Negroes Giles, Harrell, Charlotte, Alfred & Caleb; leaving $4180.95½. RtCt 16 May 1841. [C:105]

S/A with Gdn Isaac VANDEVANTER: beginning 20 Feb 1840; paid board & tuition; income from rent of farm, house and saw mill and from hire of Negroes Charlotte, Caleb, Henry & Giles, paid for board of boy Allison; leaving $7636.69. RtCt 15 Jul 1846. [C:229]

COOKE, Heirs of Henry S.
S/A of widow & infant heirs with John G. BEALE Gdn of infants: CtOD 13 Mar 1838; beginning 1 Jan 1829; expenses to Leesburg attending sale of land, income from hire of Negroes William, Austin, Tom, Nelly, Prescila, Alfred, Dicky, George, Winny & Lewis, paid Wm. H. COOKE $230.73 in full of his proportion of said money arising from the sale of land, paid John M. BAKER $230.73 in full of his proportion of said money in right of his wife Mary E. COOKE and $230.73 paid Sarah COOKE Gdn of John G. COOKE in full of his proportion . RtCt 4 Jun 1838. [C:1]

COOPER, Margaret
S/A with Gdn John SOUDER: CtOD 16 Jun 1836; paid board & tuition; suit vs. Cooper; cash from John COOPER Admr. of Geo. COOPER her late Gdn; income from rents of pasture, leaving $2456.43. RtCt 15 Aug 1838. [C:15]

JACKSON, Estate of John
S/A of estate of John JACKSON who was Gdn of his son Wm. JACKSON: CtOD 9 Jan 1838; cash from Benjamin JACKSON Admr. of Wm. JACKSON dec'd; leaving $290.61. Gdn died about the last of October 1836 but the family continued together until the 28th of Feb 1837 when the sale of the property took place. No new Gdn has been appointed. RtCt 15 Aug 1838. [C:21]

BRADEN, Estate of Flavius T.
S/A of estate of Flavius T. BRADEN dec'd with Gdn Mary VANDEVANTER: 1837 paid medical attendance on servant Henry, coffin burial of said Henry, med. attendance on Martha Jane, med. attendance of Diadama, board & nursing Martha Jane when confined with her child and afterward sick for 6 weeks, and items for servant Amanda, income from hire of Lewis, Beverly, Charles, Diadama, Amanda, Amelia & Martha Jane. S/A of Albert VANDEVANTER dec'd in account with Gdn Mary VANDEVANTER: 20 Nov 1837 cash his funeral expenses in Baltimore, leaving $176.05 ½. It appear that the ward who is also the son of the Gdn had an interest in two estates one derived from a dec'd half brother the other from his deceased father. Acct. No. 1 exhibits the estate of the dec'd half brother, the son of the Gdn by a former marriage, who together with their mother are the only heirs, and the four children being entitled to only half shares, gives her a claim to 1/3 of the estate, which I have allowed her, and the remaining two thirds I have divided equally among the four, all of which will be shown by said acct. no. 1. The rent allowed in acct. no. 2 is the wards interest in the estate of his dec'd father who left a widow & ten children including the four above mentioned. The Gdn and three surviving children. RtCt 15 Aug 1838. [C:22]

COE, Edward M., Cornelius and David J. (Heirs of Jamieson)
S/A with Gdn Elizabeth TAYLOR formerly Elizabeth COE of Edward M. COE, Cornelius COE and David J. COE, children and heirs of Jamieson COE dec'd. : CtOD 9 Jul 1838. It appears that the personal estate of Jamieson COE dec'd was exhausted by his Admr. in the payment of debts leaving an unknown amount of debts unpaid besides a debt of about $1200 due to a certain Conrad BITZER secured by a lien on a mill and some few acres of land, the only real estate of which said dec'd died seized, this mill property was sold under the lien held by BITZER and the widow of decedent who is the Gdn of the children became the purchaser at $1055, discharged BITZER's claim in part and secured him in the balance of BITZER's claim, having a surplus of $952.44 of which she was entitled to one third, and her children to the remaining two thirds surrendering the advantage derived from the purchase and sale made by her, the Gdn of those children, being also their mother, has supported them since the death of their father for which she is entitled to compensation. I have therefore allowed her the interest leaving the principle for distribution amongst them as they severally attain their ages. RtCt 10 Sep 1838. [C:24]

STRIBLING, Cecelia M.
S/A with Gdn Mor'tr. McILHANY: CtOD 13 Mar 1839; cash to send to Rockville, paid board & tuition; income from her share of rent. Scrs: C. M. STRIBLING John L. WRIGHT, John LESLIE. RtCt 9 Apr 1839. [C:33]

STONEBURNER, John Josiah, Louisa Ann and Jacob Curtis
S/A of John Josiah STONEBURNER with Gdn Elizabeth STONEBURNER: CtOD 11 May 1835; income from 7 years 1 month & 20 days interest; 6 Apr 1839 rec'd

payment in full of John J. STONEBURNER. S/A of Louisa Ann STONEBURNER with Gdn Elizabeth STONEBURNER: income from 7 years 1 month & 20 days interest; payment in full to Peter WIRE and Mary Louisa Ann WIRE. S/A of Jacob Curtis STONEBURNER with Gdn Elizabeth STONEBURNER: income from 7 years 1 month & 20 days interest. RtCt 14 May 1839 [C:35]

VANDEVANTER, Mary E.
S/A (now dec'd) with Gdn Mary VANDEVANTER: CtOD 10 Nov 1838; paid tuition, her share of Flavius J. BRADEN's estate settled with Albert VANDEVANTER acct. in Aug 1838, income from hire of Negro Charles, leaving $308.25. It appears that the ward had an interest in two estates, one derived from a deceased half brother, and the other form her deceased father, the item of $207.19 charged in the acct. in 1838 is her share of her half brothers estate in Aug 1838 the distributable fund of which estate being so nearly in whole composed of the hires of slaves that I have allowed it in this account as a fund for the use of the ward. There are two particulars in which I have thought it right to disallow the full charges made by the Gdn – the first is she claims $110 per annum for board including two weeks nursing in her sickness and serving small articles whilst going to school, and the second is the claim of $15.50 for making various articles of clothing in 1835 & 36, for the first I have allowed $75 conceiving it to be a fair charge for board under all the circumstances, and the second I have disallowed upon the grounds that the ward ought to have done those things for herself, and if she was not enabled to do so, her Gdn has failed in her duty, and not to profit by such failure for in my opinion no circumstance whatsoever can justify a parent or Gdn in failing to teach their daughter or wards to make their own clothing her claim is however presented to the consideration of the Court. RtCt 15 Oct. 1839. [C:45]

FILLER, Mary, Elizabeth, Sarah and Samuel (Heirs of Frederick)
S/A of Mary SOUDER late Mary FILLER with Gdn John COMPHER: CtOD 10 DEC 1838; received from F. FILLER's Admr. by cash received of Jacob FILLER's Admr., income from rent of lot from 1821-38, leaving $246. By the said order hereto annexed, I am directed also to settle the account of John COMPHER as Gdn of Elizabeth, Sarah, & Samuel FILLER the other three heirs of Frederick FILLER dec'd but it appears from the vouchers produced by the Gdn that they have long since been paid off respectfully reported. RtCt 13 Nov 1839. [C:49]

ROLLER, Aaron and Priscilla
S/A with Gdn Frederick ROLLER: CtOD 11 Feb 1834; 14 Mar 1834 paid Thomas J. MARLOW the present Gdn, cash rec'd from Adam KARNE Exor. of M. SHOVER dec'd. RtCt 13 Nov 1839. [C:49]

S/A with Gdn Thos. J. MARLOW: CtOD 13 Nov 1839; cash rec'd from Fred'k ROLLER former Gdn. RtCt 12 Oct 1841. [C:118]

SHEID, John H.
S/A with Gdn N. KEENE: beginning 1832; general expenses leaving $13.40¾ due to Gdn. RtCt 12 May 1840. [C:54]

VIRTS, Henry and William
S/A of Henry VERTS with Gdn Ebenezer GRUBB: CtOD 9 Dec 1839; beginning Apr 1832; paid tuition and John VIRTS for repair to house, income from John VERTS for rent in Md and from rent of house & garden in Virginia, 22 May 1839 expenses to Winchester to bind him to a trade, his car fare to Harpers Ferry returning, leaving $608.56½. S/A of Wm. VIRTS with Gdn Ebenezer GRUBB: as above, leaving $504.23 due him on 1 Apr 1840 having arrived at age. RtCt 12 May 1840. [C:75]
S/A of Henry VERTS with Gdn Ebenezer GRUBB: CtOD 16 Aug 1843; income from rents, leaving $772.28 paid in full 1 Apr 1844. RtCt 11 Feb 1843. [C:181]

BEANS, Matthew Harrison, Elizabeth Jane and Eliza J. (Orphans of Moses)
S/A of Matthew Harrison BEANS & Elizabeth Jane BEANS with Gdn D. REECE: beginning 15 Feb 1838; cash rec'd from Admr. of Aaron BEANS dec'd being 1/12 part of personal estate, leaving $300.25. Scrs: Noble S. BRADEN, G. VANDEVANTER. RtCt 11 Aug 1840. [C:73]
S/A of Elizabeth H. & Eliza J. BEANS with Gdn David REECE: beginning 1 Jul 1840; income from rents of farm, leaving $452.03. RtCt 11 Aug 1842. [C:170]

BEANS, William, Eliza Ann, Lucinda, Aaron, Patience and Amos (Orphans of Aaron)
S/A of William, Elisa Ann, Lucinda, Aaron & Patience BEANS with Gdn David REECE: CtOD 10 Feb 1840; beginning 15 Feb 1838; rent of farm, leaving $1008.07. RtCt 14 Aug 1840. [C:73]
S/A of Amos BEANS, Lucinda BEANS (now Lucinda PEACOCK), Eliza Ann BEANS, Patience BEANS and Aaron BEANS with Gdn David REECE: CtOD 11 Aug 1842; beginning 1 Jul 1840; income from rents of farm. William BEANS, one of the heirs of said Aaron BEANS, and a former ward of said REECE has been entirely paid off. RtCt 12 Jun 1844. [C:171]

CHICHESTER, Sarah E.
S/A with late Gdn George M. CHICHESTER dec'd: beginning 1 Sep 1822; paid for masonry to ADAMS House and tuition, leaving $14735.00½. It appears that George M. CHICHESTER, was appointed Gdn of his daughter in the month of March 1822, and took upon himself the control of her estate which consisted of 1150 acres of land in the German Settlement and which was divided into seven

tenements and under rent from the papers produced to me it appears that in the year 1822, 23 and 1824, as the old leases expired, new ones were given for different periods, some for five years extending down to the end of the year 1828, the Gdn appears to have kept no account of the rents as they came into his hands and the only evidence of the amount of rent received is contained in those leases, some of which were for money some for a certain quantity of wheat, and one for a share of the crop made, other than these, there is no evidence left of his transactions concerning the same except a few vouchers for material for buildings, improvements, and repairs, and receipts to a small amount for payment made for putting up those buildings, and for repairs. Those leases however with the evidence of William WENNER, who was a tenant through the whole period of the Guardianship, and of Thomas GREEN who was the overseer of said Gdn on the premises, from March 1830 until the year before he died, have enabled me to form an estimate of the rents as they are herein charged In ascertaining the rent of the tenement which was leased on the shares, I have had no guide whatever for I have not been able to get any information in relation to it, more a conjecture as to what might have been its probable size. In this dilemma conceiving that the relation of the parties, and the great disparity in their relative circumstances, would justify me in dealing liberally toward the Gdn, I have put it on a footing with the smallest tenement for which $120 was charged. From the evidence of Thomas GREEN, it appears that all the tenements were under rent, until the year 1828 when the Gdn commenced cultivating himself and about 1829 took possession of the whole except the tenement occupied by Wm. WENNER, who has continued and still continues to occupy the same, and the Gdn continued to cultivate it until his death. Upon reference to the amount of rent charge it will be discovered that it increased in amount from $980 in 1822, to $1220 in 1825 and continued at that until the Gdn took possession of it, and I have so continued it up to his death, upon the evidence of Green, who states that the crop of 1830 & 1831 were good but those of 1832 & 1833 were not good, were injured very much by smut and cheat and that that of 1834 was very indifferent. I learned from the vouchers & receipts before mentioned and from the statements of WENNER and GREEN that various buildings had been erected by the Gdn, but of their cost I could get no satisfactory information. I therefore caused two workmen of good judgment to view them and value them, and they have reported the price at which I have charged them, I have stated in the former part of this report that the estate under consideration consisted of 1150 acres of land, I will further observe that it is situated in a neighborhood in which some, if not most of the land is in a high state of cultivation, and would command high rents & that under such circumstances the rent charge would appear to be very low. I have however been governed by the following consideration. It was as I have before intimated under lease at the time it came into the hands of the Gdn and that as the old leases expired in the years 1822, 23 and 34 they were renewed by the Gdn it has been said to have been very much out of order in almost every respect at that time, and I presume the Gdn felt sufficiently interested for his ward to dispose of the lots to the best advantage. I was therefore governed by those leases in ascertaining the rents during their continuance, but after the Gdn took them under his own cultivation, I had no other alternative but to continue the rents during his occupancy at the highest estimate under the lease or to exercise my own judgment arbitrarily formed, or to the judgment of witness summoned to fix an annual value, this being an exparte settlement. I have concluded to adopt the former, and leave the parties to their future action, should it be their pleasure to take any. It is the general impression and I feel well persuaded that including the debt herein reported, the estate of the Gdn was insolvent, and the income of the ward affording a considerably more than simple support. I have made allowance to the Gdn of $200 per annum for the first eight years and of $250 for the last six year. It is, I think, a liberal allowance, but I also think I am justified by the circumstances all of which is respectfully submitted. RtCt 11 Aug 1840. [C:75]

LOVE, Henry N. and Sarah N. (Heirs of Samuel and Rebecca)

S/A of Henry N. LOVE with Gdn Eli PIERPOINT: income from rent of estate of John LOVE dec'd, and rent of estate of John & Elizabeth LOVE, payment rec'd from Jonah NICKOLS Exor. of Rich'd LOVE dec'd. Scrs: J. C. JANNEY and Samuel CLENDENING. RtCt 17 Sep 1840. [C:81]

S/A of Sarah N. LOVE with Gdn Eli PIERPOINT: income from rent rec. of estate of John & Elizabeth LOVE, rec'd from Jonah NICKOLS Exor. of Rebecca LOVE dec'd, rec'd from Fenton A. LOVE. RtCt 17 Sep 1840. [C:91]

PURCEL, James H., William Thomas W., Edgar R. and Lydia J. (Heirs of Valentine V.)

S/A of James H. PURCEL and Wm. Thomas PURCEL with late Gdn John CHAMBLIN: CtOD 13 Nov 1840; payment rec'd of the Admr. of V. V. PURCELL, income from rent for farm, paid tuition, leaving $2475.54. Scrs: Timothy TAYLOR, Townsend HEATON, and Jonah HATCHER. RtCt 11 Jan 1841. [C:93]

S/A of Edgar R. & Lydia J. PURCELL with Gdn James McIlHANY: CtOD 12 JUL 1841; income from one half of rent for mill. Scrs: Timothy TAYLOR and Townsend HEATON. RtCt 14 Sep 1841. [C:116]

S/A of Edgar R. PURCELL with Gdn James McILHANY: CtOD 14 Oct 1843; paid board and tuition, repairs of mill, and tax on land in Missouri, leaving $2038.29½. S/A of Lydia J. PURCELL with Gdn James McILHANY: paid board and tuition and tax on land in

Missouri, leaving 1988.72½. The above are the children of V. V. PURCELL dec'd who left four, of the other two Burr P. CHAMBLIN is the Gdn who accounts I have also settled simultaneously. RtCt 14 Mar 1846. [C:206]

S/A of James H. PURCELL with Gdn Burr P. CHAMBLIN: CtOD 12 Dec 1842; beginning 14 Dec 1840; paid tuition and for building spring house, income from rent of mill by McILHANY and rent of farm, leaving $44.81. S/A of Thomas W. PURCELL with Gdn Burr P. CHAMBLIN: beginning 14 Dec 1840; as above, leaving $2368.13. There are four heirs children of V. V. PURCELL dec'd the two above named & two others Edgar R. PURCELL & Lydia PURCELL represented by James McILHANY their Gdn whose accounts I have settled simultaneously with these. RtCt 14 Mar 1846. [C:209]

S/A of William Thomas PURCELL with Gdn B. P. CHAMBLIN: paid tuition and board, paid J. H. CHAMBLIN for attending to property in Missouri; leaving $702.00. Wm. T. PURCELL has been of age two or three years. RtCt 11 Apr 1854. [D:36]

SHOVER, Herod and Sophia (Children of George)
S/A of Herod SHOVER & Sophia SHOVER with Gdn Thomas J. MARLOW: CtOD 14 Feb 1837; beginning 16 May 1831; paid G. SHOVER for support of children, fee in chancery suit, cash from A. KEEN Exor. of Magdalena SHOVER dec'd, leaving $425.97. RtCt 10 Feb 1841. [C:97]

WENNER, Lydia Jane
S/A with Gdn Sarah WENNER: CtOD 13 Mar 1839; beginning Oct 1837; unsettled balance from William W. WENNER. Scrs: John EVERHART and Jacob SHAFER. RtCt 17 Jun 1841. [C:111]

S/A with Gdn Sarah WENNER: income from hire of Negro Milly and 1 load sour grapes, paid board and tuition, paid Mary YAKEY midwife to Milly; paid Abba RATTIFF midwife to Milly; 7 Sep 1851 paid Luther A. THRESHER for coffin for servant; income from rent of farm, leaving $1528.28. Gdn Sarah WENNER died some time in the fall of 1850. RtCt 17 Jun 1854. [D:52]

S/A with Gdn Jacob SHAFER: paid board & tuition and to send to her at Staunton (school); income from W. W. WENNER, ¼ of sale of Negro David, income from D. HIXSON Admr. of Sarah WENNER dec'd, from John A. WASHINGTON for rent, and from Emanuel WENNER for rent of farm; leaving $442.45 paid over to Henry J. JOHNSON, the husband of his ward. RtCt 16 Aug 1854. [D:78]

THRASHER, Margaret E.
S/A with Gdn John SOUDER: CtOD 10 Feb 1841; (now Margaret E. THRASHER) paid board and tuition, cash from F. LITTLETON bal. of decree vs. John COOPER late Gdn, leaving $54.28½ overpaid by Gdn. RtCt 17 Jun 1842. [C:112]

LOVE, Susan H. and James J. (Heirs of Thomas B.)
Sale of the real estate of the heirs of Thomas B. LOVE dec'd made by M. C. KLEIN commissioner: CtOD 11 Jan 1841; whole amt. of sale made in 3 yearly payments. S/A of Susan H. LOVE with Gdn Madison C. KLEIN: paid board & tuition, income from rents, leaving $951.20. S/A of James J. LOVE with Gdn Madison C. KLEIN: as above, leaving $897.10. RtCt 12 Jul 1841. [C:113]

S/A of Susan H. LOVE, now BALDWIN, with Gdn M. C. KLEIN: CtOD 11 Aug 1842; 2 Jan 1842 paid $1051.50 to John D. BALDWIN & Susan H. his wife in full. RtCt 14 Feb 1843. [C:149]

S/A of James J. LOVE with Gdn Madison C. KLEIN: CtOD 14 Aug 1844; beginning 26 Jan 1841, general expenses leaving $949.85, paid in full 2 October 1844. RtCt 11 Feb 1845. [C:180]

LOVE, Thomas B.
S/A with Gdn Madison C. KLEIN: CtOD 10 Jun 1846; beginning 13 May 1838; paid tuition and board, leaving $214.03 paid in full. RtCt 10 May 1847. [C:271]

WETHERALL, Nancy C.
S/A with late Gdn Israel T. GRIFFITH dec'd: CtOD 13 Apr 1840; paid tuition, cash from John SCHOOLEY Exor. of William HOUGH dec'd. her share of debt due by Amasa & Benj. HOUGH dec'd, share of debt balance due her mother, from sale of land in Ohio, 9 Aug 1841 paid Samuel S. STONE present Gdn, leaving $135.43¾. The estate of the ward consists of her share of the sale of some land in the state of Ohio, of the rents of some other land in the state of Ohio & of her share of some ground rents in the town of Alexandria—of the sale of the land in Ohio the Gdn has charged himself with an amount purporting to be her full share. RtCt 12 Nov 1841. [C:119]

S/A with Gdn Saml. S. STONE: beginning 5 Dec 1834; income from rent of land in Ohio and Israel T. GRIFFITH's Admr, paid board & tuition, leaving $758.76 ½ fully paid. RtCt 17 Aug 1849. [C321]

HICKMAN, Catherine, George, Peter and Mary (Heirs of Peter Jr.)
S/A with Guardians Michael FRY & Mary his wife: 23 Feb 1835 paid John HICKMAN Admr. of Peter HICKMAN Senr. dec'd their share of debt binding heirs, income from rent of farm. S/A of Guardians with Catherine HICKMAN, George HICKMAN, Peter HICKMAN and Mary HICKMAN: general expenses, leaving Catharine $167.97, George $85.27, Peter $69.33½, and Mary $711.04. It seems that Peter HICKMAN Jr. the father of these wards died about the year 1822 a few months before his father Peter HICKMAN Senr. Peter the younger left no real estate and upon the settlement of the administration account a balance of the personalty of $998.57 fell into the hands of Mary HICKMAN the mother of these wards who had been

appointed their Gdn upon the death of Peter the elder a small tract of land descended to the children of Peter the younger in right of their father but the personal estate of Peter the elder proving insufficient for the payment of his debts a portion of the deficiency fell on these wards amounting to $202.77 which the Gdn paid out of the fund coming into his hands. In the year 1827 the Gdn intermarried with Michael FRY who now proposes to make no charge for the support of his wards & account for the money which came into the Guardians hands and the rents of the farm from the time of his marriage with interest on the same, which I think a very fair proportion and with which Peter & George as well as the husband of Mary who has been recently married are all well satisfied, the above reported balances have been paid off and the accounts fully closed all of which will be shown upon reference to the preceding. RtCt 17 Mar 1842. [C:127]

NEER, Anna, Hannah and Elizabeth (Orphans of David)
S/A of Anna NEER with Gdn Michael DERRY: beginning 2 Apr 1842; income from rent, leaving $137.65. Scrs: Presley WIGGINTON and George ABEL. RtCt 10 May 1842. [C:143]

S/A of with Hannah NEER with Gdn Michael DERRY: CtOD 14 Mar 1842; beginning 2 Apr 1842; paid tuition, as above, leaving $4.02. RtCt 10 May 1842. [C:143]

S/A of Elizabeth SHEILER late Eli'th NEER with Gdn Michael DERRY: beginning 2 Apr 1842; paid tuition, income from rent, leaving $8.65. RtCt 10 May 1842. S/A of Hannah NEER now Hannah HOBBS with Gdn George NEER. beginning 10 Apr 1845; general expenses. RtCt 8 Nov 1847. [C:278]

MORRIS, Lucinda, Sophronia and Keziah (Orphans of Thomas)
S/A of Lucinda MORRIS, Sophronia MORRIS & Keziah MORRIS with John HESSER: income from rents. Scrs: Timothy TAYLOR and Thomas NICHOLS. RtCt 19 Nov 1842. [C:148]

STONE, Thomas, Sarah Ann and Henrietta (Heirs of James)
S/A with Gdn Henry W. TALBOTT: CtOD 10 Dec 1841; paid Mrs. STONE for support of children, cash from E. SAUNDERS, Admr. of James STONE dec'd, payment on land allowed to widow in lieu of dower; 6 Oct 1835 paid for coffin for Henrietta STONE dec'd. S/A of Thomas STONE with Gdn Henry W. TALBOTT: paid medical expenses. S/A of Sarah Ann STONE with Gdn Henry W. TALBOTT: 2 Dec 1841 payment in full to her husband Avory C. BEALL. RtCt 14 Feb 1843. [C:150]

JAMES, Mary, Sarah and Asa
S/A of Mary JAMES with Gdn Robert JAMES: paid board & tuition, leaving $2682.91. S/A of Sarah JAMES with Gdn Robert JAMES: as above, leaving $2510.45 ½. S/A of Asa JAMES with Gdn Robert JAMES: as above, paid board & tuition, leaving $1741.05½. RtCt 14 Feb 1843. [C:153]

S/A of Sarah JAMES with Gdn Robert JAMES: CtOD 15 Feb 1848; beginning 14 Apr 1845; 14 Feb 1848 paid Addison COCHRAN her husband, leaving $3217.29. RtCt 9 May 1848. [C:287]

S/A of Mary JAMES with brother Gdn Robert JAMES: CtOD 13 Mar 1845; beginning 3 Mar 1842; paid singing and music teachers, leaving $4242.50. S/A of Sarah JAMES with brother Gdn Robert JAMES: beginning Mar 1842; paid board & tuition, leaving $4576.33. RtCt 19 Apr 1845. [C:183]

S/A of Mary JAMES with brother Gdn Robert JAMES: CtOD 8 Feb 1847; paid for dancing, leaving $939.29 on 10 Sep 1846 which balance since that period has been paid. RtCt 9 Feb 1847. [C:251]

MUSE, James H.
S/A with Gdn James CAYLOR: CtOD 11 Aug 1840; income from Peter OATYER Admr. of John MOFFETT dec'd, from Peter OATYER Admr. of Walker MUSE dec'd. of Peter OATYER for Negro hire, and from rent, paid tuition, leaving $148.98. RtCt 14 Feb 1843. [C:158]

HAMILTON, Owen, John Thomas, William F. and Samuel Pugh (Orphans of Harvey)
S/A of Owen HAMILTON with Gdn Joseph P. MEGEATH: CtOD 14 Feb 1843; beginning Feb 1839; paid lawyer and clerk fees. S/A of John Thomas HAMILTON with Gdn Joseph P. MEGEATH: general expenses. S/A of Emily HAMILTON with Gdn Joseph P. MEGEATH: paid board. S/A of William F. HAMILTON with Gdn Joseph P. MEGEATH: income from rents. S/A of Samuel Pugh HAMILTON with Gdn Joseph P. MEGEATH: general expenses. RtCt 14 Oct 1843. [C:161]

S/A of John T. HAMILTON with Gdn Joseph P. MEGEATH: CtOD 16 Sep 1846; beginning 7 Aug 1843; general expenses leaving $93.96. RtCt 15 Jun 1847. [C:273]

SHUMATE, Maria
S/A with father Gdn Murphy C. SHUMATE: CtOD 11 Aug 1843; beginning 8 Mar 1837; paid board & tuition, income from hire of Negro Martha, leaving $32.05. RtCt 13 Feb 1844. [C:168]

S/A with Gdn Murphy C. SHUMATE: CtOD 8 Feb 1846; income from hire of Negro Marshall and from Martha she having a child, leaving $860.16. RtCt 11 Aug 1847. [C:275]

S/A with Gdn Murphy C. SHUMATE: (now Maria WHITE who has intermarried with R. F. WHITE) CtOD 14 May 1849; beginning 1 Jan 1847; income from hire of Martha with two children, leaving $300 paid in full. Gdn has produced for $300 in full of all accounts against him as Gdn as will be shown by the above account. RtCt 13 Dec 1849. [C:324]

CHEW, Mary Ellen, Robert, Elizabeth Ann and Margaret Jane (Orphans of Henry)

S/A of Mary Ellen CHEW, Robt. CHEW, Elizabeth Ann CHEW and Margaret Jane CHEW with Gdn Balaam OSBURN: CtOD 18 Nov 1843; beginning Aug 1839; payment rec'd. from Roger CHEW in part of their share of the residue of the estate of John CHEW dec'd. Scrs: Jno. L. POWELL and Frank T. GRADY. [C:169]

S/A of Robert CHEW, Elizabeth CHEW & Mary Jane CHEW with Gdn Balaam OSBURN: CtOD 10 Jun 1846; income from interest on accts. RtCt 12 Apr 1847. [C:270]

S/A of Elizabeth A. CHEW with Gdn Balaam OSBURN: CtOD 15 Mar 1849; income from her portion of her grand [father] John CHEW's estate equaling $339.41. [C:307]

FRY, Philip

S/A with Gdn Peter FRY dec'd: CtOD 17 Mar 1842; 2 Sep 1841 from his share of the estate of Peter FRY dec'd, paid cost of selling the estate of Peter FRY dec'd, leaving $1214.71½. The estate of Philip FRY consists of an interest in the estate of John FRY his deceased father, of which he was an only child, Peter FRY Sr. dec'd the Gdn of Philip having been also the Admr. of John, and an interest in the estate of Peter FRY Sr. dec'd his grandfather. RtCt 11 Feb 1845. [C:186]

WIRE, Mary Catharine, Susan R., Martha Jane, Sarah E., Margaret and Samuel W. (Heirs of David)

S/A of Susan R. WIRE with Gdn Jacob SMITH: paid tuition, income from rent of house and farm, leaving $660.49. S/A of Mary Catharine WIRE with Gdn Jacob Smith: as above, leaving $664.97. S/A of Sarah E. WIRE with Gdn Jacob SMITH: as above, leaving $689.12. S/A of Samuel W. WIRE with Gdn Jacob SMITH: as above, leaving $699.00. RtCt 14 June 1845. [C:187]

S/A of Mary Catharine WIRE with Gdn Jacob SMITH: tuition, leaving $652.57. S/A of Susan R. WIRE with Gdn Jacob SMITH: paid tuition, 12 Jul 1836 from John SOUDER Admr. of D. WIRE dec'd, many as above, leaving $638.60. S/A of Sarah E. WIRE with Gdn Jacob SMITH: as above, leaving $848.23. S/A of Margaret WIRE with Gdn Jacob SMITH: as above, leaving $869.19. S/A of Samuel W. WIRE with Gdn Jacob SMITH: as above, leaving $864.94. These wards being the children of David WIRE dec'd were entitled to two thirds of the personal estate after the payment of debt, and also of the annual profits of the real estate the widow their mother who is still living being entitled to the other third. The Gdn had erroneously previously rendered an account of the whole rent instead of two thirds thereof as he did of the personalty. I therefore divided the whole amount of rent among the wards and charged them with the whole amount of improvements and repairs. RtCt 9 Sep 1850. [C:339]

S/A of Mary Ann, Susan F. and Martha Jane WIRE with Gdn Peter WIRE: beginning 13 Dec 1852; infant children of David WIRE dec'd with balance of $194.60 RtCt 13 Feb 1854. [D:27]

S/A of Mary Catharine WIRE with Gdn Jacob SMITH: beginning 12 Jul 1849; paid repairs to stable, leaving $544.85. S/A of Susan R. WIRE with Gdn Jacob SMITH: beginning 12 Jul 1849; as above, leaving $827.43. S/A of Sarah E. WIRE with Gdn Jacob SMITH: beginning 12 Jul 1849; as above, leaving $788.51. S/A of Margaret WIRE with Gdn Jacob SMITH: beginning 12 Jul 1849; as above, leaving $1109.32. S/A of Samuel W. WIRE with Gdn Jacob SMITH: beginning 12 Jul 1849; as above, leaving $1109.32. RtCt 11 Apr 1854. [D:40]

S/A of Mary A., Susan F. and Martha Jane WIRE with Gdn Peter WIRE: beginning 27 Dec 1853; income from D. HIXSON wards share of Margaret FRY's dower interest in slaves of the estate Peter FRY dec'd, leaving $211.06 due to heirs jointly. RtCt 14 Jun 1855. [D:119]

S/A of Mary Catharine WIRE with Gdn Jacob SMITH: beginning 1 Aug 1853; paid for repairs, leaving $78.75. S/A of Susan R. WIRE with Gdn Jacob SMITH: as above, leaving $168.30. S/A of Sarah E. WIRE with Gdn Jacob SMITH: as above, leaving $125.68. S/A of Margaret WIRE with Gdn Jacob SMITH: as above. S/A of Samuel W. WIRE with Gdn Jacob SMITH: as above, leaving $174.46. The estate of those wards consisted of their shares of the personal estate of their father which was received of John SOUDER his administrator and charged to this Gdn in his final S/A in 1835 and a small real estate of about 21 acres of land and a house and a lot in which the widow had a life estate in 1/3. The real estate being small was rented in an undivided state for the benefit of all until Samuel W. WIRE the youngest child should arrive of age, which occurred about January 1855 when the Gdn surrendered the property to the widow and her children. Accts paid in full. RtCt 9 Sep 1856. [D:160]

KLEIN, Elizabeth

S/A with Gdn Madison C. KLEIN: (now Elizabeth DAVIS) beginning 1 Apr 1840; paid taxes and int., leaving $122.60 paid over to her husband S.? P. DAVIS. RtCt 9 Sep 1845. [C:204]

ADAMS, Samuel T.

S/A with Gdn Robert A. ISH: 18 Dec 1841 from his share of sale of the personal estate of Francis ADAMS dec'd, leaving $176.69. Scrs: Beverly HUTCHISON, Sampson HUTCHISON, and Alex'r. D. LEE. RtCt 12 Nov 1845. [C:205]

WHITE, Mary E., Josiah T. and George W. (Heirs of Beniah)

S/A of Mary E. WHITE with Gdn Thomas WHITE: CtOD 8 Feb 1841; paid tuition of Aaron & Mary, 14 Feb 1831 paid for coffins for sister & brother, 20 May 1836 paid A. R. SAUNDERS her next Gdn and to George & Josiah to make their shares equal, income from hire of Negro Bill. S/A of Josiah T. WHITE with late Gdn Thomas WHITE: paid med. bill for Negro Ann and for coat for Bill. S/A of George W. WHITE with late Gdn Thomas WHITE: paid board & tuition, leaving $945.61. This Gdn was appointed about the year 1830, and about the year 1834 Mary E. WHITE took her business out of his hands by choosing Aaron R. SAUNDERS and about the year 1837 Robert WHITE was appointed the Gdn of all three. Mary E. and Josiah T. having arrived of age, they have settled with the Gdn who is their uncle and taken his notes for the balances respectively due to them. RtCt 14 Mar 1846. [C:220]

S/A of Josiah T. WHITE with Gdn Robert WHITE: CtOD 11 Dec 1838; beginning 14 Feb 1837; paid tuition, leaving $480.25. S/A of George W. WHITE with Gdn Robert WHITE: beginning 14 Feb 1837; paid board & tuition, leaving $128.57. S/A of Mary E. WHITE with Gdn Robert WHITE: beginning 13 Feb 1837, as above, leaving $538.86. S/A of Josiah T. WHITE with Gdn Robert WHITE: beginning 9 Mar 1842, general expenses. S/A of George W. WHITE with Gdn Robert WHITE: beginning 1 Mar 1843, as above. S/A of Mary E. WHITE with Gdn Robert WHITE: beginning 18 Feb 1843, as above. Thomas WHITE was first appointed the Gdn of those children and Aaron R. SAUNDERS was appointed committee of Frances R. WHITE their mother and at her death was appointed her Admr. and was also chosen by Mary E. WHITE after she had attained the age of fourteen years as her Gdn and then about the year 1837 all three of the children chose Robert WHITE who was thereupon appointed their Gdn and who soon after instituted suit against Aaron R. SAUNDERS whose account I settled in that suit. The wards are now all three of age and have each taken the note of Robert WHITE who is their uncle for the balance respectively due to each and have requested me to close the account as settled by note of all. RtCt 12 Apr 1847. [C:256]

CHEW, James E.
S/A with Gdn Frank T. GRADY: CtOD 14 Feb 1843; 13 Jan 1840 cash from Roger CHEW in part of legacy, leaving $739.10 which under the instruction of Jonah OSBURN whose wife is a sister of James E. CHEW and the only heir now of Mary B. CHEW dec'd, I have allowed as a credit to said Gdn who is also Admr. of Mary B. CHEW dec'd in his administration acct. RtCt 14 Apr 1846. [C:227]

GALLAHER, Thomas Dorsey
S/A with Gdn Ludwell LUCKETT: CtOD 14 May 1844; 8 May 1837 cash rec'd from David GALLAHER, 10 Apr 1844 paid Joseph GALLAHER per acct. RtCt 16 Sep 1846. [C:235]

HEREFORD, Burr P.
S/A with Gdn Ludwell LUCKETT: CtOD 18 Oct 1845; beginning 8 Aug 1836; income from interest. RtCt 16 Sep 1846. [C:235]

GRAYSON, Ann F., Mary S., Benjamin, Richard O. and Thomas L. (Heirs of Richard O.)
S/A with Gdn Charles L. POWELL: CtOD 14 Nov 1844; rent rec'd of him of the tenants of the estate of E. S. FITZHUGH dec'd, to Geo. M. GRAYSON for children, 14 Jul 1843 paid Wm. FITZHUGH their distribution of estate of C. E. FITZHUGH dec'd, of George M. GRAYSON Exor. of R. O. GRAYSON. S/A of Ann F. GRAYSON with Gdn Charles L. POWELL: 15 Oct 1845 paid Geo. CARTER with whom she lived, leaving $480.07. S/A of Mary S. GRAYSON with Gdn Charles L. POWELL: beginning 10 Jan 1843; paid for clothing and dancing master, leaving $21.52. S/A of Benjamin GRAYSON with Gdn Charles L. POWELL: beginning Jan 1843; paid board and tuition. S/A of Richard O. GRAYSON with Gdn Charles L. POWELL: Jan 1843-46 paid S. S. FITZHUGH by G. M. GRAYSON for support, leaving $414.81. Thomas L. GRAYSON has balance of $414.81. RtCt 15 Oct 1846. [C:237]

S/A with Gdn Charles L. POWELL: CtOD 8 Feb 1847; income from rent, paid repairs to saw mill. S/A of Ann F. GRAYSON with Gdn Charles L. POWELL: only balances given. S/A of Mary S. GRAYSON with Gdn Charles L. POWELL: paid board and tuition including tuition in French. S/A of Benj. O. GRAYSON with Gdn Charles L. POWELL: paid board & tuition. S/A of Rich'd O. GRAYSON with Gdn Charles L. POWELL: paid board and tuition. S/A of Thomas F. GRAYSON with Gdn Charles L. POWELL: paid board. RtCt 12 Feb 1849. [C304]

S/A with Gdn Chs. L. POWELL: paid for work at saw mill and repairing corn house, income from rents. S/A of Ann F. GRAYSON with Gdn Chas. L. POWELL: 16 Jan 1849-50 paid E. O. CARTER for board, leaving $1239.62. S/A of Mary S. GRAYSON with Gdn Chas. L. POWELL: as above, leaving $401.26. S/A of Benjamin O. GRAYSON with Gdn Charles L. POWELL: paid board & tuition, leaving of $245.81. S/A of Richard O. GRAYSON with Gdn Chas. L. POWELL: paid board & tuition. S/A of Thomas F. GRAYSON with Gdn Charles L. POWELL: paid board and tuition, leaving $1381.64. The estate of these wards consists of their farms on which is a saw mill. RtCt 9 Sep 1850. [C:360]

S/A with Gdn Charles L. POWELL: paid for work on saw mill, income from rents. S/A of Benjamin O. GRAYSON with Gdn Charles L. POWELL: paid for clothing, leaving $338.97. S/A of Mary S. GRAYSON with Gdn Charles L. POWELL: 20 Apr 1851 paid Ann F. GRAYSON, leaving $709.74½. S/A of Rich'd O. GRAYSON with Gdn Charles L. POWELL: paid board and tuition, leaving $747.60. S/A of Thomas F. GRAYSON with Gdn Charles L. POWELL: paid board and tuition, leaving $1869.42. RtCt 12 Jul 1851. [C:387]

WILSON, Sarah

S/A with Gdn William KUGHN: beginning Aug 1842; 2 Aug 1846 paid fee for motion to settle, leaving $385.00 which he had paid to her and produced her receipt for the same and for which I have allowed him a credit, leaving nothing further in his hands all of which will be shown by the within account. [C:243]

CARTER, Martha E., Leonidas H., Landon F., Catharine, Presly L., Edward David and Jesse G. (Heirs of Presley)

S/A of Martha E., Leonidas H., Landon F., Catharine, Presly L., Edward David, Jesse G. CARTER with Gdn Landon S. CARTER: CtOD 13 Jan 1846; income from hire of Negroes Alexander, Ruth & Emily, and from rent of house & lot, 26 May 1843 paid midwife for Ruth, paid for coffin for burying child, leaving $801.33. RtCt 14 Apr 1846. [C:245]

S/A of Martha E., Leonidas H., Landon T., Catherine, Presley L., Edward D. and Jesse G. CARTER with Gdn Landon L. CARTER: CtOD 14 Jun 1847; 18 Aug 1846 paid Ephram JANUARY Gdn in State Missouri, leaving $75.05. RtCt 8 Nov 1847. [C:277]

LANE, Hellen E. and James W. (Orphans of Arthur)

S/A of Hellen E. LANE & James W. LANE with Gdn Dean JAMES dec'd: CtOD 10 Jun 1846; bonds paid James H. HALLEY Admr. of John H. HALLEY dec'd by decree of Court of Fairfax Co., by amt. of sale of real estate under a decree of the Court of Fairfax Co., receipt of Philo. R. CRANE present Gdn. Dean JAMES departed this life on or about 3 June 1845, and that his executrix attended to the settling of business until Philo R. CRANE qualified as Gdn and that it was upon the motion of Sally JAMES executrix of Dean JAMES dec'd. RtCt 15 Dec 1846. [C:252]

WADE, Joseph H. and John E. (Orphans of Robert)

S/A of Joseph H. WADE with Gdn Lucullus HOSPITAL: CtOD 10 Jun 1846; receipts and expenses, leaving $4.94 due Gdn. S/A of John E. WADE with Gdn Lucullus HOSPITAL: as above, leaving $10.60. RtCt 15 Dec 1846. [C:253]

THOMPSON, Hugh

S/A with Gdn S. B. T. CALDWELL: CtOD 12 May 1845; income from notes, expenses, leaving $965.47. RtCt 15 Dec 1846. [C:255]

FILLER, Jacob A., Sarah Ann, Joseph H. and Jonathan H. (Heirs of Jacob)

S/A of Jacob A. FILLER, Sarah Ann FILLER, Joseph H. FILLER, Jonathan H. FILLER with Gdn Sarah FILLER: CtOD 10 May 1847; amt. of whole acct. for four minor heirs of Jacob FILLER dec'd is $338.33 ; amt. deducted for two legatees. RtCt 15 Jun 1847. [C:273]

TRAHERN, Martha A., Enos, James and William C. (Heirs of James)

S/A of Martha A. TRAHERN with Gdn Joseph P. MEGEATH: CtOD 12 Feb 1846; cash rec'd of Thos. TRAHERN; cash of Jonathan TAVENNER. S/A of Enos TRAHERN with Gdn Joseph P. MEGEATH: as above. S/A of James TRAHERN with Gdn Joseph P. MEGEATH: cash rec'd of Thos. TRAHERN; cash of Jonathan TAVENNER. S/A of William C. TRAHERN with Gdn Joseph P. MEGEATH: as above. RtCt 13 Dec 1847. [C:279]

HATCHER, Sally Ann (Sallie Ann)

S/A of estate with Gdn Joshua HATCHER: CtOD 15 Jun 1847; paid boarding & schooling at Springdale, income from share of father's personal property, from share of her brother Addison's property and from share of school fund from J. NICHOL's estate. RtCt 13 Dec 1847. [C:282]

S/A of estate with Gdn Joshua HATCHER: CtOD 13 Aug 1849; beginning Apr 1846; paid boarding & school, income from sale of old house & 3 plough beams. RtCt 14 Jan 1850 [C327]

S/A with Joshua HATCHER: beginning Jan 1850; paid board & tuition; leaving $2761.95. RtCt 10 Jan 1853. [D:2]

S/A with Gdn Joshua HATCHER: paid school acct and for music lessons; leaving $2767.20. RtCt 15 Mar 1853. [D:8]

S/A with Gdn Joshua HATCHER: paid tuition and board, paid Wm. McCRAY ward's bill in Balto., leaving $2767.20. RtCt 9 May 1854. [D:46]

S/A with Gdn Joshua HATCHER: beginning 1 Jan 1854; 22 Jun 1854 paid John N. COMBS in right of his wife balance of $31.05. RtCt 14 Jun 1855. [D:101]

CASSADAY, Ann C. and Charles B. (Heirs of Jane)

S/A with Gdn Henry S. TAYLOR: CtOD 10 Jun 1846; paid for advertising land and for trip to Charlestown to attend the same; 20 Oct 1843 from proceeds of sale of land. S/A of Mary E. CASSADAY with Gdn Henry S. TAYLOR: income from interest. S/A of Ann C. CASSADAY with Gdn Henry S. TAYLOR: income from interest. S/A of Charles B. CASSADAY with Gdn Henry S. TAYLOR: income from interest. All have been paid off. RtCt 9 May 1848. [C:288]

WHALEY, George L.

S/A with Gdn Sandford J. RAMEY: CtOD 13 Jan 1847; cash from C. A. WHALEY Exor. of G. WHALEY, income from hire of Negro Stepney, leaving $627.72½. RtCt 10 Jul 1848. [C:289]

GRUBB, Benjamin H.

S/A with Gdn William GRUBB Jr: CtOD 11 Jun 1845; paid tuition, payments for mill wright work, income from crops and from hire of Negroes Venue & Israel, leaving $284.80. RtCt 11 Sep 1848. [C:291]

LOUDOUN COUNTY, VIRGINIA
GUARDIAN ACCOUNTS
1759-1904

HEREFORD, Mary C., William S., Minerva, Esther M. and Thomas S.

S/A of Mary C. HEREFORD, William S. HEREFORD, Minerva HEREFORD, Esther M. HEREFORD & Thomas S. HEREFORD with Gdn Ludwell LUCKETT: CtOD 11 Sep 1848; beginning 26 May 1846; paid taxes and income from interest, 23 Feb 1848 paid to Gdn in Missouri. RtCt 15 Nov 1848. [C:297]

S/A of Wm. S. HEREFORD with Gdn Ludwell LUCKETT: CtOD 13 Aug 1849; 11 Nov 1848 by draft on the Union Bank of Maryland, fully settled. RtCt 28 Dec 1850. [C:338]

S/A of Thomas S. HEREFORD with Gdn Ludwell LUCKETT: beginning Nov 1848; ward fully paid. RtCt 15 Feb 1853. [D:5]

S/A of Minerva HEREFORD with Gdn Ludwell LUCKETT: beginning 11 No 1849; paid her Gdn in the west where she resides; Minerva and her husband full paid with a certificate of deposit from the Valley Bank. RtCt 9 May 1854. [D:47]

S/A of Esther M. HEREFORD with Gdn Ludwell LUCKETT: beginning 3 Nov 1849; amt. paid ward in draft on Bank of Maryland, leaving $798.91. On 13 Jun 1859 the Gdn sent in a draft on the Union Bank of Maryland the sum of $794.92 which with its premium covered the whole amount due. I mailed the letter containing the draft to Esther M. HEREFORD, San Francisco, California. By strictness of law he was not entitled to commission, but he managed the estate so as to increase it, and in strict accordance wit the wishes of the ward's mother, with whom she lived. RtCt 15 Mar 1860. [E:26]

McDANIEL, Mary Ann and George W. (Children of Presley)

S/A of Richard E. LEE & Mary Ann (late Mary Ann McDANIEL) his wife with Gdn Tilghman GORE: CtOD 15 Jun 1847; paid fee in suit in NOBLES Admr, rec'd from George NOBLES Admr, income from hire of girl, leaving $33.80. S/A of George W. McDANIEL with Gdn Tilghman GORE: paid for store items, leaving $2.67. RtCt 11 Dec 1848. [C:300]

VANDEVANTER, Cornelius

S/A with Gdn Isaac VANDEVANTER: CtOD 9 Oct 1848; paid board and tuition, paid for attendance of servant Diadamia, and for boarding servant Maria (confined); income from hire of Negroes Presly and Catharine, leaving $404.34 due to Gdn. RtCt 12 Feb 1849. [C:303]

S/A with Gdn Isaac VANDEVANTER: CtOD 14 Jun 1850; beginning 9 Sep 1848; paid for hawling Maria and for bedtick for Diadama, income from hire of Negroes Charles, Maria, Presly, Smith, John Henry & Mary Catharine, leaving $305.67½. RtCt 4 Nov 1850. [C:384]

IRWIN, Elizabeth and Frances

From Commissioners Office Alexandria 2 Apr 1849: Gdn Peter E. HOFFMAN, paid advance to Elizabeth ERWIN of $7.15 leaving $150 in Virginia state stock that he has in his hands and owes to his other ward Marcus IRWIN $16.35 $150 of Virginia State stock. Stock is held in the name of P. E. HOFFMAN Gdn of Elizabeth IRWIN & Francis IRWIN certificate no. 895 dated Oct 23 1848. [difficult to read]. S/A of Elizabeth & Frances IRWIN with Gdn P. E. HOFFMAN: expenses. RtCt 17 May 1849. [C:308]

S/A of Frances IRWIN with Gdn P. E. HOFFMAN: CtOD 15 Oct 1850; Commissioners office Alexandria 23 Jan 1851; paid Elizabeth $8.34 and Frances $5.34 that he held $300 of Virginia state stock the joint property of Elizabeth and Frances. RtCt 25 Jan 1851. [C:382]

EVERETT, Elizabeth, Sarah and John

S/A with Gdn Benjamin DAVIS: CtOD 9 Apr 1849; rec'd from Rebecca KENWORTHY's estate; rec'd from Howell DAVIS estate; 23 Mar 1840 amt. paid Dan'l WHITE for bringing children from Indiana to Loudoun, paid board & tuition. RtCt 17 May 1849. [C:312]

S/A of John EVERETT with Gdn Benjamin DAVIS: beginning 28 Apr 1849; income from interest; leaving $1671.81. RtCt 14 Jun 1855. [D:97]

S/A of Sarah EVERETT with Gdn Benjamin DAVIS: beginning 5 Nov 1849; paid board and tuition; 1 May 1853 cash paid ward sent to her in Ohio, ward as aforesaid being now married her husband George C. POWELL rec'd balance of $1639.43 in full. RtCt 14 Jun 1835. [D:99]

S/A of John E. EVERETT with Gdn Benjamin DAVIS: beginning 1 Jul 1855; paid board, tuition and medical bill, leaving $176.90. RtCt 14 Oct 1858. [D:295]

HURST, Hannah, Sarah A. and James W.

S/A of Hannah HURST with Gdn M. C. KLEIN: CtOD 10 Apr 1848; paid board & tuition, paid for boarding hands, leaving 244.46. S/A of Sarah A. HURST with Gdn M. C. KLEIN: as above, leaving $380.94. S/A of James W. HURST with Gdn M. C. KLEIN: as above, leaving $109.92½. RtCt 12 Jun 1849. [C:314]

FRANCIS, Heirs of Lewis

S/A with Gdn John FRANCIS: CtOD 8 Oct 1850; Nov 1844 amt. for debt due estate of Enoch FRANCIS, paid for coffin, leaving $45.28. RtCt 14 Jan 1850. [C:325]

YOUNG, Ruth

S/A with Gdn Joseph WORTHINGTON: CtOD 12 Mar 1850; beginning 8 Mar 1847; 16 Mar 1847 from Craven OSBURN Exor. amt. of legacy, leaving $293.06. By reference to the will of Craven OSBURN it will appear that $300 was bequeathed to Ruth YOUNG but there is a state tax of two percent upon such legacies which was paid by the Gdn who is also the executor of Craven OSBURN dec'd and charged in his executorial account I have therefore charged the Gdn with the net amount of legacy as will be shown above. RtCt 8 Apr 1850. [C:329]

S/A with Gdn Joseph WORTHINGTON: beginning 16 May 1850; paid Elihu E. HENDRY who married Ruth YOUNG; leaving $377.35. RtCt 10 Aug 1853. [D:15]

OSBURN, William. T.
S/A with Gdn Phineas OSBURN: CtOD 12 Mar 1850; paid board and tuition, income from hire of servant boy, 22 Jan 1848 rec'd payment from Herod OSBURN's Admr, 16 Feb 1850 rec'd payment from Priscilla OSBURN's administrator. RtCt 13 May 1850 [C:329]

S/A with Gdn Phineas OSBURN: beginning 1 Apr 1850; paid tuition, income from hire of Negroes William and Mary; leaving $2820.29. RtCt 13 Feb 1854. [D:18]

S/A with Gdn Phineas OSBURN: paid tuition; leaving $2958.60. RtCt 17 Jun 1854. [D:49]

S/A with Gdn Phineas OSBURN: beginning 26 Apr 1854; paid board & tuition, income from hire of Negro boy Bill & girl Mary; leaving $3120.34. RtCt 14 Jun 1855. [D:113]

S/A with Gdn Phineas OSBURN: beginning 24 Apr 1855; income from Joab OSBURN Admr. of Volney OSBURN wards share and from hire of Negroes Bill, Mary & Harriet, leaving $3392.75. RtCt 9 Sep 1836. [D:149]

S/A with Gdn Phineas OSBURN: beginning 9 Jan 1856; paid board & tuition, share of payment on lot sold belonging to V. OSBURN's estate, leaving $3554.95. RtCt 21 Aug 1857. [D:265]

S/A with Gdn Phineas OSBURN: beginning 20 Apr 1857; paid medical bills and tuition, income from share of Volney OSBURN's estate and from hire of Negroes Bill, Mary (deducting the time of Mary's confinement), and Harriet, leaving $3669.61. RtCt 14 Apr 1858. [D:405]

S/A with Gdn Phineas OSBURN: beginning 22 May 1858; paid Addison OSBURN board, paid Mason OSBURN and Ann OSBURN, income from hire of servants, leaving $3834.76. RtCt 13 Aug 1859. [E:4]

S/A with Gdn Phineas OSBURN: beginning 23 Mar 1859; paid Addison OSBURN for board, income from hire of 3 slaves, leaving $3926.52. RtCt 14 Aug 1860. [E:91]

S/A with Gdn Phineas OSBURN: beginning 22 May 1860; paid taxes on land in Crawford Co. Iowa, leaving $4093.83. RtCt 13 Feb 1866. [E:253]

S/A with Gdn Phineas OSBURN: beginning 23 Mar 1861; paid taxes and store accts, income from hire of Negroes Bill, Mary, and Harriet, income from Jos. WORTHINGTON Exor. of Joshua OSBURN dec'd under the will of Joshua OSBURN dec'd and from Joab OSBURN Admr. of Volney OSBURN dec'd, leaving $5111.65. RtCt 13 Feb 1866. [E:255]

LOVE, Elizabeth L.
S/A with Gdn Madison C. KLEIN: CtOD 15 Mar 1849; paid tuition, leaving $9.39 which he has since paid off all. RtCt 8 Jul 1850. [C:336]

TRITTIPO, John and Eliza
S/A of John TRITTIPO with Gdn John JANNEY (of Amos): beginning 31 Dec 1841, general expenses, leaving. S/A of Reuben HOWELL & Eliza his wife late TRITTIPO with Gdn John JANNEY: beginning 31 Dec 1841, as above. Since CtOD the Gdn died leaving balance due to John TRITTIPO of $23.19 and to Reuben HOWELL & Eliza his wife of $50.84. The wards removed to the west some time in the year 1848 or 1849. The Gdn failed to pay them off but since his death his Admr. George W. JANNEY has performed that duty. RtCt 9 Sep 1850. [C:358]

SOUDER, George P., Eliza Ann, John W., Catharine E., Emily and Susan (Heirs of Michael)
S/A George P. SOUDER with Gdn George SLATER: beginning 1 Jun 1837; income rec'd from Susanna SOUDER's Exor and from Margaret SOUDER's Admr., Michael SOUDER's Admr.; leaving $948.14. S/A of Eliza Ann SOUDER with Geo. SLATER: beginning 1 Jun 1837; as above, leaving $977.94. S/A of John W. SOUDER with Geo. SLATER: beginning 1 Jun 1838; as above, leaving $1015.52. RtCt 7 Dec 1850. [C:365]

S/A of Catharine E. SOUDER with Gdn William SLATER: beginning 1 Jun 1838; income from Susanna SOUDER's Exor and from Margaret SOUDER's Admr., Michael SOUDER's Admr; leaving $339.48. S/A of Emily SOUDER with William SLATER her Gdn. beginning 1 Jun 1838; as above, leaving $1013.35. S/A of Susan SOUDER with William SLATER: beginning 1 Jun 1838; as above, leaving $989.27. RtCt 7 Dec 1850. [C:371]

S/A of Catharine E. SOUDER with Gdn Wm. SLATER: reserve for settling and recording and acct. paid in full. S/A of Emeline SOUDER with Wm. SLATER: as above, paid in full. S/A of Susan SOUDER with Wm. SLATER: as above, paid in full. RtCt 12 May 1851. [C:385]

S/A John W., Eliza A. and George P. with Gdn George SLATER: beginning 1 Jan 1860; general expenses leaving John W. S $1498.07, Eliza A. (now Eliza A. WEANING) $320, and George P. SOUDER $5.93. Jacob SMITH one of the sureties is dead. RtCt 10 Sep 1867.

S/A John W. SOUDER with Gdn George SLATER: beginning 1 Mar 1867; general payments leaving $14. [F:59]

S/A George P. SOUDER with Gdn George SLATER: beginning 1 Mar 1867; amt. due of $5.93. [F:59]

S/A Eliza A. SOUDER with Gdn George SLATER: (now Eliza A. WEANING) beginning 1 Mar 1867; payment of $350.07 to her husband J. O. WEANING. RtCt 12 Apr 1870. [F:60]

SLATER, John M. (Child of Michael)

S/A with Samuel STOUTSENBERGER dec'd Gdn: Michael SLATER the father of John M. died about the year 1825 when said John M. was an infant and in the fall of 1828 said Samuel STOUTSENBERGER married the widow and became the Gdn of said John M. and as such received of William SLATER the administrator of Michael SLATER dec'd the amount charged first in the account & about the year 1832 a small lot of land belonging to said John M. who was the only heir, was sold under a decree of the county court of Loudoun amounting to $605.43 came into the Guardians hands & with which also I have charged him. No S/A of the Guardianship account appears to have ever been made and the Gdn as appears has kept no account with his ward & under such circumstances having no materials to state an account I have concluded to let the use of the estate offset such expenses as the Gdn may have incurred until 1842 when his ward had attained about his 17th year about which time his mother dec'd and in May 1847 the Gdn dec'd also having paid his ward but $210.25. Jacob STOUTSENBERGER the executor of Samuel STOUTSENBERGER dec'd then proceeded and continued to advance to said John M. making the last advance on the 19 Dec 1848 which as appears upon an adjustment of the account over paid him and the said John M. is now indebted to him the sum of $77.63. RtCt 15 Oct. 1850. [C:377]

HOUSEHOLDER, Martha A., Drucilla and Susan (Infant children of Gideon)

S/A of Martha A. HOUS[E]HOLDER with Gdn James W. HAMILTON: beginning Oct 1845; paid for store items and clothes, leaving $209.55. S/A of Drucilla HOUSEHOLDER with James W. HAMILTON: as above, leaving $2113.81. S/A of Susan HOUSEHOLDER with James W. HAMILTON: as above, leaving $2075.70. The Gdn is also the executor of said Gideon HOUSEHOLDER dec'd the father of said wards & under the will of said testator these wards are each entitled to a legacy of $1000, and to an equal distributive share of the remainder of the estate. I settled the executorial acct. in the spring of 1850 and after reserving in the hands of the executor the amount of the legacies ascertained that the share of each of the distributees of the remained was $1236.13. RtCt 7 Feb 1851. [C:378]

CONARD, Louisa Ann and Joseph Emanuel

S/A with Gdn Abner CONARD: 20 Sep 1845 cash from Admr. of Eve AXLINE; cash from Exor. of David AXLINE dec'd and cash from Emanl. AXLINE; leaving $1378.51½. I would however state that the surety of the said Abner CONARD was Jonathan CONARD who I understand has since departed this life. RtCt 13 Jan 1851. [C380]

S/A with Gdn Abner CONARD: beginning 19 Sep 1855; rent of Emanuel AXLINE, leaving $1825.77¾. The security of the said Abner CUNARD in his bond as Gdn was Jonathan CUNARD now dec'd. RtCt 10 Jan 1853. [D:4]

S/A of Louisa A. and Joseph E. CONARD with Gdn Abner CONARD: beginning 19 Sep 1852; general expenses leaving $1929.60. RtCt 15 Mar 1853. [D:9]

S/A with Gdn Abner CONARD: paid tax on land, leaving $2108.89. RtCt 13 Feb 1854. [D:22]

S/A with Gdn Abner CONARD: beginning 5 Dec 1953; income from E. AXLINE & David AXLINE the amt. of the wards annual interest in home farm, leaving $2432.76. RtCt 14 Jun 1855. [D:105]

S/A of Louisa A. and Joseph E. CONARD with Gdn Abner CONARD: beginning 25 Dec 1854; general expenses leaving $2596.33. RtCt 9 Sep 1856. [D:154]

S/A of Louisa A. and Joseph E. CONARD with father & Gdn Abner CONARD: beginning 1 Dec 1855; general expenses leaving $2730.46. RtCt 12 Aug 1857. [D:275]

S/A with father & Gdn Abner CONARD: 7 Nov 2856 income from David AXLINE under will and from Simon ARNOLD for pasturage. Louisa Ann died 26 May 1857 and under the will of David AXLINE her grandfather, her father became her heir. The property which constitutes the bases of this fund was personal property, and the mother dying before her father, the property devised to her went to her children, and the one dying the father inherited from her. The balance due Joseph E. is $1455.96. RtCt 14 Apr 1859. [D:397]

SHEPHERD, Francis C. and Mellville R. (Infant children of Jacob R.)

S/A of Francis C. SHEPHERD and Mellville R. SHEPHERD with Gdn Nancy R. SHEPHERD: beginning 1847: payment to Carlisle College, general expenses, leaving $281.83. RtCt Feb 1851. [C381]

ALLEN, John James, Mary Elizabeth, Julia Teresa, Nathan Reed and William (Heirs of William)

S/A of John James ALLEN, Mary Elizabeth ALLEN, Julia Teresa ALLEN, Nathan Reed ALLEN and William ALLEN with Gdn Wm. H. HUGHES: beginning 1846; 12 Jun 1848-50 paid Mrs. Sarah ALLEN their Gdn in the west, 27 Mar 1846 rec'd from James ALLEN Admrs. their share of the slaves, leaving $698.95. RtCt 1 Aug 1851. [C:386]

ELGIN, Mary A.

S/A with Gdn Robert ELGIN: beginning 10 Aug 1845; income from Ignatius ELGINS, Admr. her share, general expenses leaving $124.39. RtCt 13 Sep 1852. [C:390]

S/A with Gdn Robert ELGIN: general expenses leaving $143.35. RtCt 12 Dec 1854. [D:84]

S/A with Gdn Robert ELGIN: beginning 1 Jan 1854; paid for music lessons and medical bills, leaving $64.38. RtCt 9 Sep 1856. [D:194]

S/A with Gdn Robert ELGIN: beginning 1 Jan 1856; paid for obtaining land warrant and clothing, leaving $108.40½ due to Gdn. RtCt 12 Aug 1857. [D:264]

S/A with Gdn Robert ELGIN: beginning Jan 1857; general expenses, leaving $145.77½. [D:345]

S/A with brother Gdn Robert ELGIN: general expenses leaving $145.77½. The ward is of such age as to enable her to understand accts, and her brother and Gdn can assert his claim for board, when she become of age. RtCt 18 Jun 1859 [D:411]

LYNN, Sarah G.

S/A with Gdn Pamelia LYNN: beginning Aug 1845; paid tuition and general expenses, leaving $149.71. RtCt 13 Sep 1852. [C:391]

S/A with Gdn Permelia C. LYNN: paid board & tuition, income from hire of boy, leaving $173.35. RtCt 12 Dec 1854. [D:85]

S/A with Gdn Parmelia C. LYNN: medicine, 26 May 1855 paid for coffin, leaving $25.04. Sarah G. died some time in the spring or summer of 1835 [55]. The income of Sarah G. LYNN's estate was the rent of a tract of land and the hire of a boy during her life and ascertaining that she died on 15 May 1855 I have allowed her Gdn for four and a half months of the rent and hire of the year 1855. It does not appear that said Sarah G. left any property except a gold watch and chain which her Gdn purchased for her. Balance of $25.04 for disbursement among the brothers and sisters of said Sarah G. including her mother numbering thirteen in all. RtCt 12 Aug 1857. [D:240]

TAVENER, Noble R. and Hannah V. (Children of Jonah)

S/A of Noble R. TAVENER with Gdn Solomon RUSE: rec'd cash from George WARNER Admr, leaving $272.89. S/A of Hannah V. TAVENER with Gdn Solomon RUSE: as above, leaving $272.89 The estate of these two wards consists of an interest in the estate of George WARNER dec'd devised through their deceased mother who was a daughter of said George WARNER dec'd and on interest in the estate of John NIXON dec'd devised through their deceased father Jonah TAVENER of whom said RUSE is the administrator. RtCt 15 Feb 1853. [D:1]

MEGEATH, James Townsend

S/A with Gdn Fenton FURR: beginning 13 Jul 1846; paid tuition, income from rent at Philomont and Bloomfield; leaving $1014.15. RtCt 12 Apr 1853. [D:10]

S/A with Gdn Fenton FURR: paid tuition, income from Alfred MEGEATH exc. of Gabriel MEGEATH and share of house rent at Philomont, leaving $1380.00. RtCt 13 Feb 1854. [D:23]

S/A with Gdn Fenton FURR: beginning 1 Jul 1853; paid board & tuition, leaving $1407.13. RtCt 12 Dec 1854. [D:89]

S/A with Gdn Fenton FURR: beginning 1 Jul 1854; paid board & tuition, income from rent at Philomont and Bloomfield, leaving $1418.46. RtCt 9 Sep 1856. [D:158]

S/A with Gdn Fenton FURR: beginning 1 Jul 1855; paid board and tuition, income from rent at Bloomfield and Philomont, leaving $1349.29. RtCt 14 Oct 1858. [D:349]

S/A with Gdn Fenton FURR: paid board and tuition, paid his mother for clothing, leaving $1349.29. RtCt 14 Oct 1858. [D:354]

S/A with Gdn Fenton FURR: beginning 1859; paid F. M. EDWARDS for tuition; leaving $1361.74. RtCt 13 Aug 1859. [E:2]

S/A with Gdn Fenton FURR: beginning 1859; paid board & tuition, income from Bloomfield rent, leaving $1366.70. RtCt [no date.] [E:119]

S/A with Gdn J. W. T. FURR Admr of Fenton FURR dec'd: $1000 payment in full 13 Apr 1866. RtCt 13 Mar 1882. [G:307]

BOOTH, Matilda, Henry H., Charlotte E. and James C. (Children of James)

S/A of Matilda BOOTH, Henry H. BOOTH, Charlotte E. BOOTH, and J. C. BOOTH with Gdn John GEORGE Jr: paid for repairs to house, leaving the share of each being ¼ is $8.89 which is now due to each of them except Matilda whose balance due her is $7.39. RtCt 10 Aug 1853. [D:12]

S/A of Matilda BOOTH with Gdn John GEORGE: beginning 13 Jun 1853; ¼ of rent of lot deducting 1/3 for widow share, leaving $14.62. S/A of Henry H. BOOTH with Gdn John GEORGE: beginning 13 Jun 1853; as above, leaving $17.71. S/A of Charlotte BOOTH with Gdn John GEORGE: beginning 13 Jun 1853; as above, leaving $8.82. S/A of James C. BOOTH with Gdn John GEORGE: beginning 13 Jun 1853; as above, leaving $8.82. RtCt 14 Jun 1855. [D:91]

S/A of Matilda, Henry H., Charlotte, James C. BOOTHE with Gdn John GEORGE Jr: beginning 9 Feb 1854; general expenses leaving $21.92 to Matilda, $26.69 to Henry H., $17.30 to Charlotte, and $17.30 to James C. BOOTHE. RtCt 15 Apr 1856. [D:143]

S/A of Matilda BOOTH with Gdn John GEORGE: paid for repairs to house, leaving $33.10. S/A of Henry H. BOOTH with Gdn John GEORGE: as above, leaving $38.15. S/A of Charlotte BOOTH with Gdn John GEORGE: as above, leaving $28.22. S/A of James C. BOOTH with Gdn John GEORGE: as above, leaving $28.22. RtCt 13 Jan 1857. [D:223]

S/A of Matilda BOOTH with Gdn John GEORGE: beginning 9 Feb 1856; general expenses, leaving $44.71. S/A of Charlotte BOOTH in acct with Gdn John GEORGE: as above, leaving $39.56. S/A if Henry H. BOOTH with Gdn John GEORGE: as above, leaving $50.06. S/A of James BOOTH with Gdn John GEORGE: as above, leaving $39.56. RtCt 14 Oct. 1858. [D:310]

S/A of Matilda A. BOOTHE with Gdn John GEORGE Jr: beginning 1858; 9 Feb 1857 rec'd ¼ of rent, dower paid to widow, leaving $54.64. S/A of Charlotte BOOTHE with Gdn John GEORGE Jr: as above, leaving $49.19. S/A of Henry H. BOOTHE with Gdn John GEORGE Jr: as above, leaving $61.29. S/A of James BOOTHE with Gdn John GEORGE Jr: as above, leaving $49.19. RtCt 14 Oct 1858. [D:333]

S/A with Gdn John GEORGE Jr.: beginning 9 Feb 1859; income from rents, leaving Matilda $75.70, Henry H. $82.73, Charlotte $69.94 and James C. BOOTH $69.94. RtCt 13 Jun 1861. [E:174]

S/A with Gdn John GEORGE Jr.: beginning 9 Feb 1859; income from rent, leaving Matilda $89.06, Henry H. $95.46, Charlotte $89.98 and James C. BOOTH $82.98. RtCt 13 Jun 1861. [E:176]

FRY, Annie and Emily J. (Heirs of Michael)
S/A of Annie FRY & Emily J. FRY with Gdn John LESLIE: beginning Sep 1848; income from interest on principal; leaving $2572.81. RtCt 17 Jun 1853. [D:13]

S/A with Gdn John LESLIE: beginning 29 Mar 1853; income from Enos FRY's estate, leaving $2848.39. Paid Anna half on 1 Jul 1853 as she is now 21y old. RtCt 11 Apr 1834. [D:44]

S/A of Emily J. FRY with Gdn John LESLEY: beginning 1 Jul 1854; income from Enos FRY's Exor., balance of $1727.81 due as she has now attained lawful age. RtCt 15 Apr 1836. [D:128]

THROCKMORTON, Hugh William
S/A with Gdn Richard McC. THOCKMORTON: expenses to Loudoun to rent farm; paid Ruth THOMAS in full of note executed by Sarah Mc THOCKMORTON and others for which the real estate of ward is bound and Jno. A. THOCKMORTON in consideration of his relinquishing all interest in his mother's estate, income from Negro girl sold aged 16 years, Negro girl sold aged 17 years and from hire of Negroes Lewis, Christopher, Joseph, little boy & little girl, leaving $468.02. RtCt 10 Oct 1853. [D:16]

S/A with Gdn Richard McC THROCMORTON: beginning 1 Jul 1852; paid for dividing real estate, income from hire of Lewis (yellow), Lewis (black), Christopher, Joseph, boy Henry & girl Patty, leaving $200.68. RtCt 13 Feb 1854. [D:25]

S/A with R. McC. THROCKMORTON: paid board & general expenses, leaving $1054.59. RtCt 14 Jul 1835. [D:94]

S/A with Richard McC. THROCKMORTON: paid board, income from bonds, income from Owen THOMAS hire of Negro Joe, Joseph POSTON hire of Negro Patty, Jonah THOMAS hire of Negro Henry, Joab OSBURN hire of Negro Lewis, of Mrs. BLAKELY hire of Negro Dick, Mrs. TORENSWORTH hire of Negro Dennis, and Jas. ALDER hire of yellow Lewis, leaving on 15 Aug 1855 $420.20 due to the said Gdn who is now deceased. RtCt 15 Apr 1856. [D:145]

FAWLEY, Sarah E., Jeremiah, Henry and Charles W. (Children of John)
S/A of Sarah E. FAWLEY with Gdn Samuel C. LUCKETT: income from John FAWLEY's Exor, paid tuition, leaving $289.00. S/A of Henry FAWLEY with Samuel C. LUCKETT: as above, leaving $295.66. S/A of Jeremiah FAWLEY with Samuel C. LUCKETT: as above, leaving $296.50. S/A of Charles FAWLEY with Samuel C. LUCKETT: as above, leaving $296.50. RtCt 13 Feb 1854. [D:24]

S/A of Sarah E. FAWLEY with Gdn Samuel C. LUCKETT: beginning 10 Dec 1852; paid tuition, leaving $316.82. S/A of Henry FAWLEY with Gdn Samuel C. LUCKETT: as above, leaving $322.47. S/A of Jeremiah FAWLEY with Gdn Samuel C. LUCKETT: as above, leaving $316.50. S/A of Charles W. FAWLEY with Gdn Samuel C. LUCKETT: as above, leaving $114.65. RtCt 10 Feb 1857. [D:236]

S/A of Sarah E. FAWLEY with Samuel C. LUCKETT: beginning 10 Dec 1855; paid medical bills and general expenses, leaving $301.29. S/A of Jeremiah FAWLEY with Samuel C. LUCKETT: as above, leaving $304.33. S/A of Henry FAWLEY with Samuel C. LUCKETT: as above, leaving $332.27. S/A of Charles W. FAWLEY with Samuel C. LUCKETT: as above, having become of age balance paid in full. RtCt 12 Aug 1857. [D:282]

S/A of Sarah E., Jeremiah, and Henry FAWLEY with Gdn Samuel C. LUCKETT: beginning 10 Dec 1856; general expenses leaving Sarah E. $305.30 Jeremiah $277.87, and Henry $311.76. RtCt 14 Oct 1858 [D:324]

S/A of Sarah E. FAWLEY, Jeremiah FAWLEY & Henry S. FAWLEY with Gdn Samuel C. LUCKETT: beginning 10 Dec 1858; general expenses leaving $208.03 to Sarah E., o$276.55 to Jeremiah, and $310.68 to Henry FAWLEY. RtCt 18 Jun 1859. [D:413]

S/A of Jeremiah FAWLEY with Gdn Samuel C. LUCKETT: beginning Jan 1859; general expenses leaving $257.95. S/A of Sarah E. FAWLEY with Gdn Samuel C. LUCKETT: beginning Jan 1859; expenses leaving $305.28. RtCt 14 Aug 1860. [E:77]

S/A of Jeremiah FAWLEY and others with Gdn: interest and store accts. – no dates or names; settled to 10 Aug 1867. The first acct. is that of Jeremiah FAWLEY dec'd it shows a balance due to him on said day of $19.46. Balance to Sarah E. of $197.94. and to Henry J. FAWLEY of $59.46. They are all of age. RtCt 12 Mar 1868. [E:184]

YAKEY, John W., Thomas S. and Jane A. (Heirs of Martin)
S/A of John W. YAKEY with Gdn John YAKEY: beginning 30 1849; paid tuition, leaving $221.14. S/A of Thomas S. YAKEY: basically the same as above, leaving $231.75. S/A of Jane YAKEY with Gdn John YAKEY: as

above, leaving $231.75. S/A under the will of Simon YAKEY dec'd the grandfather of said children. Amanda YAKEY the widow of Martin YAKEY dec'd was appointed the Gdn of these children, and acted as such until she intermarried of Andrew SEITZ, by which act she forfeited all interest in the real estate which under the will of Simon YAKEY dec'd father of Martin, fell under the control of John YAKEY the executor of said Simon for the benefit of their children. RtCt 15 Mar 1854. [D:28]

S/A with Gdn Amanda YAKEY now Amanda SEITZ: paid for repairs, income from John YAKEY Admr. of Martin YAKEY dec'd, paid John YAKEY their share of expense getting legacy of Ann M. COST's estate, leaving $509.83. In the will of Simon YAKEY dec'd is the following clause (after dividing his land between his son John YAKEY and the children of Martin YAKEY) my beloved Martin's widow is to have one division of the land, that is the benefit of the rents thereof for raising the children until the youngest child becomes of age, and then the lands to be equally divided among the children with this provision as long as she remains a widow in Martin YAKEY's name so as soon as she changes her name the property is to fall in the executors hands for him to rent to whom he pleases and the rents applied to the children. John YAKEY who was the executor of said Simon YAKEY administered on the estate of said Martin YAKEY and settled his administration account before about March 1847 and distributed the balance reported in his hand divided between the widow and the children, and paid over the share of the children to the widow who was then Gdn and with which I have charged her in the annexed accounts. In Oct 1848 the widow married Andrew SEITZ and surrendered the land into the possession of John YAKEY the executor of said Simon to be disposed of under the will of said Simon. Upon her marriage, according to the estate, she ceased to be the Gdn of her children and upon the settlement of the acct. a question arose as to what would be the proper arrangement in relation to the balance reported to be in her hands. I suggested the propriety of appointing a new Gdn, and that John YAKEY the executor of the Simon and testamentory Gdn of the children would be a suitable person, he however declined and time passes on until it was finally forgotten until recently the case arrested my attention, when upon mentioning the subject to said Andrew SEITZ, I suggested the propriety of returning this settlement and present the care to the Court that some disposition might be made of the funds for the use and benefit of the children and under such understanding with said SEITZ I now respectfully submit the case to the consideration of the Court. It will be discovered that the whole of the credit allowed to the Gdn relate to permanent improvement made by her, which I was satisfied from evidence, laid before me, were necessary, the whole of which I have charged to the children as they alone received the benefit derived from them, she having surrendered the land on which they were made the year they were made. RtCt 9 Sep 1856. [D:196]

S/A with Gdn John YAKEY: beginning 12 Jun 1854; paid for repairs to farm. S/A of John W. YAKEY with Gdn John YAKEY: paid tuition and board, leaving $556.47. S/A of Thomas S. YAKEY with Gdn John YAKEY: as above, leaving $499.48. S/A of Jane A. YAKEY with Gdn John YAKEY: as above, leaving 455.96. RtCt 10 Feb 1857. [D:233]

S/A with Gdn John YAKEY: beginning 9 Apr 1856; general expenses leaving $608.38. S/A of John W. YAKEY with Gdn John YAKEY: paid tuition, leaving $709.34. S/A of Thomas S. YAKEY with Gdn John YAKEY: as above, leaving $654.26. S/A of Jane A. YAKEY with Gdn John YAKEY: paid board and tuition, leaving $524.68. RtCt 12 Aug 1857. [D:280]

S/A with Gdn John YAKEY: beginning May 1857; debts of general acct leaving $397.32. S/A of John W. YAKEY with Gdn John YAKEY; beginning 6 Jan 1857; paid board and tuition, leaving $722.34. S/A of Thomas S. YAKEY with Gdn John YAKEY: as above, leaving $746.51. S/A of Jane A. YAKEY with Gdn John YAKEY as above, leaving $531.11. RtCt 14 Oct 1858. [D:325]

S/A with John YAKEY trustee under the will of Simon YAKEY: beginning 1858; paid for provisions. S/A of John W. YAKEY with acting Gdn John YAKEY: beginning 17 Apr 1858; paid board, leaving $728.34. S/A of Thomas S. YAKEY with acting Gdn John YAKEY: beginning 17 Apr 1858; general expenses leaving $856.81. S/A of Jane America YAKEY with acting Gdn John YAKEY: general expenses, leaving $638.96. RtCt 13 Aug 1859. [E:9]

S/A with Gdn John YAKEY: beginning 27 Jan 1859; Quarter Branch road case; paid for provisions. S/A of John W. YAKEY with acting Gdn John YAKEY: paid board & tuition, leaving $732.44. S/A of Thomas S. YAKEY with acting Gdn John YAKEY: paid board & tuition, leaving $880.21. S/A of Jane America YAKEY with acting Gdn John YAKEY: paid Andrew SEITZ for board & clothing. RtCt 14 Aug 1860. [E:103]

S/A with Gdn John YAKEY: beginning 9 Mar 1860; paid for various repair supplies. S/A of John W. YAKEY with Gdn John YAKEY: beginning 1 Jan 1860; income from share of rent; leaving $521.48. He is now of age. S/A of Thomas S. YAKEY with Gdn John YAKEY: beginning 6 Jan 1860; paid board & tuition, leaving $951.72. S/A of Jane A. YAKEY with Gdn John YAKEY: beginning 6 Jan 1860; general expenses leaving $658.65. She has married Thomas J. COST. John YAKEY as executor of Martin YAKEY to Amanda YAKEY his widow, and now the wife of Andrew SEITZ is fully discharged of his duties as Gdn. RtCt 13 Jun 1861. [E:192]

S/A of John W. YAKEY, Thomas S. YAKEY and Jane A. YAKEY with mother & late Gdn Amanda YAKEY (now Amanda SEITZ): beginning 13 May 1848; general expenses leaving John W. YAKEY $276.99, Thomas J. COST who married Jane S. YAKEY $276.99 and Thomas S. YAKEY $276.98 with compound interest until ___ 1861 when he became 21 years old. RtCt 17 Aug 1866. [E:294]

S/A of 14 Jan 1867. Thomas S. YAKEY paid $951.72 in full by Gdn. RtCt 9 Apr 1867. [E:351]

COCHRAN, Sarah Ann, Samuel G., Mary P., Tholemiah T. and Emily (Children of Nathan)

S/A of Sarah Ann, Samuel G., Mary P., Tholemiah T, and Emily COCHRAN with Gdn Addison COCHRAN: income from James COCHRAN's Admr, leaving $447.14. RtCt 11 Apr 1854. [D:33]

S/A of Samuel G., Sarah A, Mary P., Tholemiah T. and Emily E. COCHRAN with Gdn Addison COCHRAN: beginning 1853; income from Jas. COCHRAN Admr and from Sarah COCHRAN's Admr in full of share of her estate, 10 Nov 1854 paid $166.18 Saml. G. COCHRAN in full of his share having obtained lawful age, leaving for the rest $664.74. RtCt 14 Jun 1855. [D:115]

S/A of Sarah Ann, Mary P., Tholemiah T. and Emily COCHRAN with Gdn Addison COCHRAN: beginning 13 Feb 1855; income from James COCHRAN Admr. (from Stephen COCHRAN's estate) and from Sarah A. COCHRAN's estate, paid fee in suit COCHRAN vs COCHRAN, proceeds of land belonging to estate of Nathan COCHRAN sold under decree of Court, leaving $1554.62. RtCt 14 Oct 1858. [D:298]

DOWELL, Julia A.

S/A of Julia A. DOWELL of Fauquier Co. with Gdn Conrad R. DOWELL: beginning 1 Jun 1850; paid Henry W. WOLF (her brother in law of Fauquier Co., as agent appointed for that purpose by Julia A. DOWELL) in full of legacy bequeathed to her by Conrad BITZER dec'd per appointment (Julia now of lawful age), leaving $3379.09. RtCt 11 Apr 1854. [D:34]

SMITH, Margaret E., Malinda C. and Ryland G. (Children of William H.)

Inventory of the estate in the hands of Gdn Seth SMITH: 2/3 of net amount of arrears of pay - $13.33 1/3; 2/3 of net amount of price of land warrant taken under decree of Court – $79.17; arrears of pension forfeited by their mother by marrying – $43.31. RtCt 10 Apr 1854. [D:46]

S/A with Gdn Seth SMITH: beginning 10 Feb 1852; rec'd 2/3 of sale of land warrant, rec'd widows share of pension forfeited by marriage paid Jas. THOMPSON towards their support jointly (M. C. and M. E.), leaving $45.43 due to Ryland G. SMITH and to Margaret E. and Malinda C. SMITH jointly & equally the sum of $75.35. RtCt 12 Dec 1854. [D:86]

S/A of Margaret E. SMITH and Malinda C. SMITH with Gdn Wm. H. GILL: 10 Feb 1854 rec'd from cash first Gdn (Seth SMITH), leaving $76.22 jointly. S/A of Ryland G. SMITH with Gdn Wm. H. GILL: beginning 14 Aug 1854; same as above, leaving $52.10. RtCt 12 Aug 1857. [D:273]

S/A with Gdn William H. GILL: beginning 14 Aug 1857; general expenses leaving Margaret E. and Malinda SMITH $74.18 and Ryland G. SMITH $56.16. RtCt 13 Aug 1859. [E:5]

S/A with Gdn Wm. H. GILL: beginning 14 Aug 1859; expenses of Ryland G. SMITH leaving $56.82 transferred at his death (supposed to have died 14 Aug 1863 in the Army of Northern Virginia) to his sisters, expenses of Margaret & Malinda SMITH leaving $118 plus interest until they reach 21y old. RtCt 16 Mar 1872. [F:217]

S/A of Malinda C. & Margaret E. with Gdn W. H. GILL: full payment of $239. RtCt 9 Jul 1878. [G:109]

HOGE, Elisha H. and Anna E.

S/A with Gdn Elisha JANNEY: beginning 12 Jun 1850; income from J. G. HOGE from proceeds of land sold in the state of Ohio for their support and for rent on other lands, cash paid mother for clothes of wards, leaving $41.28 due to Elisha H. HOGE and $123.42 due to Anne E. HOGE. RtCt 17 June 1854. [D:50]

CONARD, Jonathan T.

S/A with Gdn E. J. CONARD: paid board and tuition, income from share of black girl sold and balance due from the Admrs. of his father Jonathan CONARD dec'd, leaving $1276.79. RtCt 17 Jun 1854. [D:58]

S/A with Gdn Ebenezer J. CONARD: paid tuition and medical expenses, leaving $1509.82 1/3. RtCt 13 Jan 1857. [D:198]

S/A with Gdn Ebenezer J. CONARD: paid for clothing and tuition, leaving $1651.03. RtCt 12 Aug 1857. [D:279]

S/A with Gdn Ebenezer J. CONARD: beginning 15 Jun 1857; general expenses leaving $1651.03. Thomas VICKERS one of the securities has removed to the west, the other however, William CLENDENING Jr. is perfectly good. RtCt 13 Aug 1859. [D:421]

S/A with Gdn Ebenezer J. CONARD: paid board, leaving $1758.56. RtCt 13 Aug 1859. [D:422]

S/A with Gdn Ebenezer J. CONARD: beginning 25 Jun 1859; paid board, leaving $1881.84. RtCt 14 Aug 1860. [E:73]

S/A with Gdn Ebenezer J. CONARD: beginning 13 Feb 1860; paid tuition, leaving $1982.85. RtCt 13 Jun 1861. [E:184]

S/A with Gdn Ebenezer J. CONARD: receipt for $1981.15 payment of acct in full. RtCt 17 Aug 1871. [F:172]

CONARD, Jane A.

S/A with Gdn John W. CONARD: beginning 28 May 1851; income from share from sale of black girl sold, leaving $1424.68. RtCt 17 Jun 1854. [D:60]

LORENTZ, Laura V.

S/A with Gdn Caroline O. HODSON: income from hire of Negro Catharine, paid tuition & board, income from Jas. ALDER for rent of corn field, leaving $11.46 due to Gdn. RtCt 16 Aug 1854. [D:61]

S/A with Gdn James J. LOVE: paid board & tuition, income from hire of Negroes Cash's & Henry and from rent of J. A. LORENTZ, income from E. J. LEE as administrator, leaving $380. RtCt 14 Jun 1855. [D:110]

S/A with Gdn James J. LOVE: beginning 1 Jan 1855; paid board & tuition and for shoes for Negro Catharine, leaving $839.33. RtCt 9 Sep 1856. [D:156]

S/A with Gdn James J. LOVE: beginning 1 Jan 1856; paid ferrying acct. and for clothing, leaving $839.33. RtCt 12 Aug 1857. [D:269]

S/A with Gdn James J. LOVE: beginning 1 Jan 1857; general expenses, income from hire of Negroes Catharine and Henry, leaving $839.33. RtCt 14 Oct 1855. [D:347]

S/A with Gdn James J. LOVE: beginning 1 Jan 1858; paid tuition, income from hire of Negroes Catharine & Henry, leaving $839.33. Her property consists of a small tract of land (57) fifty seven acres assessed at $1596 and the fund apparently of $839.33 principal, which is subject or not, as the Court may decide to offsets for money due the Gdn. In looking over the former S/A I find that a house and a lot was sold and the share of the ward was $485.50 and $400 was rec'd from the Admr. E. T. LEE. From this it will be seen that the original principal was $885.50 and it is now $839.33 and it is now less than it was by $46.17 and by the acct. now stated on the profit side there is due to the Gdn $590.96 and thus the whole amount sunk in the maintenance and education of the ward is $637.13. There is a considerable tract of land for which a suit is now pending in the Circuit Court of Loudoun Co. & for the defense of which the $50 were paid to John JANNEY, and the $20 to S. L. HODGSON in which this party would have an interest of probably one third, but it is a matter of very great doubt whether she will ever realize this interest. RtCt 13 Aug 1859. [D:430]

S/A with Gdn James J. LOVE: beginning 9 Jun 1859; paid various store accts., income from hire of Negro Catharine, leaving $176.93. The ward by teaching nearly supports herself, but the heavy expenses of the suit of Julia HODGSON against S. L. HODGSON have this year with her store acct. decided the balance against her. The costs of the suit above named will very nearly consume the money part of her estate. RtCt [Aug 1860?] [E:118]

SCHOOLEY, Charles G.

S/A with Gdn Mahlon SCHOOLEY: beginning 22 Feb 1852; income from Sarah S. BROWN's Exor and ward's share of legacy bequeathed to his mother by said testator, leaving $3.31 due. RtCt 16 Aug 1854. [D:63]

GRAY, Albert W.

S/A with Gdn Augustus WATERMAN: paid M. G. JONES stage fare (to Harrisburg), income from hire of Negro Charles, leaving $12464.76. The ward is now of lawful age. RtCt 16 Aug 1854. [D:64]

S/A with Gdn Augustus WATERMAN: Albert became of age on 1 May 1852, fully paid. RtCt 15 Apr 1856. [D:142]

OSBURN, Lucinda (a lunatic)

S/A with Committee Jonah OSBURN: beginning 1851; paid Jane OSBURN one years support, income from hire of black boy, leaving $2897.36. RtCt 16 Aug 1854. [D:67]

S/A with Committee Jonah OSBURN: beginning 1 Apr 1854; paid board, income from hire of black boy, leaving $3247.56. Lucinda OSBURN, a lunatic, appears departed this life about the 24th January last. RtCt 9 Sep 1856. [D:159]

PLASTER, John H., James H., Michael M., William A. and Sarah Frances (Heirs of George)

S/A of John H. PLASTER with Gdn Michael PLASTER: bal. due from Geo. PLASTER's Exor., paid tuition and general expenses, leaving $115.95. S/A of the four heirs of Geo. PLASTER (died in fall of 1845) with Gdn M. PLASTER: bal. due from Geo. PLASTER's Exor., income from rent of C. A. NEWLON for farm and house. S/A of James H. PLASTER with Gdn Michael PLASTER: beginning Jan 1848; paid tuition, leaving $45.93 due to Gdn. S/A of Michael M. PLASTER with Gdn Michael PLASTER: beginning Jan 1848; paid tuition, leaving $17.07 due to Gdn. S/A of William A. PLASTER with Gdn Michael PLASTER: beginning Jan 1848; income from interest, leaving $3.78. S/A of Sarah F. PLASTER with Gdn Michael PLASTER; beginning Jan 1848; paid tuition and general expenses, leaving $0.13. Mary PLASTER the widow of said George, died about Aug 1846 having appointed said Michael PLASTER her executor, John H. PLASTER it appears, left the family about the time of his mother's death, yet John his share being one fifth of a fair rent for the farm. In settling the account of said John H., who is now of age, I have allowed him $40. The said Mary PLASTER dec'd left her personal property to Sarah HAMILTON her mother during her natural life, who lives with and takes care of the children. Of the property left by testatrix, her executor, with the consent of the legatee for life, sold a portion, the proceeds of which he retains in his hands, and as the legatee is supported out of the proceeds in the execution hands for the maintenance of the four younger children. RtCt 16 Aug 1854. [D:69]

S/A of William Albert PLASTER with Gdn Michael PLASTER: beginning 12 Jun 1854; 10 May 1855 paid out for burial clothes, paid John Henry PLASTER share of rent. S/A of Michael M. PLASTER with Gdn Michael PLASTER: beginning 16 Mar 1854; paid his share of rent, leaving $101.47. S/A of Sarah F. PLASTER with Gdn Michael PLASTER: beginning 12 Jun 1854; paid her share of rent and tuition, leaving $107.45. S/A of James H. PLASTER with Gdn Michael PLASTER: beginning 12 Jun 1854; paid share of rent and tuition, leaving $44.09. The balance due to William Albert PLASTER at his death are credited equally among his surviving brothers & sister and also their share of their father's estate remaining in the hands of Exor. RtCt 13 Jan 1857. [D:214]

S/A of Michael M. PLASTER with Gdn Michael PLASTER: beginning 13 Mar 1856; ¼ of rent of farm due to John H. PLASTER, leaving $101.47. S/A of Sarah F. PLASTER with Gdn Michael PLASTER: beginning 13 Mar 1856; as above, leaving $107.45. S/A of James H. PLASTER with Gdn Michael PLASTER: beginning 13 Mar 1856; as above, leaving $44.09. RtCt 14 Oct 1858. [D:358]

S/A of Michael M. PLASTER with Gdn Michael PLASTER: beginning 5 Oct 1857; paid one half of MEGEATH's bill and one half of J. R. NEWLON's bill, leaving $96.10. This person is over the age of twenty one years but he is of weak mind, in fact helpless and his Gdn chooses to settle his acct. as still Gdn. S/A of Sarah Frances PLASTER with Gdn Michael PLASTER: beginning 5 Oct 1857; as above, leaving $104.09. S/A of James H. PLASTER with Gdn Michael PLASTER: beginning 5 Oct 1857; paid one third SINCLAIR's fee, leaving $55.91. RtCt 15 Mar 1860. [E:37]

S/A of Michael M. PLASTER with Gdn Michael PLASTER: beginning Oct. 1859; paid to G. H. PLASTER for stone fencing; leaving $107.12. S/A of Sarah Frances PLASTER with Gdn Michael PLASTER: beginning 10 Mar 1960; as above, leaving $115.49. S/A of James H. PLASTER with Gdn Michael PLASTER: paid for him as per acct. of M. PLASTER, leaving $71.56. RtCt 14 Aug 1860. [E:94]

GREGG, Gilford G.
S/A with Gdn Jonah HATCHER: payment from T. WHITACRE Admr. of Jemima GREGG dec'd; paid board & tuition; income from Jesse DOWELL for rent of house; cash paid to himself to go to school in New York, leaving $416.48½. RtCt 16 Aug 1854. [D:81]

S/A with Gdn Jonah HATCHER: beginning 4 Nov 1853; income from T. WHITACRE Admr. of Jemima GREGG dec'd, from Wm. McCRAY for lot of NUBBINS, from Jesse DOWELL on his rent and from crops, leaving $215.01 ½, ward who is now of age. RtCt 14 Jun 1855. [D:112]

COCHRAN, Sarah
S/A of Sarah COCHRAN dec'd (late JAMES) with Gdn Robert JAMES: beginning 3 Mar 1848; paid Addison COCHRAN & wife and Craven JAMES Admr. of Sarah COCHRAN dec'd. RtCt 12 Dec 1854. [D:83]

TRUNDLE, Esther (lunatic)
S/A with Committee Daniel T. SHREVE: beginning 13 Jun 1853; cash rec'd from Robert MOFFETT former trustee, leaving $1834.43. RtCt 12 Dec 1854. [D:87]

S/A with Committee Daniel T. SHREVE: beginning 1 May 1854; paid Solomon EVERHART for building kitchen, leaving $1857.35. RtCt 14 Jun 1855. [D:118]

SANBOWER, Samuel F. and Mary F.
S/A of Samuel F. SANBOWER with Gdn John GEORGE Jr: beginning 13 Jun 1853; paid tuition, income from Jno. SANBOWER for share 2 yrs. rent on farm, leaving $75.16. S/A of Mary F. SANBOWER with Gdn John GEORGE Jr: beginning 13 Jun 1853; paid tuition, income from Jno. SANBOWER for share 2 yrs. rent on farm, leaving Mary $73.10. RtCt 14 Jun 1855. [D:89]

S/A of Samuel F. SANBOWER with Gdn John GEORGE: beginning 9 Feb 1854; paid tuition, leaving $103.43. S/A of Mary F. SANBOWER with Gdn John GEORGE: general expenses, leaving $104.44. RtCt 15 Apr 1856. [D:131]

S/A of Samuel F. SANBOWER with Gdn John GEORGE: beginning 13 Jun 1855; paid tuition, leaving $141.21. S/A of Mary F. SANBOWER with Gdn John GEORGE: as above, leaving $144.98. RtCt 13 Jan 1857. [D:222]

S/A of Samuel F. SANBOWER with Gdn John GEORGE: beginning 12 May 1856; paid tuition, leaving $168.07. S/A of Mary F. SANBOWER with Gdn John GEORGE: as above, leaving $176.23. RtCt 14 Oct 1858. [D:286]

S/A with Gdn John GEORGE Jr: beginning 13 Mar 1857; 30 Jun 1857 paid final settlement of Mary F. SANBOWER, leaving Samuel F. SANBOWER $5.22. RtCt 13 Jun 1861. [E:167]

BROWN, William (a lunatic)
S/A of estate with Committee Jonathan HIRST: paid David BROWN in part due him on settlement as agent of Wm. BROWN, paid M. F. Insurance Co., income from bonds and notes, leaving $222.58. RtCt 14 Jun 1855. [D:93]

S/A of estate of William BROWN with Committee Jonathan HIRST: beginning 12 Oct 1854; paid David BROWN for board, paid for washing and keeping house, income from David BROWN for rent, leaving $185.52. RtCt 15 Apr 1856 [D:123]

S/A with Committee Henry S. TAYLOR: beginning 1 Jun 1855; paid expenses to Ohio and back and medical expenses, income from David BROWN for rent of farm, leaving $117.82. RtCt 13 Jan 1857. [D:213]

S/A with Committee Henry S. TAYLOR: paid board, leaving $99.17. RtCt 14 Oct 1858. [D:329]

S/A with Committee Henry S. TAYLOR: beginning 16 Sep 1857; as above, income from David BROWN for rent, leaving $156.05. RtCt 14 Oct 1858. [D:330]

S/A of with Committee Henry S. TAYLOR: beginning 14 Sep 1858; paid Fire Insurance and board, leaving $127.95. RtCt 13 Apr 1859. [D:418]

S/A with Committee Henry S. TAYLOR: beginning 10 Apr 1860; paid various store accts, leaving $21.31. The committee has considerably exceeded the income of his ward, and has allowed bills which are very questionable, especially that of G. W. JANNEY. His income of $210.00 and exceeds that which is necessary at a lunatic asylum and by all means his expenses ought to be kept within it. RtCt 13 Jun 1861. [E:142]

S/A with Committee Henry S. TAYLOR: paid various store accts and David BROWN for board, income from David BROWN for rent and sale of lumber, leaving $104.86. RtCt 13 Jun 1861. [E:183]

BURKE, Mary F., Virginia E. and Charles W.
S/A of Mary F. and Virginia E. BURKE with Gdn Washington VANDEVANTER: income from Elizabeth BURKE's Exor, leaving $771,83 to Mary F. and Virginia E. equally. S/A of Charles W. BURKE with Gdn Washington VANDEVANTER: as above, leaving $395.18 paid in full (he now being 21 years of age). RtCt 14 Jul 1855. [D:96]

S/A of Mary F. BURKE with Gdn Washington VANDEVANTER: general expenses leaving $374.69. S/A of Virginia E. BURKE with Gdn Washington VANDEVANTER: as above, leaving $404.69. RtCt 9 Sep 1856. [D:151]

VIRTZ, Margaretta, Daniel, Isaiah, Priscilla and Elizabeth C. (Children of Peter)
S/A of Margaretta, Daniel, Isaiah, Priscilla and Elizabeth C. VIRTZ with Gdn William GRAHAM: beginning 10 Aug 1853; cash rec'd from John GRUBB and from George SHOEMAKER; leaving $763.94. RtCt 14 Jun 1855. [D:98]

S/A with Gdn William GRAHAM: beginning 15 Dec 1854; cash rec'd from John GRUBB Exor. of Peter VIRTZ dec'd, leaving $1147.55. RtCt 15 Apr 1856. [D:147]

S/A of Margaretta, Daniel, Isaiah, Priscilla, and Elizabeth C. VIRTZ with Gdn William GRAHAM: beginning 12 May 1856; expenses leaving $1362.36 equally. RtCt 12 Aug 1857. [D:274]

S/A heirs of Michael VIRTZ with Gdn William GRAHAM: paid for repairs, income from rents of Matthew ORRISON. S/A OF Daniel VIRTZ with Gdn Wm. GRAHAM: beginning 13 Aug 1859; general expenses leaving $302.78. S/A of Isaiah VIRTZ with Gdn Wm. GRAHAM: beginning 13 Aug 1859; as above, leaving $316.02. S/A of Jane P. VIRTZ with Gdn Wm. GRAHAM: beginning 13 Aug. 1859; as above, leaving $316.02. S/A of Elizabeth C. VIRTZ with Gdn Wm. GRAHAM: beginning 13 Aug 1859; as above, leaving $316.02. RtCt 14 Aug 1860. [E:101]

S/A of Margaretta VIRTZ with Gdn William GRAHAM: rec'd during the year from the general acct. as stated in the acct. of Daniel VIRTZ &c, leaving $316.02. RtCt 14 Aug 1860. [E:102]

HAVENER, Mary J., Harriet E., William H. and Robert (Heirs of James)
S/A of Mary J. HAVENER, Harriet E. HAVENER, Wm. H. HAVENER, and Robert HAVENER with Gdn Lee A. SAUNDERS: beginning 5 Oct 1852; 5 Apr 1854 the share of Wm. H. HAVENNER who is now of age, rec'd from Jno. M. WILSON Admr. of James HAVENER dec'd, 6 Jul 1849 share of Mary Jane who is now of lawful age, 5 Jan 1855 balance due to date from Gdn to Mary E. DARNE, 6 Oct 1853 the share of Harriet E. who is now of lawful age. The Gdn in this S/A is charged interest on the whole amt. rec'd up to 6 Jul 1849 at which time the oldest ward attained lawful age, her ¼ part is then deducted and on 5 Jan 1855 finds the amt. due to Mary J. HAVENER (now DARNE) the sum of $38.83. On 6 Oct 1852 he finds a balance of $21.14 due to Harriet E. HAVENER (now DIGGENS) with interest thereon to 5 Jan 1855 amounting to $23.99, amt. due to Wm. H. HAVENER on 5 Jan 1855 who has lately obtained lawful age, $79.84 and to Robert HAVENER who is yet a minor the sum of $79.84 due 5 Jan 1855. RtCt 14 Jun 1855. [D:102]

DOWELL, Albert B.
S/A with Gdn Conrad R. DOWELL: 1853 paid F. LITTLETON 2/3 for Susan's coffin, paid J. ISETTS 2/3 for digging grave, paid A. R. MOTT 2/3 for medical bill, income from hire of Negro boy Enos & of Susan up to her death, leaving $1737.36. RtCt 14 Jun 1855. [D:104]

S/A with Gdn Conrad R. DOWELL: paid Ann E. DOWELL for necessary articles, income from 2/3 of hire of Negro boy Enos, leaving $1912.02. RtCt 9 Sep 1856. [D:155]

S/A with Gdn Conrad R. DOWELL: expenses with wards & mother, leaving $2071.92. RtCt 12 Aug 1857. [D:246]

S/A with Gdn Conrad R. DOWELL: beginning 31 Dec 1856; income from hire of Negro boy Enos, 1 Jul 1857 paid Samuel PURSELL this day as Gdn of the said ward (in place of C. R. DOWELL now dec'd) by his Exor. Joseph PANCOAST, leaving $2230.20. Saml. PURSELL was appointed by the said Court as the future Gdn of the said ward to whom was this day paid over the above balance of $2230.20 together with a note for the hire of Negro boy Enos the present year for $130, which constitutes the entire estate of the said ward in the hands of C. R. DOWELL at his death with interest. RtCt 14 Oct 1858. [D:308]

S/A with Gdn Samuel PURSELL: beginning 31 Dec 1857; 1 Jul 1857 rec'd from Joseph PANCOAST Exor. of C.

R. DOWELL former Gdn, leaving $2230.20. RtCt 12 Jan 1859. [D:371]

S/A with Gdn Samuel PURSEL: general expenses leaving $2373.04 . RtCt 15 May 1860. [E:22]

S/A with Gdn Samuel PURCEL: beginning 1859; paid tuition, income from hire of servant man Enos, leaving $2563.65. RtCt 13 Feb 1866. [E:215]

S/A with Gdn Samuel PURCEL: beginning Jul 1860; paid tuition, leaving $2694. RtCt 13 Feb 1866. [E:217]

S/A with Gdn Samuel PURSEL: beginning 31 May 1867; $26 & $20.35 in confederate money rec'd in 1862 & 63 from estate of Joel OSBURN dec'd, general expenses, leaving $2007.26. RtCt 18 Jun 1870. [F:66]

S/A with Gdn Samuel PURSELL: beginning 3 Aug 1868; expenses at school, leaving $2007.77. RtCt 18 Jun 1870. [F:67]

S/A with Gdn Samuel PURSELL: beginning 11 May 1869; general expenses leaving $2066.71, $95.43 over income. RtCt 17 Aug 1871. [F:172]

S/A with Gdn Samuel B. PURSELL: beginning 3 Jun 1870; general expenses leaving $1999.05. RtCt 23 Nov 1871. [F:202]

S/A with Gdn Samuel PURSELL: beginning 2 Nov 1871; general expenses leaving $1999.05. RtCt 13 Jan 1873. [F:274]

S/A with Gdn Samuel PURSEL: beginning 2 Nov 1871; general expenses leaving $1999.05. RtCt 10 Feb 1873. [F:280]

S/A with Gdn Samuel PURSELL: beginning 10 Jul 1872; general expenses leaving $2088. RtCt 14 Sep 1874. [F:423]

STOUTSENBERGER, Samuel T., Ann E., Frances A., and Emanuel W.

S/A of Samuel T. STOUTSENBERGER with Gdn Townsend M. PAXSON: 10 Jun 1854 cash paid ward to defray expenses going to the west, 12 Jan 1855 paid Solomon CRUMBAKER ward's proportion of costs in suit. CRUMBAKER vs. STOUTSENBERGER, income from D. HIXSON 1/6 of balance of his hands decreed to the children of Saml. STOUTSENBERGER, leaving $299.53. S/A of Ann E. STOUTSENBERGER with Gdn Townsend M. PAXSON: same as above, leaving $241.29. S/A of Frances A. STOUTSENBERGER with Gdn Townsend M. PAXSON: same as above, leaving $269.98. S/A of Emanuel W. STOUTSENBERGER with Gdn Townsend M. PAXSON: same as above, leaving $305.33. RtCt 14 Jun 1855. [D:107]

S/A Ann E. with Gdn Townsend M. PAXSON: beginning 12 Feb 1855; 10 Mar 1856 paid Samuel W. SLATER who married Ann E., $190.58 balance paid in full. RtCt 10 Feb 1857. [D:232]

S/A of Emanuel W. STOUTSENBERGER with Gdn Townsend M. PAXSON: beginning 12 Feb 1855; paid tuition and for division of land, leaving $307.73. S/A of Frances A. STOUTSENBERGER with Gdn Townsend M. PAXSON: as above, leaving $269.98. RtCt 12 Aug 1857. [D:242]

S/A of Emanuel W. STOUTSENBERGER with Gdn T. M. PAXSON: beginning 12 Jul 1856; paid for clothing, leaving $314.40. S/A of Francis A. STOUTSENBERGER with Gdn T. M. PAXSON: as above, leaving $269.98. RtCt 14 Oct 1858. [D:291]

S/A of Emanuel W. STOUTSENBERGER with Gdn Townsend M. PAXSON: general expenses, leaving $314.40. S/A of Frances A. STOUTSENBERGER with Gdn Townsend M. PAXSON: as above, leaving $2130.84. RtCt 12 Jan 1859. [D:379]

S/A of Francis A. STOUTSENBERGER with Gdn Townsend M. PAXSON: beginning 31 Mar 1858; general expenses leaving $180.21. She is of age and has sanctioned the expenditures made on her acct. [E:7]

S/A of Emanuel W. STOUTSENBERGER with Gdn Townsend M. PAXSON: as above; leaving $285.38. His expenditures have exceeded the income of his estate, but it is because the land belonging to him is resting having been sowed in clover seed in the Spring of 1858. He is 20 years of age. RtCt 13 Aug 1859. [E:8]

BALL, Mary A., Margaret and Elizabeth

S/A of Mary A. BALL, Margaret BALL and Elizabeth BALL with Gdn Henry T. GOVER: cash advanced to Jas. H. VANDEVANTER to defray expenses of the ward from McMinville to Pt. of Rocks, cash rec'd from the Admr. of Napolcon B. BALL by the hands of Cornelius VANDEVANTER, paid B. F. GATTAN for board at Pt. of Rocks;, paid Lial T. BEECH for bringing ward from Pt. of Rocks to Waterford, leaving due to Mary A. BALL, $396.56 due to Margaret A. BALL and $390.97 due to Elizabeth BALL. RtCt 14 Jun 1855 [D:116]

THOMPSON, Elizabeth

Sale of 7 Oct 1854 of the estate of Elizabeth THOMPSON (an insane person by order of Court) by Committee Joseph P. GRUBB: purchasers: L. D. THOMPSON, Archibald McDANIEL, Samuel CRIM, Henry EVERHART, Armstead SCOTT, Bushrod BROWN, Wesley C. SAUNDERS, Wm. H. HARDY, Joseph P. GRUBB, Amos BEANS, M. ROYSTON, Joseph MOCK, N. B. PEACOCK, Isaac CAMP, Jonathan EWERS, James CARROLL, totaling $121.08½. RtCt 15 Mar 1855. [D:120]

Appraisal/Inventory of 7 Oct 1854: (an insane person) household items totaling $128.84½, note of Archibald McDANIEL made payable to Andrew THOMPSON for $120. Aprs: Noble B. PEACOCK, Jas. McILHANY, Isaac CAMP, Joseph P. GRUBB. RtCt 12 Oct 1857. [D:284]

S/A with Committee Joseph P. GRUBB: (insane person) paid board, 3 Aug 1857 paid for coffin, income from rents, leaving $8.67 up to 10 Aug 1857 (about which time she died). RtCt 14 Apr 1859. [D:409]

LITTLETON, Bushrod
S/A of estate with Committee Richard C. LITTLETON: (insane) beginning 14 Feb 1853; paid old Nancy for services to Negro Mariah in confinement; leaving $1.87 due to the committee. RtCt 14 Jun 1855. [D:121]

S/A with Committee R. C. LITTLETON: beginning 14 Feb 1855; paid Hannah LITTLETON for board, income from hire of Negro man Edward & Minnie with one child, paid R. C. LITTLETON acct. for keeping little girl, leaving $36.85 due to Committee. RtCt 13 Jan 1857. [D:226]

S/A with Committee R. C. LITTLETON: (an insane person) beginning 7 Feb 1856; paid medical expenses and board, income from hire of Negro man Edmund, Negro woman with one child and from hire of little Negro girl; leaving $95.00 due to Committee. RtCt 14 Apr 1859. [D:401]

S/A with Committee Richard C. LITTLETON: beginning 7 Feb 1857; paid board, income from Mrs. LITTLETON for Negro man, from hire of Negro Maria with two children, and from hire of little Negro girl Delia, leaving $93.45. The expenses seem to me to be all reasonable and proper and the cost of keeping him is less than it would be in a public asylum. RtCt 13 Aug 1859. [D:429]

S/A with Committee Rich. C. LITTLETON: beginning 14 Feb 1858; paid Mrs. H. LITTLETON for board; rec'd from Jesse PORTER first bond and balance of cash payment in LITTLETON vs LITTLETON loaned to T. M. HUMPHREY, income from Mrs. H. LITTLETON for hire of Negroes Edward and Delia, leaving $1964.94. RtCt 15 Mary 1860. [E:30]

S/A with Committee Richard C. LITTLETON: (insane) paid midwife twice for Negro Maria, income from hire of Negroes Edward and Delia; paid Mrs. LITTLETON his board and for keeping boy Arthur, leaving $1945.47. His income will hereafter be greater from his distributive share of his father's personal estate. The committee has in his possession a Negro woman Maria and her three infant children, and he allows him hire for her. I think the arrangement a fair one as she seems to be in the habit of having a child almost every year. RtCt [no date] [E:117]

S/A with Committee R. C. LITTLETON: (of unsound mind) beginning 14 Feb 1860; paid H. T. FRAZIER an allotment of dower Negroes of Mrs. H. LITTLETON, paid Mrs. H. LITTLETON for board, paid for Negro woman & 4 children; income from hire of Edward, Delia, and Oscar, from T. S. LAKE 1/6 of rent of Trap farm in Confederate, and from hire of Amanda and 2 children & Armistead, leaving $1461.33. It will be perceived that the amt. of the estate has been diminished $484.14 during that time but this is unavoidable from the circumstances connected with the estate and the unavoidably large increase in the expenses of maintaining families of Negroes which composed the estate in good part. A good many of the transactions occurred in Virginia bank money and in Confederate money. RtCt Oct 1868. [E:418]

S/A with Committee Richard C. LITTLETON: beginning 9 Apr 1869; general expenses leaving $1403.20. The estate has been diminished $39.03. RtCt 10 Nov 1870. [E:506]

S/A with Committee R. C. LITTLETON: beginning 14 Feb 1865; expenses more than current income but land can be applied to support. RtCt 12 Oct 1869. [F:19]

Estate S/A with Committee Richard C. LITTLETON: beginning 2 Jun 1870; general expenses leaving $1297.80. RtCt 10 Oct 1871. [F:186]

S/A Committee with Richard C. LITTLETON: beginning 14 Feb 1871; general expenses leaving $1171.30. Ward now well advanced in life. RtCt 12 Aug 1872. [F:239]

S/A with Committee Richard C. LITTLETON: beginning 14 Feb 1872; general expenses leaving $1063.87. RtCt 9 Jun 1873. [F:327]

S/A with Committee R. C. LITTLETON: general expenses leaving $930.91. RtCt 14 Sep 1874. [F:425]

S/A with Committee R. C. LITTLETON: general expenses leaving $816.88. RtCt 8 Nov 1875. [F:486]

S/A with Committee R. C. LITTLETON: beginning 14 Jan 1875; general expenses leaving $701.45. RtCt 14 Aug 1876. [G:41]

S/A with Committee R. C. LITTLETON: beginning 14 Feb 1876; general expenses leaving $1187.71. RtCt 14 Jul 1879. [G:178]

S/A with Committee R. C. LITTLETON: beginning 14 Feb 1877; general expenses leaving $1092.73. RtCt 14 Jul 1879. [G:179]

S/A with Committee R. C. LITTLETON: beginning 14 Feb 1878; general expenses leaving $980.76. RtCt 14 Jul 1879. [G:180]

S/A with Committee R. C. LITTLETON: beginning 14 Feb 1879; general expenses leaving $859.55. RtCt 13 Oct 1880. [G:238]

S/A with Committee R. C. LITTLETON: beginning 14 Feb 1880; general expenses leaving $762.50. RtCt 9 Aug 1881. [G:280]

S/A with Committee R. C. LITTLETON: beginning 4 Feb 1881; general expenses leaving $658.68. RtCt 10 Jul 1882. [G:325]

S/A with Committee R. C. LITTLETON: beginning 14 Feb 1882; general expenses leaving $537.93. RtCt 11 Apr 1883. [G:366]

S/A with Committee R. C. LITTLETON: beginning 14 Feb 1883; $922.19 rec'd from estate of K. LITTLETON, general expenses, leaving $1282.05. RtCt 9 Sep 1884. [G:447]

S/A with Committee R. C. LITTLETON: beginning 7 Feb 1884; general expenses leaving $116.13. RtCt 11 Aug 1885. [G:482]

S/A with Committee R. C. LITTLETON: beginning 7 Feb 1885; general expenses leaving $1068.27. RtCt 15 Jun 1886. [H:9]

S/A with Committee R. C. LITTLETON: beginning 7 Feb 1886; general expenses leaving $971.53. RtCt 10 Aug 1887. [H:53]

S/A with Committee R. C. LITTLETON: beginning 7 Feb 1887; general expenses leaving $870.97. RtCt 13 Mar 1889. [H:95]

S/A with Committee R. C. LITTLETON: beginning 7 Feb 1888; general expenses leaving $768.04. RtCt 15 Jan 1890. [H:122]

S/A with Committee R. C. LITTLETON: beginning 7 Feb 1889; general expenses leaving $612.68. RtCt 12 Jan 1891. [H:127]

S/A with Committee R. C. LITTLETON: beginning 7 Feb 1890; ward died Feb 1891, leaving estate of $197.46. RtCt 10 Nov 1891. [H:149]

S/A with Committee R. C. LITTLETON: beginning 1 Jun 1891; $39.06 each to Martha the wife of ___ LAKE, Townsend FRASIER & wife, Nancy E. FRASIER & heirs of Cath. BROWN (L. P. BROWN, L. A. BROWN, C. E. BROWN & P. D. BROWN). RtCt 10 Nov 1896. [H:279]

BLEAKLY, Eliza P. and Florence L. [BLEAKLEY]

S/A of Eliza P. BLEAKLY with Gdn Craven JAMES: beginning 2 Aug 1854; paid Joseph LODGE ½ of bond due him from the said estate, leaving $95.86 due to Gdn. S/A of Florence L. BLEAKLY with Gdn Craven JAMES: beginning 10 Aug 1854; as above, leaving $95.86 due to Gdn. RtCt 15 Apr 1856. [D:124]

S/A of Eliza P. BLEAKLEY with Gdn Craven JAMES: beginning 11 Jun 1855; paid tuition, leaving $277.87 due to Gdn. S/A of Florence L. BLEAKLEY with Gdn Craven JAMES: beginning 11 Jun 1855; paid tuition, 3 Jan 1856 paid Littitia BLEAKLEY assee of Chas. BLEAKLEY, leaving $266.73 due to Gdn. RtCt 13 Jan 1857. [D:209]

S/A of Eliza P. BLEAKLY with Gdn Craven JAMES: paid tuition, income from hire of Negro boy Edward, leaving $201.76 due to Gdn. S/A of Florence L. BLEAKLY with Gdn Craven JAMES: beginning 9 May 1856; paid tuition and medical bill, leaving $188.52 due to Gdn. RtCt 14 Oct 1858. [D:293]

S/A of Eliza P. BLEAKLEY with Gdn Craven JAMES: beginning 9 May 1857; income from hire of Negro boy Edward, 22 Feb 1858 income from sale of Negro boy Elwood, leaving $83.98. S/A of Florence L. BLEAKLEY with Gdn Craven JAMES: as above, leaving $$105.73. RtCt 14 Apr 1859. [D:385]

S/A of Eliza P. BLEAKLY with Gdn Cravan JAMES: beginning 9 May 1858; paid tuition in vocal music, leaving $69.90. Balance is less than the last year by reason of the failure of crops on the land farmed by the Gdn in common with his wards he having married their mother. The board was fixed by two of the mother's brothers Burr P. and Mason CHAMBLIN. S/A of Florence L. BLEAKLY with Gdn Cravan JAMES: beginning 20 Sep 1858; paid tuition, leaving $101.48. RtCt 15 Mar 1860. [E:16]

S/A of Eliza P. BLEAKLY with Gdn Craven JAMES: 1 Jan 1860 cash from Admrs. of Wm. BLEAKLY, leaving $182.14. S/A of Florence L. BLEAKLY with Gdn Craven JAMES: as above, paid tuition, leaving $235.23. RtCt [no date.] [E:108]

S/A of Eliza P. BLEAKLY with Gdn Craven JAMES: paid board & tuition. The entire estate has been expended mainly in her board, education, clothing and expenses of her wedding trip, the last of which cost with the clothes usual on said occasions $93.82. The former were necessary expenditures made for a good purpose and the latter usual and by no means extravagant. There is due to her however a bond for $321.75 which was collected by him from Charles BLEAKLEY Admr. of Letitia BLEAKLY. S/A of Florence L. BLEAKLY with Gdn Craven JAMES: beginning 9 Sep 1865; tuition. I have settled to 9 May 1866 and report that for the same reason her whole estate has been consumed and she owes her Gdn $57.12. There is due to her a bond for $321.75 for money derived from the estate of her grandmother as stated above. Among the expenditures there is an item of $37.18 for her expenses on a wedding trip. In both cases some transactions in Virginia money and Confederate Treasury notes I have sealed according to the best information I could get. They have between them a small farm. RtCt 12 Dec 1866. [E:312]

S/A of Florence L. BLEAKLY with Gdn Craven JAMES: paid board, Oct 1869 paid for wedding outfit, leaving $211.40. 9 Oct 1869 she became of age. She is of age & married. RtCt 12 Oct 1869. [E:408]

S/A of Florence L. BLEAKLY with Gdn Craven JAMES: beginning 9 May 1866; 9 May 1867 paid Benton JAMES due $51.96. RtCt Oct 1868. [E:492]

DOWELL, Jane A.

S/A of Jane A. DOWELL now Jane A. PANCOAST with Gdn Conrad R. DOWELL: beginning 10 Jun 1849; rec'd share of legacy from Conrad BITZER's executor being wards under the will of said BITZER; 13 Mar 1852 paid Joseph PANCOAST in right of his wife Jane; rec'd cash from Albert B. DOWELL's Gdn in division of slaves; a balance of $588.49 of 1 Jun 1855 paid over to Joseph PANCOAST in right of his said wife. RtCt 15 Apr 1856. [D:126]

DOWELL, Conrad F.

S/A with Gdn Conrad R. DOWELL: rec'd share of legacy from Conrad BITZER's executor being ward's under the will of said Conrad BITZER; paid Jno. F. DOWELL amt due him in division of slaves; leaving $3233.37 paid in full as of 4 May 1855. RtCt 15 Apr 1856. [D:129]

NICEWARNER, Christian Thomas, John M., Harriet J. and Emily

S/A with Gdn Mary NICEWARNER: beginning 1854; 1 May 1854 rec'd of Christian NICEWARNER Admr. of Catharine NICEWARNER dec'd, the share of Christian Thomas NICEWARNER $23.60 this day paid him being now 21 years of age, paid Chas. H. STEWART for advertising land sold, the remaining three due $307.80. S/A of Jacob R. NICEWARNER with Gdn Mary NICEWARNER: cash rec'd of Christian NICEWARNER's Admr. of Catharine NICEWARNER dec'd being 1/8 share of his father's share in said estate; $91.15 paid Jacob being the youngest child and did not share under the will of Catharine NICEWARNER. RtCt 15 Apr 1856. [D:133]

FAWLEY, Martha A., Ann E., Mary J., William, George P., James M., Ellen C. and Samuel S. (Heirs of George)

S/A of Martha A., Ann E., Mary J., William, George P., James M., Ellen C. and Samuel S. FAWLEY with Gdn John H. WHITE: charge of Gdn for keeping idiot boy 8 ½ months, income from hire of servant Julius less Dr. EDWARDS medical acct. and from hire of Negro Ketty. 20 Oct 1854 paid Martha A. HOUSEHOLDER late Martha A. FAWLEY $27.87 her 1/8, Ellen C. FAWLEY $27.87 her 1/8 having attained lawful age, Mary J. FAWLEY $27.87 her 1/8 having attained lawful age. On 20 May 1855 balance of $231.40 due to George P. FAWLEY, $237.54 due to Ann E. FAWLEY, $235.10 due to Samuel S. FAWLEY, $233.41 due to James W. FAWLEY, and to William FAWLEY $242.80 these five last named heirs are yet minors. At the Circuit Court hold in for the County of Loudoun at the April term 1855 it was ordered by the Court that John H. WHITE the said Gdn pay over the respective balances due the said five last mentioned heirs to John SMITH their Gdn residing in Licking County, State Ohio. RtCt 15 Apr 1856. [D:138]

OSBURN, Decatur, Sanford J. R., Oscar, Octavius, Emeline M. and J. T. M.

S/A with mother & Gdn Patsy OSBURN: beginning 2 Apr 1854; income rec'd from Harrison OSBURN Admr share of personal estate, from Jonah OSBURN Admr. of Jane OSBURN (share), from Richard OSBURN Jr. Admr. share of personal estate, and from Jane OSBURN Admr share of her estate, leaving $156.41 due to Decatur, $124.62 due to Sanford J. R., $152.93 due to Oscar, $153.23 due to Octavius, $166.43 due to Emeline M. and $262.59 due to J. T. M. OSBURN. Ward J. T. M. OSBURN is now 21 years of age and has been fully paid $262.59. RtCt 15 Apr 1856. [D:137]

S/A of Emelia M. OSBURN with Gdn Patsy OSBURN: 29 Jun 1855 cash rec'd from Jonah OSBURN Admr. of Lucinda OSBURN, 20 Sept 1855 cash rec'd from Harrison OSBURN Admr. of Rich'd OSBURN Jr, 1 Jan 1856 income from sale of Negro man Beverly belonging to Lucinda OSBURN's estate, settled to 1 Apr 1856 & at that date sum of $239.41 paid C. F. DOWELL (her husband) in full. S/A of Decatur OSBURN with Gdn Patsy OSBURN: tuition, as above, leaving $231.03. S/A of Octavius OSBURN with Gdn Patsy OSBURN: as above, leaving $227.85. S/A of Oscar OSBURN: as above, leaving $226.65. S/A of Decatur OSBURN with Gdn Patsy OSBURN: as above, leaving $231.03. S/A of Sanford J. R. OSBURN with Gdn Patsy OSBURN: as above, leaving $203.08. [this acct. in jumbled order] RtCt 18 Jul 1857. [D:301]

RICHARDS, Laney A., David F. and Sarah E. (Heirs of Thomas)

S/A of Laney A., David F. and Sarah E. RICHARDS with Gdn Jonah ORRISON: beginning 10 Jun 1844; income from the Exor of Samuel RICHARDS and from Thomas RICHARDS Admr. the interest of said wards in their father's personal estate, paid tuition, leaving $15.17 due from Laney A. RICHARDS (now Laney A. BALES) to Gdn, $191.46 due to David F. Richards and $199.66 to Sarah E. Richards. RtCt 15 Apr 1856. [D:140]

S/A of David F. RICHARDS with Gdn Jonah ORRISON: beginning 14 Feb 1855; income from notes and rent, leaving $171.55 on 1 Jan 1856 (he is now 21y old). S/A of Sarah E. RICHARDS with Gdn Jonah ORRISON her Gdn: as above, leaving $206.04 (who is yet a minor) on 10 Jun 1856. RtCt 13 Jan 1857. [D:228]

S/A of Sarah E. RICHARDS with Gdn Jonah ORRISON: beginning Sep 1856; general expenses, leaving $160.94. This as his final S/A, his said ward having intermarried with Eli T. RUSE about the said 1 Jan 1858. RtCt 14 Oct 1858. [D:360]

PIERPOINT, Francis

Appraisal/Inventory of the property: acct. on Peter D. SHONG, sheriff of Lark Co., State of Ohio, note of David BYERS, household items, books, totaling $550.18. RtCt 3 Mar 1856. [D:148]

BIRDSALL, David H., Mary Etta and Rebecca Ann (Children of David)

S/A of David H., Mary E, and Rebecca A. BIRDSALL with Gdn Benjamin BIRDSALL: (children of David BIRDSALL) beginning 1 Dec 1855; general expenses leaving $157.24 each due to David H. & Mary E. and $328.49 to Rebecca A. BIRDSALL. RtCt 9 Sep 1856. [D:152]

S/A of David H. BIRDSALL with Gdn Benj'n. BIRDSALL: beginning 20 Nov 1856; general expenses, leaving $165.15. S/A of Mary E. BIRDSALL & Rebecca BIRDSALL with Gdn Benj'n BIRDSALL: as above, leaving $345.11 jointly. RtCt 14 Oct 1858. [D:305]

S/A of David H. BIRDSALL with Gdn Benjamin BIRDSALL Jr: Jan 1858 amt. of legacy from Hannah BIRDSALL, leaving $267.59. S/A of Mary E. BIRDSALL and Rebecca A. BIRDSALL with Gdn Benjamin BIRDSALL Jr: as above, leaving $546.96. RtCt 14 Apr 1859. [D:387]

S/A of David H. BIRDSALL with Gdn Benjamin BIRDSALL Jr: beginning 5 Nov 1858; general expenses, leaving $280.89. S/A of Mary Etta BIRDSALL & Rebecca A. BIRDSALL with Gdn Benjamin BIRDSALL Jr: as above, leaving $574.29. RtCt 13 Aug 1859. [D:416]

S/A of David H. BIRDSALL with Gdn Benjamin BIRDSALL: paid Sarah BIRDSALL for tuition, rec'd amt. 1/3 of Mary BIRDSALL's Admr, leaving $305.42. S/A of Mary Etta BIRDSALL with Gdn Benjamin BIRDSALL: as above. leaving $296.98. S/A of Rebecca Ann BIRDSALL with Gdn Benj'n. BIRDSALL: general expenses leaving $324.50. RtCt __ [14 Aug 1860?] [E:106]

S/A of David H. BIRDSALL with Gdn Benjamin BIRDSALL Jr: paid Sarah BIRDSALL for tuition, leaving $309.03. S/A of Mary Etta BIRDSALL with Gdn Benjamin BIRDSALL Jr: as above, leaving $270.12. S/A of Rebecca Ann BIRDSALL with Gdn Benjamin BIRDSALL Jr: as above, leaving $339.21. RtCt 13 Jun 1861. [E:137]

S/A of Mary Etta BIRDSALL with Gdn Benjamin BIRDSALL Jr: paid Sarah BIRDSALL for tuition & board, income from Execs. of E. BIRDSALL, 30 Nov 1863 at which time she died. Her income and part of her principal were consumed in her support but her grandmother from whom her expectations were considerable advised them as did her mother. The balance due at her death was $128.68. S/A of David H. BIRDSALL with Gdn Benjamin BIRDSALL Jr: as above, paid Mary BIRDSALL for board, tuition & medical attendance. He is about 20 years of age and his grandmother above alluded to, thought it would be better for him to be educated, and his mother conceiving expenditures were made trenching on his principal. Balance of $248.67. S/A of Rebecca A. BIRDSALL with Gdn Benjamin BIRDSALL Jr: beginning 18 Dec 1861; income from Execs. of E. BIRDSALL. She is about 14 years old and her friends that she might to have an education. Her estate has accumulated in the hands of her Gdn and I recommend that her Gdn be allowed to use at least that increase in her education besides the profits of her estate, balance of $500.83. RtCt 13 Feb 1866. [E:196]

S/A of David H. BIRDSALL with Gdn Benjamin BIRDSALL Jr: beginning Nov 1865; income from M. E. BIRDSALL's Admr, leaving $301.91. S/A of Rebecca Alice BIRDSALL with Gdn Benjamin BIRDSALL Jr: beginning Nov 1865; paid Sarah BIRDSALL mother for board, paid for clothing and tuition, income from M. E. BIRDSALL's Admr, leaving $472.74. RtCt 12 Dec 1866. [E:310]

S/A of Rebecca Alice BIRDSALL with Gdn Benjamin BIRDSALL: income from John BROWN's estate and amt. from J. B. BIRDSALL's estate, leaving $678.29. S/A of David H. BIRDSALL with Gdn Benjamin BIRDSALL Jr: as above, leaving $56.30. He is now of age. RtCt 9 Apr 1867. [E:324]

S/A of Rebecca Alice BIRDSALL with Gdn Benjamin BIRDSALL Jr: beginning 7 Jan 1867; general expenses leaving $561.73. The large allowance for expenses is at the suggestion of her grandmother from whom she has expectations to a considerable extent. RtCt Oct 1868. [E:407]

STOUTSENBERGER, Albert C. and Elwina T. (Orphans of Mary and Samuel)

S/A of Albert C. STOUTSENBERGER with Gdn Townsend M. PAXSON: beginning 9 Oct 1854; paid tuition, leaving $918.43. S/A of Elwina STOUTSENBERGER with Gdn Town'd M. PAXSON: beginning 9 Oct 1854; as above, leaving $917.07. Both parents, Samuel STOUTSENBERGER & Mary C. his wife, are deceased. RtCt 9 Sep 1856. [D:153]

S/A of Albert C. STOUTSENBERGER with Gdn T. M. PAXSON: beginning 4 Mar 1856; paid tuition, leaving $918.43. S/A of Elwina T. STOUTSENBERGER with Gdn T. M. PAXSON: as above, leaving $917.07. RtCt 14 Oct 1858. [D:307]

S/A Albert C. with Gdn Townsend M. PAXSON: beginning 1 Jan 1857; paid tuition. S/A of Elwina T. STOUTSENBERGER with Gdn Townsend M. PAXSON: as above. Townsend M. PAXSON laid before me on 17 Aug 1858 an acct. of his transactions as Gdn of Albert C. & Elwina T. STOUTSENBERGER for the year ending 1 Jan 1858. On examining his bond I found that his fiduciary year had properly closed on 9 Oct 1857 and I consulted with him and settled for the balance of said year and also by anticipation for the year 1858. The only items anticipated, are interest on one side and board on the other. I report that he has exceeded the income of the ward Albert C. about ten dollars & of the ward Elwina T. about eight dollars, but it is in giving them tuition in the best school in the neighborhood. RtCt 12 Jan 1859. [D:380]

S/A Elevina T. and Albert C. with Gdn Townsend M. PAXSON: beginning 9 Oct 1859; paid tuition, leaving Elevina T. $844.34 and leaving Albert C. STOUTSENBERGER $841.56. RtCt 13 Jun 1861. [E:166]

S/A of Elvina T. STOUTSENBERGER with Gdn T. M. PAXSON: beginning 9 Oct 1860; general expenses leaving $246.77. RtCt Oct 1868. [E:443]

COLSTON, Nannie F., Elizabeth M. and Susan L. (Heirs of Thomas M.)

S/A with Gdn Edward COLSTON: beginning 1 May 1841; paid Mrs. COLSTON expenses to Berkeley, 25 Apr 1843 paid Milton WALTMAN as witness at Clarke Court, 7

Mar 1845 paid for coffin for Negro child, repairs on mill, and for building barn. S/A of Nannie F. COLSTON with Gdn Edward COLSTON: paid board in Staunton, medical attendance on woman Sally & John, and sending servant Isaac to Winchester, leaving $133.63 due to Gdn. S/A of Elizabeth M. COLSTON with Gdn: paid board in Staunton, 14 Nov 1846 paid for grave for Negro child, nurse for Negro woman Julia, and medical attendance on self, leaving $8.73 due to Gdn. S/A of Susan L. COLSTON with Gdn Edward COLSTON: beginning 10 May 1845; paid board in Staunton, med. attendance on Janney & Gabe, tuition in music, 1 Jan 1850 to nurse for Caroline in confinement, and for coffin for child, leaving $1231.00. [this was a very long acct.] Elizabeth M. COLSTON, one of the children named above, died about Nov 1846. The real estate consisted of the home called Edgemont and another of about 150 acres which he had in possession, besides several large tracts in Loudoun, Fauquier, and Clarke Counties, then under leaves for lives. The personal property consisted of Negroes household and kitchen furniture stock and farming utensils and money to the amount of $1090.00 arising from the sales of Lucy A. COLSTON's estate. Soon after the death of Thomas M. COLSTON, Edward COLSTON his brother qualified as his administrator, and was at same time appointed Gdn of the three younger children, Raleigh COLSTON the fourth becoming of age early in 1842. In December 1841 the administrator made a sale of the personal property other than the slaves. Part of the real estate being chiefly under leases for life, and for other reasons then considered justifiable, no dower was assigned to the widow and it was thought most conducive to the interest and comfort of the family that they should live together on the Edgemont farm and cultivate it under the superintendance of said Raleigh COLSTON until dower was assigned, and for that purpose the Gdn purchased at the sale such articles for the widow as she needed, and for the heirs, such as was necessary for carrying on the farm, which purchases are charged in the administration acct. under the date 1 Sep 1842. The family thus living together a common joint account of the expenses of that farm, and of the widow and family were kept by the Gdn or his agent until 1844 when dower was assigned under a decree of the Circuit Sept Court in part of the Edgemont farm with the dwelling thereon, and the balance of the estate divided among the four children. Separate accounts were then opened with the three daughters commencing with the year 1845, but the common account was continued in which I have credited the Gdn with payments were for joint debts contracted by the family during the time of their living together in common down to 1 Jan 1851 which results in a balance in favour of the Gdn of $3209.20 including interest to that period as will be shown by acct. no. 1. The debts contracted by the widow and her daughters who were not finally paid off until 1847. Ann F. COLSTON became of age in 1848. I would have observe that the crop of wheat reaped and sold in 1842 whilst the family lived together in common, amounting to $1260.00 went into the hands of the administrator for the payment of a debt then pressing. It seems that only $1020.00 were used by the Admr. in paying a debt of that amount due to Mrs. FURR, but I have inadvertently charged him with the whole $1260.00. The only effect however, it has or could have had was to increase the balance found in the administrators hands, which balance is now transferred to the Guardianship account repaying the Gdn as far as that balance extends. the $1260.00 used by the administrator and charged at the end of the Guardianship acct. no. 1. The crop of wheat raised on the Edgemont farm in 1843 and assigned as dower in 1844 it not accounted for in this S/A application was made to Raleigh COLSTON the conductor and manager of the estate as the agent of the Gdn, and in his letter upon that subject which I have before me he says "Mr. JANNEY told me, that the widow was entitled to her dower and the crops thereof from the time she petitioned for it, which was in 1843. There was but the time she petitioned for it, which was in 1843. There was but very little wheat on the farm that year. The fields were rented on the share, and the crops almost an entire failure, what little there was I turned over to my mother. The widow removed to Alexandria in November 1843 & died in July 1845. Edward COLSTON the Gdn died in 1851. I have been unable to ascertain what time in the year 1851 Edward COLSTON died but I presume it must have been prior to the 4th of Nov for on that day Raleigh COLSTON was appointed the Gdn of Susan L. COLSTON his sister in the County of Albemarle. Susan L. COLSTON the third will be entitled to one third thereof when she arrives of age if she shall then claim it, but is believed she will not, but she can claim it only in the event of its having been forfeited. RtCt 9 Sep 1856. [D:164]

S/A of Susan L. COLSTON with late Gdn Edward COLSTON dec'd: beginning 1 Jan 1856; 21 Feb 1856 paid in full Chas. M. BLACKFORD her husband by Raleigh COLSTON Admr. of F. M. COLSTON dec'd and Gdn. In the month of Jan 1856 I settled and closed the acct. of said Edward COLSTON dec'd who was the administrator of said Thomas M. COLSTON dec'd and Gdn of his children. The S/A were made under the superintendance of Raleigh COLSTON one of those children who, after he had arrived of age attended in the management of the affairs of the estate as a kind of agent for his uncle the administrator. Upon the S/A of the administration account a balance appeared against the Admr. which I transferred to the credit of the children in the Guardianship acct. upon a final S/A of which I reported small balances due from Nannie F. COLSTON and from Elizabeth COLSTON who is now dead and a balance of $1231.00 due to Susan L. COLSTON on 1 Jan 1851 with interest thereon. Said Susan L. has arrived of age and recently married a Mr. Charles M. BLACKFORD and on 21 Feb 1856 said Raleigh COLSTON who had been appointed

Admr. of Thomas M. COLSTON dec'd and also Gdn of his sister the said Susan L. settled with said Charles M. BLACKFORD and paid him the full amount of the balance due to her, together with the interest due thereon, whose receipt is now before me, and is in the words and figures following viz $1231.00, paid in full 21 Feb 1856. RtCt 13 Jan 1857. [D:200]

SHAFER, Lydia, Joseph H. and Mary Ellen (Heirs of John)
S/A with Gdn Jonas P. SCHOOLEY: income from rent of farm and sale of crops. S/A of Lydia SHAFER with Gdn Jonas P. SCHOOLEY: beginning Feb 1844, paid board, and for coffin and tombstone. S/A of Joseph H. SHAFER with Gdn Jonas P. SCHOOLEY: beginning Feb 1844; paid board & tuition, 23 Oct 1848 rec'd his share of Lydia SHAFER's estate. S/A of Mary Ellen SHAFER with Gdn Jonas P. SCHOOLEY: beginning Feb 1844; same as above. [a long acct.] Balance due to John M. SHAFER of $68.15. John SHAFER the father of three children died about 1843 when they were all quite young and remained with their mother, who afterwards intermarried with William KERN said children continuing to reside with them. About October 1848, Lydia SHAFER died, showing a balance due to her of $316.10 of which the share of each of the three remaining children is one fourth, the mother being entitled to a child part thereof. It will appear that the farm was rented to Samuel FRY until 1 Apr 1849 and from that period, to said William KERN who married the widow, the Gdn during the tenancy of FRY paying said KERN and the widow before their marriage such portion of the rent and such amount for the board of the children as he thought right until the board would be adjusted and the accounts could be settled, and in the summer of 1851 the paper were laid before me which I found in a very confused state, specially those between the Gdn and said KERN who kept the children. Joseph H. SHAFER is of age, and George W. STREAM married Mary Ellen. Nothing remains unpaid except the balance due to John M. SHAFER who is not yet of age. RtCt 9 Sep 1856. [D:180]

STRIDER, Joseph L.
S/A with Gdn John NISEWARNER: beginning 19 Apr 1851; paid tuition, income from rent and from Cath. NISEWARNER's Execs. under will, leaving $157. Gdn lives in the most remote corner of the county, and not being familiar with such transactions the case was continued and forgotten and neglected, and the ward having nearly attained his age it was not pressed until last fall after he had arrived of age. RtCt 13 Jan 1857. [D:201]

ANSEL, Susan (a lunatic)
S/A with Committee William B. TYLER: 13 May 1850 rec'd cash from Everet SAUNDERS former committee, leaving $489.50. This committee was appointed and received the funds in the months of May and June 1850 and died in summer of 1851. RtCt 13 Jan 1857. [D:204]

STONEBURNER, Daniel (a lunatic)
S/A with brother & Committee Peter STONEBURNER: beginning 1 Jul 1853, paid for store goods, leaving $713.03. S/A of Catharine STONEBURNER with brother & Committee Peter STONEBURNER: beginning 1 Jul 1853; as above, leaving $348.61. RtCt 13 Jan 1857. [D:206]

S/A of Daniel STONEBURNER with Committee Peter STONEBURNER: beginning 1 Jul 1860; general expenses leaving $899.52. RtCt 10 Sep 1867. [E:378]

S/A with Committee Peter STONEBURNER: beginning 12 May 1867; paid 1/3 of bill for Cathn. STONEBURNER, paid Lutheran Church for Daniel's burial, leaving $758.58 due to estate. RtCt 12 Oct 1869. [F:23]

STONEBURNER, Catharine and Daniel (lunatics)
S/A of Catharine STONEBURNER with Committee Peter STONEBURNER: beginning Jul 1858; expenses as with Sarah STONEBURNER; leaving $334.80. Her funds have somewhat decreased because her portion of land has been uncultivated for two years past, but the expenditures for the two years for board and clothing have been only about $68. S/A of Daniel STONEBURNER with Committee Peter STONEBURNER: beginning 1 Jul 1858; as above, leaving $799.57. His funds have increased for the reason that his land has been under cultivation and his funds at interest are greater than those of the other. They are $84 more now than they were two years ago. RtCt 15 Mar 1860. [E:48]

S/A of Catharine STONEBURNER with Committee Peter STONEBURNER: beginning 1 Jul 1859; paid J. C. STONEBURNER store bill, leaving $329.05. S/A of Daniel STONEBURNER with Committee Peter STONEBURNER: beginning 1 Jul 1859; as above, leaving $810.30. RtCt [no date] [E:121]

STONEBURNER, Catharine (lunatic)
S/A with Committee Peter STONEBURNER: beginning 1 Jul 1856, general expenses leaving $366.77. S/A of Daniel STONEBURNER with Committee Peter STONEBURNER: (a lunatic) beginning 1 Jul 1856; expenses leaving $715.02. RtCt 14 Oct 1858. [D:317]

S/A of with Committee Peter STONEBURNER: beginning 1 Jul 1860; general expenses leaving $213.59. The whole amt. received during that time has been $212.66 from all sources namely rent from 13¾ acres of land and interest an annual balance and the whole expenditures has thus been $338.12 or at the rate of about $50 per annum. RtCt 10 Sep 1867. [E:376]

S/A with Committee Peter STONEBURNER: beginning 12 May 1868; general expenses leaving $105.59. RtCt 12 Oct 1869. [F:27]

S/A with Committee Peter STONEBURNER: general expenses leaving $3.68, exceeding her income by $101.91. RtCt 13 Feb 1871. [F:118]

S/A with Committee Peter STONEBURNER: income from sale of land, general expenses, leaving $8.41. RtCt 14 Jun 1875. [F:452]

S/A with Committee Peter STONEBURNER: beginning 12 May 1875; general expenses leaving $80.73 which will pay Christena FRY for board, leaving no personal estate just 15¼ acres of land. RtCt 10 Dec 1877. [G:99]

S/A with Committee Peter STONEBURNER: beginning 5 Sep 1877; general expenses leaving $1.97 due to Committee. RtCt 15 Mar 1881. [G:267]

STONEBURNER, Sarah (a lunatic)
S/A with Committee Samuel FRY: beginning 1 Jul 1853; paid for store goods, leaving $421.37. Daniel and Catharine STONEBURNER returned with this the three lunatics are the brother and sisters of said Peter STONEBURNER and the brother-in-law and sisters-in-law of said Samuel FRY. They live together and are supplied and attended to by the two committees jointly. RtCt 13 Jan 1857. [D:208]

S/A with Committee Samuel FRY: beginning 1 Jul 1856; general expenses leaving $446.98. RtCt 14 Oct 1858. [D:317]

S/A with Committee Samuel FRY: beginning 1 Jul 1858; paid Peter STONEBURNER 1/3 of flour &c used by them, leaving $433.50. The amount due her has been diminished $13.48 by the reason of the fact that her land has been lying in clover and has produced no crops. I think the charges for board and clothing have been very moderate not exceeding $33 per annum. RtCt 15 Mar 1860. [E:47]

S/A with Committee Samuel FRY: beginning 5 Nov 1859; paid J. C. STONEBURNER store bill, amt. paid Peter STONEBURNER, leaving $474.57. RtCt [no date] [E:120]

S/A with Committee Samuel FRY: beginning 1 Jul 1860. The committee is dead and J. W. GOODHART has qualified in his place. Balance is $381.65. RtCt 10 Sep 1867. [E:373]

S/A with Committee J. W. GOODHART: beginning 12 May 1868; general expenses from Peter STONEBURNER, etc, leaving $229.16. RtCt 12 Oct 1869. [F:25]

S/A with Committee J. W. GOODHART: beginning 12 May 1869; general expenses leaving $105.12. RtCt 13 Feb 1871. [F:117]

S/A with Committee J. W. GOODHART: general expenses and income leaving $97.62. RtCt 14 Jun 1875. [F:454]

CORDELL, Jacob and Margaret Jane (Children of Adam)
S/A with Gdn Adam A. CORDELL: beginning 14 Aug 1854; general expenses, leaving $43.21. RtCt 13 Jan 1857. [D:211]

S/A of Jacob and Margaret J. CORDELL with Gdn Adam A. CORDELL: (Children of Adam) beginning 31 Jul 1856; general expenses leaving $52.50 jointly. RtCt 14 Oct 1858. [D:287]

S/A with Gdn Adam A. CORDELL: general expenses, leaving $60.05. RtCt 14 Oct 1858. [D:342]

S/A of Jacob CORDELL with Gdn Adam A. CORDELL: beginning Aug 1858; rec'd cash from S. SLATER on land, income from rent of house, leaving $77.26. S/A of Margaret Jane CORDELL with Gdn Adam A. CORDELL: beginning Aug 1858; income from Susanna CORDELL's est. and per Jacob CORDELL's acct, leaving $77.26. RtCt 15 Mar 1860. [E:18]

S/A of Jacob CORDELL with Gdn Adam A. CORDELL: beginning Jun 1859; income from house rent and from Samuel SLATER on acct of land payment from Jacob SLATER's estate, leaving $88.90. S/A of Margaret Jane CORDELL with Gdn Adam A. CORDELL: beginning Jun 1859; as above, leaving $88.90. RtCt [no date.] [E:110]

S/A of Jacob CORDELL with Gdn Adam A. CORDELL: beginning 14 May 1860; reached 21y old on 11 Jun 1866 and due $76.62. S/A of Margaret CORDELL with Gdn Adam A. CORDELL: beginning 14 May 1860; 12 Apr 1867 she married and due $102.36, paid in full. RtCt 12 Oct 1869. [E:497]

CORDELL, Henrietta, John F. and Joseph H. (Children of Adam)
S/A with Gdn Joseph FAWLEY: (infant children of Adam CORDELL) beginning 14 Aug 1854; general expenses and income leaving $64.82. RtCt 13 Jan 1857. [D:212]

S/A of Henrietta, John F. and Joseph H. CORDELL with Gdn Joseph FAWLEY: (Children of Adam) beginning 31 Jul 1856; general expenses leaving $79.37 jointly. RtCt 14 Oct 1858. [D:297]

S/A with Gdn Joseph FAWLEY: general expenses leaving $19.19. RtCt 14 Oct. [D:341]

S/A of Henrietta CORDELL with Gdn Joseph FAWLEY: beginning Jun 1860; income from rent of house, leaving $90.94. S/A of John F. CORDELL with Gdn Joseph FAWLEY: beginning Jun 1860; as above, leaving $90.94. S/A of Joseph H. CORDELL with Gdn Joseph FAWLEY: beginning Jun 1860; as above, leaving $81.94. RtCt [Aug 1860?] [E:111]

S/A of Henrietta CORDELL with Gdn Joseph FAWLEY: beginning 11 Jun 1860; $95.82 due to her husband George H. LOY. RtCt 3 Feb 1871. [F:89]

WRIGHT, Edward S. and Sarah Ann

S/A of Edward S. WRIGHT with Gdn William RUSSELL: beginning Dec 1854; paid board, leaving $230.66. S/A of Sarah Ann WRIGHT with Gdn William RUSSELL: as above, leaving $230.52. The Exor holds in his hands 1/3 of the said balance of the estate by virtue of the will for the benefit of the widow and annually pass over the int to her. The other 2/3 are equally credited to the said wards. RtCt 13 Jan 1857. [D:218]

DOWELL, Archibald P. and Thomas D.

S/A of Archibald P. DOWELL with Gdn George W. DOWELL: beginning 13 Mar 1854; paid tuition & board, income from rent of dwelling store house, leaving $83.56 due to Gdn. S/A of Thomas D. DOWELL with Gdn George W. DOWELL: as above, leaving $50.98 due to Gdn. It appears no part of the funds arising from the personal estate has been paid over by the Exor. to the said Gdn and had rec'd. only the rents of the real estate which appears to be owed equal to the support of the said wards. RtCt 13 Jan 1857. [D:220]

S/A of Thomas D. DOWELL with Gdn George W. DOWELL: beginning 13 Mar 1856; paid schooling, leaving $95.15. S/A of Archibald P. DOWELL with Gdn George W. DOWELL: beginning 13 Mar 1856; as above, leaving $150.56. The Gdn has within a few days past rec'd nearly $900 from the Admr. of Thomas S. DOWELL the father of his wards. RtCt 15 Mar 1860. [E:19]

POTTS, Thomas W. and John Lewis

S/A with Gdn Nathan NEER: beginning 6 Jan 1855; 22 Jan 1855 rec'd payment from Peter DERRY Admr of Daniel DOWLING in part interest in the estate of Peter DEMORY dec'd, leaving $607.54. RtCt 13 Jan 1857. [D:225]

S/A of Thomas W. and John L. POTTS with Gdn Nathan NEER: beginning 2 Jun 1856; 22 Mar 1856 rec'd payment from Peter DERRY Admr., leaving $749.25 equally. RtCt 14 Oct 1858. [D:285]

S/A of John Lewis POTTS with Gdn Nathan NEER: beginning Nov 1856; general expenses, leaving $446.21. RtCt 14 Aug 1860. [E:96]

S/A of Thomas W. POTTS with Gdn Nathan NEER: beginning Nov 1856; as above. He is now of age and paid $210 in full. RtCt 14 Aug 1860. [E:97]

CHINN, Samuel Walter

S/A with Gdn R. C. CHINN: 30 May 1855 advance to ward going to California, paid tuition, leaving $24.27 due to Gdn. RtCt 13 Jan 1857. [D:230]

S/A with Gdn R. S. CHINN: beginning 1 Jan 1856; general expenses leaving $1229.47. RtCt 14 Oct 1858. [D:340]

KALB, Benjamin D.

S/A with Gdn Thos. D. KALB: work on farm, 2 Jun 1856 to Samuel KALB administrator, leaving $632.38. RtCt 13 Jan 1857. [D:231]

S/A with Gdn Thomas D. KALB: beginning 16 Aug 1856; paid board and tuition, cash rec'd from Admr. of Land KALB dec'd, leaving $880.76. RtCt 14 Oct. 1858. [D:290]

S/A with Gdn Thomas D. KALB: beginning 22 Apr 1857; general expenses leaving $880.76. RtCt 14 Apr 1859. [D:399]

S/A with Gdn Thomas D. KALB: beginning 1858; general expenses leaving $786.63. RtCt 15 Mar 1860. [E:29]

S/A with Gdn Thomas D. KALB: beginning 3 Jun 1859; paid Gideon HOUSHOLDER auction bill; 14 Nov 1859 paid RICKARD's note and int; leaving $809.39. RtCt [no date] [E:116]

S/A with Gdn Thomas D. KALB: beginning 16 May 1860; 19 Apr 1861 paid two muster fines; leaving $643.64. RtCt 14 Oct 1861. [E:194]

S/A of 11 Jan 1867 with Gdn Thomas D. KALB: has settled with his ward and requested it reported. RtCt 9 Apr 1867. [E:337]

KALB, Silas D.

S/A with Gdn John G. R. KALB: beginning 14 May 1855; general expenses leaving $639.85. RtCt 21 Aug 1857. [D:239]

S/A with Gdn J. G. R. KALB: 9 Sep 1856 rec'd payment from Saml. KALB's estate, leaving $943.29. Trust closed on 9 Mar 1857 when his ward became of age. RtCt 14 Oct 1858. [D:323]

GIBSON, Grace N. and Ella J. (Children of Dr. William)

S/A with Gdn Asa ROGERS: beginning 15 May 1855; paid Wm. GIBSON father of said wards on acct. of wards support under a decree of the Cir Ct, rec'd of H. B. POWELL trustee, leaving Grace $1198.32 and Ella $1398.32. RtCt 12 Aug 1857. [D:243]

S/A of Grace N. GIBSON with Gdn Asa ROGERS: paid B. P. NOLAND Admr. of Geo. C. POWELL dec'd on acct. of purchase of a ground rent of lot adjoining Middleburg which was under a ground rent to N. BEVERIDGE, 1 Jul 1856 paid Dr. Wm. GIBSON for support and education, leaving $1642.35. S/A of Ella J. GIBSON with Gdn Asa ROGERS: as above, leaving $2045.35. 16 Dec 1857. RtCt 14 Oct 1858. [D:346]

S/A Grace N. GIBSON with Gdn Asa ROGERS: beginning 19 Dec 1857; paid Dr. GIBSON sum allowed by decree of Court for maintenance, income from one half money rec'd from BEVERIDGE's trustee (H. B. POWELL), leaving $1472.39. S/A of Ella J. GIBSON with Gdn Asa ROGERS: as above, leaving $2107.88. RtCt 18 Jun 1859. [D:415]

S/A of Grace N. GIBSON with Gdn Asa ROGERS: beginning 23 Feb 1859; paid Dr. W. GIBSON maintenance of ward allowed by Court, payment from H. B. POWELL, trustee, leaving $1466.85. S/A of Ella J. GIBSON with Gdn Asa ROGERS: beginning 23 Feb. 1859; as above, leaving $2328.67. RtCt 14 Aug 1860. [E:83]

S/A of Grace N. GIBSON with Gdn Asa ROGERS: beginning 10 Jan 1860; income from trustee acct., leaving $1609.30. S/A of Ella J. GIBSON with Gdn Asa ROGERS: beginning 10 Jan 1860; as above, leaving $2720.24. RtCt 13 Jun 1861. [E:149]

S/A of Miss Grace N. GIBSON with Gdn Asa ROGERS: beginning 1 Mar 1861; payment from A. ROGERS trustee for one half of proceeds of estate for last year per S/A, leaving $2166.15. RtCt 13 Feb 1866. [E:229]

S/A of Miss Grace N. GIBSON with Gdn Asa ROGERS: beginning Oct 1861; paid Mrs. Ella McKENZIE in Balto. with whom Miss GIBSON boarded, leaving $2755.69. RtCt 13 Feb 1866. [E:230]

S/A of Grace N. GIBSON with Gdn Asa ROGERS: paid Mrs. McKENZIE for your annual allowance, leaving $3421.82. RtCt 13 Feb 1866. [E:231]

S/A of Miss Grace N. GIBSON with Gdn Asa ROGERS: beginning 29 Jul 1863; fees for investing in state bonds, ½ of net proceeds of estate of Mrs. S. R. GIBSON for last year. From copy of a decree of the Circuit Court of the City of Richmond made on 21 May 1863 that Gdn had leave to invest four thousand dollars in interest bearing bonds of the Confederate States (see copy of decree filed with acct. of said ROGERS Gdn of Ella J. GIBSON) and it is further shown that said investment was made on 29 July 1863. The Comr. further reports that on 16 Mar 1864, the Judge of the Richmond Circuit Court made an order in vacation giving said Gdn leave to invest the further sum of $400.00 upon the same terms. These investment are charged in the acct. By this acct. it appears and the Comr. reports that a balance of $489.86 was due said ward on 1 Jul 1864. The Gdn gives as a reason why he has not sent funds to his ward is, that she resides in the City of Baltimore and that he could find no safe opportunity to do so. In the Clerk's Office of the Circuit Court of the City of Richmond 16 Mar 1864. An order of the Judge of the said Court in vacation was this day received by the Clerk and the same is as follows, to wit. In consideration of the Petition of Asa ROGERS Gdn of Grace N. GIBSON and Ella J. GIBSON, the Judge of the Circuit Court of the City of Richmond, in vacation of the said Court, doth order that the said Asa ROGERS as Gdn as aforesaid hath leave to invest twelve hundred dollars the amt in his hands as Gdn of said Ella J. GIBSON and four hundred dollars the amt. in his hands as Gdn of Grace N. GIBSON in interest bearing bonds or certificates of the Confederate States or of the State of Va or any other sufficient bonds or securities of or within the said states and if the investment be made in Confederate bonds or certificates the same are not be bear a less interest than six per cent. And the said Gdn is directed in making the said investment to take the bond or certificate in his name as Gdn for his wards respectively and to have it expressed in the face there of that they are not to be transferred unless authorized by the decree of a Circuit Court of competent jurisdiction. RtCt 13 Feb 1866. [E:232]

S/A of Miss Grace N. GIBSON now Mrs. CASEY with Gdn Asa ROGERS: paid Grace and Mr. Henry G. CASEY bank money; leaving $210.04 as of 1 Jul 1865 payable in Bank notes South, leaving $58.82 due as of 1 Jul 1865. I further report that the bonds of the Confederate States for $4400 and referred to in a former report of mine were delivered to Mrs. CASEY formerly Grace N. GIBSON and her husband. RtCt 13 Feb 1866. [E:233]

S/A of Miss Ella J. GIBSON with Gdn Asa ROGERS: beginning 1 Mar 1861; general expenses leaving $3342.92. RtCt 13 Feb 1866. [E:237]

S/A of Miss Ella J. GIBSON with Gdn Asa ROGERS: beginning Oct 1861; paid her through Mrs. Ella McKENZIE of Baltimore with whom she boarded, leaving $4205.458. RtCt 13 Feb 1866. [E:238]

S/A of Miss Ella J. GIBSON with Asa ROGERS: paid Mrs. McKENZIE for you annual allowance, leaving $5280.21. RtCt 13 Feb 1866. [E:240]

S/A of Miss Ella J. GIBSON with Asa ROGERS: paid for 1 Confederate State 7 per cent bond; It appears from a copy of a decree of the Circuit Court of the City of Richmond made 21 May 1863 that the said Asa Rogers Gdn as aforesaid had leave to invest five thousand dollars in interest bearing bonds of the Confederate States (see copy of decree herewith returned) and it is further shown that said investment was made agreeably to the terms of said decree three thousand four hundred dollars were invested on 4 Sep 1863 and one thousand six hundred dollars on ___ 1866. The Comr. further reports that on 16 Mar 1861 the Judge of Richmond Circuit Court made an order in vacation giving such Gdn leave to invest the further sum of $1200.00 upon the same terms as the first named. These investments are charged in the acct. By this decree it appears and the Comr. reports a balance of $632.34 was due said ward on 1 Jul 1860. The Gdn gives as a reason why he has not sent funds to his wards is that she resides in the city of Baltimore and that he could find no safe opportunity to do so. RtCt 13 Feb 1866. [E:241]

S/A of Ella J. GIBSON with Gdn Asa ROGERS: beginning 1 Jul 1865; income from bank notes, $498.48 was due said ward on 1 Jul 1865 and is still due her $439.96 which is payable in Southern Bank notes and the balance $58.52 is payable in U. States funds. I have not charged interest on last years balance for the reason that Dr. GIBSON the father of Ella resides with his daughter in Newport Rhodes Island and the Gdn has no safe means to transmit funds to her. RtCt 13 Feb 1866. [E:243]

LOUDOUN COUNTY, VIRGINIA
GUARDIAN ACCOUNTS
1759-1904

S/A of Ella J. GIBSON with Gdn Asa ROGERS: beginning 1 Jan 1866; income from proceeds of the estate of Mrs. S. N. GIBSON, leaving $306.74. RtCt 9 Apr 1867. [E:333]

S/A of Miss Ella J. GIBSON with Gdn Asa ROGERS: beginning 17 Nov 1866; general expenses leaving $139.62. RtCt 10 Sep 1867. [E:367]

S/A of Ella J. GIBSON with Gdn Asa ROGERS: beginning 1 Jul 1867; paid H. G. CAREY now Gdn of Ella J. GIBSON in full. RtCt 15 Jun 1868. [E:396]

S/A of Ella J. GIBSON with Gdn Henry G. CAREY: beginning 2 Jul 1867; income from Jas. SMALLWOOD for rent, leaving $856.87. RtCt 15 Jun 1868. [E:403]

S/A of Ella J. GIBSON with Gdn Henry G. CAREY: beginning 13 Mar 1848; income from proceeds from crops, leaving $1096.16. RtCt 21 Jun 1869. [E:487]

S/A of Mrs. Grace A. CAREY late GIBSON with Gdn Asa ROGERS: balance in Southern State Bank, 1st National Bank at Alexandria, leaving $53.41. RtCt 9 Apr 1867. [E:236]

S/A of Henry G. CAREY and Grace A. his wife with late Gdn Asa ROGERS: beginning 17 Sep 1866; general expenses, leaving no balance. RtCt 10 Sep 1867. [E:329]

S/A of Ella J. GIBSON with Gdn Henry G. CAREY: beginning 1 Apr 1869; general expenses totaling $1976.35, acct now closed. RtCt 18 Jun 1870. [F:64]

DILLON, Anne E., Joseph Abdon and Jonah W. (Children of Isaac)

S/A of Joseph A. DILLON with Gdn Lydia Ann DILLON: beginning 21 Dec 1855; paid John J. DILLON tax on lot, rec'd payment from John J. DILLON Admr. of Isaac DILLON dec'd being wards share of his father's personal estate, 24 Jul 1855 rec'd of same as Admr of Lydia DILLON dec'd, leaving $551.39. S/A of Jonah W. DILLON and Anne E. DILLON with Gdn Lydia Ann DILLON: as above, leaving $1102.78 jointly. RtCt 12 Aug 1857. [D:245]

S/A of Joseph A., Jonah W. and Ann E. DILLON with mother & Gdn Lydia Ann DILLON: beginning 1 Jan 1856; general expenses, leaving $551.39. RtCt 14 Oct 1858. [D:288]

S/A of Joseph A. DILLON with Gdn Lydia Ann DILLON: beginning 1 Jan 1858; general expenses, leaving $489.78. S/A of Jonah W. DILLON and Ann E. DILLON with Gdn Lydia Ann DILLON: as above, leaving $1079.43. 11 May 1859 Aquilla JANNEY was appointed the new Gdn as Lydia Ann DILLON has lately married. RtCt 13 Aug 1859. [D:425]

S/A of Joseph A. DILLON with Gdn Lydia Ann DILLON: beginning 1 Jan 1858, general expenses, leaving $511.90. S/A of Jonah W. DILLON and Ann E. DILLON with Gdn Lydia Ann DILLON: as above, leaving $1079.28. RtCt 13 Aug 1859. [D:427]

S/A with Gdn Aquilla JANNEY: income from one third of the rent of the farm, leaving Joseph A. $452.99, leaving Jonah W. $452.99, and leaving Ann E. DILLON $452.99. RtCt [Aug 1860?] [E:113]

S/A of Joseph Abdon DILLON with Gdn Aquilla JANNEY: beginning Dec 1860; general expenses leaving $581.56. I also report a balance in his hands of $581.56 due to Jonah W. DILLON and the same amt. to Annie E. DILLON. The children all live with their mother Lydia Ann PRESTON (formerly DILLON) on a farm at some distance from their Guardian's residence. There will soon come into the hands of the Gdn a considerable sum from the estate of an aunt of their father (Annie DILLON) lately deceased and this will give them an income which will justify a considerable outlay for their education. RtCt 20 Aug 1866. [E:286]

S/A of Joseph Abdon DILLON with Gdn Aquilla JANNEY: beginning 12 May 1860; paid board and tuition and various store accts, income from interest. [long acct.]

S/A of Jonah William DILLON with Gdn Aquilla JANNEY: beginning 12 May 1860; as above. S/A of Anne E. DILLON with Gdn Aquilla JANNEY: beginning 12 May 1867; paid various accts. The commencement of his assumption of Guardianship to 10 Mar 1868 when he requested. This became necessary because he had accounted for the whole estate that came to his hands then as he collected the bonds of which it consisted he reported them as collected to me and I supposing them to be bonds derived from the estate of Anne DILLON has thus charged him twice with the bonds. The balances so made was of course too large and the only way to remedy it was to go back to the beginning and state the acct. as if it never had been stated at all. Upon this principal I charge him with amt. received from Lydia A. DILLON former Gdn and then with its interest every year and with interest on the bonds derived from Anne DILLON estate and the rents as they were collected. Thus I found the balance due him after charging up the bonds and crediting him with commission to be to Joseph Abdon DILLON $343.36 in cash and $3846.56 in bonds, to Jonah William DILLON $657.22 in cash and $3846.56 in bonds, and to Anne E. DILLON $930.18 in cash and $3846.56 in bonds with interest in the cash from 10 Mar 1868. Another bond upon which there has been a judgment and which bring of the bonds received from the former Gdn Lydia Ann DILLON is part of the cash above reported is now deducted from the cash and added to the bonds and it will make the whole of the cash due by the Gdn $1616.47 and the whole of the bonds $11853.97. The amt. of this bond is $314.29 and to each one of the children $104.76. The cash then due Jos. A. DILLON will be $238.60 and bonds $3951.32, to J. W. DILLON cash $552.46 and bonds $3951.22, and Anne E. DILLON cash $825.42 and bonds $3951.32. These bonds have all been turned over to J. J.

DILLON present Gdn and the cash settled with him. RtCt 12 Apr 1869. [E:450]

S/A with Gdn John J. DILLON: beginning 8 May 1868; accts with children Anne E. DILLON, Joseph Abdon DILLON and Jonah W. DILLON. RtCt 12 Oct 1869. [F:1]
S/A with Gdn John J. DILLON: duplicate of above. [F:5]

Bonds from Gdn A. JANNEY & received by Gdn John J. DILLON: [long list] $2023 worth received from division of 1 Jun 1868 of estate of Annie DILLON, bonds rec'd from estate of John PANCOAST. RtCt 17 May 1870. [F:62]

S/A with Gdn John James DILLON: $2011.34 with distributions to Annie E. DILLON (a lunatic,) Jonah Wm. DILLON & Joseph Abdon DILLON (abt 20y old.) RtCt 13 Feb 1871. [F:90]

S/A with Gdn John James DILLON: general expenses leaving $1303.09 divided amongst Annie E. DILLON, Jonah Wm. DILLON & Joseph Abdon DILLON (now of age.) Also S/A with Aquila JANNEY late Gdn. Long list of bonds. RtCt 10 Oct 1871. [F:180]

S/A with Gdn John James DILLON: beginning 15 Apr 1871; general expenses leaving $42.08 to Annie and $258.46 to Jonah. RtCt 8 Sep 1873. [F: 355]

S/A with Gdn John J. DILLON: beginning 6 Apr 1872; income from rent of Philomont farm, ROGERS farm & Purcellville farm, general expenses, leaving Annie E. $107.69, Jonah William DILLON $357 due to ward but $584.62 invested. RtCt 12 Jan 1874. [F:367]

Inventory of bonds held by Gdn John J. DILLON: totaling $6997.72½ for each child. RtCt 12 Jan 1874. [F:370]

S/A with Gdn John James DILLON: beginning 17 Mar 1874; general expenses leaving Annie E. DILLON $921.78. RtCt 8 Nov 1875. [F:477]

S/A with Gdn John James DILLON: beginning 1 Apr 1874; general expenses leaving $437.59 plus ½ of a $1000 US bond to Annie E. DILLON. RtCt 8 Nov 1875. [F:479]

DILLON, Annie E.
S/A with Gdn John J. DILLON: beginning 10 Mar 1875; investment in notes, general expenses, leaving $1012.01 due to Gdn (yet he holds several notes payable to him.) RtCt 11 Aug 1879. [G:183]

S/A with Gdn John J. DILLON: beginning 23 Jul 1876; as above, leaving $824.58 due to Gdn. RtCt 11 Aug 1879. [G:185]

S/A with Gdn John J. DILLON: beginning 10 Mar 1877; as above, leaving $785.84 due to Gdn. RtCt 11 Aug 1879. [G:187]

S/A with Gdn John J. DILLON: beginning 4 Apr 1878; as above, leaving $1052.54. Ward is now of age and needs a Committee, not a Gdn. RtCt 11 Aug 1879. [G:189]

Inventory of 14 Jun 1880 by Committee John J. DILLON: income from interest & principal on loans totaling $10879.35 and rents from Purcellville Farm, Round Hill Farm & land in Philomont totaling $136.27. RtCt 7 Jul 1880. [G:227]

S/A with Gdn J. W. GARRETT: full payment of $35.13 on 12 Jan 1880. RtCt 13 Oct 1880. [G:241]

S/A with Gdn John J. DILLON: beginning 10 Mar 1879; expenses of Purcellville farm, income from rent of farms & land, general expenses, leaving $50.84 due to Gdn who holds bonds. Annie is over 21y old but of unsound mind. RtCt 13 Oct 1880. [G:243]

S/A wit Committee John J. DILLON: beginning 14 Jun 1880; income from rent of farms, payments leaving $142.17 due to Committee yet hold a larger bond. RtCt 14 Nov 1881. [G:292]

S/A with Committee John J. DILLON: beginning 4 Jun 1882; general expenses leaving $4469.11. RtCt 9 Oct 1882. [G:340]

S/A with Committee John J. DILLON: beginning 25 Sep 1882; general expenses leaving $56.65 plus $779.58 in bonds. RtCt 11 Dec 1883. [G:413]

S/A with Committee John J. DILLON: beginning 14 Aug 1883; general expenses leaving $375.34. RtCt 11 Nov 1884. [G:452]

S/A with Committee John J. DILLON: beginning 20 Aug 1884; general expenses leaving $228.64 due to Committee, plus investments. RtCt 14 Oct 1885. [G:493]

S/A with Committee John J. DILLON: beginning 24 Aug 1885; income from rent on Philomont land, general expenses, leaving $233.64 due to Committee. RtCt 15 Feb 1886. [H:29]

S/A with Committee John J. DILLON: beginning 12 Oct 1886; general expenses leaving $271.37. RtCt 10 Jan 1888. [H:63]

S/A with Committee John J. DILLON: beginning 6 Sep 1887; general expenses leaving $274.41. RtCt 13 Mar 1889. [H:96]

S/A with Committee John J. DILLON: beginning 25 Sep 1888; general expenses leaving $165.07. RtCt 12 Jan 1891. [H:125]

S/A with Committee Jno. J. DILLON: beginning 14 Jun 1889; general expenses leaving $559.49. RtCt 10 Jun 1891. [H:136]

S/A with Committee Jno. J. DILLON: beginning 1 Dec 1890; general expenses leaving $202.35. RtCt 14 Apr 1892. [H:154]

S/A with Committee Jno. J. DILLON: beginning 14 Jun 1890; general expenses leaving $361.99. RtCt 14 Apr 1892. [H:154]

S/A with Committee John J. DILLON: beginning 14 Jun 1891; general expenses leaving $362.09. RtCt 9 Jan 1894. [H:191]

S/A with Committee J. J. DILLON: beginning 14 Jun 1892; general expenses leaving $822.05. RtCt 9 Jul 1894. [H:210]

S/A with Committee John J. DILLON: beginning 14 Jun 1893; general expenses leaving $597.62. RtCt 8 Oct 1894. [H:219]

S/A with Committee Jno. J. DILLON: beginning 14 Jun 1894; $590 loan to Jos. A. DILLON, $270.62 loan to Jas. W. SEATON, leaving $1246.56. RtCt 10 Dec 1895. [H:249]

S/A with Committee Jno. J. DILLON: beginning 14 Jun 1895; general expenses leaving $583.02. RtCt 10 Nov 1896. [H:284]

S/A with Committee John J. DILLON: beginning 14 Jun 1896; general expenses leaving $712.77. RtCt 9 Nov 1897. [H:313]

S/A with J Committee John J. DILLON: beginning 14 Jun 1897; general expenses leaving $10684.97. RtCt 10 Jan 1899. [H:357]

S/A with Committee J. J. DILLON: beginning 14 Jun 1898; general expenses leaving $1146.42 plus investments of $10684.97. RtCt 9 Jan 1900. [H:375]

S/A with Committee J. J. DILLON: beginning 15 Sep 1900; general expenses leaving $799.80. RtCt 11 Jun 1901. [H:417]

S/A with Committee J. A. DILLON: beginning 29 Sep 1900; general expenses leaving $623.83. John A. DILLON [written as Jos. A.] died 16 Mar 1901 and C. C. GAVER will be new Committee. RtCt 15 Apr 1902. [H:442]

SMITH, William G., Henry H., Joshua and John R. (Children of Jonas)

S/A of W. G., Joshua, Henry H. and John R. SMITH with Gdn Thomas R. SMITH: general expenses, leaving $4997.16. Upon examination of the will it is found that it directs all the personal property or estate in the hands of the Execs. upon the becoming of age of his oldest son Thomas R. SMITH to be sold and together with the real estate to be divided among his several children first taking out the widows ? (all the debts being first paid). Your commissioner therefore in making this S/A with the Gdn has charged him with all the estate as passed to him in said last S/A with the Execs. who in fact sold the property to him at appraisement value which appraisement of records and is believe to embrace all the personal estate of every description in their hands at that period. The debts of the estate not all having been paid off by the Execs. the Gdn (as will be seen by reference) has proceeded to pay those remaining from which he is credited in this S/A after which a distribution acct. is made up and your commissioner reports due to the widow in right of dower the sum of $2498.57 and the heirs as follows: to Wm. G. SMITH a bal. of $973.69, to Joshua SMITH a bal. of $920.99 and to Henry H. and Jno. R. SMITH jointly a bal. of $1898.92. RtCt 12 Aug 1857. [D:247]

S/A of William G. SMITH, Henry H. SMITH, Joshua SMITH & John R. SMITH with Gdn Thomas R. SMITH: beginning 12 Feb 1856; general expenses leaving $706.64 to Joshua, $936.36 Henry H. and $905.49 e to John R. SMITH. Wm. R. SMITH having attained the age of 21 years has rec'd all that was due him. RtCt 12 Aug 1857. [D:271]

S/A of Henry H. SMITH with Gdn Thomas R. SMITH: beginning 14 Feb 1857; paid board and tuition, leaving $969.81. S/A of Joshua SMITH with Gdn Thomas R. SMITH: as above, leaving $764.64. S/A of John R. SMITH with Gdn Thomas R. SMITH: as above, leaving $1039.34. RtCt 14 Apr 1859. [D:407]

S/A of Henry H. SMITH with Gdn Thomas R. SMITH: beginning 27 Mar 1858; paid board & tuition leaving $1014.06. S/A of Joshua SMITH with Gdn Thomas R. SMITH: beginning 19 Feb 1858; to W. H. FRANCIS one tithe; leaving $913.15. S/A of John R. SMITH with Gdn Thomas R. SMITH: beginning 18 Feb 1858; expenses leaving $1199.51. The rent of the Jonas SMITH's real estate was reduced from $900 to $800, in consideration of the failure of crops & general hard times. RtCt 15 Mar 1860. [E:43]

S/A of Henry W. SMITH with Gdn Thomas R. SMITH: paid board, leaving $1054.18. S/A of John R. SMITH with Gdn Thomas R. SMITH: as above, leaving $1376.95. RtCt 14 Aug 1860. [E:99]

S/A of Henry H. SMITH &c with Thomas R. SMITH: beginning 22 Jan 1860; general expenses. S/A of Henry H. SMITH with Gdn Thomas R. SMITH: beginning 12 Feb 1860; paid board & tuition and various store accts, leaving $944.31. S/A of John R. SMITH with Gdn Thomas R. SMITH: beginning 12 Feb 1860; as above, leaving $1300.69. RtCt 17 Aug 1866. [E:301]

S/A John R and Henry H. with Gdn Thomas R. SMITH: beginning 12 Feb 1861; general payments leaving $2088 to John and $1464.23 to Henry. RtCt 19 Nov 1870. [F:71]

S/A Joshua, Henry H. & John R. with Gdn Thomas R. SMITH: acct. now closed. RtCt 9 Jul 1878. [G:117]

KERCHEVAL, Robert H. (a lunatic)

S/A with Committee George KEENE: beginning 1 Apr 1855; cash receipts, leaving $1172.75. This lunatic was the son-in-law of said committee who had become involved as the security of his son-in-law to a considerable amount. RtCt 12 Aug 1857. [D:249]

STEPHENSON, James, Lloyd, John and Josephine (Children of James)

S/A with Gdn John M. ORR: beginning Jan 1851; cash sent to James & Lloyd at Georgetown, Lloyd & Josephine from Middleburg to Bentsville, paid store acct. of James, Lloyd, John, and Josephine, paid board and tuition, income from rent of house in Snickersville and rent of office, paid medical bill of Negroes Judy and Jerry, expenses to get Negroes Dick & Emily to settle with Dr. FITZHUGH, income from Ludwell LUCKETT Exor of John WHITACRE dec'd, from rent in Upperville and from hire of Negroes Mary & 2 children, Emily, Jerry, Julia Ann, Violet, Mary Jane and Margaret. S/A of James STEPHENSON with Gdn Jno. M. ORR: beginning 28 Feb 1851; paid fare from Middly to Brentsville, many of the previously listed items, leaving $518.41½. S/A of Lloyd STEPHENSON with Gdn John M. ORR: as above, leaving $360.12. S/A of John STEPHENSON with Gdn John M. ORR: as above, leaving $197.90. S/A of Josephine STEPHENSON with John M. ORR: as above, leaving $327.54. [This was a very long account.] RtCt 12 Aug 1857. [D:253]

S/A with Gdn John M. ORR: paid medical bills, income from rent of house and office and from hire of Negroes Mary & 2 children, Emily, Jerry, Janny, Julia, Violet, Margaret & Dick. S/A of Lloyd STEPHENSON with Gdn John M. ORR: paid tuition and medical bills, leaving $388.32. S/A of John STEPHENSON with Gdn John M. ORR: paid tuition and for French book, leaving $443.36. S/A of Josephine STEPHENSON with Gdn John M. ORR: paid tuition, leaving of $29.92. S/A of James STEPHENSON with Gdn John M. ORR: general expenses, leaving $352.21½. RtCt 14 Oct 1858. [D:314]

S/A with Gdn John M. ORR: amt. due the Gdn for MURPHEYs rent charged in former acct, he dying insolvent being $2500 note, paid repairs of Upperville Walker house, income from hire of Negroes Mary and her two children, Emily, Julia, Violet, Margaret, Jerry and Dick and from hire of shop in Snickersville, paid for keeping Negro Violet during her confinement, income from rent of BROWN house, from rent of Mount. farm, and cash rec'd of W. M. BUCK on acct. of WARREN farm, paid for repairs to Tavern, Dec 1859 taxes on Fauquier property. S/A of James STEPHENSON with former Gdn John M. ORR: beginning 31 Dec 1856; paid various store accts, leaving $20.97 as of 1 Jan 1860, now of age. S/A of Lloyd B. STEPHENSON with late Gdn J. M. ORR: beginning 1 Jan 1857, as above, leaving $57.94. S/A of Josephine STEPHENSON with Gdn J. M. ORR: beginning 1 Jan 1857; expenses to Charlestown, paid various store accts., paid the R. H. PHILLIPS institute, paid W. A. STEPHENSON board. S/A of John STEPHENSON with Gdn John M. ORR: paid various store accts and board and tuition. [above was a long report] On 1 Jan 1857 by the acct. formerly settled by Mr. LUCKETT there was a balance due to the Gdn of $388.32 and this was increased on 1 Jan 1858 by the great repairs done to the property which lies in and about the Village of Snickersville in Loudoun County upon which property there are a good tenements that had by long neglect fallen into a state of considerable decay, and they actually consumed the rents and a portion of the hires of the Negroes, who were of such a character as required large physicians bills. The balances due on 12 Jan 1858 was $631.82 and yet all the charges seem to be fair and proper ones. The balance on the general acct. this year was largely in favor of the heirs of James STEPHENSON and Lloyd's share of $385.69 reduced the amt. due by him so much that on 1 Jan 1859 the balance due the Gdn was $2184.03. Again during the year 1859 there was a considerable sum due to the heirs and Lloyd's share of $213.13 reduced the balance due by him to $57.94 on 1 Jan 1860. During this year he was of age. It is proper to state that two years rent was received during 1859 and that a slave Jerry was sold during this year for $1000. Jerry was sold for the following reason: Josephine STEPHENSON was a young lady of 17 years of age in 1857 and had been boarding at her cousin W. A. STEPHENSON's for several years and whose education was unfinished. The Gdn objected to the bill for board, washing &c as too high at $200 and it was finally settled at $175 per annum. The payment of this sum seems to me to have been unavoidable, the other items in this year including $269.28 expenses to at and from Staunton, where she attended the Female Institute seem to be reasonable and proper and indeed almost unavoidable, and at the years end the balance due her Gdn was $1254.46 on 12 Jan 1858. The expenses during the year 1858 exceeded her income $46.53 but they seem to me to have been reasonable & proper being for school expenses almost entirely and the balance due to the Gdn was $1290.99. During this year her bills for clothing seem to have been larger then was proper, but they were in part for clothing for the two preceding years and her education expenses were still considerable. At the end of the year the balance due the Gdn was $1531.41 viz. on 1 Jan 1860 she was now nearly 21 years of age. I submit the question of propriety of these charges to the Court. John STEPHENSON owed his Gdn on 1 Jan 1857 $443.36 and his expenses during the year were $361.00 and as he was going to boarding school I suppose them to be reasonable. During the year 1858 the expenses were $335.84 and though his clothing bill was extravagant yet on the whole the expenses were moderate as he was just finishing his education and preparing for life. During the year 1859 John was employed in the store of his brother James and served without compensation and his expenses including a large bill for clothing amounted to $322.16 being $109.03 more than his income. John without being vicious was disposed to be extravagant and the Gdn found it difficult to restrain him without proper bounds. He actually refused to pay bills which had been contracted contrary to his orders. The balance due the Gdn on 1 Jan 1860 was $845.54. RtCt 13 Jun 1861. [E:156]

S/A with Gdn Jno. M. ORR: beginning 21 Mar 1860; income from hire of Negroes Mary Cross with 2 children, Margaret, Julia, Jenny, Madison & Dick, amt. allowed on affidavit of Dr. A. H. POWELL for keeping Emily an infirm slave. S/A of Josephine STEPHENSON with Gdn John M. ORR: beginning 1 Jan 1860, general expenses, leaving $188.59. S/A of John STEPHENSON with Gdn John M. ORR.: beginning 1 Jan 1860; paid Jno. on going to

Missouri, leaving $188.60. S/A of James STEPHENSON with Gdn John M. ORR: general expenses leaving $188.59. Lloyd B. STEPHENSON has balance of $188.59. The real estate had all then been sold, and the slaves divided leaving possession in the hands of the Gdn till 1 Jan 1861. I next settled the separate acct. of Josephine STEPHENSON with her Gdn to her majority and since to 1 Apr 1861 and find due to Jno. M. ORR $64.88. In doing so I have allowed her credit for the amt. of the decree $743.79 as of 20 Oct 1860 and for one half the balance in hands of Jno. M. ORR Comr. as of 1 Apr 1861 $694.83. Jno STEPHENSON's acct. with his Gdn is settled to his majority 9 Mar 1862 and since that date to 3 Sep 1866 when there is due to John M. ORR $127.06 with interest till paid. In this S/A Jno. STEPHENSON is allowed the decree in his favor for $743.79 and $494.82 part of the funds in the hands of Jno. M. ORR one of the commissioner in STEPHENSON vs. STEPHENSON, a transaction in gold, amounting to $116.80 and a note of his to W. S. PICKETT which has been paid by Jno. M. ORR commissioner as aforesaid to the amount of $338.92. The amts. due James STEPHENSON and Lloyd B. STEPHENSON on general acct. are transferred, the first to John M. ORR his trustee and the second to a private acct. of Lloyd B. STEPHENSON, which has been settled with him by Jno. M. ORR. This Guardianship is entirely closed. RtCt 15 Jun 1868. [E:398]

HIXON, Bettie
S/A with Gdn Noble S. BRADEN: paid expenses for ward to and from Georgetown, paid board & tuition and for instruction in vocal music, leaving $1067.16. Ward has now attained the age of 21 years. RtCt 12 Aug 1857. [D:267]

CONARD, Henrietta L.
S/A with Gdn J. C. STONEBURNER: beginning 12 Jun 1854; from Jos. M. CONARD 1st payment on land under decree, paid board and tuition, income from rents, leaving $157.17. The papers relating to the first years transaction in the annexed acct. were laid before me in Mar 1856 accompanied with said STONEBURNER'S papers relating to the S/A of his acct. as administrator of John CONARD dec'd in the Circuit Ct. RtCt 12 Aug 1857. [D:276]
S/A with Gdn J. C. STONEBURNER: 22 Jan 185 rec'd payment from receiver T. P. KNOX in CONARD vs CONARD, leaving $573.49. The expenditures of the Gdn seem to be very reasonable and yet they have overrun the interest on the principal now in the hands of said Gdn. A further sum however will shortly come into his hands, and the interest on the combined sum will probably be enough to support her comfortably. RtCt 14 Oct 1858. [D:334]
S/A with Gdn Jacob C. STONEBURNER: paid board, rec'd payment from CONARD vs CONARD, leaving $1286.24. The expenditures are greater than the receipts, because the young lady bought a Melodeon during the year, which cost $40, she being nearly of age, and a competent person in mind to judge of her own wants, and being able to judge of her own affairs. RtCt 13 Aug 1859. [D:423]
S/A with J. C. STONEBURNER: beginning 9 Mar 1859; general expenses leaving $1286.34. He has over run the profits of her estate $42.75, and while I think the dentist's bill ought to be allowed, I think the store acct. rather large. It may probably be proper to allow all of it as her estate will be pretty considerably increase from the estate of an aunt, who has recently died. RtCt 14 Aug 1860. [E:71]
S/A with Gdn J. C. STONEBURNER: beginning 19 May 1860; paid store bills, payment from Jos. CONARD Admr. of Mary CONARD, leaving $1265. RtCt 13 Jun 1861. [E:111]
S/A with Gdn J. C. STONEBURNER: income from J. M. CONARD rent and from Jos. CONARD Admr. of Mary CONARD dec'd, paid medical acct and various store accts, leaving $267.00 to the time of her majority and at the request of the parties to 8 Sep 1865. RtCt 13 Feb 1866. [E:143]

CONARD, Stephen H.
S/A with Gdn Joseph M. CONARD: beginning 12 Jun 1854; paid board & tuition, income from rent, leaving $179.74½. The papers relating to the first years transactions in the annexed acct. were laid before me in March 1856 accompanied with said CONARD's papers relating to the S/A of his acct. as administrator of John CONARD dec'd in the Circuit Court. RtCt 12 Aug 1857. [D:278]
S/A with Gdn Joseph M. CONARD: beginning 27 Jul 1827; general expenses leaving $848.93½. RtCt 14 Oct 1858. [D:335]
S/A with Gdn Joseph M. CONARD: beginning 10 Mar 1858; paid tuition, leaving $1402.05. RtCt 14 Aug 1859. [D:424]
S/A with Gdn Jos. M. CONARD: beginning 1 Jul 1859; paid tuition, leaving $1384.19. RtCt 14 Aug 1860. [E:72]
S/A with Joseph M. CONARD: beginning 28 Mar 1860; paid tuition, payment from Joseph CONARD Admr. of Mary CONARD and Admr. of sale of Negro Betty, amt. of ward's interest in land rented by Jos. M. CONARD, leaving $1438.99. RtCt 14 Oct 1861. [E:186]
S/A with Gdn Joseph M. CONARD: beginning 24 Aug 1861; as above, leaving $1505.18 paid in full to 17 Apr 1862 when he became 21 yrs old. RtCt 13 Feb 1866. [E:208]

MATTHEWS, Heirs of Catharine
S/A with Gdn Bernard HOUGH is recorded in Will Book 2 G's page 94. [D:283]

OSBURN, Louisa A. and Walter C.
S/A of Louisa A. and Walter C. OSBURN with father & Gdn T. V. B. OSBURN: beginning 22 Sep 1856; cash rec'd from Joel OSBURN's Admr., leaving $2112.74. RtCt 14 Oct 1858. [D:300]

DOWELL, Catharine
 S/A with Gdn C. R. DOWELL: (now Catharine MANNING) 10 Jun 1848 rec'd payment from Conrad BITZER's Exor. being wards share of legacy under the will of said Conrad BITZER, 6 Jul 1857 paid Jacob H. MANNING $2311.36. On 28 Feb 1857 Gdn made up the foregoing acct. to that date and found a balance of $2263.10 due from the said Gdn to the said ward. Subsequently the said Gdn died. RtCt 14 Oct. 1858. [D:312]

SMITH, Eliza Jane, Susan Sophia, Samuel George and Eve Virginia (Children of Jacob)
 S/A of Eliza L. SMITH, Eve V. SMITH and Samuel George SMITH with Gdn Mary J. SMITH: beginning 14 Apr 1856; paid tuition, payment from Job SMITH Admr of George SMITH, leaving $912.64. Gdn Mary J. SMITH died on 2 Jun 1857. John SMITH the Admr owes the estate $431.53 and there is uncollected of the estate about $200. Jacob SMITH's estate owes George SMITH's estate (his father) two notes of $200. By the will of George SMITH, his three sons Jacob, John & Job are his residuary legatees in equal proportions, so that of this $400 Jacob's estate will get as of this date (the int being deducted & the commission also) about $124. His whole estate there, except which is specially devised to his widow, will not exceed $1400 which is equally divided among his four children above named & which gives each one $350 at interest only $21 per annum. At the death of their mother or upon her marrying again they are entitled to a landed estate of about the value of $5000. I have been requested by the Gdn to state all this and also the ages of the children as the basis of an application to the Court for an attachment for the support of the children beyond the interest above stated. The ages as verified by affidavit of their mother the Gdn are as follows: Eliza Jane was 18 on Feb 1857, Susan Sophia was 17 on Jul 1857, Eve Virginia will be 14 in Aug 1857, and Samuel George was 9 in May 1857. RtCt 14 Oct 1858. [D:320]
 S/A of Eliza Jane and Susan Sophia SMITH with Gdn Mary SMITH: beginning 14 Apr 1857; general expenses, leaving $456.32. S/A of Samuel George & Eve Virginia SMITH with Gdn Mary SMITH: as above, paid tuition, leaving $456.32. She has exceeded the income in this latter account, but I cannot well see how she could have clothed and educated two children one 10 and the other 13 for less than $30 unless by the excess of the strictest economy and the best judgment. RtCt 14 Oct 1858. [D:366]
 S/A of Eliza Jane SMITH and Susan Sophia SMITH with Gdn Mary SMITH: beginning Jul 1858; general expenses, payment from Job SMITH Admr. of George SMITH, leaving $460.55. RtCt 15 Mar 1860. [E:41]
 S/A of Eve Virginia SMITH and Samuel George SMITH with Gdn Mary SMITH: beginning 24 Jul 1858; paid tuition, payment from Job SMITH Admr. of Geo. SMITH, leaving $457.99. I have not yet thought it worth while to separate the fund as the expenses have been about equal. A little more money will come into the Guardians hands from George SMITH's estate, and hereafter I will keep separate accts. RtCt 15 Mar 1860. [E:42]
 S/A of Eliza Jane SMITH with Gdn Mary SMITH: beginning 18 Apr 1859; paid various store accts, leaving $219.69. S/A of Susan Sophia SMITH with Gdn Mary SMITH: beginning 18 Apr 1859; as above, leaving $221.94. RtCt 13 Jun 1861. [E:168]
 S/A of Eve Virginia SMITH with Gdn Mary SMITH: beginning 19 May 1859; paid various store accts and tuition, leaving $225.52. S/A of Samuel George SMITH with Gdn Mary SMITH: beginning 19 May 1860 [59?]; as above, leaving $221.63. RtCt 13 Jun 1861. [E:170]
 S/A of Samuel George SMITH with Gdn Mary SMITH: paid tuition and various store accts, leaving $215.35. S/A of Eve Virginia SMITH with Gdn Mary SMITH: beginning 9 Jun 1860; as above, leaving $221.52. Their Gdn and mother furnished them board from the proceeds of the farm which was devised to her form that purpose. RtCt 13 Feb 1866. [E:257]
 S/A of Samuel Geo. SMITH with Gdn Mary SMITH: beginning Jun 1861; paid various store accts, leaving $104.83. His principal during four years last past has been diminished $110.51 but considering the smallness of the income (less than $15) and the expensiveness of dress I think I am justified. RtCt 13 Feb 1866. [E:258]
 S/A of Eve Virginia SMITH with Gdn Mary SMITH: 6 Jun 1861; paid various store accts, leaving $174.00 (after providing for all future costs – at the time of her attaining the age of 21 years on 5 Aug 1864.) This may be regarded as the final S/A. RtCt 13 Feb 1866. [E:261]
 S/A of Susan Sophia SMITH with Gdn Mary SMITH: beginning 16 May 1860; paid various store accts. Susan Sophia was of age on 18 July 1861 and I have stated her acct. to that date and after reserving her proportion of fees I report a balance in her favor of $203.48. S/A of Eliza Jane SMITH with Gdn Mary SMITH: general expenses leaving $227.78, fully settled. She was of age on 11 Feb 1860. RtCt 13 Feb 1866. [E:262]
 S/A of Samuel George SMITH with Gdn Mary SMITH: beginning 25 Oct 1865; paid tuition, leaving $63. The amt. due him has been reduced some $41.57 during the year, but it seems to have been for only a reasonable amt. of clothing. RtCt 9 Apr 1867. [E:349]
 S/A of Samuel George with Gdn Mary SMITH of J.: beginning 18 Jun 1866; general expenses leaving $118.74 due to Gdn. RtCt 17 Aug 1871. [F:177]

BEANS, William H. H., Victoria, Rachel A., Josephine and David (Children of Absalom)
 Inventory of estate in the hands of Benjamin F. TAYLOR the Gdn of five of his children (William H. H. BEANS, Victoria BEANS, Rachel A. BEANS, Josephine

BEANS, and David BEANS): 9 Nov 1857 rec'd payment from Thomas E. HATCHER Admr, income from rent of farm, one sixth of which is the share of Hannah B. BEANS the deceased eldest daughter, five sixths to the wards above, and from hire of Negro man Edward. RtCt 1 Jul 1858. [D:328]

S/A of William BEANS and others with Gdn Benjamin F. Taylor: beginning 12 Oct 1857; income from hire of Negro Edward, 12 Oct 1857 rec'd payment from T. E. HATCHER Admr. in articles bought at sale, 9 Nov 1857 $163.52 rec'd payment from Absalom BEANS' Admr. S/A of William BEANS with Gdn Benjamin F. TAYLOR: paid board and tuition and for articles bought at his father's sale the sum of $40.24, leaving $207.76. S/A of Victoria BEANS with Gdn Benjamin F. TAYLOR: paid board, leaving $207.76. S/A of Rachel Anna BEANS with Gdn Benjamin F. TAYLOR: paid board and tuition, articles purchased at her father's sale amounting to $48.16, leaving $159.60. RtCt 14 Apr 1859. [D:382]

S/A with Gdn Benjamin F. TAYLOR: beginning Oct 1858; income from rent of farm, rent of blacksmith's lot, and from hire of Negro Edward, leaving $371.15. S/A of William BEANS with Gdn Benjamin F. TAYLOR: beginning 18 Jan 1859; paid board, leaving $174.03. S/A of Victoria BEANS with Gdn Benjamin F. TAYLOR: beginning 5 Mar 1859; general expenses, leaving $269.56. S/A of Rachel Anna BEANS with Gdn Benjamin F. TAYLOR: beginning 25 Nov 1858; general expenses, leaving $200.44. The tuition of William BEANS including his board makes his expenditures go beyond the income of his estate, but he is nearly twenty one years of age and is competent to act for himself in this matter and chooses to go beyond his income. RtCt 15 Mar 1860. [E:11]

S/A with Gdn Benjamin F. TAYLOR: payment from T. E. HATCHER Admr of A BEANS dec'd being Hannah B. BEANS share of the personal estate, leaving $284.10. S/A of William H. H. BEANS with Gdn B. F. TAYLOR: beginning 12 Oct 1859; paid board; income from H. B. BEAN's decree; owes Gdn $118.78; William is of age. S/A of Victoria BEANS with Gdn B. F. TAYLOR: beginning 12 Oct 1859; income from decree as above; leaving $200.92. S/A of Rachel Anna BEANS with Gdn B. F. TAYLOR: beginning 12 Oct 1859; general expenses leaving $118.64. The matters in dispute between an adult sister and these infant children in the case of BEANS vs BEANS in the Circuit Court has been settled since, and the amounts due to Hannah B. BEANS under the decree in said cause have been charged in their proper proportion in these accts. They get her share of the land and slaves. RtCt 13 Jun 1861. [E:178]

S/A of Rachel Anna BEANS with Gdn Benjamin F. TAYLOR: paid 1/5 of acct. for repairs to dwelling, paid board, credits as above, leaving $224.12. The deranged condition of the County rendered it impossible to make any progress in the S/A of such accts. I therefore postpone indefinitely all such as were in my hands with the exception of a very few in which there was no difficulty. RtCt 13 Jan 1866. [E:202]

S/A of Victoria BEANS with Gdn Benjamin F. TAYLOR: as above, leaving $304.83. The deranged condition of the county rendered it impossible to make any progress in the S/A of such accts. RtCt 13 Feb 1866. [E:203]

S/A of Victoria A. L. M. BEANS with Gdn B. F. TAYLOR: beginning 1 Nov 1861; income from rent from W. H. H. BEANS, balance due 2 Dec 1865 receipt in full ($448.66), as of Jan 1866 had reached majority and settled in full. S/A of Rachel Ann BEANS with Gdn B. F. TAYLOR: beginning 1 Nov 1861; paid board and clothing, 1 Nov 1865 amt. due ward ($326.05); is now of age. RtCt 17 Aug 1866. [E:277]

BEANS, David and Josephine

S/A of David BEANS with Gdn Benjamin F. TAYLOR: beginning 18 Oct 1858; paid board & tuition, leaving $201.82. S/A of Josephine BEANS with Gdn Benjamin F. TAYLOR: beginning 10 Nov 1858; paid board & tuition, expenses have exceeded her income by $33.68. RtCt 15 Mar 1860. [E:14]

S/A of David BEANS with Gdn B. F. TAYLOR: beginning 12 Oct 1859; paid various store accts, board & tuition, leaving $39.97 due to Gdn. S/A of Josephine BEANS with Gdn B. F. TAYLOR: beginning 12 Oct 1859; as above, leaving $31.66. The amount decreed to H. B. BEANS in the suit for the division of the land has been paid by the Gdn in large part and the whole has been charged as paid. This increases the expenditures for them so as to make them apparently very much beyond the income, but they get her share of the land and slaves as an increase to their capital. RtCt 13 Jun 1861. [E:181]

S/A of David H. BEANS with Gdn Benjamin F. TAYLOR: beginning 10 Nov 1860; paid repairs and tuition, income from sale of mountain lot, rec'd payment from Admr of Absalom BEANS, income from rent of blacksmith ship and from hire of Negro man Ed, leaving $168.31. RtCt 13 Feb 1866. [E:201]

S/A of Josephine BEANS Gdn Benjamin F. TAYLOR: as above, leaving $155.94 . RtCt 13 Feb 1866. [E:205]

S/A of David H. BEANS with Gdn Benjamin F. TAYLOR: income from his share of rent from W. H. H. BEANS, leaving $362.29. S/A of Josephine BEANS with Gdn Benjamin F. TAYLOR: board and clothing paid W. H. BEANS, leaving $255.19. For the years embraced in this S/A W. H. BEANS an elder brother rented the farm and they boarded with and accts. were kept but for the years 1864 and 1865 to 1 Nov the loss of the renter was so great from the passing of troops by his premises that these two wards as well as two older ones agreed to release him from rent, he at the same time releasing them from board. Thus they made the occupancy of the farm a joint one and the Gdn deeming the bargain a fair one has not claimed rent. RtCt 20 Aug 1866. [E:274]

S/A of David H. BEANS with Gdn Benjamin F. TAYLOR: beginning 13 Nov 1865; general expenses leaving $349.17. S/A of Josephine BEANS with Gdn Benj. F. TAYLOR: beginning 1 Nov 1865; general expenses leaving $151.50. RtCt 15 Jun 1868. [E:395]

S/A of David BEANS with Gdn Benjamin F. TAYLOR: paid medical bills, board & tuition, leaving $207.76. S/A of Josephine BEANS with Gdn Benjamin F. TAYLOR: paid board & tuition, leaving $207.76. The data for these figures will be found in the Guardianship acct. of William BEANS and others. RtCt 14 Apr 1859. [D:384]

BEANS, David H.
S/A with Gdn Benjamin F. TAYLOR: beginning 1 Nov 1866; general expenses leaving $110 paid to ward, acct is closed. RtCt 12 Apr 1870. [F:28]

MOCK, Heirs of George W.
Inventory of property belonging to the heirs of George W. MOCK dec'd.: four ninths of a tract of land supposed to be about sixty four acres, subject to the dower of Mary Ann MOCK, widow of Geo. W. MOCK dec'd. RtCt 1 Jul 1858. [D:328]

DOWELL, Charles W.
Inventory of the property and funds belonging to Charles W. DOWELL, which have come into my hands, since my qualification, as his Gdn, to wit: one Negro man named Harry, aged about 24 years, and one Negro woman named Maria aged between 18 and 19 years, and her infant child named Frances, and $3959.19. RtCt 28 Aug 1858. [D:328]

S/A with Gdn Conrad R. DOWELL: 10 Jun 1848 payment rec'd from Conrad BITZER's Exor being wards share of legacy under said BITZER's will, 18 Sep 1857 paid over this day to Sanford J. RAMEY Gdn for said ward by said Conrad R. DOWELL's Exor., leaving $3959.19 The papers were laid before your commissioner on 18 Sep 1857 by Joseph PANCOAST executor of said Conrad R. DOWELL for S/A. The comr. in stating this acct. has observed the directions of said Guardians will which directs that the said ward be settled with upon the same principles as those adopted in the S/A with his other children for whom he was Gdn, the S/As alluded to were made up and reported by your comr. as the children respectively became of age. Sanford J. RAMEY having been appointed by the Court as Gdn for the said Charles W. DOWELL in the place of his father now dec'd. RtCt 14 Oct 1858. [D:342]

S/A with Gdn Sanford J. RAMEY: paid board and tuition, 29 Dec 1857 to Negro Harry order of C. W. D., paid amt. due to John T. DOWELL, rec'd payment from Jos. PANCOAST Exor. of Conrad R. DOWELL from Gdn, income from hire of Negroes Maria and Harry, leaving $3700.61. The amount that he received from the former Gdn's executor was $3959.19 but in the division of his father's (who was his Gdn) personal estate, and slaves, his two Negroes were more valuable than those of another brother, and were charged $158.33 which with the interest accrued on it to 2 Apr 1858 was refunded to the executor. This reduces the amount received to $3800.86 and some hires received, which were used by the Gdn added, and some commission deducted, and the amount due the Gdn on the profits of $21.56 which was made principal have produced the balance now due the ward of principal of $3700.61. The Gdn seems to have used more than the income of the wards' estate, but this arises from my having charged the hires $125.55 as principal and not as profits they having been used as a borrower by the Gdn. The truth is that the estate is increased about $100 in principal. RtCt 12 Jan 1859. [D:372]

S/A with Gdn Sanford J. RAMEY: beginning 18 Nov 1858; paid board & tuition, payment from J. BITZER for five weeks hire of Negro woman Maria, leaving $3700.50. RtCt 15 Mar 1860. [E:23]

S/A with Gdn Sanford J. RAMEY: beginning Nov 1859; paid J. W. & C. B. WILDMAN for Henry?, paid Mrs. DOWELL for keeping Frank, leaving $3953.94. RtCt 13 Jun 1861. [E:144]

BOND, Eleanor C., Sarah F. and Thomas
S/A with Gdn William H. SCHOOLEY: beginning 18 Feb 1854; payments for pasturage, leaving $2.17. He had done his best with the property he could under the circumstances not being able at any time to rent it out. RtCt 14 Oct 1858. [D:331]

COMPHER, J. H. W., Jonas Curtis, Sarah C., Ann E., Marietta & William F. (Heirs of William)
S/A with Gdn: beginning 20 Oct 1856.; paid house repairs. S/A of J. H. W. COMPHER with Gdn Samuel COMPHER: beginning 31 Dec 1856; payment from Wm. COMPHER's Admr, leaving $582.36. S/A of Jonas C. COMPHER with Gdn Samuel COMPHER: beginning 31 Dec 1856; as above, paid tuition, leaving $569.14. S/A of Sarah C. COMPHER with Gdn Samuel COMPHER: beginning 31 Dec 1856; as above, leaving $587.36. S/A of Ann E. COMPHER with Gdn Henry S. WILLIAMS: beginning 31 Dec 1856; as above, leaving $587.36. S/A of Marietta COMPHER with Gdn Henry S. WILLIAMS: beginning 31 Dec 1856; as above, leaving $587.36. S/A of William F. COMPHER with Gdn Henry S. WILLIAMS: beginning 31 Dec 1856; as above, leaving $587.36. RtCt 14 Oct 1858. [D:336]

S/A with Guardians Samuel COMPHER and H. S. WILLIAMS: income from sale of crops. S/A of J. H. W. COMPHER with Gdn Samuel COMPHER: general expenses, leaving $610.12. S/A of Jonas C. COMPHER with Gdn Samuel COMPHER: beginning 18 Jun 1858; paid board and tuition, leaving $544.19. S/A of Sarah C. COMPHER with Gdn Samuel COMPHER: general expenses, leaving $642.16. RtCt 13 Aug 1859. [D:419]

S/A of Ann E., Marietta & William F. COMPHER with Gdn H. S. WILLIAMS: beginning 10 Feb 1859; general expenses leaving $642.16 each. RtCt 30 Jun 1859. [D:420]

S/A with Henry S. WILLIAMS: beginning 1 Jun 1858; proceeds from crops and division of land, paid tuition, leaving Wm. F. $740.09, Henrietta $836.13 (hereafter called Marietta) and leaving Ann E. COMPHER $788.52 (now Ann E. TRITTIPOE) the wife of G. C. TRITTIPOE. RtCt 13 Feb 1866. [E:210]

S/A of William F. COMPHER with Gdn Henry S. WILLIAMS: beginning 8 Sep 1862; paid tuition, leaving $864.12. RtCt 13 Feb 1866. [E:213]

S/A of William F. COMPHER with Gdn James M. DOWNEY: beginning 12 Feb 1866; paid tuition, leaving $542.13. RtCt 12 Oct 1869. [E:494]

S/A of William F. COMPHER with Gdn James M. DOWNEY: beginning 21 Jul 1869; general expenses leaving $280. RtCt 13 Jan 1873. [F:273]

S/A of Ann E. COMPHER with Gdn Henry S. WILLIAMS: receipt of $487.59 by husband George C. TRITAPOE. RtCt 12 May 1873. [F: 325]

S/A Jonas Curtis COMPHER with Gdn Samuel COMPHER: beginning 5 Mar 1862; payment from estate of aunt Mary COMPHER, general expenses, leaving $564. Sureties Sydnah WILLIAMS & Samuel FRY are both dead. RtCt 9 Jun 1873. [F:329]

S/A of Sarah C., Jonas Curtis and John H. W. COMPHER with Gdn Samuel COMPHER: beginning 10 Feb 1859; paid tuition, leaving Sarah C. $866.95 and Jonas Curtis COMPHER $672.16. John H. W. COMPHER due $402.18 on 23 Aug 1859 when he reached twenty one years of age. H. S. WILLIAMS Gdn of the other three children of William COMPHER was the general agent of them all, and at the end of each year turned over to the parties the amount due by him. One of the sureties Syddnah WILLIAMS is dead and probably insolvent and Samuel FRY the other seems from the assessors book to be worth $4000 to $5000. RtCt 9 Apr 1867. [E:325]

COE, Aurelius
S/A with Gdn James R. SIMPSON: paid his expenses west, cash paid ward's mother his share of compromise money in the division of estate, cash rec'd from Henderson COE Exor of Robert COE dec'd, leaving $1963.50 paid in full as was is now 21y old. RtCt 14 Oct 1858. [D:339]

McNULTY, William T.
S/A with Gdn Henry T. GOVER: beginning 26 Sep 1856; paid mother for board, rec'd payment from Wm. B. STEER Admr. of Hugh McNULTY dec'd being wards share of father's personal estate, leaving $1349.38. RtCt 14 Oct 1858. [D:350]

S/A with Gdn Henry T. GOVER: beginning Oct 1857; paid mother Mary McNULTY for board, leaving $1349.38 and a balance due him on the profits of $94.78. Before any Gdn had been appointed his mother had boarded and clothed him for three years for the sum of $205 and on 15 Jul 1857 there was a balance due to her of $108.79. RtCt 12 Jan 1859. [D:373]

S/A with Gdn Henry T. GOVER: beginning 28 Feb 1859; paid tuition, leaving $1254.60. RtCt 15 Mar 1860. [E:32]

S/A with Gdn Henry T. GOVER: paid tuition and Mary McNULTY board & clothing; leaving $1221.28. The ward is old enough to support himself. RtCt 10 Sep 1867. [E:369]

S/A with Gdn Henry T. GOVER: beginning 12 May 1866; paid Mary T. McNULTY board & clothing, paid tuition in Wilmington Del., leaving $941.56. The principal of his ward's estate has been diminished $280.00 by his being sent from house to a boarding school in Wilmington Delaware upon his own motion and the advice of discreet friends. RtCt 10 Sep 1867. [E:372]

S/A with Gdn Henry T. GOVER: beginning 15 May 1867; paid traveling expenses to & from school and Mary McNULTY for board, leaving $600. His estate has been reduced $341.36 during the year in his education which has been done at the instance of the ward & his friends. RtCt 12 Apr 1869. [E:477]

S/A with Gdn Henry T. GOVER: beginning Jul 1868; paid board in Philadelphia while studying law, general expenses, leaving $255.48. RtCt 12 Apr 1870. [F:50]

S/A with Henry T. GOVER: receipt of $37.43 acct paid in full as William is now of age. RtCt 19 Nov 1870. [F:68]

MAGILL, Thomas H. M. and Annie E. T.
S/A with Gdn N. Carroll MASON: beginning Jun 1849; paid board and tuition, 1 Sep 1856 amt. of 7 bonds drawn by Wm. T. T. MASON in favor of H. D. MAGILL dec'd rec'd of Wm. H. GRAY his Admr, income from hire of Negro Susan, leaving $21.35. This is the first and only S/A made by the Gdn though he qualified 12 Jun 1848. It will appear by reference to the foregoing statement that the Gdn received but little of his wards estate prior to 1 Sep 1856. At which time a partial S/A took place between him and the Admr. of the said decedent. At that time the said Admr. passed to the said Gdn seven separate bonds drawn by Wm. T. T. MASON in favor of the said Henry D. MAGILL in part of the said wards estate amounting in the aggregate of principal to the sum of $21.35 together with the interest due thereon amounting to $1344.63. The amt of the bonds is retained by the Gdn as principal in his hands due to the wards, the interest on which & other estate received by him from the Admr. has been applied to their support, education &c. These children were taken under the tender care and

keeping of their Grandfather Wm. T. T. MASON from the death of their father to the present time, some 10 years. It will be seen by reference to the foregoing acct. that he raised a very moderate acct. against his grand children embracing almost entirely their support, clothing, education &c, which the Gdn has paid his receipts exhibited. RtCt 14 Oct 1858. [D:352]

McFARLAND, Alice S., Maurice W. and William T. (Children of Jonathan F.)

S/A of Alice S., Maurice W. and William T. McFARLAND with Gdn William T. McFARLAND: beginning 12 May 1856, paid board, 1 May 1857 payment from James H. GULICK for land and from C. W. TURLEY on land, leaving $694.41. RtCt 14 Oct 1858. [D:352]

S/A with Gdn William T. McFARLAND: beginning 8 Jun 1858; paid Mrs. Alcinda McFARLAND the sum decreed her as cummulation of dower, paid A. S. McFARLAND widow of J. F. McFARLAND & mother of infants to board, leaving $1050.02. The reason of the different dates just states is that certain property (real estate) was sold under a decree of the Circuit Court of this County and out of the cash payment due on the confirmation a sum in gross in lieu of dower was paid to Alcinda S. McFARLAND and the remainder of the purchase money in the shape of bonds and cash was ordered to be held by the Gdn. RtCt 13 Jun 1861. [E:187]

S/A of Alice McFARLAND and Maurice McFARLAND with Gdn William T. McFARLAND: beginning 12 May 1860; paid Alcinda McFARLAND the mother for board and clothing, amt. paid Jos. McFARLAND to Alcinda McFARLAND, rec'd payment from Jos. McFARLAND Admr. of Elizabeth McFARLAND. 24 Jan 1866 - They have been living with their mother until her death which took place recently. I think their circumstances require a larger expenditure of money than the income of their estate and I respectfully recommend that the Gdn be allowed to expend fifty dollars a year each for three years in their education. RtCt 17 Aug 1866. [E:307]

S/A with Gdn W. T. McFARLAND: beginning 12 May 1865; paid tuition, leaving Alice S. $394.44, Maurice W. $397.55 and W. F. McFARLAND $406.10. RtCt Oct 1868. [E:422]

S/A of Alice, William F. & Morris W. with Gdn Wm. T. McFARLAND: beginning 10 Apr 1868; general expenses leaving Alice S. $290.56, Morris W. $393.60 & Wm. F. $406.58 (reached 21 on 23 Aug 1873.) RtCt 12 Jan 1874. [F:371]

ORAM, Enos and Lucinda Jane (Children of Henry)

S/A of Enos ORAM with Committee Henson ELLIOT: beginning 14 Apr 1847; general expenses leaving $35.66 up to 14 Apr 1848 (when he died). S/A of Lucinda Jane ORAM with Gdn Henson ELLIOT: beginning 14 Apr 1846; paid tuition, leaving $394.17 (up to 11 Apr 1855 when ward became of age). It will be seen by reference that 1/10 of the annual rent of the farm has been reserved by the Gdn and amts. to $45.00 this amt. is due to Amanda ORAM who is a pretermitted child of Henry ORAM the deceased father and is due to her from the said Gdn on the said 14 Apr 1855. RtCt 14 Oct 1858. [D:355]

SKINNER, Heirs of Gabriel

S/A with Gdn James SKINNER: income from hire of Negroes Flora and Lucy Ann. S/A of Bettie J. SKINNER with Gdn James SKINNER: beginning 8 Mar 1851; paid tuition, leaving $508.27. S/A of Sarah DEAN with Gdn James SKINNER, as above, leaving $9.88. S/A of Dennis McCARTY with Gdn James SKINNER: as above, leaving $3.81. S/A of Joseph AMOS & wife with Gdn James SKINNER: as above, leaving $40.08. S/A of Benjamin F. SKINNER with Gdn James SKINNER: as above, leaving $54.31. S/A of Elizabeth SKINNER (widow) with James SKINNER Admr: beginning 24 Feb 1851; general expenses, leaving $284.54. There are two other distributees, namely Nathaniel J. SKINNER and Henry W. SKINNER whose accts. were closed under their written authority as will be shown by my report of August 1851. Having ascertained the balances due to and from the Administrator and Gdn at his request, a return of my report is withheld, until he can have an opportunity of settling those balances the distributees being all now of age. RtCt 14 Apr 1858. [D:361]

SULLIVAN, Mary F., Samuel M. and Anna Bell (Children of Samuel by Rubanion TILLETT)

S/A of Mary F. TILLETT, Samuel M. TILLETT, and Anna Bell TILLETT with Gdn Henrietta TILLETT: 12 May 1856 rec'd payment from F. LITTLETON Shff & Committee Admr. of Samuel SULLIVAN dec'd by A. H. ROGERS, cash from F. W. SHAFFER trustee for Samuel SULLIVAN, board, leaving Mary F. TILLETT $93.51, Saml. M. TILLETT $10.54 and Anna B. TILLETT $14.85. These children are entitled to the annual rent of a house and lot in the Town of Leesburg, conveyed by Samuel SULLIVAN to F. W. SHAFFER as his trustee for their benefit. The said trustee has settled his acct. to 12 May 1856, the bal. then due from him was paid over to the Gdn and is credited to the children is in fact in the hands of the said trustee who is the security of the said Gdn who has recently married & her powers as such consequently annulled. RtCt 14 Oct 1858. [D:368]

S/A of Samuel M. SULLIVAN with Gdn Eleanor GULLATT: beginning 12 Dec 1857; $296 distributed to sisters Mary F. POWER, Anna Belle SULLIVAN, Henrietta WRIGHT (sister of half blood) & Giles E. TILLET (brother of half blood.) Samuel died Aug 1864. He was a minor and estate survived by the will of his father to his two sisters and John E. WRIGHT & Giles E. TILLET. RtCt 13 Feb 1871. [F:111]

S/A of Anna Belle SULLIVAN with Gdn Eleanor GULLATT: beginning 12 Nov 1870; general expenses $42.08 due to Gdn but not claimed. RtCt 12 Apr 1875. [F:444]

WORSLEY, Elizabeth, Thomas L. and Ann Edwards

S/A with Gdn Mrs. Virginia G. WORSLEY: beginning 15 Aug 1856; paid fee bills of Presley SAUNDERS, leaving $232.52. The rent was fixed by David SHAWEN at $225 which was $25 more than any one else would say it was worth. I have allowed $100 each for board, tuition and clothing which I think moderate. Her bond is in a penalty of five thousand dollars, but the funds in her hands as be decree of the Court in WORSLEY vs WORSLEY will be about $7000 which would require a bond of $14000. The money however is not yet collect, and will not be for about two years. RtCt 14 Oct 1858. [D:370]

DOWELL, Virginia E. and Laura

Inventory of what belongs to Virginia E. and Laura DOWELL with Gdn Sanford J. RAMEY: $847.77. RtCt 8 Dec 1858. [D:371]

S/A with Gdn Sanford J. RAMEY: rec'd payment from C. R. DOWELL's Execs., leaving $851. RtCt [Aug 1860?] [E:115]

WOOD, Joseph (a lunatic)

Appraisal/Inventory: one bond, one desk, and one trunk totaling $1934.00. Scrs: Joseph TAYLOR, Stephen GREGG, E. R. PURCELL. RtCt 10 Dec 1858. [D:371]

S/A with Committee Asa M. JANNEY: beginning 14 Aug 1858; paid six months board while sane, paid two years board, washing, &c since his insanity, other general expenses, leaving $117.39. It would seem that the interest on the funds belonging to him will not pay his expenses, and that every day his estate is becoming less. RtCt 15 Mar 1860. [E:50]

S/A with Committee Asa M. JANNEY: beginning 14 Aug 1859; paid Josiah WOOD for expenses in conveying Joseph to Philadelphia and in the city for medical advice and attention, leaving $167.51. RtCt 13 Jun 1861. [E:191]

S/A with Committee Asa M. JANNEY: beginning 14 Aug 1860; paid board and store accts., leaving $297.52 due to Committee. RtCt 13 Feb 1866. [E:264]

S/A with Committee Asa M. JANNEY: beginning 14 Aug 1865; general expenses leaving $225.75. RtCt 9 Apr 1867. [E:349]

S/A with Committee Asa M. JANNEY: beginning 14 Aug 1866; general expenses leaving $2150.03 due to Committee. RtCt 15 Jun 1868. [E:405]

S/A with Committee Asa M. JANNEY: beginning 14 Aug 1867; general expenses leaving $322.85 due to Committee, income is not sufficient for support. RtCt 19 Nov 1867. [F:72]

S/A with Committee Asa M. JANNEY: beginning 12 Aug 1869; general expenses leaving $441.86 due to Committee. RtCt 12 Apr 1871. [F:134]

S/A with Committee Asa M. JANNEY: beginning 14 Aug 1870; general expenses and income leaving $344.18 due to Committee. RtCt 12 Aug 1872. [F:246]

S/A with Committee Asa M. JANNEY: beginning 14 Aug 1871; general expenses and income leaving $381.77. RtCt 14 Oct 1872. [F:253]

S/A with Committee Asa M. JANNEY: beginning 14 Aug 1872; paid brother Josiah WOOD for board, leaving $489.03. RtCt 9 Feb 1875. [F:435]

S/A with Committee Asa M. JANNEY: beginning 15 Aug 1874; general expenses leaving $1092.98. RtCt 8 Nov 1875. [F:496]

S/A with Committee Asa M. JANNEY: beginning 15 Aug 1877; general expenses leaving $835.08. RtCt 12 Jan 1880. [G:208]

S/A with Committee Asa M. JANNEY: beginning 15 Aug 1878; general expenses leaving $639.93. RtCt 14 Dec 1880. [G:255]

S/A with Committee Asa M. JANNEY: 14 Aug 1880; general expenses leaving $526.05. RtCt 9 Jan 1882. [G:303]

S/A with Committee Asa M. JANNEY: beginning 1881; general expenses leaving $569.61. RtCt 9 Jan 1883. [G:356]

S/A with Committee A. M. JANNEY: beginning 15 Aug 1882; general expenses leaving $24.76. RtCt 14 Oct 1885. [G:489]

NUTT, George Whitfield

S/A with Gdn Cuthbert B. ROGERS: beginning 11 Jul 1857; income from interest on notes, general expenses, leaving $237.91. RtCt 12 Jan 1859. [D:374]

S/A with Gdn Cuthbert B. ROGERS: beginning 4 Dec 1858; paid tuition, leaving $223.59. RtCt 15 Mar 1860. [E:33]

S/A with Gdn C. B. ROGERS: beginning 11 Jul 1859; general expenses leaving $220.00 paid in full. RtCt 4 Mar 1861. [E:125]

ROWLES, Edmund J. (a lunatic)

S/A with Committee Robert JOHNSON: beginning 1839; general expenses, 7 Jun 1853 rec'd payment from T. ROGERS, receiver for Edmund JENNINGS' estate, leaving $367.16. An order for settlement was obtained on 13 Sep when, as the acct. will show, the committee was in advance of the assets which had come into his hands, and whilst a suit was in progress against Amos Janney which was not made available until Oct 1854. RtCt 12 Jan 1859. [D:375]

JEFFRIES, Mary Francis and Joseph O. (Children of B. B. and Tacey)

Inventory 11 Jan 1859 of the estate of Mary Francis & Joseph O. JEFFRIES and the other children by Gdn: one house and lot in Leesburg, occupied by Thos. LITTLETON as a shop. Nine acres of land near Dover. RtCt 12 Jan 1859. [D:382]

BEDINGER, George R.

S/A with Gdn Henry T. HARRISON: 5 Jul 1858 sent check for expenses to N. Y., 6 Oct 1858 check to self at University of Va, leaving $940.73. Also four [bonds], three of Virginia & one of Missouri into which the principal of the estate has been converted. The expenses have largely exceeded the income this year because the estate of the ward has not come into the Guardian's hands, but they are not greater than were absolutely necessary for the education and other indispensable expenses of the ward. I think the investment in state bonds was a judicious one. RtCt 14 Apr 1858. [D:389]

S/A with Gdn Henry T. HARRISON: beginning 7 Feb 1859; paid expenses at Uni. of Va. and various store accts. The Gdn has invested all the money received for his ward in State Bonds with the exception of $106.52. The ward has expended more than his income by the sum of $489.53. I am very reluctant to all the charges and have informed the Gdn that his ward must be limited to the income of his estate as the very furthest point to which I can go. The ward is at the University of Virginia probably an expensive school, but I judge that he does not take care of his funds. RtCt 14 Aug 1860. [E:67]

S/A with Gdn Henry T. HARRISON: beginning 11 Jan 1860; as above, 1 Jan 1861 ½ medical bill of Negro Mary, one half of Negroes Jack, Mary, Daniel & Jacob. Due to the ward $81.67. He has not come up to his income this year by nearly $465.00 and the Gdn now starts with him out of debt and with a sufficient income for all reasonable wants. RtCt 13 Jun 1861. [E:140]

S/A with Gdn Henry T. HARRISON: beginning 14 Feb 1861; payment from A. T. M. RUST Exor of G. RUST, paid for maintenance of Negro Mary while sick, no balance in the hands of said Gdn or agent except a bond of J. P. SMART & Co. for $1350.00 an investment made in May 1861. RtCt 10 Sep 1867. [E:352]

BEDINGER, Virginia

S/A with Gdn Henry T. HARRISON: beginning 11 Jan 1858; 5 Jul 1858 paid expenses in N. Y., 3 Nov 1858 paid A. T. STEWART one set of furs, cash sent to you from Philadelphia, 2 Dec 1858 check to you at Shepherdstown, leaving $856.57. Also four Virginia State bonds in which the money paid to him for them has been judiciously invested, and which at par amount to $4000. The expenditures of the ward have far exceeded this years income, but they have been necessary, the ward being a young lady finishing her education, and but a part of her funds having yet come into the Guardian's hands. RtCt 14 Apr 1859. [D:390]

S/A with Gdn Henry T. HARRISON: investment of 3 Va. coupon bonds, paid T. LITTLETON for packing furniture for Mo. bond per contra; rec'd payment from Geo. RUST's Execs; income from hires of Negroes Daniel, Jack, Mary and Jacob and from int on 9 state bonds, actual expenses of $739.73 and her income will be about $864. Her expenses will be less for the future, as she will soon stop going to school, and they cannot well be curtailed while she is at school. She has exceeded her income $220.75 and there is due to the Gdn by her $195.91. RtCt 14 Aug 1860. [E:65]

S/A with Gdn Henry T. HARRISON: beginning 11 Jan 1860; cash sent you in Baltimore, leaving $149.30. RtCt 13 Jun 1861. [E:139]

S/A with Gdn Henry T. HARRISON: beginning 15 Feb 1861; as above, leaving $29.97. RtCt 10 Sep 1867. [E:355]

CLARKE, Archie M., Elizabeth J., Mollie A. and Isaac V. (Heirs of A. H.)

S/A with Gdn Mary CLARKE: beginning Dec 1854; income from sale of cattle and harvest, profits of both farms: paid the widows dower share, the remaining 2/3, the share of each legatee, 4 in no. S/A of Archie M. CLARKE with Gdn Mary CLARKE: beginning 1854; paid tuition, Oct 1856 cash given to ward to go to Baltimore looking for a situation, long list of sundry business accts. paid, leaving $1405.99. S/A of Elizabeth J. CLARKE (now Elizabeth J. SLAYMAKER) with Gdn Mary CLARKE: paid music and tuition, paid business accts, leaving $1406.11. S/A of Mollie A. CLARKE with Gdn Mary CLARKE: as above, leaving $1436.46. S/A of Isaac V. CLARKE with Gdn Mary CLARKE: paid tuition and long list of sundry business accts. paid, leaving $1705.49. Proceeds of the two farms, charged the estate with the cash actually paid out by her in carrying on the farms and credited all the money rec'd by her (during the same period) for produce &c sold taking no account of the seed or of such as was used in the support of the family. She and all her children living in common, no interest account has been raised on balance due from or to her but continued from the beginning to the end without making an annual vest. The Gdn charges no commission nor does she make any charge for the support of her children wards. RtCt 14 Apr 1859. [D:391]

CONARD, Joseph E.

S/A with Gdn Abner CONARD: 4 Nov 1857 rec'd payment from Emanuel AXLINE, leaving $1611.61 on 1 Jul 1858. The ward being now 17 years old, the amt. of his estate at his majority including the land, will not exceed $2800. RtCt 14 Apr 1859. [D:398]

S/A with Gdn Abner CONARD: beginning 16 Nov 1858; payment from Emanuel AXLINE and David AXLINE, leaving $1695.42. RtCt 14 Aug 1860. [E:70]

S/A with Gdn Abner CONARD: beginning Feb 1860; general expenses leaving $1826.02. RtCt 13 Jun 1861. [E:185]

S/A with Gdn Abner CONARD: beginning 12 Oct 1860; income from sale of crops leaving $2099.48. RtCt 10 Sep 1867. [E:358]

MINOR, Benjamin W.
S/A with Gdn Daniel SHREVE: paid tuition and for items for Negro Henrietta, income from hire of Negroes Bet & Jane, leaving $30.13. The security in the Gdn's bond (Charles SHREVE) is dead. RtCt 14 Apr 1859. [D:402]

S/A with Gdn Daniel SHREVE: beginning Dec 1856; paid tuition, income from hire of Negroes Jane, Betty and Henrietta, leaving $62.12. RtCt 14 Apr 1858. [D:404]

S/A with Gdn Daniel SHREVE: beginning 6 Feb 1859; paid tuition, income from hire of Negroes Betsey, Jane & Henrietta, leaving $251.45. RtCt 14 Aug 1860. [E:86]

VIRTS, Heirs of Michael
S/A with Gdn Wm. GRAHAM: beginning 1857; general expenses leaving $1503.06. RtCt 14 Apr 1859. [D:410]

FRY, Marietta C. E. C. and O. J. C. C.
S/A with Gdn David E. FRY: beginning 9 Nov 1857; general expenses, leaving $185. S/A of Marietta C. E. C. FRY with Gdn David E. FRY: paid medical bill and general expenses, leaving $92.50. S/A of O. J. C. C. FRY with Gdn David E. FRY: had no listed expenses. RtCt 18 Jun 1859. [D:412]

BOND, Thomas D.
S/A with Gdn William H. SCHOOLEY: beginning 18 Feb 1858; income from sale of Watt farm. Account is to 18 Feb 1859 at which time his ward was of age, and find a balance due to the ward of $6.29 but this should be retained to meet fee bills for recording accts. RtCt 13 Aug 1859. [D:417]

MOFFETT, Louisa (a lunatic)
S/A with Committee M. C. KLEIN: 11 Jan 1858 paid for tombstone for her son's grave in the April 1857, paid L. asylum at Mt. Hope, taxes on land in Iowa, and board, income from her squatter claim on land in Iowa, leaving $436.43. RtCt 13 Aug 1859. [E:3]

S/A with Committee M. C. KLEIN: beginning 16 Mar 1859; paid Mt. Hope lunatic asylum, taxes in Iowa, and board, leaving $218.75. The estate consists of an annuity of $250.00 which is devoted necessarily to her support. RtCt 13 Jun 1861. [E:189]

EWERS, Laura C. and James Isaac
S/A of Laura C. EWERS with Gdn Franklin EWERS: beginning 14 Aug 1856; general expenses leaving $24.69. S/A of James Isaac EWERS with Gdn Franklin EWERS: beginning 14 Aug 1856; general expenses leaving $24.69. RtCt 15 Mar 1860. [E:25]

OVERFIELD, Jessie
S/A with Gdn H. H. GREGG: beginning 9 Jul 1856; amt. rec'd from Admr. of Richard OSBURN Sr, paid board, leaving $942.08. RtCt 15 Mar 1860. [E:34]

S/A with Gdn Henry H. GREGG: beginning 9 Jul 1860; paid board and clothing; statement to 22 Jun 1865 the day of her death and report a balance due to her administration at that time of $940.00 with interest till paid. RtCt 12 Dec 1866. [E:321]

OVERFIELD, Richard
S/A with Gdn Henry H. GREGG: beginning 9 Jul 1856; rec'd payment from Exor of R. OSBURN Sr., paid board and medical bills, paid for coffin and tombstones, until 10 Sep 1858 when he died leaving $767.71. This I suppose is to be distributed according to the laws of the child's domicile wherever that may have been. He was removed to Ohio by his father, who now resides in some Southern State. It will be perceived that during the last year the ward's estate decreased considerably. RtCt 15 Mar 1860. [E:35]

JEFFRIES, Joseph D., Ann C., Mary T., Martha J. and Hannah (Children of B. B.)
Inventory of the property belonging to Joseph D. JEFFRIES & others by Gdn John T. LYNN: one house and lot in the Town of Leesburg, 9 acres of land near Dover. RtCt 13 Feb 1860. [E:51]

S/A with Gdn John T. LYNN: general provisions. S/A of Mary T. JEFFRIES with Gdn John T. LYNN: general expenses leaving $41.70 due to Gdn. S/A of Joseph D. JEFFRIES with Gdn John T. LYNN: beginning 11 Jan 1860; paid B. B. JEFFRIES board & clothing; amt due Jos. D. JEFFRIES and descending to his father B. B. JEFFRIES; at time of his death on 17 Sep 1862 $3.28 due him (which belongs to B. B. JEFFRIES his father as his distributee.) First acct is general one of Mary T. JEFFRIES with the five children. RtCt 20 Aug 1866. [E:288]

S/A of Ann C. JEFFRIES with Gdn John T. LYNN: 11 Jan 1860 general payment from acct. of M. T. JEFFRIES accompanying this acct.; amt. due Ann C. JEFFRIES, due Martha J. JEFFRIES, and due Hannah V. JEFFRIES; with $1.77 due to each ward. RtCt 20 Aug 1866. [E:290]

S/A of Mary T. JEFFRIES with Gdn John T. LYNN: beginning 11 Jan 1863; general expenses leaving $3.53. RtCt 20 Aug 1866.

S/A of Ann C. JEFFRIES with Gdn John T. LYNN: beginning 11 Jan 1863; general expenses leaving $6.96. There was also due at the same date to Martha J. JEFFRIES and to Hannah V. JEFFRIES each $6.96 the transactions being precisely the same for each one of them. RtCt 20 Aug 1866. [E:292]

S/A of Mary T. JEFFRIES: 18 May 1867 paid in full. RtCt Oct 1868. [E:292]

S/A of Hannah JEFFRIES with Gdn John T. LYNN: beginning 11 Jan 1865; income from sale in the case of JEFFRIES vs JEFFRIES and from rent of land in Aldie; leaving $95.67. S/A of Martha J. JEFFRIES with Gdn John T. LYNN: beginning 11 Jan 1865; as above, leaving $102.87. The Guardianship of Ann C. JEFFRIES terminated by her marriage on 26 Nov 1866 and the amount due her has been paid by him to her husband. RtCt Oct 1868. [E:416]

CRIM, John

Sale of 11 Nov 1856 by Committees Wm. & S. CRIM: Purchasers were [long inventory totaling $836.36 ¼]: Wm. CRIM, Henry GAVER, N. B. PEACOCK, C. F. CRIM, H. EVERHART, Peter COMPHER, U. BEANS, R. TAVENNER, Samuel CRIM, John FILLER, Landon MERCHANT, Lewis TORRISON, George PRESTON, Benjamin LESLIE, Jos. P. GRUBB, S. C. E. RAMSEY, A. McDANIEL, H. W. HARDY, Thomas McARTOR, Jos. WIGHTMAN, Samuel CLENDENING, Armistead SCOTT, Jas. CARROLL, Aaron SCATTERDAY, Hugh THOMPSON, John SEXTON, Burr W. HAMILTON, Richard HOOE, Thomas W. WHITE, Ran'd WHITE, Thomas JAMES. Appraisal: household items totaling $10.54. RtCt 13 Apr 1860. [E:52]

S/A with Committees William & Saml. CRIM: beginning 14 Jul 1857; income from hire of Negroes Jordan & George, paid various accts. & notes, paid board; leaving $499.24 due to Committee as of date of his death on 25 Dec 1863. RtCt 10 Sep 1867. [E:74]

S/A with Committees Wm. CRIM & Saml. CRIM: paid expenses to Charlestown, paid W. CRIM for board, R. TAVENNER for support of child, and S. CRIM for support and attention, leaving due to Guardians $40.67. RtCt 14 Aug 1860. [E:359]

RAWLINGS, Mrs. Lucinda

Appraisal/Inventory of 18 Jun 1860 of estate in the hands of Committee Andrew ROBEY: household items, numerous bonds, house and lot in Middleburg and out lot adjoining the said town (40 acres), totaling $30315.05; a Negro man named Frank now hired to Samuel HEFFLEBOWER in Alexandria Va. & a horse & carriage. Aprs: R. S. CHINN, John M. MORAN, S. A. CHANCELLOR. RtCt 26 Jun 1860. [E:60]

S/A with Committee Andrew ROBEY: beginning 10 Jun 1860; paid many store accts.. int of notes (very long acct.) and board. On___ 186- the said Lucinda RAWLINGS departed this life and on 13 Feb 1865 administration on her estate was granted by the County Court of Rappahannock to the said Andrew ROBEY late her committee. Transferred certain securities amounting to $5562.00 from ROBEY's acct. as committee to his acct. as Admr. Balance of $706.18 as of 13 Feb 1865. RtCt 13 Nov 1867. [E:384]

Final settlement of 30 Dec 1867: bond for $1400.72 for full payment. RtCt 12 Mar 1868. [E:391]

FRAZIER, Thomas J., Catharine America, William C., Mary Jane, Margaret and Samuel H. (Heirs of Samuel H.)

S/A with Mary A. FRAZIER: paid for repairs of Spring house, paid M. A. FRAZIER widow 1/3, shares to M. E. FRAZIER, W. C. FRAZIER, M. J. FRAZIER, E. J. FRAZIER, C. A. FRAZIER, income from hire of Negroes Maria, Kitty, John, George, Ann & Milton. S/A of William C. FRAZIER with Gdn Mary A. FRAZIER: beginning 9 Mar 1857; general expenses, leaving $324.47. S/A of Maria J. FRAZIER with Gdn Mary A. FRAZIER: paid tuition, leaving $218.50. S/A of Thomas J. FRAZIER with Gdn Mary A. FRAZIER: paid tuition, leaving $219.32. S/A of Catharine America FRAZIER with Gdn Mary A. FRAZIER: paid board, leaving $234.42. $40.62 due to S. H. FRAZIER and $40.62 to Margaret E. FRAZIER, who are both of age. Similar sums were due to each of the minor children which are transferred to their Gdn accts. To produce this result I have charged the board of some little servants to the general fund (its amt. being $147.30) and then allowed the widow one third of the balance due the estate and the children each one ninth. RtCt 14 Aug 1860. [E:79]

S/A with Gdn Mary A. FRAZIER: income from hire of Negroes John Wesley, George Henry, Kitty, Milton, Maria, and Ann, income from rent of house in Petersville Md, from sale of crops, and from hires of Maria Charity & Joseph. S/A of Wm. C. FRAZIER with Gdn Mary A. FRAZIER: paid tuition and various store accts. S/A of Maria Jane FRAZIER with Gdn Mary A. FRAZIER: paid board, tuition, and various store accts. S/A of Thomas J. FRAZIER with Gdn Mary A. FRAZIER: paid tuition. S/A of Catharine America FRAZIER with Gdn Mary A. FRAZIER: paid tuition. [the above was a long accounting] 24 Nov 1865. The widow of Samuel H. FRAZIER is the Gdn of the children and has managed the farm with singularly good judgment through out the war, and has made it almost as profitable as it was in time of peace. I have stated in acct. no. 1 her said transactions allowing her 1/3 of the net proceed and passing 1/6 of the remaining two thirds to each of the six children, namely Samuel H. FRAZIER who is of age, Margaret who is of age and married, William C., Maria J., Thomas J., and Catharine A. FRAZIER for whom she is Gdn. W. C. FRAZIER reached majority on 13 May 1865 and due $403.15. Acct. no. 4 shows the transactions as Gdn of Maria Jane FRAZIER to 9 Mar 1865 at which time there was due to her the sum of $85.87. It will be perceived that her estate has been diminished $155.73 besides using all the income, she was part of the time boarding away from home going to school and her expenses seem to be entirely reasonable, the board having been fixed by two neighbors of good judgment as was the case also with the hires of the Negroes. Acct. no. 5 shows the transactions as Gdn of

Thomas J. FRAZIER and shows a balance due to him on 9 Mar 1865 of $266.12 an increase of $55.17. Acct. no. 6 shows the transactions as Gdn of Catharine America FRAZIER to the same date and that her estate has been diminished by expenses very unusual and unavoidable in clothing in consequences of the circumstances of the country, and for board and tuition while at school $78.69 and there is due to her $157.05. RtCt 13 Feb 1866. [E:145]

S/A with agent and Gdn Mary A. FRAZIER: beginning 10 Mar 1866; income from rent of property in Petersville Maryland and sale of crops. S/A of Thomas J. FRAZIER with Gdn Mary A. FRAZIER: beginning 10 Mar 1865; paid board and tuition. S/A of Mary Jane FRAZIER with Gdn Mary A. FRAZIER: beginning 10 Mar 1865; paid for clothing. S/A of Catharine FRAZIER with Gdn Mary A. FRAZIER: beginning 10 Mar 1865; paid board. Statement to 10 Mar 1867. On the general acct. she is indebted to those who are of age or married in the sum of $34.82 each and to the others to whom she is Gdn in the sum of $34.83 each. I have further stated her acct. as Gdn of Thomas J. FRAZIER to 10 Mar 1867 and find that he is indebted to her in the sum of $28.51, she having expended $83.68 more than his income in his education. I think it ought to be allowed as she is the mother and not acting for her own aggrandizement but for the welfare of her son. He has an interest of one sixth in a farm of [blank] acres in the German Settlement assessed at $10325. It is manifestly proper therefore that an education is advisable, if not indispensible. I have also settled her acct. as Gdn of Mary Jane FRAZIER to the same time and find a balance due to the ward of $81.69 which shows a loss of capital in the years of $4.18 and this only for clothing not charge being made for board. I have settled her acct. as Gdn of Catharine FRAZIER to the same time and find due to the Gdn the sum of $13.19 she having expended the income and $170.26 of principal in her education and clothing, no charge having been made for board. I think this ought to be allowed for the reasons stated above with regards to Thomas J. FRAZIER. James W. RUST, one of the sureties is dead. RtCt 12 Apr 1869. [E:218]

S/A with agent and Gdn Mary A. FRAZIER: beginning 13 Apr 1867; income from sale of crops and rent of Maryland house. S/A of Thomas J. FRAZIER, Mary J. FRAZIER, and Catharine A. FRAZIER with Gdn Mary A. FRAZIER: beginning 10 Mary 1867; finds due to each of the children the sum of $90.77. I have stated their separate accts. to the same date, and find due to Thomas J. FRAZIER $31.33, to Mary Jane FRAZIER $134.23 and to Catharine A. FRAZIER $62.25. RtCt 12 Apr 1867. [E:457]

S/A with Gdn Mary A. FRAZIER: beginning 10 Jun 1859; income from hire of Negroes John, George, Kitty, and Maria. S/A of William C. FRAZIER with Gdn Mary A. FRAZIER: beginning 1 Apr 1859; paid store accts, leaving $390.76. S/A of Maria J. FRAZIER with Gdn Mary A. FRAZIER: paid self board not allowed in last acct. and tuition, leaving $241.60. S/A of Thomas J. FRAZIER with Gdn Mary A. FRAZIER: beginning 1 Apr 1859; paid store accts, general expenses causing principal has been diminished $7.77. He goes to school, and boards with his mother, who with an elder brother farms the lands paying hire for the Negroes and a rent of two fifths for the land they being undivided. S/A of Catharine A. FRAZIER with Gdn Mary A. FRAZIER: beginning 1 Oct 1859; paid store accts, leaving $235.74 RtCt 13 Jun 1861. [E:460]

S/A with agent & Gdn Mary A. FRAZIER: beginning 10 May 1869; distributions to widow, W. C. FRAZIER, S. H. FRAZIER, Margaret, Mary, Catharine FRAZIER & Thomas J. FRAZIER. RtCt 13 Dec 1870. [F:78]

S/A with Gdn Mary A. FRAZIER: beginning 10 Mar 1870; general expenses leaving Catharine A. FRAZIER $172.31. RtCt 12 Jun 1871. [F:138]

S/A with Gdn Mary A. FRAZIER: general expenses leaving Catharine A. FRAZIER $172.31. [very faint on microfilm] RtCt 16 Mar 1872. [F:212]

S/A with Mrs. Mary A. FRAZIER: receipt of A. A. WENNER and C. A. WENNER late FRAZIER for full acct. S/A. RtCt 9 Feb 1875. [F:430]

GREGG, Mary Virginia

S/A with Gdn Guilford G. GREGG: payment from M. CHAMBLIN Exor. of Mary GREGG, leaving $1106.96 and that he has exceeded her income for the year, but she will receive further funds, which will make her income in future amply sufficient for her support. RtCt 11 Aug 1860. [E:85]

S/A with Gdn Guilford G. GREGG: beginning 31 Dec 1860; payment from M. CHAMBLIN Exor. of Thos. GREGG, leaving $2091.70 with lawful interest from that day. The estate has been very well managed, the Gdn having continued to transact the business so as even to increase the estate in a slight degree. RtCt 9 Apr 1867. [E:331]

S/A with Gdn Guilford G. GREGG: beginning 13 Jan 1866; paid for material and clothes, leaving $2052.97. The expenses have exceeded her income by nearly $49.00 but they have been more than usually heavy in order to equip her for going to school. RtCt 10 Sep 1867. [E:366]

S/A with Gdn Guilford G. GREGG: paid board and tuition at Belmont, leaving $130.58 and that this excess was wholly on account of her education. RtCt Oct 1868. [E:433]

S/A with Gdn Guilford G. GREGG: beginning 4 Feb 1868; paid board and tuition, etc, leaving $1736.93. RtCt 13 Dec 1870. [F:81]

S/A with Gdn Guilford G. GREGG: beginning 11 Jan 1871; paid board and clothing, leaving $1733. Ward nearly of age. RtCt 14 Apr 1873. [F: 316]

NIXON, John E., Joel R., Hannah E. and Parelia F.

S/A of John E. NIXON with Gdn Gustavus L. ELGIN: 14 Dec 1857; payment from R. ELGIN Comr. in the case of

WILLIAMS vs NIXON, paid ¼ of amt. due R. J. NIXON (now WHITACRE) former Gdn. S/A of Joel R. NIXON with Gdn Gustavus L. ELGIN: paid R. WHITACRE tuition, leaving $420.57. S/A of Hannah E. NIXON with Gdn Gustavus L. ELGIN: beginning 18 Jan 1858; as above, leaving $380.18. S/A of Parelia F. NIXON with Gdn Gustavus L. ELGIN: beginning 14 Dec 1858; as above, leaving $393.43. A very considerable amount will come to them from the estate of their grandfather Joel NIXON dec'd. which will swell their income to about $36 to $40 each. RtCt 14 Aug 1860. [E:87]

S/A of John E. NIXON with Gdn G. L. ELGIN: beginning 14 Dec 1859; paid R. WHITACRE for tuition, leaving $483.69. S/A of Joel R. NIXON with Gdn G. L. ELGIN: 14 Dec 1859; as above, leaving $432.09. S/A of Hannah E. NIXON with Gdn G. L. ELGIN: beginning 14 Dec 1859; as above, leaving $435.36. S/A of Parelia F. NIXON with Gdn G. L. ELGIN: beginning 14 Dec 1859; as above, leaving $394.98. New Gdn J. T. LYNN on 15 Sep. RtCt 9 Apr 1867. [E:343]

S/A of John E. NIXON with Gdn John T. LYNN: beginning 15 Jan 1866; paid board & tuition, leaving $7.76. S/A of Joel R. NIXON with Gdn John T. LYNN: beginning 15 Sep 1866; general expenses leaving $3.23 due to Gdn. S/A of Hannah E. NIXON with Gdn John T. LYNN: beginning 15 Sep 1866; paid WHITACRE for board & tuition, leaving $10.02. S/A of Parelia F. NIXON with Gdn John T. LYNN: beginning 15 Sep 1866; as above, owes $1.06 to Gdn. These expenses with the former Gdn G. L. ELGIN were unequal and rather exceeded their income and the same has been the case for this year, and may be for two of them John E. and Parelia F. NIXON next year, but so far this excess has been entirely unavoidable. They live with their mother who is married a second time and are treated kindly and considerately by Mr. WHITACRE her husband, to whom they have been going to school. RtCt 9 Apr 1867. [E:347]

S/A of John E. NIXON with Gdn John T. LYNN: from G. L. ELGIN's estate her being the former Gdn, paid R. WHITACRE board, leaving $680.71. S/A of Joel R. NIXON with Gdn John T. LYNN: beginning 15 Sep 1666; general expenses as above, leaving $625.54. S/A of Parelia F. NIXON with Gdn John T. LYNN: beginning 15 Sep 1866; as above, leaving $624.78. Hereafter their income will be increased by the falling in of the dower of the mother, who died 16 Jul 1867 and it will be about $53. RtCt 12 Apr 1869. [E:483]

S/A with Gdn John T. LYNN: beginning 15 Sep 1867; accts. of John E. NIXON, Joel R. NIXON & Parelia F. NIXON general expenses leaving over $874 to each. RtCt 12 Oct 1869. [F:21]

S/A of John E. NIXON with Gdn John T. LYNN: beginning 15 Sep 1868; general expenses leaving $933.48. RtCt 12 Jun 1871. [F:143]

S/A of Parelia F. NIXON with Gdn John T. LYNN: beginning 1 Jan 1870; general expenses leaving $885.12. RtCt 12 Jun 1871. [F:144]

S/A of John E. NIXON with Gdn John T. LYNN: beginning 1 Jan 1870; general expenses leaving $933.48. RtCt 12 Jun 1871. [F:145]

S/A of Parelia F. NIXON with Gdn John T. LYNN: general expenses leaving $885.42. RtCt 12 Jun 1871. [F:145]

S/A of Parelia F. NIXON with Gdn John T. LYNN: beginning Nov 1870; general expenses leaving $908.26. RtCt 16 Mar 1872. [F:215]

S/A of John E. NIXON with Gdn John T. LYNN: beginning 1870; general expenses leaving $965.31. RtCt 16 Mar 1872. [F:216]

OVERFIELD, Marshall
S/A with Gdn John P. H. GREEN: paid tuition, rec'd payment from Richard OSBURN's estate, general expenses, leaving $895.50. His estate has been increased by the death of a brother upwards of $400, and will hereafter be sufficient for his support and education. RtCt 14 Aug 1860. [E:92]

STUCK, Jane C. and Margaret Ann
S/A with Gdn F. F. STUCK: income from hire of Negro Charles from S. H. PRICE Exor. of Elizabeth STUCK, paid for tuition at Frederick, leaving Jane C. STUCK $84.48 and leaving Margaret Ann STUCK $.91; she having authorized the payment of her estate to the education of Jane C. STUCK her sister. The other ward Mary Ellen was of age before he received any money for her. RtCt [Aug 1860] [E:123]

REDMOND, Ann (a lunatic)
S/A of estate with Committee A. D. LOVE: (now dec'd) beginning 15 May 1846; paid for removing her and her furniture to his house and for removing her and her furniture back to her own house, leaving $441.78 with interest thereon from 1 June 1850, the period of her death. Her estate consisted of a small farm in which she had a life estate, and $732.37 in bonds. The farm was rented out for $35 per annum, and she resided in a house on a small lot belonging to John BAYLEY, at a rent of $25 per annum. The last year or so of her life, she became very offensive from her filthyness, requiring the daily attendance of a servant to keep her and her room clean. RtCt 11 Mar 1861. [E:125]

HOUSHOLDER, Adam M. [HOUSEHOLDER]
Sale by Committee Gideon HOUSHOLDER: two colts about 1 Dec last for $51.50, a stack of hay on 26 Feb last for $6.50. RtCt 2 Apr 1861. [E:128]

S/A of estate with Committee Gideon HOUSEHOLDER: (insane) beginning 30 Mar 1860; expenses to Staunton, income from notes and from rents, leaving $138.55. RtCt 17 Aug 1866. [E:271]

S/A with Committee Gideon HOUSHOLDER: beginning 12 Nov 1865; income from rent, leaving $98.49. RtCt 10 Sep 1867. [E:368]

S/A with Committee Gideon HOUSHOLDER: beginning 12 Nov 1866; income from rent, leaving $231.42. RtCt Oct 1868. [E:414]

S/A with Committee Gideon HOUSHOLDER: beginning 9 Nov 1868; payment to Western Lunatic Asylum, income from rents of land, leaving $244.94. RtCt 12 Jun 1871. [F:139]

S/A with Committee Gideon HOUSHOLDER: beginning 9 Nov 1868; paid Western Lunatic Asylum, income from rents, leaving $244.94. RtCt 17 Aug 1871. [F:174]

S/A with Committee Gideon HOUSHOLDER: beginning 12 Nov 1872; $70 each distributed to brothers & sisters Alice M. HOUSEHOLDER only child of Columbus HOUSEHOLDER dec'd, children of Caroline HAMILTON first wife of James W. HAMILTON, Samuel SPRECKERS who married Martha A. HOUSEHOLDER, Susan HAMILTON second wife of James W. HAMILTON, John L. JORDAN who married Julia HOUSEHOLDER & Drusilla HOUSEHOLDER. RtCt 8 Sep 1873. [F:351]

S/A with Committee Gideon HOUSEHOLDER: beginning 12 Apr 1873; $260 distributed to Alice M. HOUSHOLDER child of Columbus HOUSHOLDER, children of Caroline HAMILTON (Eli W. HAMILTON one of the children can not be heard from,) Samuel SPRECKER, Susan HAMILTON & John L. JORDAN. Adam is suppose to be dead as he has not been heard from since 1862 when he wandered off in the night and is thought to have drowned in the Potomac. RtCt 8 Jun 1874. F:416]

S/A with Committee Gideon HOUSHOLDER: beginning 12 Feb 1874; $43.33 each distributed to Alice M. child of Columbus HOUSHOLDER, children of Carolina HAMILTON (Maria & Lydia HAMILTON,) Samuel SPRECKER, Susan HAMILTON, John L. JORDAN & Drusilla HOUSHOLDER. Eli J. HAMILTON was supposedly dead but appears not to be. RtCt 14 Oct 1885. [G:495]

HOUGH, William H. Sr
Appraisal/Inventory of 8 Apr 1861 by Committee Isaac S. HOUGH: 103 ¾ acres of land, amt. of notes against his children totaling $19668.38, notes against other individuals both good and worthless with principal of $8528.64, household furniture, stock & farming implements worth $808.00, $683.44 cash in possession. RtCt 8 Jun 1861. [E:129]

S/A of estate with Committee Isaac S. HOUGH: (lunatic) beginning 8 Apr 1861; paid various store accts and general expenses leaving $529.14 with interest on $518.28 part there of from 7 Aug 1862. W. H. HOUGH died about that time. Some Virginia money coming into his hands in payment of a note in Feb 1862, and upon the advance of the U. S. troops in March this kind of currency becoming much depreciated he sold it and his own in Baltimore and I have charged him with its proceeds. RtCt 13 Feb 1866. [E:244]

BEALES, Jefferson F., Benjamin C., Margaret, Rodney D. and Norval V.
S/A of Jefferson F. BEALES with Gdn Richard WHITE: beginning 22 May 1845; 1/5 from D. CARR, paid A. F. MILLBURN note for house, overpaid a few dollars since he became of age. S/A of Benjamin C. BEALES with Gdn Richard WHITE: general expenses leaving $2.21 with interest from 19 Jun 1853 when he became 21y old. S/A of Margaret BEALES (now LOWE) with Gdn Richard WHITE: as above, paid Moses LOWE, husband of Margaret V. BEALES, leaving $33.26 with interest from 19 Jun 1853. S/A of Rodney D. BEALES with Gdn Richard WHITE: paid tuition, leaving $264.64. S/A of Norval V. BEALES with Gdn Richard WHITE: paid tuition, leaving $371.20. RtCt 13 Jun 1861. [E:129]

ORRISON, Townshend and Laney Ellen
S/A of Townshend ORRISON with Gdn Wilson C. SANDERS: beginning 12 Sep 1854; paid tuition, payment from John WILLIAM's Admr. of David A. & America ORRISON, leaving $1600. S/A of Laney Ellen ORRISON with Gdn Wilson C. SANDERS: paid tuition and for clothing, leaving $1470.00. RtCt 13 Jun 1861. [E:150]

ORRISON, Amanda
S/A with Gdn Wilson C. SANDERS: beginning 4 Nov 1853; paid Betsey ORRISON for Amanda's support, leaving $202.00. RtCt 13 Jun 1861. [E:154]

WILEY, William Decatur
S/A with Gdn Charlotte E. WILEY: payment from Lewis TAYLOR Admr. of William WILEY, paid board and tuition. As of 1 Jul 1860, Charlotte E. WILEY has married sometime since and thus ceased to be Gdn and another person has qualified, but she is a debtor to the estate, and therefore compelled to pay compound interest. RtCt 13 Jun 1861. [E:172]

S/A with Gdn Lewis TAYLOR: beginning 10 Mar 1860; general expenses leaving $514.99. RtCt 19 Jun 1866. [E:309]

S/A with Gdn Lewis TAYLOR his Gdn: beginning 10 Mar 1862. The ward reached the age of 21 on 20 Dec 1868 at which time there was due to him $760.00. RtCt 12 Apr 1869. [E:485]

JAMES, Florida C., Sarah C., Mary V., Robert M. and Thomas B.
S/A of Florida C. JAMES and others with Gdn Craven JAMES: beginning 9 Nov 1859; amt. due wards legacy from their grandfather Mahlon MORRIS, leaving $552.46. RtCt 13 Feb 1866. [E:247]

S/A with Gdn Craven JAMES: beginning 9 Nov 1860; payment from M. MORRIS Exor; general expenses leaving Florida C. $156.79, Sarah C. J $156.79, Mary V. $156.79, Robert M. $157.27 and Thomas B. JAMES $156.21. RtCt 9 Apr 1867. [E:335]

S/A of Florida C. JAMES with Gdn Craven JAMES: payment from C. JAMES executor of Mahlon MORRIS dec'd, leaving $172.65. The like sum is due to Sarah C. JAMES and Mary V. JAMES. RtCt Oct 1868. [E:415]

S/A of Florida C. & Sarah C. JAMES with Gdn Craven JAMES: beginning 9 Nov 1868; general expenses leaving $209.99 to each. RtCt 12 Apr 1870. [F:44]

S/A of Florida C. & Sarah C. JAMES with Gdn Craven JAMES: beginning Nov 1868; general expenses leaving Florida C. $349.30. RtCt 13 Feb 1871. [F:99]

JAMES, Mary V., Sarah C. & Cecelia
S/A with Gdn Craven JAMES: receipt of final S/A. RtCt 11 Nov 1873. [F:365]

MANN, John W., Mary L., Joseph William, Abner W. and Franklin S. L. (Heirs of George W.)
S/A with Gdn Joseph M. CONARD: beginning 3 Apr 1863; paid tuition, leaving John W. $437.75, Mary L. $411.81, Joseph Wm. $437.51, Abner W. $424.82 and Franklin S. L. MANN $341.11. The Gdn was also administrator with the will annexed of George W. MANN from whom the estate is derived so far as it has been reduced into possession. Franklin S. L. MANN was a mere infant at the death of his father, who died in Missouri where he had gone to settle, and before he had settled and the father devised the whole estate to his wife for the benefit of herself and children, and the Gdn has acted on the presumption that this will gives him a right in his case of the children to go for their comfort beyond the mere income. He has therefore paid the mother the moderate sum of $25 per annum for board and clothing of this child and for one year the same sum for Abner W. As the children grow up they seem to be self supporting. RtCt 13 Feb 1866. [E:248]

S/A with Gdn Joseph M. CONARD: beginning 12 Sep 1865; paid Leanna MANN for board, deduct 1/6 for Ida's coffin, leaving John W. C. funds due, Mary Laura $383.60, Joseph Wm. $362.42, Abner W. $341.12 and Franklin S. L. MANN $326.22. I had formerly allowed the board which had been paid to Leanna MANN the widow of George Wm. MANN and mother of the wards by the Gdn, but she complained of its insufficiency, and the Gdn at my suggestion got several neighbors to fix upon a suitable board for all the children including one (Ida) who had died in 1862. This additional board and his share (one sixth) of the expenses of Ida have reduced the balance as above stated. The will leaves the whole estate to Leanna MANN for the use of herself and children but she would not qualify either as personal representative or as Gdn and devolved the responsibility upon her brother J. M. CONARD. It became then necessary to determine what share she should have, and I gave her one third of the estate not a child's part and not the whole of it after payment of debts. RtCt 12 Dec 1866. [E:318]

S/A with Gdn Joseph M. CONARD: paid expenses of Ida S. L. MANN now dec'd, and for her coffin and grave, to be apportioned among her distributees: Leanna MANN mother, J. W. C. MANN brother, Jos. W. MANN brother, Mary L. MANN sister, Abner W. MANN brother, Franklin S. L. MANN brother. 3 Mar 1868 - I have charged a child's share of Ida's expenses to John W. C. MANN, Joseph W. MANN, Abner W., Franklin S. L. and Mary Laura MANN. Mary Laura MANN is of age and the amount due to 8 Mar 1868 is $165.05. The amount due John W. C. is $381.10, Joseph W. is $327.46, Abner W. $296.11 and Franklin S. L. MANN $324.87 all of 12 Sep 1866. RtCt Oct 1868. [E:409]

S/A with Gdn Joseph M. CONARD: beginning 12 Sep 1866; paid tuition, John W. MANN having reached 21y on 1 Nov 1868 paid in full $421.09, leaving Joseph W. $360.68, Abner Walter $308.42 and Franklin S. L. MANN $353.14. RtCt 12 Apr 1869. [E:475]

S/A of Joseph William MANN with Gdn Joseph M. CONARD: beginning 16 Sep 1869; general expenses leaving $418. Other children are in Missouri, don't need the income and not having annual S/A to save funds. RtCt 17 Aug 1871. [F:175]

S/A of Joseph William MANN with late Gdn Joseph M. CONARD: receipt for $485 paid acct in full. RtCt 12 Aug 1872. [F:240]

S/A of A. Walker MANN with Gdn Joseph M. CONARD: receipt of $418, acct. paid in full. RtCt 14 Jul 1873. [F:336]

GOCHNAUER, Pembroke S., Preston B. and Charles W. (Heirs of David)
S/A of Pembroke S. GOCHNAUER with Gdn Joseph GOCHNAUER (Original filed with will 2R:36): paid him when going to college in Baltimore, paid E. A. GOCHNAUER for the estate, paid various store accts, leaving $431.39. S/A of Preston B. GOCHNAUER with Gdn Joseph GOCHNAUER: paid tuition and various store accts, leaving $154.47. S/A of Charles W. GOCHNAUER with Gdn Joseph GOCHNAUER: beginning 14 Dec 1860; paid E. GOCHNAUER for board, leaving $213.05. On 18 Aug 1859 Exor made sale of the real and personal property according to the will. RtCt 13 Feb 1866. [E:266]

S/A of Pembroke S. GOCHNAUER with Gdn Jos. GOCHNAUER: beginning 10 Dec 1861; general expenses leaving $396.75. S/A of Preston B. GOCHNAUER with Gdn Joseph GOCHNAUER: board, leaving $175.87. Charles W. GOCHNAUER's acct. settled to 10 Dec 1864 and $249.49 paid. RtCt 10 Sep 1867. [E:363]

LOUDOUN COUNTY, VIRGINIA
GUARDIAN ACCOUNTS
1759-1904

GOCHNAUER, Charles W.

S/A of Charles W. GOCHNAUER with Gdn Joseph GOCHNAUER: beginning 11 Jul 1867; general expenses leaving $1600.00. RtCt 12 Apr 1869. [E:462]

S/A with Gdn Joseph GOCHNAUER: beginning 10 Dec 1868; $696.75 payment from Exor of E. A. GOCHNAUER, general expenses, leaving $2168.97. RtCt 12 Aug 1872. [F:236]

S/A with Gdn Joseph GOCHNAUER: beginning 4 Apr 1873; general expenses leaving $1965.44. RtCt 8 Jun 1874. [F:395]

S/A with Gdn Joseph GOCHNAUER: beginning 12 Dec 1873; general expenses leaving $2058.57. RtCt 9 Aug 1875. [F:459]

S/A with Gdn Joseph GOUCHNAUER: beginning 10 Dec 1871; general expenses including for education leaving $1877.73. RtCt 14 Apr 1873. [F:315]

S/A with Gdn Joseph GOCHNAUER: beginning 10 Dec 1874; general expenses leaving $2158.30. RtCt 14 Aug 1876. [G:39]

S/A with Gdn Joseph GOCHNAUER: beginning 10 Dec 1875; general expenses leaving $2305.81. RtCt 10 Dec 1877. [G:93]

NICHOLS, William

Sale of 23 Feb 1866 by Committee John COCKERILLE: purchasers: John W. COCKERILLE, Henry ROGERS, Joseph FURR, Joseph NICHOLS, Elias HUGHES, Thomas MYERS, Wm. HOGE, Wm. J. CRAIG, John MEAD, William HOGUE, John GREGG, John L. TILLETT, David J. WEADON, Wm. J. SMITH, Michael MULLEN, Gabriel WARNER, Smith HIRST, Albert TAYLOR, Aquilla MEAD, Samuel COLBERT, James HOGUE, Daniel HOGUE, David BEALL, Saml. N. BROWN, Elijah HUTCHISON, Ed. J. SMITH, Owen HOLMES, Geo. W. NOLDAN, Thornton WHITACRE, Robt. VANSICKLER, Henson SIMPSON, David ACRES, Thomas GORE, Arnelius COE, George LICKEY, Saml. M. JANNEY, Lot TAVENNER, James LACOCK, Addison HAINE, totaling $1202.31. RtCt 15 Jun 1866. [E:279]

S/A with Committee John COCKERILLE: (unsound mind) The ward died in June and he paid some matters that ought to have been paid by the administrator, but as he had funds in his hands they only diminished the balance to be paid by him which is $130.79. RtCt 9 Apr 1867. [E:341]

S/A with Committee John COCKERILLE: (a lunatic) beginning 1 Sep 1866; income from notes, general expenses, leaving $23.67. RtCt 14 Dec 1880. [G:252]

GEORGE, Anna Belle, Olivia and William S. (Children of Solomon)

S/A of Anna Belle GEORGE and others with Gdn Samuel W. GEORGE Jr. on general acct: income from hire of Negro woman, paid S. W. GEORGE expenses in trying to recover runaway Negro. S/A of Olivia GEORGE, Anna Belle GEORGE, and William S. GEORGE with Gdn Samuel W. GEORGE Jr: beginning 12 Feb 1862; paid board, tuition, and clothing. The only estate belonging to them is a farm devised by their grandfather Jno. GEORGE Sr. who died in or about 1860. I had the rent of this farm fixed by Saml. W. GEORGE an uncle of all the parties and Charles W. JOHNSON a near neighbor and they appraised it at $100 per annum for each of the years 1861, 1862, 1863 & 1864 and, of this ¼ belongs to Samuel W. GEORGE the Gdn. The two elder children both now of age. The balance due to Gdn S. W. GEORGE Jr. by Olivia E. GEORGE on 11 Feb 1865 was $84.60, that due by Annabelle GEORGE was $46.00 and that by W. S. GEORGE was $129.41. RtCt 19 Jun 1866. [E:282]

S/A with agent Samuel W. GEORGE Jr: beginning 6 Mar 1865; accts of Annabell GEORGE & William S. GEORGE. RtCt 12 Oct 1869. [F:13]

WIRE, Mary Ann, Susannah F. and Martha J.

S/A with Gdn Peter WIRE: beginning 13 Dec 1854, general expenses. S/A of Susannah F. WIRE with Gdn Peter WIRE: beginning 13 Dec 1860; 28 Nov 1860 from int on $98.85 to date of marriage ($128.42). S/A of Mary Ann WIRE with Gdn Peter WIRE: beginning 13 Dec 1860; 11 Mar 1863 from compound int to date of majority ($129.87). S/A of Martha J. WIRE with Gdn Peter WIRE: beginning 13 Dec 1860, $130.27 awaiting the call of Martha J. WIRE Gdn in Ohio. RtCt 17 Aug 1866. [E:297]

S/A of Martha J. WIRE with Gdn Peter J. WIRE: on 1 Nov 1868 $152 paid in full. RtCt [no date.] [E:485]

WRIGHT, Ella and Elizabeth

S/A with Gdn Robert L. WRIGHT: amt. paid Mrs. E. CARTER for family supplies under will of Jonathan CARTER, payment rec'd from F. M. CARTER trustee, income from rent of farm and from hire of Negroes Ellen and Jane. $6734.92 due to the wards on 8 Jul 1866 (on which day R. L. WRIGHT died). But since his death his executors have paid two small claims upon the trust fund and I have therefore report that on 11 Sep 1866 there is due to the wards of $6771.66. The will of Jonathan CARTER is the basis of this acct. he having left certain land and slaves to be rented and hired out unto the wards his grandchildren should arrive at the age of 21 years, the interest to be added to the principal until such time, said principal fund being the accruing rents and hires. The surviving trustee is Francis M. CARTER and he has complied with the requirements of the will of Jonathan CARTER in regard to this fund. RtCt 17 Aug 1866. [E:298]

SHAFER, John M.

S/A with Gdn Jonas P. SCHOOLEY: beginning 1 Jul 1855; paid board & tuition. John M. SHAFER arrived at the age of 21 years on 30 Nov 1861 and on 12 Feb 1866 he is due $954.31. RtCt 17 Aug 1866. [E:303]

ARNOLD, Thomas Clayton
　　S/A with Gdn Richard JAMES: beginning 23 Dec 1865; paid tuition, payment from Jacob ARNOLD's estate part legacy, leaving $693.12. RtCt 9 Apr 1867. [E:323]
　　S/A with Gdn Richard JAMES: beginning 13 Nov 1866; payment from Joseph ARNOLD executor of Jacob ARNOLD, tuition, leaving $744.73. RtCt Oct 1868. [E:407]
　　S/A with stepfather & Gdn Richard JAMES: no Settlement made since 13 Nov 1867 so balance still $744.73. RtCt 14 Sep 1874. [F:423]
　　S/A with Gdn Richard JAMES: $744.73 on hand, interest charged to ward for board. RtCt 16 Mar 1876. [G:9]
　　Inventory by Gdn Mary C. JAMES: $830.37 from Wm. SMITH Exor of Richard JAMES. RtCt 14 Jun 1877. [G:59]
　　S/A of 13 Jul 1880 with Gdn Mary C. JAMES: $854.60 full payment when he reached majority. RtCt 7 Aug 1880. [G:241]

LOVE, Samuel H.
　　S/A with Gdn Joseph P. GRUBB: beginning 11 May 1865; paid board and tuition, leaving $2492.00. RtCt 9 Apr 1867. [E:338]
　　S/A with Gdn Joseph P. GRUBB: 26 Oct 1870 $408.63 paid acct in full. RtCt 12 Jun 1871. [F:142]

ARNOLD, Americus S. and Annie E.
　　S/A with Gdn Simon ARNOLD: beginning 14 Nov 1865; payment rec'd from estate of Michael ARNOLD, leaving $101.68. Since his bond for $800 was executed the mother of the children had died and they succeed to her estate, and to her share in her father Jacob SMITH's estate and that was a fund in the hands of their late Gdn Jacob SMITH. RtCt 10 Sep 1867. [E:351]
　　S/A with Gdn Jacob SMITH: amt. of proceeds of house and lot sold in case of SMITH vs ARNOLD, paid tuition. At the death of Jacob SMITH on or about 1 Feb 1862 the balance due the wards was $569.60 with interest from that date. Some shoe bills I have charged in equal proportions to the mother and her children not being able to separate them fully, in doing this I am sure substantial justice has been done to the wards. Two thirds of the amount due on the administration acct. have been transferred to the Gdn acct. RtCt 12 Apr 1869. [E:446]
　　S/A with Gdn Simon ARNOLD: beginning 14 Nov 1865; settlement under his first bond from 14 Nov 1865 to 9 Apr 1867 when he gave a new bond. The amount due by him on 9 Apr 1867 have been transferred to his acct. under the second bond. RtCt 12 APR 1869. [E:447]
　　S/A with Gdn Simon ARNOLD: beginning 9 Apr 1867; payment from E. ARNOLD's Admr from M. ARNOLD's Admr, leaving $2234.23. S/A of Americus ARNOLD with Gdn Simon ARNOLD: beginning 9 Apr 1868; paid for clothes and board, he is finishing his education. S/A of Annie ARNOLD with Gdn Simon ARNOLD: beginning 9 Apr 1868; paid board; leaving $152.32. RtCt 12 Apr 1869. [E:448]
　　S/A with Gdn Simon ARNOLD: beginning 2 Jan 1869; $850 from W. M. SMITH Admr of E. ARNOLD, paid school expenses for Americus in Gettysburg, leaving $807.50. RtCt 13 Dec 1870. [F:76]
　　S/A of Anna: beginning 24 Nov 1868; general expenses leaving $544.33. RtCt 13 Dec 1870. [F:77]
　　Appraisal/Inventory of Annie H. ARNOLD with Gdn Samuel SMITH: $1046.61 rec'd from Admr of Eliz. ARNOLD, $735.28 from Samuel SMITH for land, crops, balance from estate of Simon ARNOLD dec'd former Gdn. RtCt 13 Nov 1871. [F:191]
　　S/A with Gdn Simon ARNOLD: beginning 8 Apr 1869; general expenses leaving Americus S. ARNOLD $10.36. RtCt 13 May 1872. [F:221]
　　S/A of Annie A. ARNOLD with Gdn Samuel SMITH: beginning 9 Jan 1871; rec'd funds from Admr of E. ARNOLD and from Admr of Simon ARNOLD, income of interest, leaving $2223.10. RtCt 14 Apr 1873. [F:308]
　　S/A with Job SMITH Admr of Gdn Simon ARNOLD: final payment of $109.62 to Anna ARNOLD's husband John H. BEATTY. RtCt 8 Jun 1874. [F:391]

TAYLOR, Samuel Townsend
　　Guardianship of Samuel Townsend TAYLOR and others with Gdn Mary S. TAYLOR is fully closed as of 27 Sep 1867. RtCt 12 Mar 1868. [E:394]

WHITE, Rachel (a lunatic)
　　S/A with Committee Eli H. NICHOLS: beginning 1 Apr 1866; paid J. M. ORR fee for mother, paid board, leaving $334.84. RtCt 12 Mar 1868. [E:394]
　　S/A with Committee Eli H. NICHOLS: paid board til her death on 10 Aug 1867 and find due the estate 57 cents and this acct. is final. RtCt 15 Jun 1868. [E:402]

HAMPTON, Jonah Nichols and James Franklin
　　S/A with Gdn Sallie W. HAMPTON: paid tuition. The money was a gift from her to her children and the care and attention required by two children is certainly a full offset to interest. Thomas J. NICHOLS her present husband is the Gdn and the amount coming to his hands 11 Nov 1867 is $922.70. RtCt 15 Jun 1868. [E:397]
　　S/A with Gdn Thomas J. NICHOLS: payment from J. W. NICHOLS Exor of Jonah NICHOLS in part of legacy; leaving $907.99. S/A of Jonah Nichols HAMPTON with Gdn Thomas J. NICHOLS: paid tuition and Virginia NICHOLS, leaving $895.89. RtCt 12 Apr 1869. [E:463]
　　S/A of Jonah Nichols HAMPTON with Gdn Thomas J. NICHOLS: beginning 24 Nov 1868; general expenses leaving $895.89. RtCt 12 Apr 1870. [F:32]

S/A of James F. HAMPTON with Gdn Thomas J. NICHOLS: beginning 24 Nov 1868; payments leaving $894.80, expenses went a little above income because of a spell of sickness. RtCt 12 Apr 1870. [F:33]

S/A with Gdn Thomas J. NICHOLS: has $895.89 since 1869 without settling acct, ward went to farming in company with his brother J. F. HAMPTON on 1 Apr 1877 and will be using money for farm equipment. RtCt 9 Jul 1877. [G:60]

S/A with Gdn Thomas J. NICHOLS: wards rented a farm on 1 Apr 1877 and can now take care of themselves, J. N. has $895.89 and J. F. has $894.80. RtCt 13 Feb 1878. [G:104]

S/A with Gdn T. J. NICHOLS: have settled. RtCt 12 Mar 1884. [G:429]

HOLMES, Joseph F.
S/A with Gdn Charles E. MOUNT: $207.32 paid in full on 21 Jan 1868, account closed. RtCt 15 Jun 1868. [E:398]

COOPER, George T. or F.
Inventory of estate by Gdn John H. LYNN: cash received from estate of Mary COOPER dec'd per George COOPER of George, cash received from estate of Solomon COOPER dec'd. RtCt 8 Jun 1868. [E:406]

S/A with Gdn John H. LYNN: $115.52 payment of acct in full. RtCt 13 Feb 1871. [F:90]

WASHINGTON, Sally B., Lily and Rosa (Children of Samuel E.)
Inventory of the estate of Sally B., Lalla and Rosa WASHINGTON children of Gdn Samuel E. WASHINGTON: $400 rec'd from David HIXSON Shff. of Loudoun Co. Admr. of Sarah WENNER dec'd as of 17 Feb 1868. Also from same a bond executed by Archibald J. WIGHTMAN, Joseph M. L. WIGHTMAN and William GRAHAM for $1487.29 dated 4 May 1860 and payable twelve months after date with interest from date received on same day. Also $2000.00 received on 18 Jun 1868. RtCt 18 Jun 1868. [E:406]

S/A with Gdn E. Fletcher POTTS: beginning 10 Feb 1868; $400 from estate of S. E. WENNER, $2000 from A. T. M. FILLER, $760 each to Sally WASHINGTON, Lily WASHINGTON & Rosa WASHINGTON. RtCt 12 Apr 1870. [F:60]

S/A with Gdn E. F. POTTS: beginning 10 Feb 1869; general expenses leaving Lily WASHINGTON $780.28, exceeding income by $12.56. RtCt 13 Feb 1871. [F:119]

S/A with Gdn E. F. POTTS: beginning 10 Feb 1870; general expenses leaving Rosa WASHINGTON $779.77. RtCt 13 Feb 1871. [F:1120]

S/A with Gdn E. Fletcher POTTS: beginning 10 Feb 1869; Sallie B.'s majority of 10 May 1870, advancement to go west, leaving Sallie B. WASHINGTON $155.23. RtCt 13 Feb 1871. [F:121]

S/A with Gdn E. F. POTTS: beginning 30 Mar 1870; general expenses leaving Lily WASHINGTON $714.28 & Rose L. WASHINGTON $773.77. RtCt 10 Oct 1871. [F:189]

S/A with Gdn E. F. POTTS: beginning 10 Feb 1871; paid board to father, general expenses, leaving Lily WASHINGTON $774.18, leaving Rosa WASHINGTON $778.77. RtCt 12 Aug 1872. [F:243]

S/A with Gdn E. F. POTTS: beginning 10 Jun 1872; general expenses leaving Rosa $773.77 & Lilly $774.28. RtCt 11 Aug 1873. [F:349]

S/A with Gdn E. F. POTTS: beginning 10 Jun 1872; general expenses leaving Rosa $773.77 and Lily $774.28. RtCt 8 Sep 1873. [F:363]

S/A with Gdn E. F. POTTS: beginning 10 Feb 1873; general expenses leaving Lily $774.28 & Rosa $773.77. They are boarding with father S. E. WASHINGTON. RtCt 14 Sep 1874. [F:428]

S/A of Rosa & Lily with Gdn E. F. POTTS: beginning 20 Mar 1874; general expenses leaving $651.28 to be sent to her husband & $801.76 to Lily WASHINGTON. RtCt 15 Jul 1876. [G:25]

S/A of Rosa & Lily with Gdn E. F. POTTS: beginning 10 Feb 1875; general leaving Lillie WASHINGTON $148.15 due to her husband. RtCt 9 Oct 1876. [G:48]

COOPER, Sarah R.
S/A with Gdn Thomas J. BROWN: payment from G. HOUSHOLDER Admr. of John COOPER of George, (now wife of George H. SNOOTS) to 15 Nov 1866 when she was married and I find due to her husband $103.95. RtCt Oct 1868. [E:412]

NICHOLS, Maria, M. Virginia, L. Ellen, Louisa and George W. (Children of Henry H.)
S/A of Maria NICHOLS widow and the children of H. H. NICHOLS with agent & Gdn Eli H. NICHOLS: beginning 11 Nov 1861; income from rent. S/A of Maria NICHOLS, M. Virginia NICHOLS, L. Ellen NICHOLS, Louisa NICHOLS, and George W. NICHOLS with Eli H. NICHOLS: beginning 11 Nov 1861, general expenses. [above are long accts.] 27 Jun 1867 - Gdn of the children of Henry H. NICHOLS to 14 Nov 1866, the fifth anniversary of his qualification. There are funds from two sources involved in the accts. settled, the first arising from rents of real estate, which belonged to Henry H. NICHOLS, and the second from the land which Henry H. NICHOLS children inherited from their grandfather Thomas NICHOLS (Esq.) The first named funds are shared by the widow and four children and upon these lands some buildings have been erected and the costs of them charged to the widow & children in the proportion of one third and two thirds. Of the family supplies I have charged them by heads sometimes one fourth to each and sometimes one fifth in consequence of the absence or presence of L. Ellen NICHOLS who was at

school for some time. I have settled first the acct. of the funds arising from the lands of H. H. NICHOLS and transferred the balances for or against the parties entitled to their separate accts. and next I have done the same with the funds arising from the lands inherited from Thomas NICHOLS Esq. I have then stated their separate accts. including that of the widow as her agent and find that on 11 Nov 1835 Maria NICHOLS widow owed Eli H. NICHOLS her agent the sum of $9.17, M. Virginia NICHOLS owed her said Gdn $44.26, L. Ellen NICHOLS owed him $209.64, Louisa NICHOLS owed him $17.03 and Geo. W. NICHOLS owed him $4.14. The reason why so much is due from L. Ellen NICHOLS is that she was at boarding school for nearly two years of the time, when her elder sister and her younger brother and sister were at home at less expense. Eli H. NICHOLS as Gdn of the children received from himself and Thomas J. NICHOLS administrator of Thomas Nichols (Esq.) $350 in Confederate notes, which had come into their hands from the sale of property in the fall of 1861, this was only the equal distributive share of the children. RtCt Oct 1868. [E:424]

S/A of widow and children with Eli H. NICHOLS: paid for food supplies. S/A of children with Gdn Eli H. NICHOLS: income from sale of wheat. S/A of Maria NICHOLS widow, M. Virginia NICHOLS, L. Ellen NICHOLS, Louisa NICHOLS, AND George H. NICHOLS with Eli H. NICHOLS his Gdn: beginning 11 Nov 1866; general expenses. 7 Apr 1868 - the first is a statement of the rents derived of the lands of H. H. NICHOLS, the second that from the lands of the children of said Henry which descended from their grandfather Thomas NICHOLS (Esq) and lastly the separate accts. of Maria NICHOLS widow, M. Virginia NICHOLS who is now of age, of L. Ellen NICHOLS and of Louisa NICHOLS and George W. NICHOLS. The accts. are very seriously affected by expenditures for necessary buildings on the real estate, but for which their income would have increased their capital. The acct. of the widow and of Virginia NICHOLS are here included for convenience of reference. The balances due to Eli H. NICHOLS as agent are as follows, from Maria NICHOLS $32.16 and from M. Virginia NICHOLS $28.25 while L. Ellen NICHOLS owes him as her Gdn $170.55 and he owes his wards Louisa A. NICHOLS and George W. NICHOLS respectively $19.47 and $11.07 respectively. RtCt 12 Apr 1869. [E:478]

S/A with agent and Gdn Eli H. NICHOLS: beginning 16 Nov 1867; real estate which descended to the children from their grandfather Thomas NICHOLS; distributions to widow Maria NICHOLS, M. Virginia NICHOLS, L. Ellen NICHOLS, Louisiana NICHOLS & Geo. W. NICHOLS. RtCt 12 Apr 1870. [F:51]

S/A with agent Eli H. NICHOLS: beginning Nov 1868; shares to widow Maria NICHOLS and children M. Virginia NICHOLS, L. Ellen NICHOLS, Louisa Anna NICHOLS & George W. NICHOLS, all except George are now of age. RtCt 13 Dec 1870. [F:82]

RUST, Sallie J., Manley T., John C., Mary Ellen, James Buckannan and Margaret Virginia (Children of James W.)

S/A with Gdn Charles L. MANKIN: beginning 9 Apr 1866; paid various store accts. and tuition, all are children under 14y old, leaving Mary Ellen RUST at the end of the second year on 9 Apr 1868 $107.90, leaving James Buchanan RUST $1219.69 and leaving Margaret V. B. RUST $144.24. RtCt Oct 1868. [E:435]

S/A with Gdn Charles L. MANKIN: beginning 21 Nov 1866; paid various store accts. and tuition, leaving Sally J. RUST $108.46, leaving Mandley T. RUST $115.59 and leaving John C. RUST $117.27. RtCt Oct 1868. [E:439]

S/A with Gdn Charles L. MANKINS: beginning Mar 1868; $138.44 each to Sallie J. RUST (now married), Manley T. RUST, John C. RUST, Mary Ellen RUST, James Buckannan & Margaret Virginia RUST. The last 3 children are going to school. Funds are proceeds from sale of their uncle John HICKMAN's & their grandmother Catharine HICKMAN's lands. RtCt 13 Feb 1871. [F:100]

S/A with Gdn Charles L. MANKINS: beginning 14 Nov 1870; general expenses leaving $33.60 each to B. F. FOLEY, Mandley T. RUST, John C. RUST, Mary Ellen RUST, James B. RUST & Margaret V. RUST. Margaret is under 14y old and James and Margaret are a little older. RtCt 13 Feb 1871. [F:107]

S/A with Gdn Benj. F. FOLEY: beginning 14 Nov 1872; paid general expenses of Margaret V. RUST leaving $74.58, James B. RUST leaving $36.23 & Mary Ellen RUST leaving $24.97 owed to Gdn. RtCt 20 Feb 1873. [F:297]

S/A with Gdn Charles L. MANKIN: beginning Mar 1868; income from sale of real estate to W. B. DOWNEY & J. M. ORR, distributions to Sallie J. RUST (married,) Mandley T. RUST, John C. RUST, Mary Ellen RUST, James B. RUST & Margaret Virginia RUST. RtCt 12 Apr 1871. [F:128]

Inventory of Mary Ellen & James B. RUST by Benjamin F. FOLEY: $150.62 from former Gdn C. L. MANKIN, 1/6 of rents of a farm. RtCt 3 May 1871. [F:135]

Inventory of Margaret V. W. RUST by Gdn Benjamin F. FOLEY: $128.48 from former Gdn C. L. MANKIN, 1/6 rent of a farm. RtCt 3 May 1871. [F:136]

S/A with Gdn Charles L. MANKIN: beginning 9 Apr 1871; general expenses leaving John C. RUST $370.93. Ward now of age. RtCt 11 Aug 1873. [F:348]

S/A with agent B. F. FOLEY agent: beginning 1 Nov 1871; general expenses leaving Margaret V. RUST $72.58, James B. RUST $35.73 & Mary Ella RUST $29.85. James B. is very delicate and can no support himself. RtCt 9 Mar 1874. [F:383]

S/A with agent & Gdn B. F. FOLEY: beginning 14 Nov 1871; general expenses leaving Margaret V. RUST $74.84, James B. RUST (very delicate) $36.36 & Mary Ellen RUST (at such an age to be almost helpless) $27.35. RtCt 8 Nov 1875. [F:490]

S/A with agent & Gdn B. F. FOLEY: beginning 15 Dec 1871; general expenses leaving Margaret V. RUST $223.68, James B. RUST $142.52 & Mary Ellen RUST $118.45. RtCt 8 Nov 1875. [F:493]

S/A with Gdn Benjamin F. FOLEY: beginning 14 Nov 1874; general expenses, 6 children including James B., Marg. V. has $179.38 & Mary Ellen owes Gdn. All are of age. RtCt 11 Jun 1879. [G:165]

S/A with Gdn B. F. FOLEY: beginning 1 Jan 1879; $.87 due B. F. FOLEY after $179.39 acct of 15 Sep 1878. RtCt 11 Mar 1880. [G:213]

TAYLOR, Emma D.
S/A with Gdn Thomas E. TAYLOR: beginning Aug 1866; paid various store accts, 22 Jul 1866 paid her trip to Baltimore to get wedding clothes, leaving $473.96. Balance of $473.86 was sent to Barclay D. EYRE, the husband of Emma D. TAYLOR. RtCt Oct 1868. [E:441]

HICKMAN, George S., Luther W., Etchison H. and Margaret Susan Mary (Children of Peter)
S/A of George S. HICKMAN with Gdn George HICKMAN: paid board, tuition, expenses & clothing at Gettysburg College, payment from estate of Peter HICKMAN. Acct. as Gdn of Geo. S. HICKMAN to 14 Aug 1866 which was the anniversary of his qualification and the termination of his Guardianship his death having taken place between that time and 11 Sep 1866. I have raised no interest acct. until Aug 1865 at which time interest commenced against him in the estate acct. of Geo. S. HICKMAN's father Peter HICKMAN. The friends of the ward, his uncles and aunts by the mother's side, and his family physician recommend his being sent to school and his funds have been so applied. RtCt 12 Apr 1869. [E:464]

S/A of Luther W. HICKMAN with George HICKMAN: paid tuition, leaving $419.50. S/A of Etchison H. HICKMAN with Gdn George HICKMAN: tuition, leaving $329.39. S/A of Margaret Susan Mary HICKMAN with Gdn George HICKMAN: paid tuition, leaving $407.67. George HICKMAN took charge of the children of his brother Peter HICKMAN immediately after his death and expended money for their actual support charging board at a rate fair by two of his neighbors. The reason why the balance due to Etchison H. HICKMAN is so much less than those due to the others is that he has been sick and has had large doctor bills to pay, his clothing also has cost a little more. RtCt 12 Apr 1869. [E:465]

S/A with uncle & Gdn John G. R. KALB: beginning 8 Oct 1866; $297.69 each to children George S. HICKMAN (school at Gettysburg,) and 3 other unnamed. RtCt 12 Apr 1870. [F:34]

S/A with Gdn John G. R. KALB: beginning 19 Oct 1867; accts of children Geo. S. HICKMAN, M. Susan M. HICKMAN, Etchison H. HICKMAN & Luther W. HICKMAN with $249.97 to each. RtCt 12 Apr 1870. [F:35]

S/A with Gdn John G. R. KALB: beginning 5 Nov 1868; distributive share from Admr of Susannah KALB, payments leaving $1376.43. RtCt 12 Apr 1870. [F:37]

S/A of M. Susan M. HICKMAN with Gdn John G. R. KALB: beginning 13 Oct 1866; paid tuition at Sharpsburg, general expenses, leaving $371.69. [F:38]

S/A of Etchison H. HICKMAN with Gdn John R. KALB: beginning 16 Oct 1866; general expenses leaving $595.87. [F:39]

S/A of Luther W. HICKMAN with Gdn John R. KALB: beginning 3 Nov 1866; general expenses leaving $807.88. RtCt 12 Apr 1870. [F:40]

S/A of M. Susan M. HICKMAN with Gdn John R. KALB: beginning 27 Oct 1868; paid tuition at Hagarstown, general expenses, leaving $345.29. RtCt 12 Apr 1870. [F:42]

S/A of Luther W. HICKMAN with Gdn John G. R. KALB: beginning 4 Jan 1869; paid tuition at Springdale, general expenses, leaving $1080.10. RtCt 12 Apr 1870. [F:43]

S/A of Etchison H. HICKMAN with Gdn John G. R. KALB: beginning 29 Dec 1868; paid Mrs. E. HICKMAN for board (children is delicate and requires attention,) general expenses, leaving $851.48. RtCt 12 Apr 1870. [F:43]

S/A with Gdn John G. R. KALB: $1190.86 divided between Geo. S. HICKMAN (now of age,) Etchison H. HICKMAN, M. Susan M. HICKMAN & Luther W. HICKMAN. RtCt 8 Jun 1874. [F:396]

S/A with John G. R. KALB: beginning 22 Dec 1869; general expenses leaving M. Susan M. $360.39, Luther W. $1402.88 & Etchison H. $849.46. RtCt 8 Jun 1874. [F:403]

S/A with John G. R. KALB: beginning 25 Jan 1871; $106.41 each to Geo. S. HICKMAN (of age,) M. S. M. HICKMAN, Luther W. HICKMAN & Etchison H. HUTCHISON. RtCt 8 Jun 1874. [F:406]

S/A with John G. R. KALB: beginning 19 Oct 1871; $444.04 to G. S. & M. S. M, $461.80 to Luther W. & Etchison H. HICKMAN. RtCt 8 Jun 1874. [F:409]

S/A with John G. R. KALB: beginning 5 May 1873; $16.60 each as above. Luther reached majority on 14 Nov 1873. RtCt 8 Jun 1874. [F:412]

S/A with Gdn J. G. K. KALB: beginning 20 Nov 1873; payment from S. J. KALB rent of dower, $129.05 each leaving E. H. HICKMAN $1497.22, M. S. M. HICKMAN $262.80 & two other children. RtCt 9 Oct 1876. [G:42]

S/A with Gdn John G. K. KALB: beginning 31 Oct 1874; income from sale of crops, general expenses, $125.71 each leaving M. Susan M. HICKMAN (reached 21y old on 8 Jan 1876) $130.10, Etchison HICKMAN $1640.57. RtCt 9 Oct 1876. [G:44]

S/A with Gdn J. G. R. KALB: beginning 4 Jan 1876; general expenses leaving Etchison HICKMAN $1524.96. Ward is very delicate. RtCt 13 Aug 1877. [G:73]

S/A with Gdn J. G. R. KALB: beginning 1 Jan 1877; general expenses leaving E. H. HICKMAN $1642.79. RtCt 9 Dec 1878. [G:141]

S/A with Gdn J. G. R. KALB: beginning 8 Oct 1877; income from rent of dower land, crops, general expenses, leaving Etchison H. HICKMAN $1891.85. RtCt 11 Aug 1880. [G:232]

S/A with Gdn J. R. KALB: beginning 8 Oct 1879; income from sale of crops, general expenses, leaving Etchison H. HICKMAN $2141.93 final S/A as of 4 May 1881 when he became of age. RtCt 13 Jun 1882. [G:318]

S/A with Gdn J. G. R. KALB: E. H. HICKMAN reached majority on 4 May 1881 and due $2141.03, closing acct. RtCt 13 Jan 1885. [G:467]

LEITH, Nellie E., Susan V., Richard D., Theodore and George Ernest (Heirs of Theodore)

The real estate with agent George E. PLASTER: beginning 30 Sep 1867; listing of repairs and crop necessities, income from rent for 2 shops in Unison and from sale of crops, distributions to : adult ___ LEITH, and minors Nellie E., Susan V., Rich'd D., Theodore, and Geo. Ernest LEITH – each 1/6th ($80.73). RtCt 12 Apr 1869. [E:468]

S/A of George Ernest LEITH with Gdn Geo. E. PLASTER: beginning 31 Dec 1867; general expenses leaving $130.83. RtCt 12 Apr 1869. [E:470]

S/A of Miss Nellie E. LEITH with Gdn George PLASTER: traveling expenses to Staunton, paid tuition & board at Weslyan Female Institute. RtCt 12 Apr 1869. [E:471]

S/A of Theodore LEITH with Gdn George PLASTER: paid tuition. RtCt 12 Apr 1869. [E:472]

S/A of Richard D. LEITH with Gdn George PLASTER: paid tuition, dancing lessons and singing lessons. RtCt 12 Apr 1869. [E:473]

S/A of Susan V. LEITH with Gdn George E. PLASTER: no receipts as the property from which the ward derives support or as necessarily ? with improvements. RtCt 12 Apr 1869. [E:474]

S/A with Gdn Geo. E. PLASTER: beginning 1 Jan 1869; general expenses leaving Nellie LEITH $658.76 due to Gdn. RtCt 12 Apr 1870. [F:45]

S/A with Gdn Geo. E. PLASTER: beginning 1 Jan 1869; general expenses leaving George Ernest LEITH $150.87 due to Gdn. RtCt 12 Apr 1870. [F:46]

S/A with Gdn George E. PLASTER: beginning 1 Jan 1869; general expenses leaving Susan V. LEITH $101.76 due to Gdn. RtCt 12 Apr 1870. [F:47]

S/A with Gdn George. E. PLASTER: beginning 1 Jan 1869; general expenses leaving Theodore LEITH $168.27 due to Gdn. RtCt 12 Apr 1870. [F:48]

S/A with Gdn George E. PLASTER: beginning 1 Jan 1869; general expenses leaving Richard D. LEITH $448.75 due to Gdn. RtCt 12 Apr 1870. [F:49]

Inventory: 5/6 of 63½ acres of land, 105 acres of land, ½ of store house & lot which sold for $650, ¼ acre with shop, lot with old shop, dower lands of 61 acres & 15 acres of Mrs. Veturia A. LEITH. Their share of personal estate of father Theodorick LEITH not yet distributed. RtCt 6 Jan 1871. [F:88]

S/A with Gdn George E. PLASTER: general expenses leaving $83.85 due to Gdn from Susan V., $128.79 due to Gdn from George Earnest & $61.95 due to Gdn from Theodore. Gdn has received nothing from the personal estate as Exor is not ready to distribute. He has made advances for support and education of wards, his sister's children. RtCt 12 Apr 1871. [F:124]

S/A with agent G. E. PLASTER: beginning 9 Sep 1870; income from rents of real estate, distributions to F. M. LEITH who married J. W. LEITH, Nellie LEITH, Richard D. LEITH (college expenses,) Theodore LEITH, Susan V. LEITH & George E. LEITH. RtCt 12 Apr 1871. [F:126]

S/A with Gdn Geo. PLASTER: income from sale of farm items, leaving $148.08 each to Theoderick LEITH, George E. LEITH, Susan V. LEITH, Richard D. LEITH, Nellie E. LEITH (now of age.) RtCt 11 Aug 1873. [F:341]

S/A with Gdn Geo. E. PLASTER: beginning 9 Sep 1872; $53.46 each to Richard D. LEITH, Theodore LEITH, Susan V. LEITH & Geo. E. LEITH. RtCt 8 Sep 1873. [F:352]

S/A with Gdn Geo. E. PLASTER: beginning 9 Oct 1872; income from sale of crops and cattle and rent of shop, leaving $27.71 each to Richard D. LEITH, Theodore LEITH, Susan V. LEITH & George E. LEITH. RtCt 9 Mar 1874. [F:380]

S/A with Gdn George E. PLASTER: beginning 9 Sep 1874; $55.03 each to Richard D. LEITH, Theodore LEITH, Susan V. LEITH & Geo. E. LEITH. RtCt 9 Feb 1875. [F:433]

S/A with Geo. E. PLASTER: beginning 9 Sep 1875; income from ½ of rents, general expenses, leaving Theodore LEITH $576.64, Susan V. LEITH $1342.62 & Geo. E. LEITH $1394.90. RtCt 12 Nov 1877. [G:83]

S/A with George E. PLASTER on general acct: $62.03 to each, leaving Susan V. LEITH $985.49, Geo. E. LEITH $1425.07 & T. D. LEITH $666.64. RtCt 12 Nov 1877. [G:85]

S/A with Geo. E. PLASTER: general expenses leaving Susan V. LEITH $999.73, Geo. E. LEITH $1571.10. RtCt 10 Dec 1877. [G:94]

S/A with Gdn Geo. E. PLASTER: beginning 9 Sep 1877; general expenses leaving Susan V. LEITH $1106.40 & Geo. E. LEITH $99.28. RtCt 10 Mar 1879. [G:155]

S/A with agent & Gdn George E. PLASTER: beginning 9 Sep 1879; general expenses, leaving George E. LEITH $41.67 (after paying him $775 at majority) & Susan V. LEITH (nearly of age) $890.32. RtCt 12 Jan 1880. [G:205]

S/A with Gdn Geo. E. PLASTER: beginning 9 Sep 1871; general expenses leaving Susan V. LEITH $47.60 to 21 Mar 1882 when she attained her majority, other children have been paid in full. RtCt 10 Jul 1882. [G:321]

COE, Elizabeth
Inventory of the personal property coming into the hands of Shff & Committee Summerfield BOLYN: note of $50 by Arulius COE & Duane COE, note of $1000 executed by Stephen McCARTY & John FRANCIS. RtCt 26 Apr 1869. [E:486]

POTTERFIELD, Julius W.
S/A Committee with L. H. POTTERFIELD: (insane) paid for one bed at sale of property of Saml. POTTERFIELD and medicine, payment from J. EVERHART Admr of M. EVERHART. The whole personal estate has been exhausted. RtCt 21 Jun 1869. [E:488]

S/A with Shff & Committee S. BOLYN: beginning 21 Mar 1870; general expenses leaving $130.78. RtCt 13 May 1872. [F:230]

S/A with Shff & Committee E. V. WHITE: beginning 6 Oct 1868; general expenses leaving $179.91. RtCt 12 Aug 1872. [F:242]

Inventory by Committee L. H. POTTERFIELD: $607.14 in receipts. RtCt 7 Sep 1872. [F:247]

S/A with Committee Luther H. POTTERFIELD: beginning 2 May 1872; general expenses leaving $367.04. RtCt 14 Jul 1873. [F:337]

S/A with Committee L. H. POTTERFIELD: beginning 14 Dec 1872; general expenses leaving $23.49. Ward is now dead and money may be claimed by hospital in Frederick Co MD where he died. RtCt 12 Nov 1877. [G:87]

POTTERFIELD, Silas (insane)
S/A with Committee L. H. POTTERFIELD: beginning 13 Nov 1866; same as with Julius W. POTTERFIELD. The whole personal estate is exhausted, and the rents of the real estate are not sufficient to support him. RtCt 21 Jun 1869. [E:489]

POTTERFIELD, Catharine (insane)
S/A with Committee Luther H. POTTERFIELD: beginning 12 Nov 1866; same as with Julius W. POTTERFIELD. This S/A is final, the trust having been transferred to E. V. WHITE Shff. of Loudoun. RtCt 21 Jun 1869. [E:491]

S/A with Shff & Committee S. BOLYN: beginning 21 Mar 1870; general expenses leaving $85.44. RtCt 13 May 1872. [F:231]

Inventory by Committee L. H. POTTERFIELD: $561.15 in receipts. RtCt 7 Sep 1872. [F:248]

S/A with Shff Committee E. V. WHITE: beginning 6 Oct 1868; paid L. H. POTTERFIELD for support of ward, general expenses, leaving $179.91. RtCt 12 Aug 1872. [F:279]

S/A with Committee Luther H. POTTERFIELD: beginning 2 May 1872; general expenses leaving $437.06. RtCt 14 Jul 1873. [F:337]

S/A with Committee Luther H. POTTERFIELD: beginning 14 Dec 1872; general expenses leaving $295.94. RtCt 12 Nov 1877. [G:89]

S/A with Committee L. H. POTTERFIELD: beginning 18 May 1876; general expenses leaving $88.75 RtCt 9 Oct 1883. [G:410]

BROWN, Joseph J.
S/A with Gdn Wm. JANNEY: paid Edward BROWN for board & tuition, paid for clothing, leaving $6.78 due to Gdn. His expenses considering the removal from Ohio to Loudoun and back again to Ohio have been very moderate. His board while not at school was charged by his Gdn at a very moderate rate. RtCt 12 Oct 1869. [E:493]

STOUT, George W.
Inventory of entire estate: Amt. rec'd from Pension Office ($621.11), further pension of $8.00 per month commencing 10 Nov 1870. RtCt 7 Nov 1870. [E:500]

S/A with grandfather & Gdn John L. STOUT: beginning 17 Mar 1870; general expenses, income from pension of $8/month from US government, leaving $531.11. His mother is married again. RtCt 13 Feb 1871. [F:110]

S/A with Gdn John L. STOUT: beginning 1870; general expenses leaving $654.17, income from pension of $8/month until he reaches 16y old. Ward lives with his mother who has remarried, but Gdn wants child with him as he has two sons one older and one younger and feels the ward would be better off with them. RtCt 23 Nov 1871. [F:199]

S/A with Gdn Jno. L. STOUT: beginning 14 Jun 1871; general expenses leaving $713.88. New Gdn is Cornelius William PAXSON. RtCt 12 Aug 1872. [F:245]

S/A with Gdn Jno. L. STOUT: beginning 14 Jun 1871; same as above. RtCt 14 Oct 1872. [F:258]

COOPER, Benjamin and Thomas
S/A with Gdn Israel G. POWELL: beginning 9 Nov 1868; general expenses leaving Thomas COOPER $159.10 and Benjamin COOPER $161.07. RtCt 19 Nov 1870. [E:500]

COOPER, Thomas
Inventory: $144.05 rec'd from Henry HEATON in the case of COOPER vs COOPER. RtCt 5 Jan 1871. [F:87]

COOPER, Benjamin
Inventory: $141.16 rec'd from Henry HEATON in the case of COOPER vs COOPER. RtCt 5 Jan 1871. [F:88]

HOGE, Henrietta and Elizabeth G.
S/A with Gdn Jesse HOGE: beginning 13 Aug 1867; payment rec'd from D. HOGE Exor. of H. B. TAYLOR dec'd and from Thomas E. TAYLOR for rent, leaving Henrietta HOGE $536.31 and Elizabeth G. HOGE $536.41. RtCt 19 Nov 1870. [E:501]

S/A with Gdn Jesse HOGE: beginning 14 Feb 1870; general expenses leaving $1275.37. RtCt 16 Mar 1872. [F:214]

S/A with Gdn Jesse HOGE: general expenses leaving Elizabeth G. HOGE $1379.94. RtCt 9 Mar 1874. [F:379]

S/A with Gdn Jessie HOGE: Henrietta died an infant & her father inherited her share of property, $773.54 goes to Jessie HOGE & $773.55 to Elizabeth. RtCt 14 Jun 1875. [F:447]

S/A of Elizabeth G. HOGE with father & Gdn Jesse HOGE: beginning 13 Aug 1874; general expenses leaving $829.88. RtCt 16 Mar 1875. [G:11]

S/A of Elizabeth G. HOGE with Gdn Jesse HOGE: beginning 13 Aug 1875; paid tuition & travel expenses, leaving $769.71. RtCt 10 Dec 1877. [G:94]

S/A of Elizabeth G. HOGE with Gdn Jesse HOGE: beginning 13 Aug 1877; general expenses leaving $483.83. RtCt 11 Sep 1878. [G:129]

HOUSEHOLDER, Alice M.
S/A with Gdn George W. JANNEY: beginning 10 Jun 1869; rec'd payment from Comr. of sale of real estate of Adam HOUSEHOLDER, leaving $698.52. RtCt 19 Nov 1870. [E:503]

S/A with Gdn George W. JANNEY: beginning 10 Jun 1870; general expenses leaving $524.58. [very faint on microfilm] RtCt 16 Mar 1872. [F:213]

S/A with Gdn George W. JANNEY: beginning Nov 1871; general expenses leaving $517.52. Ward is exceedingly delicate and mother Mrs. VINNEDGE & child lives in the Western Country. RtCt 14 Oct 1872. [F:251]

S/A with Gdn George W. JANNEY: general expenses leaving $362.27. She is very delicate and has had a limb broken. Gdn now lives in MD. RtCt 11 Aug 1873. [F: 340]

S/A with Gdn George W. JANNEY : beginning May 1873; Gdn now dead, $253.53 paid to attorney. RtCt 9 Feb 1875. [F:432]

LEITH, Louisa
S/A with late Gdn Bushrod OSBORN: beginning 5 Feb 1868; payment to Laurence LEITH, share bal. of acct. against B. OSBORN Admr. T. V. B. OSBORN, leaving 863.46. RtCt [Jun 1870?] [E:504]

S/A with late Gdn Bushrod OSBURN: beginning 15 Aug 1869; funds from Admr of T. V. B. OSBURN, $1010.23 paid to her husband Lawrence LEITH. RtCt 12 Aug 1872. [F:238]

ELGIN, Robert, Rosalie and Ida (Children of Robert E.)
S/A with acting Gdn Margaret E. ELGIN: beginning 1 Jan 1867; paid for building of tenants house (rent of George W. FLING the current tenant), distributions to widow Margaret E. ELGIN of $83.89, $41.94 each to Robert ELGIN, Rosalie ELGIN & Ida ELGIN. RtCt 12 Oct 1859. [F:9]

HUMPHREY, Virginia G., Ann Eliza and Abner Edward (Children of Abner G.)
S/A with Gdn Mary C. HUMPHREY: beginning 10 Sep 1867; $110 each to Virginia G. HUMPHREY, Ann Eliza HUMPREY & Abner Edward HUMPREY. RtCt 12 Oct 1869. [F:17]

Inventory: 2/3 of 315 acres of land. RtCt 7 Jan 1871. [F:89]

S/A with Gdn Mrs. Mary C. HUMPHREY: $451.29 distributed to Virginia G. HUMPREY, Ann Eliza HUMPHREY & Abner Edward HUMPHREY. RtCt 13 Feb 1871. [F:95]

S/A with Gdn Mary C. HUMPHREY: beginning 12 Sep 1871; accts. of Virginia G. HUMPHREY, Annie G. HUMPHREY, Abner Edward HUMPHREY. RtCt 20 Feb 1873. [F: 281]

S/A with mother Gdn Mary G. HUMPHREY: beginning 24 Aug 1872; $100.06 each leaving Virginia G. HUMPHREY $11.71, Annie E. HUMPHREY $37.73, Abner E. HUMPHREY $313.66. RtCt 8 Nov 1875. [F:480]

S/A with Gdn Mary G. HUMPHREY: general expenses leaving Annie C. HUMPHREY $59.18 on 20 Oct 1874 when she married Mason THROCKMORTON, Virginia G. HUMPHREY (now of age) $96.20 & Abner Edward $4.35. RtCt 8 Nov 1875. [F:484]

NEER, Nathan
S/A with Admr Potts NEER: receipt of Jonas POTTS for $27.53 in full of all demands against Nathan NEER dec'd Gdn of John L. POTTS, the said Jonas POTTS being his dec'd father and he being dead intestate & without issue. RtCt. 12 Oct 1869. [F:23]

LOUDOUN COUNTY, VIRGINIA
GUARDIAN ACCOUNTS
1759-1904

BIRDSALL, Children of Benjamin Jr.

S/A with Gdn Benjamin BIRDSALL Jr: beginning 10 Feb 1868; paid mother Sarah BIRDSALL for board, general expenses leaving Rebecca Alice BIRDSALL $359.16. Gdn died 1 Aug 1868; Deborah B. BIRDSALL is his Admr. RtCt 12 Apr 1870. [F:29]

Inventory by Gdn D. B. BIRDSALL: Wards Charles W. BIRDSALL, Mary Ann BIRDSALL, Rebecca BIRDSALL, Eliza BIRDSALL & Ellen H. BIRDSALL, income from rents of 120 acres of lands of which 1/3 is dower rights of the Gdn. RtCt 25 Jan 1872. [F:208]

S/A with mother Gdn D. B. BIRDSALL: paid for items for family, children Charles BIRDSALL, Mary Anna BIRDSALL, Rebecca BIRDSALL, Elizabeth BIRDSALL & Ellen H. BIRDSALL all owe the Gdn. RtCt 13 May 1872. [F:220]

S/A with widow Deborah BIRDSALL including Ann BIRDSALL's share: beginning 7 Nov 1871; paid for items used by Deborah B. BIRDSALL, Ann BIRDSALL, Charles W. BIRDSALL, Rebecca BIRDSALL, Eliza H. BIRDSALL, Ellen H. BIRDSALL & oldest daughter Mary Anna BIRDSALL who was away at school for 10 months. RtCt 14 Apr 1873. [F:309]

S/A with agent D. B. BIRDSALL: income from sale of crops and general expenses leaving $.80, acct. of Ann BIRDSALL joint tenant who pays nothing for board, C. W. BIRDSALL (now of age), Rebecca K. BIRDSALL, Eliza H. BIRDSALL, Ella BIRDSALL, Mariana BIRDSALL & widow. RtCt 9 Mar 1874. [F:376]

S/A with Gdn D. B. BIRDSALL: beginning 30 Oct 1873; income from sale of crops, payments to Ann BIRDSALL, C. W. BIRDSALL, Marianna BIRDSALL, Eliza H. BIRDSALL, Rebecca BIRDSALL, Ellen H. BIRDSALL & widow. RtCt 14 Aug 1876. [G:29]

S/A with Gdn D. B. BIRDSALL: beginning Nov 1874; as above. RtCt 14 Aug 1876. [G:32]

S/A with Gdn Deborah B. BIRDSALL: beginning 12 Nov 1875; income from sale of crops, general expenses, giving $6.67 to Ann BIRDSALL, $49.46 to widow D. B. BIRDSALL, leaving C. W. BIRDSALL $114.92, Marianna BIRDSALL $128.77, Rebecca BIRDSALL $45.22, Eliza BIRDSALL $5.05 & Ellen BIRDSALL $13.75. RtCt 9 Jul 1877. [G:65]

S/A with agent & Gdn Deborah B. BIRDSALL: beginning 20 Oct 1876; income from sale of crops, general expenses, $41.33 to Ann BIRDSALL, $74.81 to widow Deborah, leaving due by C. W. BIRDSALL $124.09, Marianna BIRDSALL $175.85, Rebecca BIRDSALL $61.82, Elizabeth BIRDSALL $12.62 & Ella BIRDSALL $21.38. RtCt 11 Sep 1878. [G:125]

S/A with Deborah B. BIRDSALL: beginning 22 Nov 1877; general expenses to Ann BIRDSALL & Deborah BIRDSALL, leaving C. W. BIRDSALL $128.43, Marianna BIRDSALL $186.86, Rebecca BIRDSALL $72.40, Eliza BIRDSALL $19.24 & Ella BIRDSALL $29.10. RtCt 10 Nov 1879. [G:198]

BOGER, Catharine

S/A with Gdn Benjamin J. GRUBB: beginning 12 Aug 1867; $2784.98 her distributive share from estate of Saml. BOGER, payments leaving $2505.90. RtCt 12 Apr 1870. [F:30]

S/A with Gdn Benj. J. GRUBB: beginning 12 Sep 1869; general expenses leaving $2562.89, child is not able in mind to care for herself. RtCt 12 Apr 1871. [F:122]

S/A with Gdn Benjamin J. GRUBB: beginning 1 Nov 1869; general expenses leaving $2561.40. RtCt 12 Jun 1871. [F:137]

S/A with Gdn Benjamin J. GRUBB: beginning 14 Aug 1871; general expenses leaving $2763.21. Ward is now dead and her mother Mary Ann BOGER is her heir. RtCt 8 Jun 1874. [F:393]

OSBURN, Walter C.

S/A with Gdn Bushrod OSBURN: beginning 15 Aug 1866; general expenses leaving $1294.95. RtCt 12 Apr 1870. [F:55]

S/A with Gdn Bushrod OSBURN: beginning 31 Oct 1867; general expenses leaving $1175.82. RtCt 10 Nov 1870. [F:69]

S/A Gdn Bushrod OSBURN: beginning Mar 1870; general expenses leaving $1390.40 with $299.15 due to Gdn. RtCt 10 Oct 1871. [F:187]

S/A with Gdn Bushrod OSBURN: beginning 15 Aug 1870; general expenses leaving $1057.50. Ward is now of age. RtCt 12 Aug 1872. [F:240]

OSBURN, Children of T. V. B.

S/A with Gdn Bushrod OSBURN: beginning 15 Aug 1867; general expenses, including acct of Louisa A. OSBURN who is now married, leaving $553.65. RtCt 12 Apr 1870. [F:56]

PUSEY, William N. (Child of Joshua)

S/A with Committee James M. WALTER: (a non compos person) beginning 9 Mar 1868; $800 annuity from father Joshua PUSEY, general expenses, leaving $97.83. RtCt 12 Apr 1870. [F:58]

S/A with Committee James M. WALKER: (a non compos person) beginning 4 Oct 1869; board & care paid to Saml. & Mary HOUGH, general expenses, leaving $57.74. RtCt 13 Feb 1871. [F:100]

S/A with Committee James M. WALKER: (of unsound mind) beginning 4 Jul 1870; general expenses leaving $507, will of father Joshua PUSEY provides for $800/annum. RtCt 11 Jul 1871. [F:170]

S/A with Committee Joshua PUSEY: beginning 31 May 1871; general expenses leaving $507.92. RtCt 12 Aug 1872. [F:244]

S/A with Committee James M. WALKER: (of infirm mind) beginning 2 Jul 1872; general expenses leaving $103.17 due to Committee. RtCt 11 Aug 1873. [F: 347]

S/A with Committee James M. WALKER: beginning 1 Apr 1873; general expenses leaving $125.56. RtCt 8 Jun 1874. [F:419]

S/A with Committee James M. WALKER: beginning 1 Apr 1874; general expenses leaving $164.20. RtCt 9 Aug 1875. [F:471]

S/A with Committee James M. WALKER: beginning 1 Apr 1875; general expenses leaving $148 plus bond. RtCt 15 Jul 1876. [G:21]

S/A with Committee James M. WALKER: beginning Apr 1875; general expenses leaving $216.10. RtCt 9 Jul 1877. [G:63]

S/A with Committee James M. WALKER: beginning 1 Apr 1877; general expenses leaving $132.87. RtCt 9 Jul 1878. [G:116]

S/A with Committee Jas. M. WALKER: beginning 1 Apr 1879; general expenses leaving $39.39. RtCt 15 Jun 1880. [G:222]

S/A with Committee Jas. M. WALKER: beginning 7 Apr 1880; general expenses leaving $77.46. RtCt 13 Jun 1881. [G:274]

S/A with Committee James M. Walker: beginning 1881; general expenses leaving $101.87. RtCt 13 Jun 1882. [G:317]

S/A with Committee J. M. WALKER: beginning 1 Apr 1882; income from interest on bonds, general expenses, leaving $13.15. RtCt 14 Aug 1883. [G:382]

S/A with Committee James M. WALKER: beginning 1 Apr 1883; general expenses leaving $15.14. RtCt 9 Jun 1884. [G:443]

S/A with Committee James M. WALKER: beginning 1 Apr 1884; general expenses leaving $37.21. RtCt 11 Aug 1885. [G:479]

S/A with Committee James M. WALKER: beginning 1 Apr 1885; general expenses leaving $1.33. RtCt 15 Jun 1886. [H:12]

S/A with Committee James M. WALKER: beginning 1 Apr 1886; general expenses leaving $30.10. RtCt 10 Aug 1887. [H:54]

S/A with Committee J. M. WALKER: beginning 1 Apr 1887; general expenses leaving $62.63. RtCt 14 Aug 1888. [H:84]

MANN, J. W. C.
S/A with Joseph M. CONARD: receipt of $421.09 acct paid in full. RtCt 19 Nov 1870. [F:69]

BROWN, Addison
Inventory with John N. BROWN Admr of Committee Benjamin BROWN: sums totaling abt $1000, also entitled to share of the bonds of Daniel SHAFER the purchaser of real estate. RtCt 23 Nov 1870. [F:75]

S/A with Committee Benjamin BROWN: (of unsound mind) beginning 14 Feb 1870; general expenses leaving $776.66. RtCt 17 Aug 1871. [F:171]

S/A with Committee Benjamin BROWN: beginning 17 Feb 1872; general expenses leaving $1597.19 to estate. RtCt 14 Jul 1873. [F: 332]

S/A with Committee Benjamin BROWN: beginning 14 Feb 1873; general expenses leaving $2514.91. RtCt 8 Jun 1874. [F:392]

S/A with Committee Benj. BROWN: beginning 14 Feb 1874; general expenses leaving $2509.08. RtCt 14 Jun 1875. [F:445]

S/A with Committee Benjamin BROWN: beginning 14 Feb 1875; general expenses leaving $2517.21. RtCt 15 Jul 1876. [G:24]

S/A with Committee Benjamin BROWN: beginning 14 Feb 1876; general expenses leaving $2513.44. RtCt 11 Jun 1877. [G:51]

S/A with Committee Benjamin BROWN: beginning 14 Feb 1877; general expenses leaving $2529.52. RtCt 9 Jul 1878. [G:112]

S/A with Committee Benjamin BROWN: beginning 14 Feb 1878; general expenses leaving $2528.83. RtCt 11 Jun 1879. [G:162]

S/A with Committee Benjamin BROWN: beginning 14 Feb 1878; general expenses leaving $2528.83. RtCt 14 Jul 1879. [G:177]

S/A with Committee Benj. BROWN: beginning 14 Feb 1879; paid board to Wesley CARRUTHERS, general expenses, leaving $2621.70. RtCt 17 Apr 1880. [G:216]

S/A with Committee Benjamin BROWN: beginning 14 Feb 1880; general expenses leaving $2666.21. RtCt 10 May 1881. [G:270]

S/A with Committee B. BROWN: beginning 14 Feb 1881; general expenses leaving $2657.14. RtCt 13 Jun 1882. [G:315]

S/A with Committee Benjamin BROWN: beginning 14 Feb 1882; general expenses leaving $2670.71. RtCt 14 May 1883. [G:374]

S/A with Committee Benj. BROWN: beginning 14 Feb 1883; general expenses leaving $2688.26. RtCt 9 Sep 1884. [G:446]

S/A with Committee Benjamin BROWN: beginning 14 Feb 1884; general expenses leaving $2688.26. RtCt 11 Aug 1885. [G:482]

S/A with Committee Benjamin BROWN: beginning 14 Feb 1885; fee to Clark Co. Court, general expenses leaving $3406.32. RtCt 10 Sep 1894. [H:215]

HAMILTON, Lydia A.
Inventory: $332.16 from M. HARRISON. RtCt 4 Jan 1871. [F:87]

LOUDOUN COUNTY, VIRGINIA
GUARDIAN ACCOUNTS
1759-1904

ANDERSON, Lulah, Thomas E. & Nannie D.
Inventory: income from sale of dower land of Mrs. Eleanor ANDERSON. RtCt 2 Mar 1871. [F:122]

S/A with Gdn Martha ANDERSON: beginning 12 Dec 1870; general expenses leaving $297.87. RtCt 10 Aug 1874. [F:421]

S/A with mother & Gdn Martha D. ANDERSON: beginning 12 Dec 1873; general expenses leaving $313.75. RtCt 9 Aug 1875. [F:456]

S/A with Gdn Martha D. ANDERSON: beginning 1 Jul 1875; $175 from Admr of E. ANDERSON, general expenses, leaving $16.82. RtCt 16 Mar 1876. [G:9]

PHILLIPS, Richard S. & Arthur W.
Inventory of 6 Jun 1871 by mother Elizabeth J. PHILLIPS: $771.82 each as distribution from estate of their father, rents of 548 acres of land. RtCt 8 May 1871. [F:136]

Barn acct: $1627.84 expenditures toward rebuilding a barn. RtCt 8 May 1861. [F:137]

S/A with Gdn E. J. PHILLIPS: income from 1/3 of rents and general expenses, leaving Arthur PHILLIPS $713.55. RtCt 13 May 1872. [F:228]

S/A with Gdn E. J. PHILLIPS: income from 1/3 of rents and general expenses, leaving Richard PHILLIPS $405.94. RtCt 13 May 1872. [F:229]

S/A with Gdn Elizabeth J. WHITE: beginning Feb 1870; payments including education, leaving Richard S. PHILLIPS $574.43. RtCt 14 Apr 1873. [F:319]

S/A with Gdn Elizabeth J. PHILLIPS: beginning 12 Dec 1871; general expenses leaving Arthur W. PHILLIPS $1118.89. RtCt 14 Apr 1873. [F:321]

S/A with Gdn Elizth. J. PHILLIPS: beginning 12 Dec 1873; general expenses leaving Arthur W. PHILLIPS $1459.62. RtCt 8 Jun 1874. [F:417]

S/A with Gdn Elizth. J. PHILLIPS: beginning 12 Dec 1873; general expenses leaving Richard S. PHILLIPS $591.70. RtCt 8 Jun 1874. [F:418]

S/A with Gdn Elizabeth J. PHILLIPS: general expenses leaving Richard S. PHILLIPS $784.35. RtCt 14 Jun 1875. [F:449]

S/A with Gdn E. J. PHILLIPS: beginning 12 Dec 1874; general expenses leaving Arthur W. PHILLIPS $1668.50. RtCt 14 Jun 1875. [F:450]

S/A of Arthur W. with Gdn Elizabeth J. PHILLIPS: share of roof on tenant's house, from rents, general expenses, leaving $1887. RtCt 14 Jun 1876. [G:17]

S/A of Richard S. with Gdn Elizabeth J. PHILLIPS: share of roof on tenant's house, from rents, general expenses, leaving $816.50. RtCt 14 Jun 1876. [G:18]

S/A of Arthur W. with Gdn Elizabeth J. PHILLIPS: beginning 2 Dec 1875; general expenses leaving $2050.48. RtCt 9 Jul 1877. [G:62]

S/A of Arthur W. with Gdn E. J. PHILLIPS: general expenses leaving $1844.67. RtCt 10 Mar 1879. [G:157]

S/A of Arthur W. with Gdn Elizabeth J. PHILLIPS: income from share of rent, general expenses, leaving $2034.15. RtCt 11 Jun 1870. [G:170]

S/A of Richard S. with Gdn Elizth. J. PHILLIPS: beginning 23 Feb 1875; general expenses leaving $1208.18 due to Gdn. Ward reached majority on 23 Feb 1876. RtCt 15 Jun 1880. [G:219]

S/A of Arthur W. with Gdn Elizth J. PHILLIPS: beginning 1879; general expenses leaving $1091.94. Ward came of age 8 Apr 1880. RtCt 15 Jun 1880. [G:221]

JEFFRIES, Hannah V.
S/A with Gdn John T. LYNN: beginning 11 Jan 1870; general expenses leaving $157.25. RtCt 12 Jun 1871. [F:141]

S/A with former Gdn John T. LYNN: beginning 11 Dec 1867; general expenses leaving $123.54. RtCt 12 Jun 1871. [F:142]

PIGGOTT, William, Thomas, John, Bushrod, Mary J. and Isaac (Children of Burr)
S/A with Thomas J. NICHOLS Admr of Gdn Thomas NICHOLS: payment in full to William PIGGOTT, Thomas PIGGOTT, John PIGGOTT, Bushrod PIGGOTT, Thomas E. TAYLOR & Mary J. TAYLOR his wife and Isaac PIGGOTT. All are of age. RtCt 12 Jun 1871. [F:146]

SMITH, William B.
S/A with Gdn John ANDERSON: beginning 13 Jan 1868; farm property needed repairs, income from rents, leaving $62.20 due to Gdn. RtCt 12 Jun 1871. [F:147]

S/A with Gdn John ANDERSON. (an infant) beginning 13 Jan 1869; paid for travel to Columbian College, income from crops, leaving $39.49 due to Gdn. Guardianship given to John CARR of Fauquier where ward resides. RtCt 10 Feb 1873. [F:302]

VIRTS, Henry J. J., Clara Hannah C., Rosella V., Mary L., Orra J., America Elizabeth and Annie Rachel (Children of Henry)
S/A with mother & Gdn Virginia VIRTS: beginning 11 Nov 1862; income from 1/7 each of rents, $812.38 from estate of Henry VIRTS of Jacob, general expenses, leaving $615.25 to Henry J. J. VIRTS, leaving $583.22 to Clara Hannah C. VIRTS, leaving $540.62 to Rosella V. VIRTS, leaving $489.30 to Mary L. VIRTS, leaving $555.56 to Orra J. VIRTS, leaving $233.40 to America Elizabeth VIRTS (at boarding school,) leaving $343.77 to Annie Rachel VIRTS (at boarding school.) RtCt 12 Jun 1871. [F:149]

Proceeds of crops of the land and S/As: for widow, Wm. F. BEANS (husband of Annie Rachel VIRTS) and 6 other children. RtCt 12 Jun 1871. [F:157]

S/A with mother & Gdn Virginia VIRTS: beginning 11 Nov 1868; paid American Elizabeth VIRTS' tuition at St. Mary's Springs, general expenses, leaving her $416.66, Rosella V. VIRTS' expenses leaving her $603.77, Clara H.

C. VIRTS' expenses leaving her $93.90, Henry J. VIRTS' expenses leaving him $813.88, Orra J. has $552.88; Henry, Clara & Rosella are quite young and going to school. RtCt 12 Jun 1871. [F:164]

S/A with widow & Gdn Virginia VIRTS: beginning 11 Nov 1869; shares to children Orra J. VIRTS (now of age,) Mary L. VIRTS, Rosella V. VIRTS, Clara H. C. VIRTS & Henry J. J. VIRTS. Annie R. VIRTS is now of age and married, America Elizabeth VIRTS is now of age. RtCt 13 Jan 1873. [F:275]

S/A with widow & Gdn Virginia VIRTS: beginning 11 Nov 1869; income from sale of crops, shares as above. Orra J. reached 21y old on 18 May 1872, America Elizabeth was 21y old on 26 Nov 1869. Annie R. VIRTS married to ___ VIRTS. RtCt 10 Feb 1873. [F:304]

S/A with Gdn Virginia VIRTS: expenses leaving Henry J. J. VIRTS $865.35, Hannah C. VIRTS $629.95, Rosella V. VIRTS $607.27 & Mary L. VIRTS $458.71. RtCt 9 Mar 1874. [F:386]

S/A with agent Virginia VIRTS: beginning 11 Nov 1873; expenses leaving Henry J. J. $926.23, Hannah C. $614.86, Rosella V. $587.44 & Mary L. $459.55. RtCt 9 Mar 1874. [F:388]

S/A with Virginia VIRTS: expenses leaving Henry J. J. $1006.36, Hannah C. $650.82, Rosella V. VIRTS $626.79 & Mary L. VIRTS $487.10. Security of John Leslie is now dead. RtCt 9 Aug 1875. [F:473]

Inventory by Gdn J. E. CARRUTHERS: $1068.09 paid to Henry J. J. VIRTS from former Gdn Mrs. Virginia VIRTS, $673.38 paid to Rosella VIRTS from former Gdn, $622.76 paid to Clara H. A. VIRTS from former Gdn. RtCt 27 Jun 1876. [G:19]

S/A with Virginia VIRTS: $49.39 each leaving Henry J. J. VIRTS $1068.09, Hannah Clara VIRTS $692.76, Rosella V. VIRTS $673.38 & Mary S. VIRTS $533. RtCt 15 Jul 1876. [G:27]

S/A with Gdn James E. CARRUTHERS: beginning 1 Mar 1876; income from mother's estate sale, general expenses, leaving Henry J. J. $35.70 due to Gdn, Clara H. A. $42.36 (teaches music and bought our married sister's share of a piano) due to Gdn & Rosella V. VIRTS (expense of a wedding outfit) $85.93 due to Gdn. RtCt 9 Jul 1877. [G:69]

S/A with Gdn J. E. CARRUTHERS: beginning 14 Feb 1877; general expenses leaving Henry J. J. $16.71 due Gdn, Clara H. VIRTZ $101.72, Rosella VIRTZ (now married) $227.83. RtCt 9 Jul 1878. [G:121]

S/A with Gdn James E. CARRUTHERS: beginning 14 Feb 1878; expenses leaving Clara H. H. (now 21y old since close of year) $203.76 due to Gdn & H. J. J. $67.18 due to Gdn. RtCt 11 Aug 1879. [G:181]

S/A with Gdn Jas. E. CARRUTHERS: beginning 14 Feb 1879; general expenses leaving H. J. J. $145.05; final settlement made with Clara H. A. on 14 Nov 1870. RtCt 15 Jun 1880. [G:226]

S/A with Gdn James E. CARRUTHERS: beginning 14 Feb 1880; general expenses leaving Henry J. J. VIRTZ $139.88. RtCt 13 Jun 1881. [G:278]

S/A with Gdn Jas. E. CARRUTHERS: beginning 14 Feb 1881; paid Henry J. J. $147.81 when he reached age 21y on 24 Jan 1882. RtCt 9 May 1882. [G:311]

HOUGH, Elizabeth H.

S/A with Gdn James C. JANNEY: beginning 4 Apr 1869; legacy from William SWART, general expenses, leaving $.85. RtCt 17 Aug 1871. [F:173]

BOGER, Ella Virginia

Appraisal/Inventory of 10 Oct 1871 by Gdn Andrew ROBEY: CtOD 9 Oct 1871; 2/3 of farm and household items, bonds, totaling $5160.68. Aprs: Jerome W. GOODHART, Jacob SHUMAKER, Peter H. FRY. RtCt 11 Oct 1871. [F:178]

S/A with Gdn Andrew ROBEY: income from land of Mrs. Mollie J. BOGER now LENG and estate of Jacob BOGER. RtCt 9 Jun 1873. [F:326]

S/A with Gdn Andrew ROBEY: beginning 12 Feb 1873; investments totaling $2090.96, mother Mollie J. COTES. RtCt 9 Aug 1875. [F:457]

S/A with Gdn Andrew ROBEY: beginning 12 Feb 1875; general expenses leaving $2065.85 in investments. RtCt 14 Aug 1876. [G:35]

S/A with Gdn Andrew ROBEY: beginning 12 Feb 1876; farm and general expenses leaving $3517.11. RtCt 9 Jul 1877. [G:61]

S/A with Gdn Andrew ROBEY: beginning 12 Feb 1877; general expenses leaving $4441.51 RtCt 9 Jul 1878. [G:111]

S/A with Gdn Andrew ROBEY: beginning 20 Feb 1878; 2 bonds totaling $425, $25.07 left. RtCt 14 Jul 1879. [G:176]

S/A with Gdn Andrew ROBEY: beginning 20 Feb 1879; $5306.94 in bonds, $630.27 legacy from Admr of Mary BOGER, estate increased by $885. RtCt 13 Oct 1880. [G:239]

S/A with Gdn Andrew ROBEY: beginning 23 Jun 1880; income from bonds & interest totaling $5550.34. RtCt 14 Nov 1881. [G:285]

S/A with Gdn Andrew ROBEY: beginning 13 Feb 1881; general expenses, income from bonds, leaving $5813.30. RtCt 9 Oct 1882. [G:339]

S/A with Gdn Andrew ROBEY: beginning 30 Sep 1882; income from bonds, general expenses, leaving $6163.80. RtCt 9 Oct 1883. [G:404]

S/A with Gdn Andrew ROBEY: beginning 13 Feb 1883; general expenses leaving $6432.98. RtCt 9 Sep 1884. [G:444]

S/A with Gdn Andrew ROBEY: beginning 1 Mar 1884; general expenses and investment leaving $6506.20. RtCt 14 Oct 1885. [G:491]

S/A with Gdn H. H. RUSSELL: beginning 1 Apr 1887; general expenses leaving $9031.68, $9020 is invested. RtCt 14 Aug 1888. [H:88]

S/A with Gdn H. H. RUSSELL: beginning 1 Apr 1888; general expenses leaving $343.32 with $9120 loaned out. RtCt 15 Jan 1890. [H:116]

S/A with Gdn H. H. RUSSELL: beginning 1 Apr 1889; general expenses leaving $249.84. RtCt 10 Jun 1891. [H:133]

S/A with Gdn H. H. RUSSELL: beginning 1 Apr 1890; general expenses leaving $202.35. RtCt 14 Apr 1892. [H:153]

S/A with Gdn H. H. RUSSELL: beginning 1 Apr 1891; general expenses leaving $9396.64 paid in full 3 May 1892 to Ella V. now Ella V. VIRTZ. RtCt 14 Nov 1893. [H:181]

BRADEN, Cecelia L., Robert & Rodney Walter

S/A with Gdn Oscar S. BRADEN: beginning Jun 1869; expenses of Cecelia L. BRADEN leaving $125.76 due to Gdn, expenses of Robert BRADEN including tuition at Roanoke College, leaving $137.28 due to Gdn. RtCt 23 Nov 1871. [F:190]

S/A with Gdn Oscar S. BRADEN: beginning Jun 1869; general expenses leaving Rodney Walter BRADEN $157.33. RtCt 23 Nov 1871. [F:192]

S/A with Gdn O. S. BRADEN: beginning 12 Jun 1871; paid board to Mrs. BRADEN, payments leaving R. Walter BRADEN $33.81 & Cecelia V. BRADEN $526.51 due to Gdn (some debt from surgery to her eyes.) RtCt 14 Aug 1876. [G:36]

S/A with Gdn: Cecelia V. became of age on 12 Jun 1876, owed Gdn $526.50, acct. closed. RtCt 11 Jun 1879. [G:168]

S/A of Robert BRADEN with Gdn O. S. BRADEN: beginning 12 Jun 1871; general expenses leaving $97.24 due to Gdn. RtCt 14 Aug 1876. [G:38]

SHREVE, Virginia, Francis, Mary and Daniel S. (Children of William)

S/A with Gdn William E. GARRETT: beginning 18 Nov 1868; accts. of Virginia SHREVE, Francis SHREVE, Mary SHREVE & Daniel Trundle SHREVE, expenses from repairing a mill. RtCt 23 Nov 1871. [F:193]

S/A with Gdn Wm. E. GARRETT: beginning 16 Nov 1870; income from sale of land in Missouri, shares to Virginia SHREVE, Francis SHREVE, Mary SHREVE & Daniel Trundle SHREVE, leaving $53.49 due to Gdn. RtCt 14 Oct 1872. [F:256]

S/A with Gdn Wm. E. GARRETT: income from farm rents and rents of tenant house, general expenses and for mill repairs, leaving Virginia SHREVE $91.20 due to Gdn, Francis SHREVE $98.36 due to Gdn, Mary SHREVE $117.61 & Daniel S. SHREVE $84.78. RtCt 10 Jan 1876. [G:6]

S/A with Gdn Wm. E. GARRETT: beginning 14 Apr 1874; general expenses to Mary, William, Danl. & Frances from Daniel T. SHREVE. RtCt 9 Jul 1878. [G:107]

STOCKS, William (of unsound mind)

Appraisal/Inventory of 16 Nov 1871 by Committee Mahlon STOCKS: CtOD 11 Sep 1871; farm and household items totaling $817.55, notes, crops. Aprs: William FAWLEY, John WILLIAMS, Lewen T. JONES. RtCt 25 Nov 1871. [F:196]

Sale by Committee Mahlon STOCKS: purchasers: Jackson MINOR, Saml SWANK, Rich'd JAMES, Jas. MATHEWS, Geo. HICKMAN, Geo. BAKER, Geo. EVERHART, Jno. WILLIAMS, Jno. TITUS, Geo. SHOEMAKER, Saml. MONEY, Saml. SNOOTS, Ed WHITE, Wm. H. SCHOOLEY, Jas. WILLIAMS, Wilson BARRETT, Jonas COMPHER, Danl. FRY, Syd. TITUS, Mary E. STOCKS, Jonas SLATER, Henry VIRTS, Jno. BEATTY, Wm. SPRING, totaling $917.02. RtCt 10 Jan 1872. [F:203]

S/A with father & Committee Mahlon STOCKS: beginning 14 Jun 1872; general expenses leaving $689.64. RtCt 9 Jun 1873. [F:328]

S/A with Committee Mahlon STOCKS: beginning 14 Apr 1873; general expenses leaving $621.80. RtCt 8 Jun 1874. [F:420]

STOCKS, John H. (of unsound mind)

Inventory by Committee J. R. RODERICK: $110 from Mahlon STOCKS. RtCt 30 Mar 1874. [F:390]

S/A with Committee Mahlon STOCKS: beginning 1 Feb 1874; $112 payable to new Committee Jacob R. RODERICK. RtCt 8 Jun 1874. [F:420]

S/A with Committee Mahlon STOCKS: beginning 1 Feb 1874; funds from estate of Wm. STOCKS, leaving $112. RtCt 10 Aug 1874. [F:422]

S/A with Committee Jacob R. RODERICK: beginning 17 Mar 1874; general expenses leaving $266.42. RtCt 9 Jul 1878. [G:120]

S/A with Committee Jacob R. RODERICK: beginning 10 Nov 1877; general expenses leaving $248.25. RtCt 11 Jun 1879. [G:171]

S/A with Committee Jacob R. RODERICK: beginning 10 Nov 1878; general expenses leaving $194.44. RtCt 13 Oct 1880. [G:242]

S/A with Committee Jacob P. RODERICK: beginning 10 Nov 1879; general expenses leaving $145.78. RtCt 9 Jan 1882. [G:303]

S/A with Committee J. R. RODERICK: beginning 10 Nov 1881; general expenses leaving $25.64, needs to dispose of the land or ward will go on public cost. RtCt 11 Dec 1883. [G:416]

S/A with Committee J. R. RODERICK: beginning 10 Nov 1883; income from rent of land, general expenses, leaving $65.31. RtCt 11 Nov 1884. [G:454]

S/A with Committee J. R. RODERICK: beginning 13 Jun 1885; income from sale of land and crops, general expenses, leaving $409.20. Committee Jacob R. RODERICK has died and Geo. P. HUNTER become new Committee: RtCt 10 Jan 1888. [H:59]

S/A with Committee G. V. WARNER: beginning 10 Apr 1888; general expenses leaving estate $229.27. RtCt 15 Jan 1890. [H:123]

SHRIVER, Emily Gertrude, Martha Ellen & Willie
S/A with Gdn W. H. GRUBB: beginning 4 Sep 1869; income from sale of land in Illinois, general expenses, leaving $217.76. RtCt 23 Nov 1871. [F:200]

S/A with Gdn Wm. H. GRUBB: beginning 1 Nov 1871; general expenses, $72.27 to each ward. RtCt 12 Apr 1875. [F:442]

S/A of Emily Gertrude with Gdn Wm. H. GRUBB: beginning 14 Dec 1874; $208.96 due to Mrs. Ann SHRIVER, expenses, leaving $187.57 each to Emily, Ellen & Willie SHRIVER. RtCt 9 Jul 1878. [G:119]

SHRIVER, Alice R. & Annie Mariah
S/A with Gdn Wm. H. GRUBB: beginning 4 Sep 1869; general expenses leaving $140.89. RtCt 23 Nov 1871. [F:201]

S/A with Gdn Wm. H. GRUBB: beginning 14 Dec 1871; payments to mother, general expenses, leaving $284.96. Small sum to widow for life with remainder to her five children. RtCt 12 Apr 1875. [F:441]

S/A of Alice R. with Gdn Wm. H. GRUBB: beginning 12 Dec 1874; general expenses leaving $114.94. Alice R. is now of age and Annie M. is married. RtCt 9 Jul 1878. [G:117]

BRADEN, Florence M.
Inventory by Gdn Wm. C. SHAWEN: money from estate of grandfather Joshua PUSEY. RtCt 1 Feb 1872. [F:208]

S/A with Gdn Wm. C. SHAWEN: beginning 13 Mar 1871; paid tuition and general expenses, leaving $551.29. RtCt 14 Oct 1872. [F:248]

WHITLOCK, Henry and Mattie E. (ROBERTS)
Inventory by Gdn Henry WHITLOCK: $300 from legacy from the state of Connecticut. RtCt 10 Feb 1872. [F:209]

ROGERS, Maria C., Ellen V., George R., Laura Lee and Charlotte R. (Children of Arthur L. and Charlotte)
Inventory by Gdn A. T. M. RUST: insurance policy. Children Laura Lee, George K. & Charlotte K. ROGERS. [very faint on microfilm] RtCt 4 Mar 1872. [F:209]

S/A with Gdn A. T. M. RUST: mother C. A. ROGERS, general expenses leaving $3905. RtCt 14 Sep 1874. [F:426]

S/A with Gdn A. T. M. RUST: beginning 9 Jun 1874; paid mother C. A. ROGERS, general expenses, leaving $22.31 to ware and $113.95 due to Gdn. Bulk of estate is $3905.02 at 8% interest. RtCt 14 Jun 1875. [F:451]

S/A with Gdn A. T. M. RUST: beginning 8 Jan 1875; paid mother C. A. ROGERS, general expenses leaving $22.31 to wards and $109.74 to Gdn. RtCt 16 Mar 1876. [G:14]

S/A with Gdn A. T. M. RUST: beginning 31 Dec 1875; payments to mother C. A. ROGERS, general expenses, leaving $23.24 due to Gdn. RtCt 11 Jun 1877. [G:58]

S/A with Gdn A. T. M. RUST: beginning 9 Jan 1877; mother C. A. ROGERS, children Maria C., Ellen V., George R., Laura Lee & Charlotte R., expenses leaving $79.52 due to Gdn. RtCt 11 Sep 1878. [G:134]

S/A with Gdn A. T. M. RUST: beginning 9 Jan 1878; mother C. A. ROGERS, general expenses leaving $3405. RtCt 11 Jun 1879. [G:163]

S/A with Gdn A. T. M. RUST: beginning 9 Jan 1879; general income & expenses leaving $3405. RtCt 15 Jun 1880. [G:224]

S/A with Gdn A. T. M. RUST: beginning 9 Jan 1880; general expenses leaving $781 to Maria C. Rogers (came of age in Oct or Nov) and $1974 to other wards. All living with mother. RtCt 10 May 1881. [G:272]

S/A with Gdn A. T. M. RUST: beginning 9 Jan 1881; general expenses leaving $1974. RtCt 9 May 1882. [G:310]

S/A with Gdn A. T. M. RUST: beginning 9 Jan 1882; general expenses leaving $1974. RtCt 14 May 1883. [G:373]

S/A with Gdn A. T. M. RUST: beginning 9 Jan 1883; general expenses leaving $1974. RtCt 13 May 1884. [G:434]

S/A with Gdn A. T. M. RUST: beginning 9 Jan 1884; general expenses leaving $1974. RtCt 14 Apr 1885. [G:475]

S/A of Ella V. and Laura L. with Gdn A. L. M. RUST: beginning 9 Jan 1885; $781 to Ella V. ROGERS on 5 Mar 1885 as she is now 21y old, general expenses, leaving $2343. RtCt 11 May 1886. [H:7]

S/A of Ella V. and Laura L. with Gdn A. T. M. RUST: beginning 9 Jan 1886; general expenses leaving $2343. RtCt 10 May 1887. [H:36]

S/A of Ella V. and Laura L. with Gdn A. T. M. RUST: beginning 9 Jan 1887; interest to Mrs. ROGERS, general expenses, leaving Laura L. (now of age) $534.94 & $781 to unnamed sibling. RtCt 12 Jan 1891. [H:130]

HOUSEHOLDER, Kate C. & Daniel P.
Inventory: proceeds of sale of estate. [very faint on microfilm] RtCt 7 Mar 1872. [F:210]

S/A with Gdn George W. JANNEY: beginning 10 Apr 1871; general expenses leaving Daniel $1791.28 & Kate C. $1787.74. RtCt 14 Oct 1872. [F:250]

S/A with Gdn George W. JANNEY: beginning 1 Jun 1872; general expenses leaving Daniel P. HOUSEHOLDER $3070.57. Gdn has removed to Baltimore. RtCt 14 Jul 1873. [F: 333]

S/A with Gdn George W. JANNEY: general expenses leaving Kate C. HOUSEHOLDER $2962.82. Gdn has removed to Baltimore. RtCt 14 Jul 1873. [F: 334]

S/A with Gdn George W. JANNEY: general expenses leaving Kate C. HOUSEHOLDER $3040. RtCt 8 Jun 1874. [F:395]

S/A with Gdn Luther A. MANN: general expenses leaving Kate C. HOUSEHOLDER $2842.55. RtCt 14 Jun 1875. [F:448]

S/A of Kate C. HOUSEHOLDER with Gdn Luther A. MANN: beginning 8 Apr 1875; general expenses leaving $2842.55 to ward and $18.32 of profits to Gdn. RtCt 14 Aug 1876. [G:40]

S/A of Kate C. HOUSEHOLDER with Gdn L. A. MANN: beginning 13 Apr 1876; general expenses leaving $2993.57. RtCt 11 Sep 1878. [G:132]

S/A of Kate C. HOUSEHOLDER with Gdn Luther A. MANN: beginning 13 Apr 1877; general expenses leaving $2876.47. RtCt 11 Sep 1878. [G:133]

S/A of Kate C. HOUSEHOLDER with Gdn Luther A. MANN: beginning 13 Apr 1878; general expenses leaving $2916.30 to 13 Aug 1880 when she attained age. RtCt 14 Dec 1880. [G:247]

S/A of Daniel P. HOUSHOLDER with Gdn George W. JANNEY: beginning 1873; general expenses leaving $2859.40. Ward reached 21y old on 2 Aug 1874. RtCt 11 Sep 1878. [G:130]

S/A of Daniel P. HOUSHOLDER with Gdn Geo. W. JANNEY: expenses leaving $1772.54. Ward now of age, acct. closed. RtCt 11 Aug 1879. [G:191]

PAXON, Lillie
Inventory by Gdn Westwood PAXSON: receipts from Lillie PAXSON, Rosa PAXSON & Clara PAXSON. [very faint on microfilm] RtCt 7 Mar 1872. [F:211]

BUSSARD, M. W.
S/A with Gdn O. M. BUSSARD: general expenses leaving $333.08. [very faint on microfilm] RtCt 16 Mar 1872. [F:211]

HOUGH, Edgar
S/A with Gdn James M. WALKER: beginning 14 Jan 1868; general expenses, income from interest on loans, leaving $952.06. RtCt 13 May 1872. [F:222]

S/A with Gdn James M. WALKER: beginning 14 Jan 1869; general expenses leaving $1082.91. RtCt 11 Aug 1873. [F: 345]

S/A with Gdn Jas. M. WALKER: beginning 1 May 1873; reached majority by 19 Apr 1874, leaving $1173. RtCt 8 Jun 1874. [F:415]

HICKS, Kimble G. Jr.
S/A with Gdn Kimble G. HICKS: beginning 14 Aug 1854; $1000 legacy from Thomas SHEARMAN, income from rent of farm and from hire of Negroes Webster Mitchell, Jenny, Julia Ann, Ann Matilda, Winney, Jim, Jack Taylor, Scott, Lettice & Mary, leaving $7790.48. Gdn died 23 May 1861. Information furnished by A. C. BYRNE who married the sister of ward who was Gdn's son. RtCt 13 May 1872. [F:224]

SCHOOLEY, Annette F. & Kate F.
Inventory by Gdn Mrs. Sarah Ann SCHOOLEY: rents and profits from 2/11 of 2/3 of 276 ¼ acres of land. RtCt 5 Aug 1872. [F:232]

S/A with Gdn Sarah A. SCHOOLEY: all monies have been paid. RtCt 9 Jul 1877. [G:65]

FOSTER, F. H.
Inventory by Jas. W. WORKS: sales totaling $47.25, small sums arising from the purchase money of a house & lot in Aldie. RtCt 5 Aug 1872. [F:233]

BEAMER, Michael T.
S/A with Gdn John LESLIE: beginning 10 Dec 1867; funds from H. HEATON in case of Edward MORRISON's estate, expenses, leaving $180. RtCt 12 Aug 1872. [F:233]

RUST, R. L. B. & M. A. E.
S/A with Gdn Simon SANBOWER: beginning 9 Apr 1866; division of land, general expenses, leaving $19.80 due to Gdn. RtCt 14 Oct 1872. [F:253]

MATTHEWS, Jonathan, Rodney & Mary C., John and Jesse
S/A with Bernard HOUGH: beginning 1 Apr 1853; general expenses, Jonathan reached majority by 7 Feb 1863, mother Susan MATTHEWS, L. S. MOORE the husband of Mary C. MATTHEWS, shares of John & Jesse MATTHEWS not stated (one is dead and the other is a nonresident of state.) RtCt 14 Oct 1872. [F:259]

BENTLEY, Maria W., Robert, Elizabeth P. and Ann C. (Children of R. M.)
S/A with Gdn A. C. BENTLEY: $1000 each from insurance policy loaned out to Maria W. BENTLEY, Robert L. BENTLEY, Elizabeth P. BENTLEY & Ann C. BENTLEY. RtCt 14 Nov 1872. [F:271]

PANCOAST, Alberta M., Lillias and Rosa Lee (Children of Joseph) [PANCOST]
Inventory by Gdn Henry HEATON: Loans to Alberta M. PANCOAST, Lillias PANCOAST, Rosa Lee PANCOAST, income from bonds, rents of 182 ½ acre farm

after 1/3 to widow, and interest on $1000 from will of Joel OSBURN. RtCt 1 Jan 1873. [F:271]

S/A with Henry HEATON: beginning 28 Oct 1868; income from rents & sale of crops, payment rec'd from estates of great uncle John PANCOAST & Sidney HAWLING, widow Mrs. J. A. PANCOAST & children Alberta M. PANCOAST, Lillias PANCOAST & Rosa Lee PANCOAST (too young to go to school, while others have completed their schooling) RtCt 10 Feb 1873. [F:283]

S/A with Gdn Henry HEATON: beginning 1 Nov 1871; income from crops, general expenses, as above. RtCt 10 Feb 1873. [F:292]

S/A with Gdn Henry HEATON: beginning 10 Jun 1872; expenses and proceeds of real estate leaving Alberta M. PANCOAST who married Maurice OSBURN $2228.70, Lilias PANCOAST $1745.57 & youngest child Rosa Lee PANCOAST $5742.02. RtCt 8 Sep 1873. [F:358]

S/A with Gdn Henry HEATON: beginning 10 Jun 1873; general expenses leaving Rosa Lee PANCOAST $460.06. RtCt 13 Aug 1877. [G:75]

S/A with agent & Gdn Henry HEATON: beginning 6 Sep 1873; $57.63 to widow Jane A. PANCOST, $58.51 each to Morris OSBURN, Lilias PANCOST (who is now 21y old) & Rosa Lee PANCOST. RtCt 13 Aug 1877. [G:77]

S/A of Lilias PANCOST with Gdn Henry HEATON: her acct. settled in full with her husband R. Bentley GRAY. RtCt 13 Aug 1877. [G:82]

S/A with Henry HEATON: beginning 1 Jan 1877; income from rents, general expenses to widow Mrs. Jane A. PANCOAST, Rosa Lee has $5738.78 bearing interest. RtCt 12 Nov 1877. [G:90]

S/A with Gdn Henry HEATON: beginning 6 Jul 1877; expenses leaving Rosa Lee PANCOAST $6052.07. Ward soon old enough to go to school. RtCt 9 Dec 1878. [G:138]

S/A of Rosa Lee PANCOAST with Gdn Henry HEATON: beginning 24 Jun 1878; reached majority on 15 Feb 1886, general expenses leaving $3864.96. RtCt 10 Aug 1886. [H:14]

HAWLING, Children of Joseph L.
Money received by his children as their Gdn: $1000 each to Mary HAWLING, Martha HAWLING, Anne HAWLING & Rose HAWLING. RtCt 1 Mar 1873. [F:307]

LLOYD, Annie & Maud
S/A with Gdn Samuel ORRISON: beginning 8 May 1871; payments from Admrs of C. E. LLOYD, Geo. LLOYD & H. LLOYD; $898.25 due ward at death on 16 Feb 1872 divided between mother Emily E. LLOYD & Maud LLOYD; $1372.58 due Maud at death on 25 Mar 1872. RtCt 14 Apr 1873. [F:317]

SHOEMAKER, George, William, Sarah, Elizabeth and Mary (Children of Josiah)
S/A with Gdn John H. TITUS: beginning 9 Mar 1869; payments of $175 each to George SHOEMAKER, Wm. SHOEMAKER, Sarah SHOEMAKER, Elizabeth SHOEMAKER & Mary SHOEMAKER. Father Josiah SHOEMAKER was in default as Admr of Solomon COOPER. RtCt 14 Apr 1873. [F:322]

PAXSON, Alice B.
Inventory of Gdn Thomas J. MAFFETT: $31.42 rec'd from father W. B. PAXSON in May 1873. RtCt 14 Jul 1873. [F: 336]

FRY, Isabella
S/A with Gdn Christian FRY: beginning 12 Aug 1868; distribution from estate of S. FRY, general expenses, leaving $139.50. RtCt 11 Aug 1873. [F: 338]

THOMPSON, George S., Ann Eliza and Barbara Cornelia (Children of Joseph)
Inventory: $166.67 from estate of Saml. THOMPSON invested in house & lot occupied by mother Sarah THOMPSON & children George S. THOMPSON, Ann Eliza THOMPSON & Barbara Cornelia THOMPSON. RtCt 26 Aug 1873. [F: 350]

DABNEY, R. Heath
S/A with Gdn V. DABNEY: beginning 18 Jun 1872; paid taxes on lands in Iowa, general expenses, leaving $203.35. RtCt 11 Nov 1873. [F:364]

S/A with Gdn Virginia DABNEY: beginning 11 Aug 1873; land in Jackson Co & Calhoun Co IA, $1600 legacy from Mrs. HALL. Gdn is a teacher in NY City. RtCt 10 Mar 1879. [G:150]

S/A with Gdn Virginia DABNEY: beginning 10 Jun 1876; general expenses leaving $1560.89. RtCt 11 Mar 1880. [G:211]

BEAMER, John Samuel
S/A with Gdn Michael BEAMER: beginning 1 Jan 1868; $309.69 from legacy of Jos. MORRISON, expenses leaving $958.50. He has paid Bassett LEE the husband of Julietta BEAMER and he was father & distributee of George E. BEAMER the other has inherited the interest. RtCt 12 Jan 1874. [F:365]

JONES, Henrietta, John William & Arthur Lee
Inventory by Gdn James H. JONES: interest of abt $100 in personal estate of grandfather Moses P. WATSON, income from rents of 20 of land. RtCt 16 Apr 1874. [F:391]

S/A with Gdn James H. JONES: beginning Nov 1873; Henrietta & John W. each paid $361.85 when they came of age, Arthur L. is the only one <21y. RtCt 11 Mar 1880. [G:208]

S/A with Gdn Jas. H. JONES: beginning 6 Jan 1879; general expenses leaving Arthur Lee JONES $358.69 paid in full on 6 Dec 1882. RtCt 13 Feb 1883. [G:362]

FILLER, William H. & Sarah J.
S/A with Gdn Ezekiel POTTS: beginning 10 Nov 1860; general expenses leaving $79.20 for both. RtCt 14 Sep 1874. [F:424]

S/A with Gdn Ezekiel POTTS: W. H. FILLER's acct of $10.20 paid in full. RtCt 12 Apr 1875. [F:436]

PIGGOTT, Ruth Hannah
Inventory by Committee John W. PIGGOTT: $2032 in cash, income from rent of 22 1/3 acres of land. RtCt 1 Dec 1874. [F:429]

S/A with Committee John W. PIGGOTT: beginning 10 Nov 1874; income from dower rent of T. H. PIGGOTT, general expenses leaving $224.24. RtCt 15 Jul 1876. [G:22]

S/A with Committee John W. PIGGOTT: income from share of rent dower and rent of land, general expenses, leaving $340.44 to ward and $17.93 to Committee. RtCt 11 Jun 1877. [G:57]

S/A with DShff & Committee William GAINES: beginning 14 Sep 1886; general expenses leaving $86.28. RtCt 14 Aug 1888. [H:83]

S/A with Gdn Henry VIRTS: beginning 1 Jan 1886; general expenses leaving estate $397.19 turned over to Geo. W. TITUS the new Gdn. RtCt 14 Aug 1888. [H:85]

GREGG, Phebe A.
S/A with Gdn Martha A. GREGG: beginning 10 Jun 1868; paid board & tuition in PA, income from rent of farm, leaving $5375.08. Became of age on 17 Oct 1873. RtCt 9 Feb 1875. [F:430]

HAWLING, Eugene
S/A with Gdn Eliza HAWLING: beginning 15 Feb 1871; general expenses leaving $266.30. RtCt 12 Apr 1875. [F:437]

HAWLING, Cecil
S/A with Gdn Eliza HAWLING: beginning 15 Feb 1871; general expenses leaving $474.25 due to Gdn. RtCt 12 Apr 1875. [F:439]

BEAMER, Julia E.
S/A with Gdn Michael BEAMER: balance in full paid to Bassett LEE. RtCt 14 Jun 1875. [F:446]

CRIM, John Edward
S/A with Committee Saml. CRIM: beginning 15 Oct 1872; general expenses leaving $125.56. RtCt 14 Jun 1875. [F:446]

HATCHER, Lindig and Lucy (Children of Rodney G.)
S/A with Gdn M. G. & T. A. HATCHER: $3489.96 received from Wm. McCRAY Admr of Rodney G. HATCHER, bond of estate of W. Byron LOVETT, bond on estate of Nancy L. HATCHER dec'd, bond assigned to widow Fanny HATCHER as her dower; children Lindig & Lucy HATCHER. RtCt 13 Jul 1875. [F:455]

HUTCHISON, James
S/A with Committee Silas HUTCHISON: beginning 1839; income from hire of servants and rent of farm, paid John HUTCHISON for board, general expenses leaving $794.85. RtCt in Fairfax 30 Jun 1871. RtCt Loudoun 9 Aug 1875. [F:459]

S/A with Committee Silas M. HUTCHISON: beginning 1 Jan 1870; general expenses and income from interest leaving $1973.50 RtCt 11 Apr 1883. [G:367]

S/A with Committee Silas M. HUTCHISON: beginning 1 Jan 1870; $794.88 per report from Fairfax Co, general expenses leaving $749.99. RtCt 12 Jun 1883. [G:378]

SMITH, William P., Mary J., Thomas J. and Samuel J. (Heirs of Phebe)
S/A with Gdn John W. PIGGOTT: $95.48 due equally to Wm. P., Mary J., Thos. J. & Samuel J. SMITH. RtCt 9 Aug 1875. [F:472]

STEADMAN, Carrie H.
Inventory by Gdn Susan F. STEADMAN: $150 from sale of her father's real estate and invested by Gdn in a house & lot with her own dower interest in said estate. RtCt 10 Aug 1875. [F:475]

CARTER, Alice V.
S/A with Gdn C. W. JOHNSON: beginning 18 Nov 1872; general expenses, leaving $68. Wards funds ordered to be removed to OH. RtCt 8 Nov 1875. [F:476]

NEER, Florence
S/A with Gdn Charles W. JOHNSON: beginning 10 Apr 1866; payment to collector of White Co. IN, general expenses, leaving $30.44. RtCt 8 Nov 1875. [F:487]

BENTLEY, Nellie, Belle & Kate (Children of E. L.)
Inventory by Hy C. SELLMAN: $52 each from Mutual Benefit Life Insurance Co. of NJ, $990 each from Protection Insurance Co. of Chicago, rents from Dr. A. R. MOTT. RtCt 13 Nov 1875. [F:497]

S/A with Gdn H. C. SELLMAN: (children of E. L. BENTLEY) paid insurance and general expenses, leaving Nellie $0, Kate $80.12 due to Gdn, and Bell (tuition at Emmettsburg) $143.09 due to Gdn. RtCt 11 Jun 1877. [G:49]

S/A with Gdn H. C. SELLMAN: beginning 11 May 1877; general expenses leaving Belle BENTLEY $1112.83. RtCt 9 Dec 1878. [G:140]

S/A with late Gdn H. C. SELLMAN: Nellie BENTLEY now wife of M. McABEE and acct. settled in full with $250 payment of 28 Aug 1878. RtCt 10 Mar 1879. [G:149]

S/A with Gdn H. C. SELLMAN: beginning 11 May 1877; income from sale of house and land, paid tuition in Emittsburg, general expenses, leaving Kate BENTLEY $1388.48. RtCt 11 Aug 1880. [G:228]

S/A with Gdn H. C. SELLMAN: beginning 1a May 1878; income from sale of land, general expenses, leaving Belle BENTLEY $1508.39. RtCt 11 Aug 1880. [G:231]

S/A with Gdn H. C. SELLMAN: beginning 11 May 1880; paid tuition at Emittsburg, general expenses, leaving Kate BENTLEY $1247.93. RtCt 9 Oct 1882. [G:336]

S/A with Gdn H. C. SELLMAN: beginning 11 May 1880; general expenses leaving Belle BENTLEY $1523.25. RtCt 9 Oct 1882. [G:338]

S/A with Gdn H. C. SELLMAN: beginning 11 May 1882; general expenses leaving Kate BENTLEY $1154.19. RtCt 13 May 1884. [G:431]

S/A with Gdn H. C. SELLMAN: beginning 19 Jul 1875; general expenses leaving Nelly BENTLEY $415.98 due when of age. RtCt 10 Mar 1885. [G:471]

MOORE, Sarah A. & Mary S.
Inventory by C. W. BARTON: $440 interest in said estate, house & lot of 5 acres occupied since 1866, widow is now my wife. RtCt 13 Dec 1875. [G:1]

S/A with Gdn C. W. BARTON: beginning 13 Sep 1875; general expenses leaving Sarah A. MOORE bonds of $220 less $9.79 Gdn expenses. RtCt 11 Jun 1877. [G:53]

RUSSELL, Emily M.
S/A with Gdn Louisa RUSSELL: beginning 14 Aug 1869; income from share of rent, expenses, leaving $156.78 due to Gdn and $2163.73 due to ward. RtCt 10 Jan 1876. [G:1]

S/A with Gdn Mrs. J. Louisa RUSSELL: beginning 11 Jun 1880; general expenses leaving $2375.63. RtCt 13 Jun 1881. [G:276]

RUSSELL, Matilda
S/A with Gdn Louisa RUSSELL: beginning 14 Aug 1869; income from share of rent, general expenses, leaving $2163.73 less $425.88 in advancements. RtCt 10 Jan 1876. [G:4]

VIRTS, Rosa A.
Inventory by Gdn John W. VIRTS: $900 from Saml. CLENDENING and Joseph P. GRUBB Execs of Saml. CLENDENING. RtCt 10 Mar 1876. [G:9]

S/A with Gdn Jno. W. VIRTS: payments leaving $1823.57 due to her husband. RtCt 10 Mar 1879. [G:158]

BROWN, Children of Albert O.
S/A with Gdn A. J. BRADFIELD: beginning 10 Nov 1873; paid mother Mrs. BROWN, general expenses, leaving $733.17. RtCt 16 Mar 1876. [G:10]

S/A with Gdn A. J. BRADFIELD: beginning 14 Jun 1876; general expenses leaving $733.17. RtCt 10 Dec 1877. [G:92]

S/A with Gdn A. J. BRADFIELD: beginning 10 Nov 1873; general expenses leaving Arthur BROWN & others $733.17. RtCt 13 Feb 1878. [G:100]

S/A with Gdn A. J. BRADFIELD: beginning 6 Dec 1876; $60 allotted mother for support of children, leaving $706.75. RtCt 13 Feb 1878. [G:101]

S/A with Gdn A. J. BRADFIELD: beginning 19 Nov 1878; general expenses leaving $641.05. RtCt 11 Mar 1880. [G:215]

S/A with Gdn A. J. BRADFIELD: beginning 10 Nov 1879; general expenses leaving $609.30. RtCt 15 Feb 1881. [G:258]

S/A with Gdn A. J. BRADFIELD: beginning 10 Nov 1880; general expenses leaving $578.55. RtCt 9 Jan 1882. [G:300]

S/A with Gdn A. J. BRADFIELD: beginning 10 Nov 1881; general expenses leaving $548.25. RtCt 13 Feb 1883. [G:365]

S/A with Gdn A. J. BRADFIELD: beginning 10 Nov 1882; paid Mrs. BROWN for maintanence, general expenses, leaving $497.55. RtCt 13 May 1884. [G:429]

S/A with Gdn A. J. BRADFIELD: beginning 1o Nov 1883; general expenses leaving $459.55. RtCt 14 Apr 1885. [G:476]

S/A with Gdn A. J. BRADFIELD: beginning 10 Nov 1884; general expenses leaving $328.19. RtCt 11 May 1886. [H:4]

S/A with Gdn A. J. BRADFIELD: beginning 10 Nov 1885; paid Mrs. Eliza D. BROWN, general expenses leaving $172.32. RtCt 14 May 1889. [H:102]

S/A with Gdn A. J. BRADFIELD: beginning 19 Nov 1877; general expenses leaving $674.02. RtCt 14 Apr 1892. [H:151]

S/A with Gdn A. J. BRADFIELD: beginning 10 Nov 1888; general expenses leaving $89.41. RtCt 14 Apr 1892. [H:151]

S/A with Gdn A. J. BRADFIELD: beginning 10 Nov 1890; general expenses leaving $16.17, they have attained their majority. RtCt 14 Apr 1892. [H:152]

HILLEARY, H. C.
S/A with Committee Wm. SMITH: beginning 26 Dec 1874; general expenses leaving $42.68 due to Admr. RtCt 16 Mar 1875. [G:12]

LYNN, Gertrude & Fanny
S/A wit Gdn Edgar ISH: beginning Oct 1874; general expenses leaving Gertrude $21.99 due to Gdn & Fanny $27.12 due to Gdn. RtCt 16 Mar 1876. [G:13]

VANSICKLER, Rosa Bell
　S/A with Gdn John MEAD: general expenses leaving $176.34. RtCt 16 Mar 1876. [G:15]
　S/A with Gdn John MEAD: beginning 11 Mar 1874; general expenses leaving $175.57. RtCt 16 Mar 1876. [G:16]
　S/A wit Gdn John MEAD: beginning 11 Mar 1875; general expenses leaving $250.75. RtCt 10 Nov 1879. [G:201]
　S/A with Gdn John MEAD: beginning 1879; Rosa became 21y old on 14 May 1880 and due $250.75. RtCt 12 Jan 1883. [G:381]

ELGIN, Ida F. (Child of Robert & Margaret)
　Inventory with Gdn P. H. CARR: $75 or ¼ of rents of a farm from estate of father Robert ELGIN dec'd & mother Margaret ELGIN dec'd. RtCt 6 Jun 1876. [G:17]
　S/A with Gdn P. H. CARR: beginning 10 Apr 1876; expenses leaving $5.30 due to Gdn. RtCt 13 Feb 1878. [G:103]
　S/A with Gdn Peter H. CARR: beginning 10 Apr 1877; general expenses leaving 20.28. RtCt 10 Nov 1879. [G:194]
　S/A with Gdn Peter H. CARR: beginning Apr 1879; general expenses leaving $18.10. RtCt 10 Nov 1879. [G:195]
　S/A with Gdn Peter H. CARR: beginning 1 Apr 1879; general expenses leaving $706.11. RtCt 15 Feb 1881. [G:259]
　S/A with Gdn Peter H. CARR: beginning 1 Apr 1880; general expenses leaving $768.67. RtCt 14 Nov 1881. [G:294]
　S/A with Gdn P. H. CARR: beginning 1 Apr 1881; income from rent and from mother, general expenses leaving $829.53 paid on 17 Oct 1882 when she became of age. RtCt 9 Jan 1883. [G:358]

STEER, James M.
　Appraisal/Inventory of 9 Jun 1876: real estate in Waterford known as lots no. 47 & 48 in the new addition of the town. Admr says not enough funds to pay the 3 heirs or all the debts. Aprs: Wm. WILLIAMS, S. A. GOVER, C. L. HOLLINGSWORTH. RtCt 27 Jun 1876. [G:20]

DOUGLAS, James E.
　Inventory at Aldie by Gdn Andrew J. FLEMING: $612.68 at Citizens National Bank of Alexandria. RtCt 27 Jun 1876. [G:21]
　S/A with Gdn Andrew J. FLEMING: beginning 18 Jul 1876; $612.68 from life insurance policy, general expenses, leaving $575.61. RtCt 12 Nov 1877. [G:83]

RUST, Frederick G.
　S/A with Committee A. T. M. RUST: beginning 29 Sep 1874; income from Walter B. LAWRENCE, payments leaving $23.67 due to Committee. RtCt 15 Jul 1876. [G:23]
　S/A with Committee A. T. M. RUST: beginning 14 Feb 1876; general expenses leaving $573.67. RtCt 11 Jun 1877. [G:56]
　S/A with Committee A. T. M. RUST: beginning 14 Feb 1877; general expenses leaving $1186.17. RtCt 11 Sep 1878. [G:135]
　S/A with Committee A. T. M. RUST: beginning 14 Feb 1878; $300 to Western Lunatic Asylum, other expenses, leaving $1844.80. RtCt 11 Jun 1879. [G:164]
　S/A with Committee A. T. M. RUST: beginning 28 Feb 1879; paid Western Lunatic Asylum, general expenses, leaving $2622.48. RtCt 15 Jun 1880. [G:225]
　S/A with Committee A. T. M. RUST: beginning 27 Feb 1880; paid Western Lunatic Asylum, general expenses, leaving $3384.73. RtCt 10 May 1881. [G:271]
　S/A with Committee A. T. M. RUST: beginning 14 Feb 1881; general expenses leaving $4125.13. RtCt 9 May 1882. [G:309]
　S/A with Committee A. T. M. RUST: beginning 14 Feb 1882; $1197.50 rec'd from John H. WILSON, general expenses, leaving $4857.17. RtCt 14 May 1883. [G:372]
　S/A with Committee A. T. M. RUST: beginning 14 Feb 1883; income from John H. WILSON, general expenses, leaving $5627.12. RtCt 13 May 1884. [G:435]
　S/A with Committee A. T. M. RUST: beginning 14 Feb 1884; general expenses leaving $6176.59. RtCt 11 Aug 1885. [G:486]
　S/A with Committee A. T. M. RUST: beginning 14 Feb 1885; $1320.59 income from Jno. H. WILSON, general expenses, leaving $7071.37. RtCt 11 May 1886. [H:8]
　S/A with Committee A. T. M. RUST: beginning 14 Feb 1886; $1320.59 income from Jno. H. WILSON, general expenses, leaving $6146.32. Litigation costs over custody of ward's estate in Courts of Staunton VA. RtCt 10 May 1887. [H:41]
　S/A with Committee A. T. M. RUST: beginning 14 Feb 1887; general expenses leaving $6413.09. RtCt 10 Jan 1888. [H:61]
　S/A with Committee E. J. LEE: beginning Oct 1888; payments including to Penn Hospital, leaving $2759.81. RtCt 11 Jul 1892. [H:162]
　S/A with Committee E. J. LEE: beginning 11 Aug 1891; general expenses leaving $2224.18. RtCt 10 Oct 1892. [H:165]
　S/A with Committee E. J. LEE: beginning Aug 1892; income from rent of Rockland farm, general expenses leaving $2877.70 on 11 Aug 1893 to ward's estate. RtCt 9 Jul 1894. [H:208]
　S/A with Committee E. J. LEE: beginning 1 Aug 1893; general expenses leaving $4522.32. RtCt 8 Apr 1895. [H:242]
　S/A with Committee E. J. LEE: beginning 1 Aug 1894; income from rent of 17 North St. NY City and rent of

Rockland farm, paid Penn Hospital, general expenses, leaving $6690.01. RtCt 10 Nov 1896. [H:282]

S/A with Committee R. T. W. DUKE Jr: RUST was committed to Western State Hospital on 2 Oct 1897, property includes 235 acre farm in Loudoun, house in NY City, bonds, $3788.13 from previous Committee, $8000 fund in NY, stock. RtCt 13 Dec 1897. [H:315]

S/A with Committee R. T. W. DUKE Jr: beginning 23 Aug 1896; general expenses leaving $1094.62. RtCt 15 Mar 1898. [H:329]

S/A with Committee R. T. W. DUKE Jr: beginning 11 Jan 1898; general expenses leaving $715.97. RtCt 10 Apr 1899. [H:363]

S/A with Committee R. T. W. DUKE Jr: beginning Jan 1899; general expenses leaving $1264.77 plus notes, bonds & rents turned over to Frederick on 19 Jun 1899. RtCt 12 Sep 1900. [H:397]

LESLIE, John B., John A. and John E. (Children of John)
S/A with Gdn John B. LESLIE: beginning 12 Oct 1874; children John A. and others, general expenses leaving $70.02 due to Gdn, no income until debts have been paid. RtCt 9 Oct 1876. [G:46]

Inventory of John B., John A. & John E. LESLIE children by his second marriage, by Gdn John W. GARRETT: income from rent and funds from estate, totaling $800. RtCt 20 Apr 1878. [G:106]

S/A with Gdn J. W. GARRETT: beginning 2 Feb 1878; general expenses leaving $418.55. RtCt 14 Jul 1879. [G:174]

S/A with Gdn Jno. W. GARRETT: beginning 8 Oct 1878; general expenses leaving $466.80 to J. A., J. E. & J. B. LESLIE. RtCt 11 Mar 1880. [G:214]

S/A with Gdn J. W. GARRETT: beginning 8 Oct 1879; general expenses leaving $411.18 to J. A., J. E. & J. B. LESLIE. RtCt 14 Dec 1880. [G:251]

S/A with Gdn J. W. GARRETT: beginning 8 Oct 1880; income from rents, general expenses, leaving $402.61. RtCt 9 Jan 1882. [G:302]

S/A with Gdn J. W. GARRETT: beginning 8 Oct 1881; payments to Mrs. LESLIE, etc., leaving $412.12. RtCt 9 Jan 1883. [G:361]

S/A with Gdn John W. GARRETT: beginning 8 Oct 1882; income from rents, paid Mrs. LESLIE on maintanence, leaving $432.85. RtCt 12 Feb 1884. [G:427]

S/A with Gdn J. W. GARRETT: beginning 8 Oct 1883; general expenses leaving $432.83. RtCt 11 Aug 1885. [G:487]

S/A with Gdn John W. GARRETT: beginning 8 Oct 1884; income from rent of farm, board paid Mrs. LESLIE, general expenses, leaving $1.72 due to Gdn. RtCt 11 May 1886. [H:3]

S/A with Gdn J. W. GARRETT: beginning 6 Feb 1886; general expenses leaving $.06. RtCt 10 May 1887. [H:35]

S/A with Gdn Jno. W. GARRETT: beginning 1 Jan 1887; general expenses leaving $.27. RtCt 14 Aug 1888. [H:86]

PAXSON, Derizo C.
S/A with Gdn C. W. PAXSON: beginning 13 Jul 1869; reached majority by 26 Sep 1870, general expenses leaving $115.42. RtCt 9 Oct 1876. [G:47]

WHITE, John K., Robert A., George Anna S., & Mary Louisa
Inventory by Gdn Robert J. WHITE: $3796.65. RtCt 30 Jan 1877. [G:49]

HUNTER, Virginia D., Mary M., John B. & Margaret E.
Inventory by Gdn William J. STONE: $1023 from George P. HUNTER Admr of their father Michael L. HUNTER, rents from the land of their father. RtCt 11 Jun 1877. [G:52]

S/A with Gdn Wm. J. STONE: beginning 21 Feb 1877; each has $313.75. RtCt 9 Dec 1878. [G:142]

S/A with Gdn Wm. J. STONE: beginning Apr 1878; general expenses leaving Margaret E. $338.30, Mary M. $372.97, Virginia E. $372.97 & John D. $372.97. RtCt 11 Jun 1879. [G:169]

S/A with Gdn Wm. J. STONE: beginning 18 Mar 1879; expenses leaving Mary M. HUNTER $408.77, John D. HUNTER $401.92, Virginia HUNTER $263.89 (came of age 11 Jan 1880) and Margaret E. $372.02. RtCt 11 Aug 1880. [G:236]

S/A with Gdn Wm. J. STONE: beginning 1880; expenses leaving Margaret $405.91, John D. $437.51, Mary M. $450.48, Virginia paid $450.48 when she came of age 20 May 1881. RtCt 10 Oct 1881. [G:288]

S/A with Gdn Wm. J. STONE: beginning 14 Feb 1882; expenses leaving John D. $478.36, Mary M. already paid in full when she reached 21y old & Margaret E. (now married to __ COOPER) $444.98. RtCt 9 Mar 1882. [G:308]

S/A with Gdn Wm. STONE: beginning 10 Apr 1882; expenses leaving John D. HUNTER $509.71. RtCt 9 Jan 1883. [G:357]

MANN, F. S. L.
S/A with Gdn J. M. CONARD: beginning 12 Sep 1868; interest and fee leaving $505.12. RtCt 11 Jun 1877. [G:54]

JAMES, Fleet, Eliza, Mollie, Alice J. & Matson
S/A with Gdn Mason JAMES: Gdn fully paid and his Guardianship ceased. RtCt 11 Jun 1877. [G:55]

MOORE, Nancy

S/A with Gdn C. W. BARTON: beginning 13 Sep 1875; $220 in bonds, $8.41 to Gdn for expenses. RtCt 11 Jun 1877. [G:59]

S/A with Gdn C. W. BARTON: beginning 13 Sep 1876; expenses leaving $220. Additional funds coming at the death of Sally Ann wife of C. W. BARTON rec'd from estate of Wm. MOORE dec'd. RtCt 15 Mar 1881. RtCt 15 Mar 1881. [G:266]

S/A with Gdn C. W. BARTON: beginning 13 Sep 1880; expenses leaving $195.99. RtCt 15 Aug 1882. [G:335]

HOLLIDAY, Rosa Lee & Anna

S/A with Gdn R. S. CHINN: beginning 12 Jun 1876; $153 distributive share, expenses, leaving $936.23. RtCt 9 Jul 1877. [G:64]

S/A with Gdn R. S. CHINN: beginning 12 Jun 1877; general expenses leaving $1036.23 each to Rosa & Anna. RtCt 9 Dec 1878. [G:136]

S/A with Gdn R. S. CHINN: beginning 12 Jul 1878; general expenses leaving Anna HOLLIDAY $1036.26. RtCt 10 Nov 1879. [G:193]

S/A with Gdn R. S. CHINN: beginning 12 Jul 1878; general expenses leaving Rosa HOLLIDAY $1036.26. RtCt 10 Nov 1879. [G:193]

S/A with Gdn R. S. CHINN: beginning 12 Jan 1879; general expenses leaving Rosa HOLLIDAY $1091.31. RtCt 14 Dec 1880. [G:246]

S/A with Gdn R. S. CHINN: beginning 12 Jul 1879; general expenses leaving Anna HOLLIDAY $1091.36. RtCt 14 Dec 1880. [G:247]

S/A with Gdn R. S. CHINN: beginning 12 Jul 1880; expenses annually paid by stepfather W. REDMAN, leaving each $1091.31. RtCt 10 Oct 1881. [G:286]

S/A with Gdn R. S. CHINN: beginning 12 Jul 1881; general expenses leaving $1091.31 each to Anna & Rosa. RtCt 9 Oct 1882. [G:342]

S/A with Gdn R. S. CHINN: beginning 12 Jul 1882; general expenses leaving Rosa $1091.31 and Anna $1091.31. RtCt 11 Dec 1883. [G:414]

S/A with Gdn R. S. CHINN: beginning 12 Jul 1883; general expenses leaving $1091.31 each to Rosa & Anna HOLLIDAY. RtCt 13 Jan 1885. [G:464]

S/A with Gdn R. S. CHINN: (now REDMON) beginning 12 Jul 1884; general expenses leaving Rosa Lee HOLLIDAY $1110.78 paid in full. RtCt 11 Nov 1885. [G:497]

S/A with Gdn R. S. CHINN: beginning 12 Jul 1884; general expenses leaving Anna HOLLIDAY $1091.31. RtCt 11 Nov 1885. [G:498]

S/A of Anna HOLLIDAY with Gdn R. S. CHINN: beginning 12 Jul 1885; general expenses leaving $1101.81, 1/3 of rent to widow. RtCt 15 Feb 1887. [H:28]

S/A of Anna HOLLIDAY with Gdn R. S. CHINN: beginning 12 Jul 1886; payment leaving $1020.81, $51.90 in interest payable to Wilfred REDMAN for board and maintanence. RtCt 10 Jan 1888. [H:60]

S/A of Anna HOLLIDAY with late Gdn R. S. CHINN: beginning 12 Jul 1887; general expenses leaving $1101.81 in principal paid to new Gdn Wm. GAINES and interest of $51.34 paid to father for board. RtCt 14 May 1889. [H:108]

S/A of Anna HOLLIDAY with Gdn Wm. GAINES: beginning Oct 1888; general expenses leaving $1043.12. RtCt 12 Jan 1891. [H:127]

PAXSON, Anna Beall

S/A with Gdn C. W. PAXSON: beginning 26 Sep 1868; general expenses leaving $483.68 due to husband J. H. DAVIS (married shortly after 13 Jul 1877.) RtCt 13 Aug 1877. [G:71]

BEAMER, Rachel

S/A with Committee N. B. PEACOCK: beginning Jul 1876; general expenses leaving $33.40 due to Committee. RtCt 13 Aug 1877. [G:74]

S/A with Committee N. B. PEACOCK: beginning 13 Jul 1877; income from sale of land & rent, general expenses, leaving $44.35. RtCt 11 Sep 1878. [G:124]

S/A with Committee N. B. PEACOCK: acct is final as all have been expended. RtCt 9 Dec 1878. [G:137]

S/A with Committee John MILTON: beginning 12 Jan 1880; general expenses leaving $331.20. RtCt 10 Jul 1882. [G:319]

BEAMER, William Francis Augustus, George Henry Thomas, Joseph Michael Bronaugh, Maggie Ellen Frances, Daniel Wine Washington, Mary Alice Virginia, Mary Lina May and Samuel Randolph William (Children of Michael)

S/A with Gdn Jonathan MATTHEW: $1714.08 from N. B. PEACOCK Admr of M. BEAMER. Children: William Francis Augustus BEAMER, George Henry Thomas BEAMER, Joseph Michael Bronaugh BEAMER, Maggie Ellen Frances BEAMER, Daniel Wine Washington BEAMER, Mary Alice Virginia BEAMER, Mary Lina May BEAMER & Samuel Randolph William BEAMER. RtCt 9 Nov 1877. [G:91]

S/A with Gdn Jonathan MATTHEW: expenses leaving W. F. A. BEAMER (now of age) $5.08, Geo. H. T. BEAMER, Joseph M. BEAMER, Danl. W. W. BEAMER, Mary A. V. BEAMER, Mary L. M. BEAMER & Saml. R. W. BEAMER have $226.67 & Maggie E. BEAMER $221.67. RtCt 9 Jul 1878. [G:109]

Inventory by Gdn Jno. MILTON: funds from Jonathan MATHEW late Gdn, rent from Mrs. Caroline BEAMER & from N. B. PEACOCK Admr of Michael BEAMER, income from land division and residue with W. F. BARRETT Exor of Geo. BEAMER. RtCt 10 Jul 1879. [G:173]

S/A with Gdn Jonathan MATTHEWS: beginning Nov 1878; mother Caroline BEAMER, general expenses leaving Maggie E. (under 21y old) $162.55, Geo. H. T., Jos. M., M. E. B., M. W. V, Mary L. M. & S. R. W. each $249. RtCt 10 Nov 1879. [G:196]

S/A with Gdn John MILTON: beginning 28 Jul 1879; $508.16 in full paid Geo. H. T. BEAMER on 28 Jul 1879, balance of $615.18 each for Jos. M. B. BEAMER, Danl. W. W. BEAMER, M. A. V. BEAMER, M. L. M. BEAMER & Saml. R. W. BEAMER. RtCt 15 Feb 1881. [G:256]

S/A with Gdn John MILTON: beginning 10 Dec 1880; expenses leaving Joseph M. V. $655.91 paid in full on 24 Feb 1881, M. A. V. BEAMER $709.58 paid in full on 26 Dec 1882 as she is now married, Danl. W. W., M. L. M. & Saml. R. W. BEAMER each $725.29. RtCt 14 May 1883. [G:369]

S/A with Gdn John MILTON: beginning 1 Apr 1883; rent paid Mrs. BEAMER, general expenses, leaving Danl. W. W. BEAMER $877.86, Samuel R. W. BEAMER $877.86 & M. L. M. BEAMER $877.87. RtCt 10 May 1884. [G:435]

S/A with Gdn John MILTON: beginning 10 Dec 1883; general expenses leaving S. R. W. $1061.96 & M. L. M. BEAMER $1007.55. Danl. W. W. BEAMER reached his majority in 1884 and was paid in full. RtCt 10 Aug 1886. [H:20]

NICHOLS, George W.
S/A with Gdn Eli H. NICHOLS: beginning 11 Nov 1869; general expenses leaving $6.20. Final statement as ward now of age. RtCt 10 Dec 1877. [G:96]

NIXON, George
S/A with Committee Jonah NIXON: beginning 25 Nov 1875; payments until 10 Sep 1876 leaving $42.15. Ward is now dead. RtCt 10 Dec 1877. [G:97]

CHAMBLIN, Rosa & Laura
S/A with Gdn Joshua HATCHER: beginning 7 May 1877; general expenses leaving each $48.36. Rosa is of age and Laura wishes to go to school. Abt $2200 from estate of their grandfather Mason CHAMBLIN. RtCt 13 Feb 1878. [G:102]

S/A with Gdn Joshua HATCHER: beginning 1 Nov 1877; general expenses leaving Laura CHAMBLIN $472.29. RtCt 16 Apr 1879. [G:160]

S/A with Gdn Joshua HATCHER: beginning 11 Jul 1878; general expenses leaving Laura CHAMBLIN $5.98 after paying $1229.18 to ward when she reached age on 10 Dec 1880. RtCt 15 Mar 1881. [G:263]

McFARLAND, Edgar
S/A with Gdn John F. RYAN, Admr of father: beginning 1 Jun 1875; expenses leaving $1840.52. Edgar received the full balance on 25 Nov 1877. RtCt 13 Feb 1877. [G:105]

LAYCOCK, Edward & Lulu
Inventory by Gdn John W. GARRETT: $500 from case of DAVIS heirs vs. LAYCOCK. RtCt 20 Apr 1878. [G:107]

S/A with Gdn J. W. GARRETT: beginning 11 Feb 1878; general expenses leaving $472.30. RtCt 14 Jul 1879. [G:175]

S/A with Gdn Jno. W. GARRETT: beginning 11 Feb 1879; general expenses leaving $472.30. RtCt 11 Mar 1880. [G:215]

S/A with Gdn J. W. GARRETT: beginning 11 Feb 1880; general expenses leaving $487.58. RtCt 13 Jun 1881. [G:274]

S/A with Gdn J. W. GARRETT: beginning 11 Feb 1881; general expenses leaving $474.84. RtCt 15 Aug 1882. [G:329]

S/A with Gdn J. W. GARRETT: beginning 11 Feb 1882; general expenses leaving $467.90. RtCt 14 May 1883. [G:376]

S/A with Gdn J. W. GARRETT: beginning 11 Feb 1883; paid father for maintenance, general expenses, leaving $436.02. RtCt 9 Jun 1884. [G:439]

S/A with Gdn Jno. W. GARRETT: beginning 11 Feb 1884; paid father for maintenance, general expenses, leaving $460.37. RtCt 11 Aug 1885. [G:488]

S/A with Gdn J. W. GARRETT: beginning 11 Feb 1885; general expenses leaving $460.37. RtCt 10 Aug 1886. [H:22]

S/A with Gdn J. W. GARRETT: beginning 11 Feb 1886; general expenses leaving $460.37 plus $15.38 paid to their father for their board & maintenance. RtCt 10 May 1887. [H:39]

S/A with Gdn John W. GARRETT: beginning 11 Feb 1887; general expenses leaving $460.37. RtCt 14 May 1889. [H:98]

S/A with Gdn John W. GARRETT: beginning 11 Feb 1889; general expenses leaving $460.37 with payment to father for maintenance. RtCt 10 Nov 1891. [H:141]

S/A with Gdn John W. GARRETT: beginning 11 Feb 1890; general expenses leaving $460.37. RtCt 14 Apr 1892. [H:156]

S/A with Gdn John W. GARRETT: beginning 11 Feb 1891; general expenses leaving $234.68 to Lula & Edward, now both 21y old. RtCt 9 Jan 1894. [H:193]

COOMBS, Mrs. Sallie A.
S/A with Committee William McCRAY: beginning 14 Nov 1875; income from rent of various lands and bonds, general expenses, leaving $27881.02. Ward is daughter of his wife by a former marriage and her mother, brothers & sisters are the heirs apparent of her estate. RtCt 9 Jul 1878. [G:113]

S/A with Committee Wm. McCRAY: beginning 19 Jan 1878; general expenses leaving $293.61 due to Committee. RtCt 9 Aug 1881. [G:280]

S/A with Committee William McCRAY: beginning 1 Jan 1881; income from sale of Fairfax land, general expenses, leaving $1635.87. RtCt 11 Nov 1884. [G:461]

COOMBS, Mrs. Sarah A.

S/A with Committee Wm. McCRAY: beginning 15 Jan 1884; general expenses leaving $964.90. RtCt 10 Jan 1888. [H:56]

S/A with Committee Wm. McCRAY: beginning Jan 1886; general expenses leaving $183.89 due to Committee. RtCt 14 May 1888. [H:69]

S/A with Committee Wm. McCRAY: beginning 15 Jan 1888; general expenses leaving $911.96. RtCt 15 Jan 1890. [H:117]

S/A with Committee Wm. McCRAY: beginning 15 Jan 1889; general expenses leaving $495.69. RtCt 10 Nov 1891. [H:145]

S/A with Committee Wm. McCRAY: beginning 15 Jan 1891; general expenses leaving $837.01. RtCt 14 Nov 1893. [H:183]

S/A with Committee Wm. McCRAY: beginning 9 Jan 1893; general expenses leaving $1271.87 plus bonds. RtCt 12 Feb 1896. [H:251]

S/A with Committee Edgar McCRAY: beginning 15 Jan 1895; general expenses leaving $489.28. RtCt 10 Mar 1896. [H:257]

S/A with Committee Edgar McCRAY: beginning 15 Jan 1895; general expenses leaving $66.65 due to Committee. RtCt 12 May 1896. [H:258]

S/A with Committee Edgar McCRAY; beginning 1896; receipts from BOWMAN farm & VANDEVANTER farm, payments leaving $131.08. RtCt 11 May 1897. [H:293]

S/A with Committee Edgar McCRAY: beginning 15 Jan 1897; as above, expenses, leaving $124.46. RtCt 9 Aug 1898. [H:343]

S/A with Committee Edgar McCRAY: beginning 15 Jan 1898; as above, general expenses, leaving $606.45 payable to McCRAY as Admr; Sarah having died 15 Sep 1899. RtCt 13 Feb 1901. [H:412]

LICKEY, Eugenia D.

S/A with Gdn John MEAD: now 21y old and acct. is settled. RtCt 11 Sep 1878. [G:134]

JANNEY, Mary G., Robert W., Cora and John C. (Children of George W.)

S/A with mother & Gdn Mary JANNEY: beginning 12 Mar 1877; general expenses leaving Mary G. JANNEY $264.35, Robt. W. JANNEY $265.11, Cora JANNEY (now of age) $561.99, John C. JANNEY $74.39 & $74.39 each to children T. H. VANDEVANTER, Townsend HEATON & Ella JANNEY. RtCt 9 Dec 1878. [G:144]

S/A with mother & Gdn Mary JANNEY: beginning 12 Mar 1877; general expenses leaving Mary G. JANNEY $164.35, Robert W. JANNEY $592.78, Cora JANNEY $561.99 (now of age.) RtCt 10 Mar 1879. [G:151]

S/A with Gdn Mary JANNEY: beginning 12 Mar 1878; payments leaving Mary G. JANNEY $12.25, Robert W. JANNEY owing Gdn $353.47 on 4 May 1879 when he reached majority. RtCt 15 Feb 1881. [G:260]

S/A with Gdn Mary JANNEY: beginning 12 Jun 1880; final payments to ward of $35.49 on 4 Jul 1881 as ward has reached majority. RtCt 13 Feb 1883. [G:362]

S/A of Cora W. JANNEY with Gdn Mrs. Mary JANNEY: (now Mrs. SHUEY) beginning 12 Mar 1878; general expenses leaving 910.33 paid in full 12 Jul 1888. RtCt 9 Oct 1888. [H:94]

STEER, William E.

S/A with Committee Milton SCHOOLEY: beginning 20 Aug 1878; proceeds from sale of real estate of father James M. STEER, general expenses leaving $858.68. RtCt 16 Apr 1879. [G:161]

S/A with Committee Milton SCHOOLEY: (of unsound mind) beginning 20 Aug 1878; income from bonds, general expenses, leaving $300.76 plus $600 invested. RtCt 14 Dec 1880. [G:253]

S/A with Committee Milton SCHOOLEY: beginning 6 Sep 1880; general expenses leaving $249.79 plus $600 bond. RtCt 14 Nov 1881. [G:298]

S/A with Committee Milton SCHOOLEY: beginning 20 Aug 1881; general expenses leaving $819.79. RtCt 9 Oct 1883. [G:403]

S/A with Committee Milton SCHOOLEY: beginning Aug 1882; general expenses leaving $821.22. RtCt 9 Oct 1883. [G:404]

S/A with Committee Milton SCHOOLEY: beginning 20 Aug 1883; general expenses leaving $821.22. RtCt 11 Nov 1884. [G:460]

S/A with Committee Milton SCHOOLEY: beginning 2 Aug 1884; general expenses leaving $821.22. RtCt 14 Oct 1885. [G:490]

S/A with Committee Milton SCHOOLEY: beginning 20 Aug 1885; general expenses leaving $821.22. RtCt 15 Feb 1887. [H:33]

S/A with Committee Milton SCHOOLEY: beginning 21 Aug 1886; general expenses leaving $821.22. RtCt 10 Jan 1888. [H:62]

S/A with Committee Milton SCHOOLEY: beginning 21 Aug 1889; general expenses leaving $821.22. RtCt 10 Jun 1891. [H:138]

S/A with Committee B. L. FOX: beginning 20 Aug 1893; general expenses leaving $37.05 interest on $787.19 principal payable for board. RtCt 12 Sep 1898. [H:349]

S/A with Committee B. L. FOX: beginning 20 Aug 1898; general expenses leaving $45.59. RtCt 13 Jan 1903. [H:471]

S/A with Committee B. L. FOX: beginning 20 Aug 1902; general expenses leaving $26.11 paid to Mrs. Mary J. HOUGH for his benefit. RtCt 12 Nov 1903. [H:482]

PINKARD, C. F.
S/A with Gdn J. W. GARRETT: beginning 12 Jan 1877; general expenses leaving $23.73. RtCt 11 Jun 1879. [G:162]

S/A with Gdn J. W. GARRETT: beginning 12 Jan 1879; general expenses leaving $35.13. RtCt 11 Aug 1880. [G:233]

WARNER, Malinda E. & Mary E.
S/A with Gdn Jas. M. HOGE: $380.50 rec'd from Henry HEATON. RtCt 27 Jun 1879. [G:172]

S/A with Gdn James M. HOGE: beginning 23 Sep 1878; general expenses leaving Malinda E. $216.42 (fully settled) & Mary E. $180.73. RtCt 17 Apr 1880. [G:217]

S/A with Gdn Jas. M. HOGE: beginning Jun 1880; general expenses leaving Mary E. Warner $229.39. RtCt 14 Feb 1882. [G:306]

S/A with Gdn James M. HOGE: beginning 23 Sep 1881; general expenses leaving Mary E. WARNER $234.52. RtCt 13 Feb 1883. [G:364]

GRAHAM, James E.
Inventory by Gdn Mrs. E. GRAHAM: $208.33 from Admr. of Mrs. P. HAMILTON, $380.25 from Ct. decree. RtCt 27 Jun 1879. [G:172]

LOVELESS, Elizabeth
Inventory by Committee T. William WEADON: $96/yr pension for life by the US, barely sufficient to support her, no annual S/A required. RtCt 26 Jun 1879. [G:173]

MOORE, M. E. & C.
Inventory by William MOORE: 1/5 of land inherited from grandmother Margaret WRIGHT (some of the adult children of the grandmother have sold their shares,) wards <21y old. RtCt 14 Jul 1879. [G:180]

TITUS, Wilbur F.
S/A with Gdn T. S. TITUS: general expenses leaving $1875.50. RtCt 11 Aug 1879. [G:191]

S/A with Gdn T. Sydney TITUS: beginning 8 Apr 1879; general expenses leaving $1875.50. RtCt 15 Feb 1881. [G:262]

S/A with Gdn T. Sydney TITUS: beginning 8 Apr 1880; board paid Mrs. Nancy HOOE, general expenses leaving $1879.96. RtCt 10 Oct 1881. [G:292]

S/A with Gdn T. Sidney TITUS: beginning 1881; general expenses leaving $1896.42. RtCt 15 Aug 1882. [G:332]

S/A with Gdn T. Sidney TITUS: beginning 12 Jun 1882; general expenses leaving $1901.45. RtCt 11 Dec 1883. [G:417]

S/A with Gdn T. Sydney TITUS: beginning 2 Jun 1883; general expenses leaving $1910.65. RtCt 10 Mar 1885. [G:474]

S/A with Gdn T. S. TITUS: beginning 2 Jun 1884; general expenses leaving $1995.93. RtCt 10 Aug 1886. [H:22]

S/A with Gdn T. S. TITUS: beginning 2 Jun 1885; general expenses leaving $2474.31. RtCt 15 Feb 1887. [H:27]

S/A with Gdn T. S. TITUS: beginning 2 Jun 1886; general expenses leaving $2491.55. RtCt 9 Oct 1888. [H:92]

S/A with Gdn T. S. TITUS: beginning 1889; $1809.41 paid in full to ward on 27 Oct 1893. RtCt 13 Mar 1894. [H:199]

SLAYMAKER, Edmund W., Archie C., Amos, Wm. J. & Mary E.
Inventory by Gdn A. B. SLAYMAKER: $100 rent of land all used for support, no annual S/A required. RtCt 10 Sep 1879. [G:192]

HEFNER, Carrie
Inventory by Gdn Isaac YOUNG: $226.87 from case of SAUNDERS vs. RHODES, $142 from land damages case against Leesburg Magisterial District, rents from small tract near Leesburg to support her grandmother Mrs. RHODES. RtCt 9 Dec 1879. [G:202]

HARPER, Wells A., Robert N., Charles E. and James W. (Children of Robert)
Inventory by Gdn A. J. BRADFIELD: $4000 VA bond, $500 Alexandria bond, 2 shares RR stock, cash. Children Wells A., Robert N., C. E. & James W. HARPER. RtCt 9 Dec 1879. [G:203]

S/A with Gdn A. J. BRADFIELD: beginning 19 Jul 1879; Wells is of age and rec'd $1162.19 of the $4648.78 balance. RtCt 13 Oct 1880. [G:245]

S/A with Gdn A. J. BRADFIELD: beginning 19 Jul 1880; general expenses leaving $2557.55. RtCt 9 Jan 1882. [G:301]

S/A with Gdn A. J. BRADFIELD: beginning 19 Jul 1881; $634.91 paid to Robert HARPER on 31 Jan 1882 now of age, leaving $1812.85. RtCt 14 Nov 1882. [G:350]

S/A with Gdn A. J. BRADFIELD: beginning 19 Jul 1882; general expenses leaving John W. HARPER $864.43 & Chas. E. HARPER $839.42. RtCt 13 May 1884. [G:430]

S/A with Gdn A. J. BRADFIELD: beginning 19 Jul 1884; general expenses leaving Charles E. HARPER $861.57. RtCt 14 Apr 1885. [G:476]

S/A with Gdn A. J. BRADFIELD: beginning 19 Jul 1884; general expenses leaving J. William HARPER $908. RtCt 14 Apr 1885. [G:477]

S/A of John William HARPER with Gdn A. J. BRADFIELD: beginning 19 Jul 1884; general expenses leaving $963.83. RtCt 11 May 1886. [H:5]

S/A of John William HARPER with Gdn A. J. BRADFIELD: beginning 19 Jul 1885; general expenses leaving $951.58. RtCt 15 Oct 1886. [H:23]

S/A of John William HARPER with Gdn A. J. BRADFIELD: (written as James William HARPER) beginning Nov 1886; general expenses leaving $1017.19 paid on 19 Dec 1888 when he reached majority. RtCt 14 May 1889. [H:100]

S/A of Charles E. HARPER with Gdn A. J. BRADFIELD: beginning 19 Jul 1884; Chas. paid $1026.76 on 24 Jul 1886 by Gdn, paid in full. RtCt 15 Oct 1886. [H:24]

S/A of Robert W. HARPER with Gdn A. J. BRADFIELD: beginning 19 Jul 1882; general expenses leaving $168.51 paid in full on 20 Sep 1886. RtCt 15 Feb 1887. [H:33]

MANN, Joseph H.
Appraisal/Inventory by Committee Wm. F. COOPER: farm items totaling $81.10. Aprs: Silas D. KALB, Robert BOOTH, S. W. GEORGE Jr. RtCt 22 Dec 1879. [G:203]

Sale of 2 Aug 1879: purchasers: Wm. F. COOPER, Geo. EVERHART, Rebecca MANN, Robt. BOOTH, Wm. BUTTS, Jos. RIVERS, John MANN, John WIGGINTON, Sand. N. GRUBB, John S. MANN, Benj. CARNES, Saml. W. GEORGE, totaling $108.75. RtCt 22 Dec 1879. [G:204]

WHITLOCK, Robert T. & Henry W.
S/A of 11 Dec 1879 with Gdn Henry WHITLOCK: (the two youngest) satisfied with estate S/A for sale of land in CT. RtCt 11 Mar 1880. [G:212]

FILLER, Sarah J. M.
S/A with Gdn Ezekiel POTTS: $48 due to ward. RtCt 11 Mar 1880. [G:213]

SMALE, Emma S. & Mary M.
Inventory by Gdn G. J. SMALE: $45.50 each from case of SWART vs SMALE, shares from estate of father John SMALE. RtCt 19 Apr 1880. [G:218]

S/A with Gdn Mrs. G. J. SMALE: beginning 10 May 1879; general expenses leaving Emma S. SMALE $163.15. RtCt 10 Jul 1882. [G:326]

S/A with Gdn A. J. SMALE: beginning 10 May 1879; general expenses leaving Mary M. SMALE $150.94. RtCt 10 Jul 1882. [G:327]

S/A with Gdn Olivia J. SMALE: beginning 10 May 1882; general expenses leaving Emma C. SMALE $100.24 & Mary M. SMALE $100.65. Income not sufficient to maintain principal. RtCt 14 Aug 1883. [G:383]

S/A of Mary M. SMALE with Gdn Olivia J. SMALE: beginning May 1883; $108.58 paid and wished released from liability. RtCt 10 Nov 1891. [H:144]

S/A of Emma C. SMALE with Gdn Olivia J. SMALE: beginning 10 May 1883 $100.39 paid and wished released from liability. RtCt 10 Nov 1891. [H:144]

HAVENNER, William A.
Inventory of Gdn Benj. BRIDGES: bonds, house & 20 acres of land, totaling $526.53. RtCt 8 Jun 1880. [G:219]

S/A with Gdn Benj. BRIDGES: beginning Oct 1879; Jul 1881 coffin for mother, general expenses, leaving $9.59. RtCt 10 Oct 1881. [G:287]

S/A with Gdn Benj. BRIDGES Jr.: beginning 27 Apr 1881; general expenses leaving $20.69. RtCt 15 Aug 1882. [G:330]

SHRUEEY, Mrs. Sarah
S/A with Committee N. B. PEACOCK: beginning 10 Jul 1879; paid Sally J. ATLEE for board, general expenses, leaving $30.42. RtCt 11 Aug 1880. [G:235]

S/A with Committee N. B. PEACOCK: beginning 11 Mar 1880; general expenses leaving $35.29. RtCt 13 Jun 1881. [G:277]

S/A with Committee N. B. PEACOCK: beginning 19 Jun 1881; income from rent of store house, stable, shop, and house, general expenses, leaving $983.54. RtCt 9 Oct 1882. [G:344]

SHUMAKER, Maggie E.
S/A with Gdn J. MATTHEW: (nee BEAMER) beginning 1879; $169.93 from rents & interest. Ward married & bearing children. RtCt 14 Dec 1880. [G:249]

S/A with Gdn Jonathan MATTHEW: beginning 19 Oct 1880; general expenses leaving $144.40. RtCt 10 Oct 1881. [G:291]

S/A with Gdn James S. SHUMAKER: paid full amount at her majority. RtCt 15 Aug 1882. [G:331]

STOUTSENBERGER, Clara
Inventory by Gdn John W. WENNER: $250 legacy from the will of John W. WENNER. RtCt 3 Feb 1881. [G:256]

BARTON, Sarah Amanda
S/A with Gdn C. W. BARTON: (wife of Jno. A. HESS) beginning 13 Sep 1876; to receive ½ of $224.11 upon the death of her mother Sally Ann BARTON rec'd from estate of Wm. MOORE dec'd, general expenses, leaving $38.37. RtCt 15 Mar 1881. [G:264]

WHITE, Daniel
Inventory by Committee Jonah NIXON: income from bonds and rent from farm, house & lot. RtCt 17 Mar 1881. [G:268]

JAMES, Sarah
　　Inventory by Committee Joseph & Chas. E. JAMES: income on $5000 under will of Elijah JAMES dec'd, 50 acres of land under will. RtCt 11 Apr 1881. [G:269]
　　S/A with Committee Joseph & C. E. JAMES: beginning 1 Jan 1881; general expenses leaving $261.39 upon death at 7 Apr 1882. RtCt 10 Jul 1882. [G:320]

GARDNER, James
　　S/A of 30 Mar 1881 with Committee Thos. BROWN: Ward recently died and had no assets. RtCt 16 Apr 1881. [G:269]

LOVETT, Caroline
　　Inventory by Gdn T. LOVETT: ¼ interest of $87.50 annual rent in farm descended from Jefferson C. THOMAS, also interest in his estate. RtCt 10 May 1881. [G:270]
　　S/A with Gdn Tazwell LOVETT: beginning 16 Jan 1880; general expenses leaving payments $162.26 due to Gdn. RtCt 9 Oct 1882. [G:343]
　　S/A with Gdn Tazwell LOVETT: beginning 1882; general expenses leaving $126.51 due to Gdn. RtCt 9 Oct 1883. [G:402]

RUSSELL, Louisa
　　S/A with Martin? W. RUSSELL: receipt of final S/A as ward is now of age. RtCt 13 Jun 1881. [G:275]

HUGHES, John
　　S/A with Gdn C. B. WILDMAN: beginning 12 May 1877; full S/A of $123.31 on 8 Mar 1881. Ward now of age. RtCt 9 Aug 1881. [G:279]

LOGAN, Anna
　　Inventory by Gdn C. R. BITZER: (Annie) ¼ of legacy (or $465.61 plus interest) devised to her mother Mrs. Sarah D. LOGAN under the will of George BITZER dec'd. RtCt 19 Sep 1881. [G:284]
　　S/A with Gdn C. R. BITZER: beginning 14 Jun 1881; general expenses leaving $442.33. RtCt 11 Aug 1885. [G::484]
　　S/A with Gdn C. R. BITZER: beginning 15 Jun 1883; general expenses leaving $442.53 on 19 Sep 1884 when she became of age. RtCt 11 Aug 1885. [G:485]

KEENE, Washington
　　S/A with Committee W. W. PRESGRAVES: beginning 1869; income from interest, general expenses, leaving $274.98. RtCt 14 Nov 1881. [G:295]
　　S/A with Committee W. W. PRESGRAVES: beginning 12 Apr 1881; general expenses leaving $274.98. RtCt 15 Aug 1882. [G:331]
　　S/A with Committee W. W. PRESGRAVES: beginning 12 Apr 1882; general expenses leaving $359.29. RtCt 11 Dec 1883. [G:425]
　　S/A with Committee W. W. PRESGRAVES: beginning 12 Apr 1883; general expenses leaving $356.55. RtCt 11 Nov 1884. [G:457]
　　S/A with Committee W. W. PRESGRAVES: beginning 12 Apr 1884; general expenses leaving $216.32 due Committee with a $350 bond. RtCt 14 May 1889. [H:99]
　　S/A with Committee W. W. PRESGRAVES: Committee allowed $4 more per month for support, leaving $719.62. [H:444]
　　Inventory of Committee H. R. MOCK: income from crops totaling $696.81. RtCt 28 Dec 1903. [H:498]

BALDWIN, Orion
　　Inventory by Gdn Mary E. BALDWIN: $398.99 from life insurance policy of M. K. BALDWIN, also real estate and distribution from the estate of M. K. BALDWIN. RtCt 23 Dec 1881. [G:299]
　　S/A with Gdn Mrs. M. E. BALDWIN: beginning Dec 1881; general expenses leaving $396.23. RtCt 9 Jan 1883. [G:359]
　　S/A with Gdn Mary E. BALDWIN: beginning 15 Oct 1882; became of age on 17 Jan 1884, $416.33 paid over to him. RtCt 11 Nov 1884. [G:455]

YELLOTT, W. R., Florence & R. E.
　　Inventory by Gdn A. T. M. RUST: $113.50 from Rockbridge Co. RtCt 23 Dec 1881. [G:300]
　　S/A with Gdn A. T. M. RUST: beginning 14 Jul 1881; $113.50 from Rockbridge Co., general expenses, leaving $34.28 each to A. R. & Florence, $32.20 to R. E. YELLOTT who came of age 18 Aug 1881. RtCt 14 Feb 1882. [G:305]

YELLOTT, Mrs. Virginia & children
　　S/A with trustee A. T. M. RUST: beginning 9 Nov 1883; $9068.01 in fund (S/A & insurance), $9071.69 for rebuilding dwelling and furniture destroyed by fire. RtCt 10 May 1887. [H:51]

NIXON, Mary A.
　　Inventory by Committee Burr W. PAXSON: $6.75 due by Jonah NIXON Admr of Geo. NIXON dec'd, $93.12 pension from H. VIRTS, $26 pension, rent of farm in which she has life interest. RtCt 11 Feb 1882. [G:304]
　　S/A with Committee B. W. PAXSON: beginning 15 Aug 1881; general expenses leaving $25.37 due to Committee. RtCt 14 May 1883. [G:374]
　　S/A with Committee B. W. PAXSON: beginning 2 Sep 1882; general expenses leaving $13.75 due to Committee. RtCt 9 Oct 1883. [G:400]
　　S/A with Committee B. W. PAXSON: beginning 12 Sep 1883; income from pension and rent of farm, general expenses, leaving $206.44. RtCt 11 Nov 1884. [G:458]
　　S/A with Committee B. W. PAXSON: beginning 13 Aug 1884; general expenses leaving $63.52 due to Committee. RtCt 12 Jan 1886. [G:499]

BYRNE, Henry M., Thomas W., Uriah E., Annie L., Virginia M., Sydnor B. & George M.

Inventory by Gdn Virginia S. Francis: $67.97 each. RtCt 6 May 1882. [G:307]

S/A with Gdn Virginia S. FRANCIS: beginning 9 Jan 1882; expenses leaving Henry M. BYRNE $76.73, Thomas W. BYRNE $76.73, Uriah E. BYRNE $76.73, Annie L. BYRNE $76.73, Virginia M. BYRNE $76.73, Sydnor B. BYRNE $76.73 & Geo. M. BYRNE $76.73. RtCt 11 Dec 1883. [G:418]

S/A wit Gdn Virginia L. FRANCIS: beginning 9 Jan 1883; expenses leaving $77.86 to Henry M. BYRNE upon his majority on 2 Oct 1884, $78.44 each to Thomas W., Sarah E., Annie L., Virginia, Sydnor B. & Geo. W. BYRNE. RtCt 11 Aug 1885. [G:478]

KEEN, Lucy

S/A with Gdn Fenton FURR: beginning 1 Jan 1874; income from rent of land and sale of crops, general expenses, leaving $78.77 final S/A. RtCt 13 Jun 1882. [G:312]

ROLLINS, V. G. S. & Mary

S/A with Gdn Saml. ORRISON: beginning 30 Jun 1882; expenses leaving V. G. S. & Mary each $213.69. RtCt 13 Jun 1882. [G:316]

LAUCK, W. C.

Inventory by Gdn Geo. W. NICHOLS: no personal estate, 38 acres of land near Silcott Springs. RtCt 15 Aug 1882. [G:329]

S/A with Gdn George W. NICHOLS: beginning 1882; board paid Maria NICHOLS, general expenses, leaving $48.84 due to Gdn. RtCt 14 May 1883. [G:377]

S/A with Gdn Geo. W. NICHOLS: beginning 9 Jan 1883; general expenses leaving $3.73 which will be applied to S/A cost leaving nothing. RtCt 13 May 1884. [G:433]

S/A with Gdn Geo. W. NICHOLS: beginning 1 Jan 1884; general expenses leaving $35.81. RtCt 11 Aug 1885. [G:488]

S/A with Gdn George W. NICHOLS: beginning 1 Jan 1885; income from rents, general expenses, leaving $49.65. RtCt 15 Oct 1886. [H:25]

S/A with Gdn Geo. W. NICHOLS: beginning 1 Jan 1885; general expenses leaving $27.54. RtCt 10 May 1997. [H:43]

S/A with Gdn Geo. W. NICHOLS: beginning 31 Dec 1886; general expenses leaving $94.44. RtCt 9 Oct 1888. [H:93]

S/A with Gdn Geo. W. NICHOLS: beginning 31 Dec 1887; general expenses leaving $33.01. RtCt 15 Jan 1890. [H:115]

S/A with Gdn Geo. W. NICHOLS: beginning 31 Dec 1888; general expenses leaving $8.89. RtCt 14 Apr 1892. [H:157]

S/A with Gdn G. W. NICHOLS: beginning 1 Jul 1891; general expenses leaving $44.57. RtCt 9 Jan 1894. [H:194]

S/A with Gdn Geo. W. NICHOLS: beginning 1 Jan 1893; general expenses leaving $22.14. RtCt 10 Sep 1895. [H:237]

S/A with Gdn Geo. W. NICHOLS: beginning 1 Jan 1894; general expenses leaving $93.65 paid at reaching majority on 21 Nov 1894. RtCt 12 Nov 1895. [H:241]

YAKEY, Minnie Belle

S/A with Gdn John W. YAKEY: (named written as Mary Bell) beginning 12 Aug 1878; $1000 from BEAMER's estate, expenses, leaving $1157.87. RtCt 15 Aug 1882. [G:333]

S/A with Gdn John W. YAKEY: beginning 10 Jun 1882; general expenses leaving $1157.87. RtCt 14 Aug 1883. [G:384]

S/A with Gdn John W. YAKEY: beginning 10 Jan 1883; general expenses leaving $1157.87. RtCt 9 Sep 1884. [G:448]

S/A with Gdn John W. YAKEY: beginning 10 Jan 1884; general expenses leaving $1157.87. RtCt 14 Oct 1885. [G:496]

S/A with Gdn John W. YAKEY: beginning 10 Jan 1885; general expenses leaving $1157.87 paid in full on 30 Jul 1886 when she reached majority. RtCt 15 Oct 1886. [H:26]

PAXSON, Clara

Inventory by Gdn E. G. CAUFMAN: $60 from Edward NICHOLS and $81.20 from Jno. H. ALEXANDER. RtCt 4 Aug 1882. [G:336]

S/A with Gdn E. G. CAUFMAN: beginning 11 Feb 1882; expenses leaving $262.82 due on 6 Sep 1883 when she became of age. RtCt 11 Dec 1883. [G:415]

DILLON, J. W.

Appraisal/Inventory by Committee J. T. GRUBB: goods, notes, household items, totaling $5820.21. Aprs: F. M. BOLYN, Henry VANDERHOFF, J. R. JANNEY. RtCt 10 Oct 1882. [G:345]

Sale of 24 Oct 1882 by Committee J. T. GRUBB: purchasers: John BENEDUM, T. M. BOLYN, Geo. H. BOLYN, Mrs. Will DILLON, Harmon GREGG, Fred FRITTS, John GRUBB, Frank JANNEY, Joe JANNEY, Cornelius SHAWEN, Wm. STROUD, Wm. POOL, W. P. PANCOAST (bought store & goods,) totaling $2787.56. RtCt 14 Nov 1882. [G:351]

S/A with Committee J. T. GRUBB: request for debts published in the newspaper Mirror, submissions totaling $3303. RtCt 9 Jan 1883. [G:359]

S/A with Committee J. T. GRUBB: expenses leaving $2336.44 paid to ward. RtCt 11 Apr 1883. [G:365]

SHUMAKER, William B., George J., Sarah, Mary and Elizabeth (Children of Josiah) [SHOEMAKER]

S/A with Gdn Jno. H. TITUS: beginning 9 Mar 1878; paid board to mother, expenses leaving Wm. B. SHUMAKER $172.70 on 9 Mar 1878 upon coming of age, George J. SHUMAKER $172.70 to 24 Aug 1879 upon coming of age, $175.75 to Sarah (of age and now Sarah CAMPBELL,) and $179.99 each to Mary & Elizabeth. RtCt 14 Nov 1882. [G:348]

S/A with Gdn John H. TITUS: (spelled SHOEMAKER) beginning 9 Mar 1882; general expenses leaving Maria Elizabeth SHOEMAKER $185.41 when she came of age on 9 May 1883 & Mary SHOEMAKER $179.99. RtCt 12 Feb 1884. [G:426]

S/A with Gdn John H. TITUS: (spelled SHOEMAKER) beginning 9 May 1883; $200.81 due to Mary SHUMAKER on 23 May 1885 when she reached majority. RtCt 11 Aug 1885. [G:480]

RAMSEY, Samuel T.

Inventory by Gdn W. V. MOORE: income from sale of wheat totaling $35.27. RtCt 13 Dec 1882. [G:352]

Inventory of Wm. V. MOORE: from sale of mountain land & estate of Jonathan BROWN, totaling $195.31. RtCt 15 Sep 1883. [G:389]

S/A with Gdn Wm. MOORE: beginning 12 Jun 1882; general expenses leaving $210.98 paid in full as ward now of age. RtCt 12 Mar 1884. [G:428]

FOLEY, Miss Margaret J.

Appraisal/Inventory by Committee B. F. SAFFER: household items, note, bond. Aprs: Bushrod SKILMAN, James B. RUST, George POLAND. RtCt 13 Dec 1882. [G:352]

Sale of 13 Sep 1883 by Committee B. F. SAFFER: purchasers: Jacob LORENTZ, Grimes FOLEY, Richd. SUMMERS, Ludwell HUTCHISON, Mrs. Francis GREGG, Millard BROWN, Philip KEYES, Charles DEAN, John HUTCHISON, Reuben DEAN, Alonzo OBANNON, Alexander ALLEN, Nelson SETTLE, Mary NEWMAN, John McCARTY, Thos. SUMMERS, Saml. BYRNES, David EATON, Frank DEMORY, totaling $117.30. RtCt 15 Oct 1883. [G:407]

S/A with Committee B. F. SAFFER: beginning 14 Aug 1882; expenses leaving $204.57. RtCt 11 Nov 1884. [G:459]

S/A with Committee B. F. SAFFER: beginning 14 Aug 1883; $86.70 due ward on 14 Aug 1892. RtCt 15 Feb 1893. [H:167]

MILBOURNE, Orra & Blanche

Inventory: by Gdn G. H. NIXON: $100 each from O. S. BRADEN Admr of A. J. MILBOURNE. RtCt 9 Dec 1882. [G:353]

S/A with Geo. H. NIXON: (now Orra L. CARTER) receipt of 25 Mar 1885 for payment in full of $100, Orra L. having reach majority. RtCt 11 Aug 1885. [G:481]

KERCHEVAL, George E.

Appraisal/Inventory of 18 May 1882: CtOD 13 Mar 1882; Minor F. CHAMBLIN Admr; farm and household items, totaling $1285.07. Aprs: David H. PLASTER, L. E. HUTCHISON, Madison MONROE. RtCt 28 Dec 1882. [G:354]

S/A with DShff Wm. GAINES: beginning 1 Feb 1885; $310 from Thomas A. HALL, general expenses, leaving $87.70. RtCt 10 Aug 1886. [H:13]

S/A with DShff & Committee Wm. GAINES: beginning 1 Feb 1887; general expenses leaving $532.66 [long acct]. RtCt 14 Dec 1897. [H:316]

S/A with DShff & Committee Wm. GAINES: beginning 1 Jun 1897; general expenses leaving $486.45. RtCt 11 Oct 1900. [H:401]

S/A with DShff & Committee Wm. GAINES: beginning 1 Jun 1900; income from crops, payments to Mrs. KERCHEVAL, general expenses, leaving $309.90. RtCt 13 Nov 1901. [H:423]

S/A with Committee Wm. GAINES: beginning 1 Aug 1901; general expenses leaving $323.19. RtCt 11 Mar 1903. [H:461]

S/A with DShff & Committee Wm. GAINES: beginning 1 Feb 1886; general expenses leaving $127.54. RtCt 10 Jan 1888. [H:58]

COOPER, Margaret E.

S/A with Gdn Wm. STONE: beginning Apr 1882; expenses leaving $444.98. [G:356]

TAYLOR, Harriet B.

S/A with Committee C. SHAWEN: beginning 16 Feb 1882; income from rent of farm, general expenses, leaving $598.06 paid to Admr (she is now dead.) RtCt 13 Feb 1883. [G:363]

WRIGHT, Joseph & Beverley

S/A with Gdn J. L. NORRIS: receipt of $1492.50 from Valley Mutual Insurance Co, no need for appraisal. RtCt 10 Jul 1883. [G:381]

CRAIG, John A. Jr.

S/A with Gdn John FLEMING: receipt of $306.20, no need for appraisal. RtCt 10 Jul 1883. [G:382]

WALKER, R. L.

S/A with Gdn Barcklay LLOYD: beginning 11 Jun 1878; general expenses leaving $440.30. RtCt 14 Aug 1883. [G:385]

MASON, Mary A. V. B.

Inventory by Gdn Temple C. MASON: payment from former Gdn, income from sale of land, payment from W. F.

BARRETT Admr. of George BEAMER, totaling $1485. RtCt 14 Aug 1883. [G:387]

HAMMERLY, Mary E.
Inventory by Gdn J. A. HAMMERLY: $2500 from life insurance, lien on small tract of land where she lives. RtCt 20 Aug 1883. [G:387]

CHAMBLIN, John R. & H. C.
Inventory by Gdn A. G. CHAMBLIN: receipt $1000 22 Aug 1882. RtCt 20 Aug 1883. [G:388]

FIELDS, Emily J. [FIELD]
Inventory of Committee Saml. CLENDENING: $343.60 from sale of real estate. RtCt 20 Aug 1883. [G:388]
S/A with Committee Saml. CLENDENING: beginning 15 Jun 1884; cost of keeping Mrs. Mary FIELDS during last sickness, etc. leaving $227.53. RtCt 15 Jun 1886. [H:10]

CRAVEN, Giles T.
Inventory by Committee G. G. CRAVEN: (now dec'd?) bonds, funds exhausted by boarding the lunatic at Asylum. RtCt 23 Aug 1883. [G:388]
S/A with Committee G. G. CRAVEN: beginning 1 May 1883; expenses including to West. L. Asylum, leaving $5280. RtCt 8 Apr 1895. [H:222]
S/A with Committee G. G. CRAVEN: beginning 1 May 1894; paid Western Hospital, general expenses, leaving $357.05 and $4938.64 in investments. RtCt 11 May 1903. [H:467]
Inventory of Mar 1902 by Committee F. G. WELSH: cash in bank, bonds, totaling $4938.67. RtCt 15 Apr 1903. [H:494]

HICKMAN, G. L. Kurtz, Elnora A., Benjamin J., William S. and John E.
S/A with Gdn Eleanor M. HICKMAN: beginning 17 Sep 1867; income from sale of crops, expenses, full payment to G. L. Kurtz HICKMAN of $655.45 on 15 Sep 1875, Elnora A. HICKMAN payment of $450.58 in full on 15 Sep 1876, Benjamin J. HICKMAN due $301.39 on 15 Sep 1872, Wm. S. HICKMAN paid $493.31 on 15 Sep 1873, John E. HICKMAN due $688.36. [G:390]

PAXSON, Fannie H., Hattie A., Wm. C. J., Charles & Louisa E.
Inventory of Gdn Mrs. C. W. PAXSON: received $87.57 for each. RtCt 28 Sep 1883. [G:400]

ARNIS, Annie R., William H., Chista V.
Inventory by Gdn Margaret C. ARNIS: $128.64 for each. RtCt 10 Oct 1883. [G:406]

HUTCHISON, Mary E., Franklin, Maria L. & Melville
Inventory by Gdn A. M. HUTCHISON: $11.31 each. RtCt 12 Oct 1883. [G:407]

HOUSE, Samuel M. J. & Mary H.
Inventory by Gdn C. C. GAVER: $748.20 from estate of E. C. H. HOUSE. RtCt 13 Nov 1883. [G:412]
S/A with Gdn C. C. GAVER: beginning 1 Aug 1883; general expenses leaving Samuel M. J. HOUSE $382.40. RtCt 11 Nov 1884. [G:455]
S/A with Gdn C. C. GAVER: beginning 1 Aug 1883; general expenses leaving Mary H. HOUSE $382.40. RtCt 11 Nov 1884. [G:456]

PETERS, Walter G., William R., Edward W. & Robert J.
Inventory by Gdn John GEORGE: $351.52½ each. RtCt 28 Nov 1883. [G:412]
S/A with Gdn John GEORGE: beginning 1 Nov 1883; $1406.10 from estate of Rosanna W. GEORGE, expenses leaving William PETERS $341.63, Walter PETERS $401.65, Edward PETERS $401.66 & Robert PETERS $401.66. RtCt 15 Feb 1887. [H:31]
S/A with Gdn John GEORGE: beginning 1 Nov 1886; expenses leaving William R. PETERS $147.11 paid 1 May 1888 when he reached majority, Robert J. PETERS $401.66 & Edward PETERS $422. RtCt 14 May 1889. [H:110]

GLASCOCK, Orra M., May, Fenton F., Lilly and Alfred
S/A with Gdn H. B. GLASCOCK: beginning 12 Sep 1881; income from sale of farm in Fauquier, expenses, leaving Orra M. GLASSCOCK $559.36, May GLASCOCK $559.40, F. Fadeley GLASCOCK $559.31, Lilly GLASCOCK $559.31 & Alfred GLASCOCK $559.31, but they also owe the Gdn. RtCt 11 Dec 1883. [G:420]
S/A with Gdn Hattie B. GLASCOCK: beginning 12 Sep 1883; income from sale of land, expenses, leaving Orra M. GLASCOCK $1106.96, May GLASCOCK $1107, Fenton F. GLASCOCK $1106.91, Lilly GLASCOCK $1106.91 & Alfred GLASCOCK $1106.91. RtCt 11 Nov 1884. [G:450]

HOUGH, E. Stanley
Inventory by Gdn Cor. SHAWEN: rec'd $891.71 from estate of E. P. HOUGH. RtCt 11 Dec 1883. [G:425]
S/A with Gdn Cornelius SHAWEN: beginning 30 Apr 1883; general expenses leaving $944.35. RtCt 13 Jan 1885. [G:465]

HAWS, Ella & Oscar
Inventory by Gdn R. C. CHAMBLIN: (written as Ellen & Asker) rec'd $409.96 from Wm. Matthew. RtCt 29 Jan 1884. [G:426]
S/A with Gdn R. C. CHAMBLIN: beginning 12 Dec 1883; general expenses leaving $397.09. RtCt 11 Aug 1885. [G:483]
S/A with Gdn R. C. CHAMBLIN: beginning 12 Dec 1884; general expenses leaving $414.99. RtCt 15 Jun 1886. [H:12]

S/A with Gdn R. C. CHAMBLIN: beginning 12 Dec 1885; general expenses leaving $351.96. RtCt 10 Jan 1888. [H:55]

S/A with Gdn R. C. CHAMBLIN: beginning 12 Dec 1886; general expenses leaving $727.32. RtCt 14 May 1889. [H:105]

S/A with Gdn R. C. CHAMBLIN: beginning 1 Jan 1889; general expenses leaving $1292.12. RtCt 15 Jan 1890. [H:120]

S/A with Gdn R. C. CHAMBLIN: beginning 12 Dec 1888; general expenses leaving $1264.61. RtCt 10 Nov 1891. [H:146]

S/A with Gdn R. C. CHAMBLIN: beginning 31 Dec 1890; paid A. E. HAWS for maintenence, general expenses, leaving Oscar HAWS $654.62 & Ella HAWS $629.62. RtCt 10 Nov 1896. [H:280]

S/A with Gdn R. C. CHAMBLIN: beginning 1 Jan 1896; general expenses leaving $79.62 due Oscar on 19 Nov 1896, $633.12 due Ella on 25 May 1897 when she married Louis SAUNDERS. RtCt 15 Jun 1898. [H:339]

OSBURN, Maurice
Appraisal/Inventory: farm items, stock of store goods, acct agst estate of Jonah OSBURN, store accts, totaling $1643.91. Aprs: Craven JAMES, J. H. PURCELL, Owen THOMAS. RtCt 18 Mar 1884. [G:438]

Sale of 3 Oct 1883: purchasers: Rodney GRAY, Theo. BELL, Ed. BALLENGER, Geo. GIBSON, Oscar TAYLOR, sale of store goods, totaling $1097.85. RtCt 18 Mar 1884. [G:438]

S/A with Committee Jas. E. CARRUTHERS: beginning 4 Sep 1883; general expenses leaving $618.74, confirmed by deed entered in the case of Jonah OSBURN Admrs vs OSBURN. [G:467]

S/A with DShff & Committee C. SHAWEN: distributions to creditors, totaling $332.21. [G:470]

NIXON, J. Ellwood
S/A with Gdn John F. LYNN: beginning 15 Sep 1871; became of age 11 Oct 1875, leaving $108.91 still due. Hannah E. NIXON is wife of Jno. A. LYNN. John F. LYNN now dec'd. RtCt 9 Jun 1884. [G:440]

NIXON, Parelia
S/A with Gdn J. T. LYNN: beginning 15 Sep 1871; became of age 21 Dec 1871, leaving $165 still due. Gdn is dec'd. RtCt 9 Jun 1884. [G:441]

HESSER, Martha E.
Inventory by Committee S. A. MARSHALL: (now dec'd) $300 to $350 from suit of HUMPHREY's Admr vs HESSER. RtCt 2 Jun 1884. [G:444]

S/A with Committee Sarah A. MARSHALL: beginning 1892; general expenses leaving $261.53. RtCt 10 Jan 1899. [H:356]

KING, Randolph
S/A with Gdn T. H. CARTER: beginning 12 May 1884; general expenses leaving $129.76. RtCt 11 Nov 1884. [G:449]

S/A with Gdn T. H. CARTER: beginning Apr 1884; general expenses leaving $113.98. RtCt 11 Aug 1885. [G:481]

S/A with Gdn T. H. CARTER: beginning 30 Apr 1885; general expenses leaving $134.23 on 14 Aug 1887 when he reached his majority. RtCt 10 Jan 1888. [H:66]

TIPPETT, Henry, Elizabeth & Sarah
Inventory by Gdn John W. TIPPETT: land sold in TIPPETT vs. PALMER totaling $183. RtCt 13 Nov 1884. [G:464]

CHICK, Edward
Inventory by Gdn George W. CHICK: $109.88 from estate of Geo. W. CHICK dec'd. RtCt 16 Jan 1885. [G:473]

LOVE, E. Dilley
Inventory by Gdn Armida E. LOVE: $247.18 from estate of Louis N. B. LOVE. RtCt 6 Mar 1885. [G:473]

SNOUFFER, Ashton
Inventory by Gdn G. A. T. SNOUFFER: Abt $300 proceeds from MINOR vs. SHREVE. RtCt 21 Sep 1885. [G:497]

WILEY, Edgar T.
S/A with Gdn Jas. M. HOGE: beginning 2 Aug 1884; $225 from father's estate, general expenses leaving $225. RtCt 11 May 1886. [H:1]

S/A with Gdn James M. HOGE: beginning 2 Aug 1885; general expenses leaving $276.10. RtCt 15 Jun 1886. [H:11]

WILEY, Charles H.
S/A with Gdn Jas. M. HOGE: beginning 2 Aug 1884; $225 from father's estate, general expenses leaving $225. RtCt 11 May 1886. [H:1]

S/A with Gdn Jas. M. HOGE: beginning 2 Aug 1884; general expenses leaving $260.70. RtCt 14 May 1888. [H:74]

S/A with Gdn James H. HOGE: beginning 2 Aug 1887; $258.36 paid ward on 28 Aug 1890 when he reached majority. RtCt 13 Mar 1894. [H:196]

WILEY, Annie J.
S/A with Gdn Jas. M. HOGE: beginning 2 Aug 1884; $225 from father's estate, general expenses leaving $275. RtCt 11 May 1886. [H:2]

S/A with Gdn Jas. M. HOGE: beginning 2 Aug 1883; general expenses leaving $321.22. RtCt 14 May 1888. [H:72]

LOUDOUN COUNTY, VIRGINIA
GUARDIAN ACCOUNTS
1759-1904

S/A with Gdn Jas. M. HOGE: beginning 2 Aug 1887; $311.31 due at her majority in Sep 1892. RtCt 13 Mar 1894. [H:198]

BEATTY, Bettie Jane, Harry W. and Chester M. (Children of William)

S/A with Gdn W. R. CHINN: beginning 26 May 1884; $2923.56 from estate of Wm. BEATTY, $2200 from S. J. BEATTY, general expenses, leaving $1639.04 to each to Bettie Jane, Harry W. & Chester M. BEATTY. RtCt 11 May 1886. [H:6]

S/A with Gdn W. R. CHINN: beginning 1 Jun 1885; paid Lydia BEATTY for maintenance of wards, general expenses, leaving $5294.80. RtCt 15 Jan 1890. [H:118]

S/A with Gdn K. C. CHINN: beginning 1 Jun 1889; general expenses leaving $5030.06. RtCt 16 Sep 1891. [H:140]

S/A with Gdn K. C. CHINN: beginning 1 Jun 1890; general expenses leaving $5527.61. RtCt 9 Jan 1894. [H:190]

S/A with Gdn K. C. CHINN: beginning 1 Jun 1892; expenses leaving $6989.15. RtCt 14 Sep 1897. [H:306]

S/A with Gdn K. C. CHINN: beginning 1 Jun 1897; general expenses leaving Betty on 10 Oct 1898 $2448.21 at majority & $5073.49 to Harry & Chester. RtCt 10 Jul 1899. [H:371]

MERCHANT, Leroy W.

S/A with Gdn A. W. MERCHANT: beginning 24 Dec 1885; expenses leaving $37.34. RtCt 15 Jan 1886. [H:9]

MOFFETT, Mary C., John L., Charles H. and Gracie A. (Children of L. C. [Maffett])

Inventory by Gdn John T. THOMPSON: $1218.54 from estate of L. C. MOFFETT on 1 Feb 1887. Children are Mary C., John L., Chas. H. & Gracie A. MOFFETT. RtCt 1 Feb 1887. [H:34]

S/A with mother Mary A. MOFFETT (now Mary A. THOMPSON wife of Jno. T. THOMPSON): husband now to become Gdn. [H:40]

S/A with Gdn Jno. T. THOMPSON: beginning 12 Jan 1887; $1218.52 rec'd from former Gdn. RtCt 14 May 1888. [H:68]

S/A with Gdn Jno. T. THOMPSON: beginning 1 Feb 1887; Mary C. MOFFETT (now Mrs. GOODHART) of age 1 Feb 1893 paid $224.27, Jno. L. MOFFETT of age Jul 1895 paid $304.63, Chas. H. MOFFETT of age Oct 1897 paid $304.63, Grace A. MOFFETT of age May 1899 paid $304.65. RtCt 15 Feb 1898. [H:327]

DODD, Mary E., Lilly S., Robert A., Ethel A., William H., John G., Ruth V., Nora J., Ida G. and Bettie (Children of Margaret E.)

Inventory by father & Gdn Chas. H. DODD: $909.10 insurance policy to benefit children Mary E. age 19y, Lilly S. age 16y, Robert A. age 15y, Ethel A. age 13y, William H. age 11y, Jno. G. age 8y, Ruth V. age 6y, Nora J. age 4y, Ida G. age 2y & Bettie age 6m. RtCt 16 Feb 1887. [H:35]

S/A with Gdn Chas. H. DODD: beginning 10 Apr 1887; shares of $88.51 each, Mary E. DODD of age on 7 Dec 1888, Lilly S. DODD of age 14 Jul 1890, Robt. A. DODD of age 5 Apr 1892, Ethel A. DODD of age 24 Feb 1894, Wm. H. DODD of age 21 May 1897, Jno. G. DODD of age May 1900, Ruth V. DODD of age 25 Jan 1902, Nora J. DODD of age 30 Apr 1904, Ida G. DODD of age 27 Jan 1906 & Bettie DODD of age 5 Aug 1907. RtCt 14 May 1889. [H:107]

S/A with Gdn Chas. H. DODD: Lillie S. DODD has married Wm. P. GIBSON and will be 21y old on 14 Jul 1890, Gdn wants to pay her $88.51 share of her mother's life insurance policy. RtCt 14 Sep 1889. [H:113]

S/A with Gdn Ida G. DODD: beginning May 1894; general expenses leaving Ruth V. DODD $93.03, Nora J. DODD $103.33, Ida G. DODD $103.30 & Bettie DODD $105.18. Gdn has resigned and W. P. HEFLIN takes her place. RtCt 10 Sep 1895. [H:238]

S/A with Gdn Robert A. DODD: beginning 25 May 1894; payments from estates of Robert COSTELLO & C. H. DODD, general expenses, leaving John G. DODD $202.60. RtCt 16 Sep 1896. [H:274]

S/A with W. C. HEFLIN: beginning 19 Jun 1895; general expenses leaving $492.28 plus $400 bond. RtCt 16 Sep 1896. [H:278]

S/A with Gdn Jno. G. UTTERBACK: William H. became 21y old on 21 May 1897, $353.70 paid to him in full. RtCt 25 Jun 1897. [H:304]

S/A with Gdn W. C. HEFLIN: beginning 19 Jun 1896; general expenses leaving $213.12 to Nora G. DODD, Ruth V. ATWELL, Grace DODD & Betty DODD. RtCt 15 Jan 1901. [H:409]

S/A with Gdn W. C. HEFLIN: beginning 19 Jun 1900; general expenses leaving Grace DODD $329.85. RtCt 11 Aug 1903. [H:474]

S/A with Gdn W. C. HEFLIN: beginning 19 Jun 1900; general expenses leaving Nora G. DODD $329.85. RtCt 11 Aug 1903. [H:475]

S/A with Gdn W. C. HEFLIN: beginning 19 Jun 1900; general expenses leaving Betty DODD $329.85. RtCt 11 Aug 1903. [H:480]

S/A with Gdn W. C. HEFLIN: (now Grace HUMPHRIES) beginning 19 Oct 1903; $846.64 paid to new Gdn & husband Henry HUMPHRIES on 19 Oct 1903. RtCt 14 Dec 1903. [H:496]

DODD, J. B.

S/A with Gdn R. A. DODD: beginning 1 Jun 1896; general expenses leaving $387.35 on 1 Jun 1900 at majority, fully paid. RtCt 15 Aug 1900. [H:396]

THOMPSON, Irving P.
S/A with Gdn W. D. THOMPSON: beginning 13 Apr 1885; payment from estate of Hugh S. & R. H. THOMPSON, general expenses, leaving $124.87. RtCt 10 May 1887. [H:37]

S/A with Gdn W. D. THOMPSON: beginning 10 Jan 1887; ward now dec'd, $140.45 distributed to brothers & sisters W. D. THOMPSON, J. O. THOMPSON, H. A. THOMPSON, J. H. THOMPSON & S. M. GRUBB. RtCt 14 May 1888. [H:75]

S/A with Gdn W. D. THOMPSON: beginning 2 Jun 1888; $45.26 each to next of kin W. D. THOMPSON, J. A. THOMPSON, H. A. THOMPSON, J. H. THOMPSON & S. M. GRUBB. RtCt 15 Jan 1890. [H:119]

THOMPSON, J. Harry
S/A with Gdn J. A. THOMPSON: beginning 16 Feb 1886; general expenses leaving $2864.60 which was invested. RtCt 10 May 1887. [H:38]

S/A with Gdn J. A. THOMPSON: beginning 10 Jan 1887; general expenses leaving $3080.20, $3390 is loaned out. RtCt 14 May 1888. [H:70]

S/A with Gdn J. A. THOMPSON: beginning 6 Feb 1888; general expenses leaving $213.88. RtCt 14 Sep 1889. [H:112]

S/A with Gdn J. A. THOMPSON: beginning Feb 1889; general expenses leaving $1495.91. RtCt 10 Jun 1891. [H:139]

S/A with Gdn J. A. THOMPSON: beginning 10 Jan 1890; general expenses leaving $276.94. RtCt 10 Nov 1891. [H:143]

S/A with Gdn J. A. THOMPSON: beginning 10 Jan 1891; general expenses leaving $512.23 on 10 Jan 1892 paid as he has reach his majority. RtCt 10 Oct 1892. [H:166]

BARTLETT, William
S/A with Gdn Geo. F. EAMICH: beginning 11 Sep 1886; expenses leaving $91.46 paid in full on 17 Sep 1887 when he reached majority. RtCt 10 May 1887. [H:40]

HOUGH, L. W. S.
S/A with Committee H. H. RUSSELL: beginning 1 May 1886; deposits in bank, general expenses leaving $966.53. RtCt 10 May 1887. [H:44]

FURR, John L.
S/A with Gdn Minor F. CHAMBLIN: beginning 1 Nov 1885; expenses leaving $130.65 paid on 21 Feb 1887 when he reached his majority. RtCt 10 May 1887. [H:46]

SKINNER, Mary C.
S/A with Gdn E. W. SKINNER: beginning Aug 1885; expenses leaving $109.35. RtCt 10 May 1887. [H:47]

SKINNER, Willie H.
S/A with Gdn E. W. SKINNER: beginning 10 Aug 1885; expenses leaving $93.41 due to Gdn. RtCt 10 May 1887. [H:48]

RICE, J. E.
S/A with trustee H. H. RUSSELL: beginning 4 Oct 1886; income from sale of stock and notes, general expenses, leaving $1213.19. RtCt 10 May 1887. [H:49]

MILBURN, Ann E.
S/A with Shff & trustee S. BOLYN: beginning 1 Jul 1885; expenses leaving $1398.06. RtCt 10 May 1887. [H:52]

BEACH, Martha E.
S/A with Shff & trustee S. BOLYN: beginning 1 Jul 1885; general expenses leaving $1398.06. RtCt 10 May 1887. [H:52]

CARTER, Eleanor H. & Robt. C.
S/A with Gdn Anna W. BALDWIN: beginning Apr 1885; general expenses leaving $1700, invested in real estate. RtCt 10 Jan 1888. [H:65]

HESS, Sarah Amanda
S/A with Gdn C. W. BARTER: beginning 10 May 1880; Mrs. BARTON died 31 Aug 1883 so Amanda receives her share of interest. Amanda became of age before the death of her mother. $126.92 due on 10 May 1884. RtCt 10 Jan 1888. [H:67]

BOGER, John E.
S/A with Gdn J. W. FRY: beginning 20 Dec 1886; general expenses leaving $211.75. RtCt 14 May 1888. [H:72]

S/A with Gdn J. W. FRY: beginning 20 Dec 1887; general expenses leaving $241.82. RtCt 10 Jun 1891. [H:136]

HEATON, Cecelia D.
S/A of 9 Jan 1888 of J. H. VANDEVENTER Exor of late Gdn Gabriel VANDEVENTER dec'd: (now married to R. W. BRADEN and reached her majority) acct. paid in full. RtCt 14 May 1888. [H:76]

SURVICK, Nora, Carrie and Mary B. (Children of Benjamin)
S/A with Gdn Samuel ORRISON: beginning 10 May 1884; children Nora, Carrie & Mary B. SURVICK; expenses leaving $1572.93. RtCt 14 May 1888. [H:77]

ROLLINS, Virginia G. R. & Margaret M.
S/A with Gdn Samuel ORRISON: beginning 11 Apr 1882; general expenses leaving Virginia G. L. ROLLINS $130.04 & Margaret M. ROLLINS $223.82. RtCt 14 May 1888. [H:79]

S/A with Gdn Saml. ORRISON: beginning 1887; principal & interest of $137.84 for Virginia ROLLINS. RtCt 10 Sep 1894. [H:217]

S/A with Gdn Saml. ORRISON: ward Maggie ROLLINS is now of age. RtCt 10 Sep 1894. [H:218]

VIRTZ, Henry T.
Inventory by Gdn G. W. TITUS: $4501.01 from Admr, $458.73 from late Gdn, ¼ of 2/3 rent of farm at $300. RtCt 21 May 1888. [H:82]

S/A with Gdn Geo. W. TITUS: beginning 9 May 1888; $1501.01 from estate of Henry VIRTZ, payments to Mrs. Delia VIRTZ, leaving $2026.42. RtCt 10 Nov 1891. [H:147]

S/A with Gdn Geo. W. TITUS: beginning 9 Mar 1891; paid Mrs. Delia VIRTZ for maintanence, general expenses, leaving $1701.09 due ward's estate on 9 Mar 1896. RtCt 14 Jul 1896. [H:265]

S/A with Gdn Geo. W. TITUS: beginning 11 Mar 1896; from D. VIRTS' estate, general expenses, leaving $1527.17. RtCt 9 Aug 1897. [H:303]

S/A with Gdn G. W. TITUS: beginning 1 Mar 1897; general expenses leaving $1514.90 on 16 Sep 1897, paid in full. RtCt 9 Aug 1898. [H:347]

HOUSE, Mary H.
S/A with Gdn C. C. GAVER: beginning 1 Aug 1884; general expenses leaving $549.41 paid on 5 Feb 1888 when she reached majority. RtCt 14 Aug 1888. [H:87]

RICKARD, Jesse L. & Walter C.
S/A with Gdn Mrs. Kate RICKARD: beginning 9 Feb 1886; expenses leaving $634.10. RtCt 9 Oct 1888. [H:91]

S/A with Gdn Kate RICKARD (now PAXSON): beginning 9 Feb 1888; receipt of 1 Oct 1895 from Jessie L. RICKARD for full payment of $320.97. RtCt 10 Mar 1897. [H:289]

S/A with Gdn Kate RICKARD: W. C. RICKARD rec'd $317.05 on 22 Aug 1897 as payment in full. RtCt 9 Nov 1897. [H:312]

MINOR, Annie M.
Appraisal/Inventory of 10 Apr 1888 by Committee H. H. RUSSELL: notes & interest, bank deposits. Will of Annie M. MINOR dated 19 Nov 1878 is with the Committee. Aprs: John GRAY, W. W. ATHEY, Herbert OSBURN. RtCt 24 May 1888. [H:94]

S/A with Shff & Committee H. H. RUSSELL: beginning 17 Apr 1888; expenses to asylum, general payments, leaving $783.51. RtCt 15 Jan 1890. [H:121]

S/A with Shff & Committee H. H. RUSSELL: beginning 1 May 1889; general expenses leaving $607.19. RtCt 12 Jan 1891. [H:128]

S/A with Committee H. H. RUSSELL: beginning 1 May 1890; general expenses leaving estate $282.73. RtCt 14 Apr 1892. [H:158]

S/A with Shff & Committee H. H. RUSSELL: beginning 1 May 1891; expenses leaving $73.51 payable to S. W. Lunatic Asylum. RtCt 15 Aug 1893. [H:181]

CHICK, Charles Edward
S/A with Gdn Geo. W. CHICK: beginning 13 Jan 1885; payments in full by sale of real estate to him, final settlement. RtCt 14 May 1889. [H:103]

McCARTY, George B.
S/A with Committee C. E. MOUNT: beginning 15 May 1888; general expenses leaving $15.88 to estate as ward has died. RtCt 14 May 1889. [H:104]

SILCOTT, Mary
S/A with Gdn Jno. W. SILCOTT: beginning 4 May 1887; $2676.43 from estate of M. SILCOTT, expenses, leaving $2875.13. RtCt 14 May 1889. [H:106]

S/A with Gdn Jno. W. SILCOTT: beginning 1 May 1888; expenses leaving $3068.71. RtCt 15 Jan 1890. [H:114]

S/A with Gdn Jno. W. SILCOTT: beginning 4 May 1889; ward of age 18 Jan 1890 and paid $3252.19 final S/A. RtCt 12 Jan 1891. [H:132]

WOODS, Blanch
S/A with Gdn Edgar JACKSON: beginning Aug 1884; $400.62 share of parents estate, income from rent of farm, became of age on 20 Jul 1886, leaving $206 paid in full 12 Mar 1889. RtCt 14 May 1889. [H:109]

YOUNG, Susannah B.
S/A with Committee J. W. FOSTER: beginning 23 Oct 1883; she has died and estate of $389.87 turned over to the Shff. [H:123]

PIGGOTT, Mary E. & Albert S.
Inventory by Gdn Alberta J. PIGGOTT: $2105.30 from personal estate of their father, income from a few bonds and 2/3 rent of 160 acre farm. RtCt 10 May 1890. [H:124]

S/A with Gdn Alberta J. PIGGOTT: beginning 1890; income from 2/3 rent of farm, expenses leaving $208.63 plus $2120 in investments. RtCt 15 Aug 1893. [H:179]

S/A with Gdn Alberta J. PIGGOTT: beginning Apr 1891; general expenses leaving $260.64 plus $1770 invested. RtCt 9 Jan 1894. [H:195]

S/A with mother Gdn Alberta J. PIGGOTT: beginning 1 Apr 1893; income from investments plus interest and rents, leaving $2690.98. Wants to buy a piano for Mary, age 12y. RtCt 15 Jul 1896. [H:262]

S/A with Gdn Alberta J. PIGGOTT: beginning 20 Mar 1897; expenses leaving $123.07 to mother, $246.16 to children, $152.51 distributive share of estate of Mary PIGGOTT, leaving $86.03 due to Gdn. RtCt 13 Sep 1899. [H:372]

S/A with Gdn Alberta J. PIGGOTT: beginning 3 Nov 1899; income from rents, expenses leaving $117.93 due to Gdn. RtCt 5 Oct 1901. [H:421]

S/A with Gdn Alberta J. PIGGOTT: beginning 1901; expenses leaving $95.46. RtCt 12 Jan 1904. [H:498]

PEYTON, Cabel Y.
S/A with Gdn Oscar S. BRADEN: beginning 9 Feb 1889; $2129.09 from estate of W. N. PUSEY, general expenses leaving $1664.25. RtCt 12 Jan 1891. [H:129]

S/A with Gdn O. S. BRADEN: beginning 9 Feb 1889; general expenses leaving $1606.54. RtCt 10 Jun 1891. [H:138]

S/A with Gdn O. S. BRADEN: beginning 9 Feb 1890; general expenses leaving $1288. RtCt 9 Jul 1894. [H:211]

S/A with Gdn O. S. BRADEN: beginning 9 Feb 1894; general expenses leaving $1118.73. RtCt 10 Dec 1895. [H:248]

S/A with Gdn O. S. BRADEN: beginning Feb 1895; general expenses leaving $921.98. O. S. BRADEN is now dec'd, before 2 Jul 1896. RtCt 11 Aug 1896 [H:272]

BEVERLEY, R. A.
S/A with Gdn J. B. BRONLEY: beginning 2 May 1881; general expenses leaving $1357.76. [H:134]

DIVINE, Arthur Fairfax and Jessie (Children of Emily)
Inventory of 22 Sep 1891 by Gdn John H. NELSON: children Arthur Fairfax & Jessie Divine; bond of $1190, bond of $170, $109.28 in cash. RtCt 22 Sep 1891. [H:141]

S/A with Gdn John H. NELSON: beginning 1894; $512.44 paid Arthur Divine upon reaching age on 22 Jun 1894, payments leaving Jessie Divine $510. RtCt 12 May 1896. [H:260]

BARTLETT, Ella
S/A with Gdn Geo. F. EAMICK: beginning 2 Oct 1887; $100.32 paid on 1 Sep 1889 when she reached her majority. RtCt 10 Nov 1891. [H:142]

CLAPHAM, Elizabeth
Inventory by Committee J. H. CLAPHAM: bonds and interest, totaling $327.88. RtCt 9 Feb 1892. [H:150]

S/A with Committee J. H. CLAPHAM: (she now dec'd) beginning 1 Nov 1896; general expenses leaving $74.55 paid to heirs at law J. H. CLAPHAM & Saul CLAPHAM. RtCt 15 Dec 1896. [H:286]

FURR, Minor
S/A with M. F. CHAMBLIN: beginning 1 Nov 1885; general expenses leaving $179.99 to ward on 4 Aug 1891 when he reached majority. RtCt 14 Apr 1892. [H:155]

PANCOAST, Lula, Carrie & Harry
S/A with Gdn Mrs. L. Alice PANCOAST: $281.42 from estate of S. T. PANCOAST, 2/3 of $300 from real estate, Lula was kept at school for 7y at $100/y, Carrie was at boarding school for 4y & Harry for 3y. Harry will be of age Mar 1892. RtCt 14 Apr 1892. [H:159]

FLING, W. F.
Appraisal/Inventory by Committee H. H. RUSSELL: farm items totaling $676.25. Appraisal/Inventory of joint property of BRADFIELD & FLING 23 May 1892: farm animals totaling $1087.50 with $411.25 being W. F. FLING's. Aprs: Geo. W. HOLMES, John C. CARR, C. H. HIGDON. RtCt 31 May 1892. [H:160]

S/A with Committee H. H. RUSSELL: beginning 9 May 1892; income from sale of farm items, general expenses leaving $613.74 [H:172]

S/A with Committee H. H. RUSSELL: general expenses totaling $986.35. [H:176]

ROWLES, Mary C.
Inventory by Committee J. C. COLEMAN: bonds totaling $1278.48. RtCt 7 Dec 1891. [H:161]

S/A with Committee J. C. COLEMAN: beginning 1 Mar 1892; expenses leaving $307.77 payable to J. P. MACHEN her Admr with will amended. RtCt 10 Dec 1895. [H:244]

HUMPHREY, William D.
S/A with Gdn Thomas C. HUMPHREY: beginning 21 May 1892; $400 paid on 21 May 1892 as he has reached his majority. RtCt 15 Feb 1893. [H:169]

CARTER, John F.
S/A with Gdn F. M. CARTER: beginning 1 Jan 1889; payments to mother Pattsy W. CARTER totaling $469.83. RtCt 11 Apr 1893. [H:169]

S/A with Gdn F. M. CARTER: beginning 1 Jan 1892; payments to mother, general expenses, leaving $237.16. RtCt 12 Nov 1903. [H:483]

CARTER, Francis M. Jr.
S/A with Gdn F. M. CARTER: beginning 1 Jan 1889; expenses leaving $12.97. RtCt 11 Apr 1893. [H:170]

S/A with Gdn Francis M. CARTER: beginning 1 Jan 1892; share of father's estate, general expenses, leaving $197.02 due to Gdn, ward has attained his majority. RtCt 12 Nov 1903. [H:489]

CARTER, William Maulsby
S/A with Gdn F. M. CARTER: beginning 1 Jan 1889; expenses leaving $10.47. RtCt 11 Apr 1893. [H:171]

S/A with Gdn F. M. CARTER: beginning 1 Jan 1892; share of father's estate, general expenses, leaving $275.74 due to Gdn, ward has attained his majority. RtCt 12 Nov 1903. [H:486]

LOUDOUN COUNTY, VIRGINIA
GUARDIAN ACCOUNTS
1759-1904

RAWLINGS, Corrie Lee, Emma Mary and Eva V. (Children of John M. Jr.)

S/A with Gdn Jno. M. RAWLINGS: beginning 8 Mar 1886; Children Corrie Lee, Emma Mary & Eva V. RAWLINGS. General expenses leaving $236.58. RtCt 15 Aug 1893. [H:180]

S/A with Gdn Jno. M .RAWLINGS: beginning 8 Mar 1890; expenses leaving $65.67. Children are very poor and Gdn is their grandfather who let their mother spend entire principal on their education, grandfather will provide for them in the future. RtCt 11 May 1897. [H:295]

S/A with Gdn Jno. M. RAWLINGS: beginning 27 Apr 1897; payments including to mother for support, leaving $108.91 due to Gdn. RtCt 15 Jan 1899. [H:359]

LOVE, F. T.

S/A with Gdn C. C. GAVER: beginning 11 Apr 1891; expenses leaving $843.97. RtCt 14 Nov 1893. [H:185]

S/A with Gdn C. C. GAVER: beginning 1 Apr 1893; payment from estate of Eli A. LOVE, general expenses leaving $892.24 at majority on 21 Dec 1897, paid in full. RtCt 15 Mar 1898. [H:335]

LOVE, C. C., Edgar L., Rufus T. & Lacey R.

S/A with Gdn C. C. GAVER: beginning 11 Apr 1891; expenses leaving $3415.26. RtCt 14 Nov 1893. [H: 186]

S/A with Gdn C. C. GAVER: beginning 1 Apr 1893; payment from estate of Eli A. Love, maintenance to Mrs. LOVE & Mrs. BEANS, general expenses, leaving $3804.47. RtCt 15 Mar 1898. [H:333]

S/A with Gdn C. C. GAVER: beginning 1 Apr 1897; general expenses leaving $1011.83 due to C. C. LOVE on 1 Apr 1901 abt the time of his majority. RtCt 11 Feb 1902. [H:429]

S/A with Gdn C. C. GAVER: beginning 1 Apr 1897; general expenses leaving Edgar L., Rufus T. & Lacey R. $3068.75. RtCt 11 Feb 1902. [H:431]

GARRETT, Thomas E. & John B.

Cause of Samuel E. GARRETT Gdn vs. Thomas E. GARRETT & others: Gdn to spend $150 per annum on Thomas' education. Oct 1892. [H:188]

Gdn to spend $200 per annum on Thomas' education. Oct 1893. [H:188]

S/A with Gdn John W. GARRETT: beginning 1 Oct 1892; general expenses leaving $335.41. RtCt 9 Jul 1895. [H:227]

S/A with Gdn John W. GARRETT: beginning 1 Oct 1892; general expenses leaving John B. GARRETT $768.09. RtCt 9 Jul 1895. [H:230]

S/A with Gdn Jno. W. GARRETT: beginning 1 Oct 1894; general expenses leaving Thomas E. GARRETT $150.32. RtCt 11 Aug 1896. [H:270]

S/A with Gdn Jno. W. GARRETT: beginning 1 Oct 1894; general expenses leaving J. B. GARRETT $750.97. RtCt 11 Aug 1896. [H:271]

S/A with Gdn Jno. W. GARRETT: beginning 1 Oct 1895; general expenses leaving Thos. E. $37.27 due at majority, receipt of 1 Sep 1896. RtCt 10 Nov 1896. [H:281]

S/A with Gdn Jno. W. GARRETT: beginning 1 Oct 1895; general expenses leaving J. B. $746.53. RtCt 10 Oct 1898. [H:351]

S/A with Gdn Jno. W. GARRETT: beginning 1 Oct 1897; general expenses leaving J. B. $749.35. RtCt 15 Jan 1901. [H:406]

S/A with Gdn Jno. W. GARRETT: beginning 1 Oct 1899; general expenses leaving J. B. $750.69. RtCt 13 Nov 1901. [H:424]

CLINE, Beulah, Corrie V., A. T., Gracie J., Fannie B. & Mabel R.

S/A with agent & Gdn Corrie V. CLINE: beginning 1 Dec 1892; $31.87 to Beulah CLINE, $31.88 to Corrie V. CLINE, $127.48 to Corrie V. CLINE for 4 others. RtCt 12 Dec 1893. [H:188]

S/A with Gdn Corrie V. CLINE: beginning 1 May 1894; $27.93 to Bulah CLINE, $27.93 to Corrie V. CLINE, $111.76 to Corrie V. CLINE for 4 children. RtCt 13 May 1895. [H:226]

S/A with Gdn Corrie V. CLINE: beginning 1 Apr 1895; children Gracie J., Fannie B. & Mabel R. CLINE; $34.18 each to Bulah CLINE of age, Corrie V. CLINE of age & A. T. CLINE of age, $102.54 to Corrie V. CLINE for 3 wards. RtCt 9 Jul 1895. [H:229]

S/A with Gdn Corrie V. CLINE: beginning 1 Apr 1896; income from rents, paid care of cemetery lot in Middleburg, leaving $34.58 each for Corrie V. CLINE, Beulah CLINE, A. T. CLINE, Gracie CLINE, Fannie B. CLINE & Mabel R. CLINE. RtCt 11 Aug 1896. [H:267]

S/A with Gdn Corrie V. CLINE: beginning 15 Apr 1897; general expenses leaving $35.52 each to the 6 children. RtCt 16 Jun 1897. [H:297]

S/A with Gdn Corrie V. CLINE: beginning 1 Apr 1898; general expenses leaving $35.76 each to the 6 children. RtCt 9 Aug 1898. [H:345]

S/A with Gdn Corrie V. CLINE: beginning 1 Oct 1898; general expenses leaving $9.97 each to the 6 children. RtCt 11 Dec 1899. [H:374]

TAVENNER, J. Wilmer

Inventory by Gdn Albert MILHOLLEN: house & lot in Philomont, rent from house, note, totaling $995.02. RtCt 13 Dec 1893. [H:189]

S/A with Gdn Albert MILHOLLEN: beginning Dec 1893; income from rents, general expenses leaving $86.84. RtCt 13 Jul 1897. [H:298]

S/A with Gdn Albert MILHOLLEN: beginning 14 Aug 1896; general expenses leaving $164.21 paid at majority on 14 Feb 1900. RtCt 9 Jul 1900. [H:390]

LACEY, Charles H.
Appraisal/Inventory by DShff & Committee Eugene MONROE: (of unsound mind) farm and household items, totaling $387.20. Aprs: A. V. THOMAS, Danl. SHAFER, W. H. FLING. RtCt 9 Jan 1894. [H:190]

S/A with Shff & Committee H. H. RUSSELL: beginning Apr 1893; income from rents and note, general expenses leaving $2.82. RtCt 13 Aug 1901. [H:419]

DARR, Alice & Maggie
S/A with Gdn Robt. W. GRUBB: beginning 27 May 1892; $538 from estate of Rosa A. DARR, general expenses leaving $511.10. RtCt 9 Jan 1894. [H:192]

S/A with Gdn Robt. W. GRUBB: beginning 28 May 1893; general expenses leaving $25.57 on income. RtCt 9 Jul 1895. [H:232]

FOX, Manly
Appraisal/Inventory by Shff & Committee H. H. RUSSELL: household items, $814 in bank, totaling $991.40. Aprs: E. G. CAUFMAN, Jacob CARSON, M. H. WHITMORE. RtCt 5 May 1894. [H:202]

Sale of 27 Mar 1894: purchasers: Budd ARNOLD, Mrs. Robert BRADY, James BROOKS, Jacob CARSON, James COX, John FLETCHER, Jos. HOUGH, Chas. JOHNSON, James RUSSELL, George SHOEMAKER, Mrs. Geo. TITUS, totaling $139.06. RtCt 5 May 1894. [H:204]

S/A with Shff & Committee H. H. RUSSELL: beginning 14 Mar 1894; paid Western Lunatic Asylum, etc, leaving $562.34 plus $500 in bonds. RtCt 16 Oct 1895. [H:240]

S/A with Committee H. H. RUSSELL: beginning 16 Jul 1895; expenses leaving $181.68 plus bonds; ward was discharged from the asylum at Staunton on 9 Aug 1895, closing the Committees acct. RtCt 12 May 1896. [H:261]

DUNBAR, Edward McVeigh
S/A with Gdn S. E. ROGERS: beginning May 1894; general expenses leaving $119.17. RtCt 9 Jul 1894. [H:208]

S/A with Gdn J. T. McGAVACK: beginning 13 May 1895; general expenses leaving $1252.60. RtCt 11 Aug 1896. [H:268]

S/A with Gdn J. T. McGAVACK: beginning 12 May 1896; to mother for support, general expenses, leaving $1336.71. RtCt 11 May 1903. [H:462]

NICHOLS, Thomas W.
S/A with Gdn Thos. H. PIGGOTT: beginning 2 Oct 1891; May 1893 paid ¼ of digging mother's grave, general expenses leaving $20.96. RtCt 9 Jul 1894. [H:212]

LUCIUS, Katie & Charles
S/A with Gdn E. A. MILHOLLEN: beginning Sep 1891; general expenses leaving Katie LUCIUS $43.14. RtCt 10 Sep 1894. [H:213]

S/A with Gdn E. A. MILHOLLEN: beginning Sep 1891; general expenses leaving Charles LUCIUS $55.14. RtCt 10 Sep 1894. [H:214]

S/A with Gdn E. A. MILHOLLEN: beginning 1 Apr 1894; general expenses leaving Charles $72.47 & Kate $3.29. RtCt 13 Jul 1897. [H:299]

S/A with Gdn E. A. MILHOLLEN: beginning 1 Apr 1896; general expenses leaving Katie $4.69 & Charles $104.15. RtCt 9 Aug 1898. [H:340]

HELM, Lizzie C. & Thomas M.
Inventory by Gdn M. C. HELM: cash and bonds totaling $3427.75. RtCt 5 Oct 1894. [H:220]

CRAVEN, Lillie B.
S/A with Gdn C. J. C. MOFFETT: (now Lillie B. WELLS) beginning 14 Jan 1889; $472.38 paid in full on 14 Feb 1895. RtCt 8 Apr 1895. [H:221]

TRITTAPOE, Walter T. [TRITAPOE]
S/A with Gdn H. A. TRITTAPOE: beginning 1 Sep 1894; expenses leaving $168. RtCt 9 Jul 1895. [H:231]

S/A with Gdn H. A. TRITAPOE: beginning 1 Apr 1895; general expenses leaving $203.71 on 1 Mar 1899 at majority. RtCt 14 Jun 1899. [H:367]

WRIGHT, B. Oden & Jos. E.
S/A with Gdn Joseph L. NORRIS: $749 payment in full on 23 Jan 1895. RtCt 9 Jul 1895. [H:233]

SWANK, Samuel
Sale of 20 Feb 1895 by George C. STREAM: purchasers: Edgar COOPER, Wm. BARTLETT, Charles FAWLEY, John LENHART, Luther FRY, Hadd COOPER, totaling $195.70. RtCt 7 Sep 1895. [H:233]

WENNER, Bessie
S/A with Gdn S. T. HICKMAN: beginning 29 Mar 1886; payment from C. C. WENNER Admr for S. E. WENNER, general expenses, leaving $1060.15. RtCt 10 Sep 1895. [H:234]

MATTINGLY, Hattie
S/A with Gdn D. H. VANDEVANTER: beginning May 1895: $132.74 from estate of Mary HOUGH, general expenses, leaving $72.89 paid to ward and her husband having married on 25 Jun. RtCt 10 Sep 1895. [H:238]

RITICOR, Joseph
Appraisal/Inventory by Committee Joshua L. RITICOR: $600 bond, $1427.83 in Peoples National Bank of Leesburg, $272 in Loudoun National Bank, horse & buggy, rents. Aprs: James W. HOGAN, Marvin GALLEHER, B. Frank LEISH. RtCt 11 Nov 1895. [H:244]

S/A with Committee J. L. RITICOR: beginning 15 Sep 1894; income from rents and bank deposits, general expenses leaving $1068.29 plus $816 bond. RtCt 10 Mar 1897. [H:291]

S/A with Committee J. L. RITICOR: beginning 1 Dec 1896; income from rents, payment to Western State Hospital, leaving $1103.69. RtCt 15 Feb 1898. [H:326]

S/A with Committee Joshua L. RITICOR: beginning 9 Feb 1898; general expenses leaving $94.13 plus investment of $1068.29. RtCt 13 Feb 1899. [H:361]

S/A with Committee Joshua L. RITICOR: beginning 1 Dec 1898; payments including to Western State Hospital leaving $152.63 plus $868.29 in investments. RtCt 12 Mar 1900. [H:383]

S/A with Committee Joshua L. RITICOR: beginning 1 Dec 1899; income from rents, general expenses and Hospital payment, leaving $164.85 in interest paid to Western State Hospital. RtCt 11 Apr 1901. [H:416]

S/A with Committee Joshua L. RITICOR: beginning 1 Dec 1900; paid Western Hospital & other expenses, leaving $122.70 in interest on $1868.29. RtCt 15 Apr 1902. [H:443]

S/A with Committee Joshua L. RITICOR: beginning 1 Dec 1901; paid Western Hospital & other expenses, leaving $108.71 in interest on $1868.29. RtCt 11 May 1903. [H:466]

KEYS, Louisa
S/A with Committee A. W. HOSKINSON: (of unsound mind) beginning 31 Mar 1894; income from sale of personal and real estate, general expenses, leaving $342.20. RtCt 10 Dec 1895. [H:246]

FOSTER, Margaret M.
S/A with Gdn Jas. R. FOSTER: beginning 10 Oct 1892; $3800 from legacy, check to Mrs. J. W. FOSTER, general expenses leaving $3700. RtCt 10 Dec 1895. [H:247]

S/A with Gdn Jas. R. FOSTER: beginning 10 Oct 1894; general expenses leaving $3700. RtCt 10 Mar 1896. [H:357]

S/A with Gdn Jas. R. FOSTER: beginning 16 Oct 1895; general expenses leaving $.91 due to Gdn, plus $3700 principal. RtCt 10 Mar 1897. [H:287]

S/A with Gdn Jas. R. FOSTER: beginning 19 Oct 1897; general expenses totaling $222, principal of $3700. RtCt 12 Jan 1898. [H:328]

S/A with Gdn James R. FOSTER: beginning 24 Nov 1897; general expenses leaving $222. RtCt 13 Feb 1899. [H:360]

S/A with Gdn James R. FOSTER: beginning 10 Oct 1898; general expenses leaving $127.45. RtCt 12 Feb 1900. [H:381]

S/A with Gdn James. R. FOSTER: beginning 10 Oct 1899; general expenses leaving $349.45. RtCt 15 Jan 1901. [H:408]

S/A with Gdn James R. FOSTER: beginning 1901; general expenses leaving $132.97 paid 12 Oct 1901 to Miss Foster. RtCt 11 Feb 1902. [H:428]

S/A with Gdn James R. FOSTER: beginning 21 Apr 1902; general expenses leaving $3800 due on 21 Apr 1902 when she attained her majority. RtCt 13 Aug 1902. [H:448]

DISHMAN, Edna E. & Charles E.
S/A with Gdn Rosa B. DISHMAN: beginning 1 May 1893; from decree of DISHMAN vs DISHMAN, general expenses, leaving $882.97. RtCt 14 Jan 1896. [H:250]

GIST, Harry S.
S/A with Gdn Jno. R. HUTCHISON: beginning 10 Jul 1893; $73.83 from estate of Geo. RHODES, general expenses, leaving $74.53 paid in full to ward on 20 Jul 1895. RtCt 12 Feb 1896. [H:252]

MORRIS, George H.
S/A with Committee F. M. LOVE Sr: (of unsound mind) beginning Apr 1860; payment from estate of M. MORRIS, general expenses, leaving $43.82 due Committee, entire estate was consumed, ward is still alive and maintained by the Committee. RtCt 12 Feb 1896. [H:253]

GIBSON, W. B. & W. E.
S/A with Gdn Jos. A. GIBSON: $250 paid to W. B. GIBSON on 15 Jan 1892 and $288.12 paid to W. E. GIBSON on 2 Jun 1894. RtCt 10 Mar 1896, both paid in full. [H:256]

JACKSON, Charles H. & Hannie
S/A with Gdn Jesse MOTON: beginning 30 May 1895; expenses leaving Charles H. $33.60 on 7 May, his majority & $33.82 to Hannie JACKSON, not yet of age. RtCt 14 Jul 1896. [H:264]

TURNER, Lucy
S/A with Gdn C. C. GAVER: (now 20y old) beginning 30 Mar 1894; general expenses leaving $296.44. RtCt 11 Aug 1896. [H:269]

S/A with Gdn C. C. GAVER: beginning 1 May 1894; $223.56 due ward 2 Apr 1896 at majority. RtCt 15 Dec 1896. [H:285]

JORDAN, Claretta, Robert, Bertha, Katie & Lizzie
S/A with Gdn Jno. W. GARRETT: beginning 12 Sep 1895; $382.47 income from pension (made trips to Washington DC because hard to get), paid mother for maintanence, expenses, leaving $241.80. Lizzie became 16y old before 21 Sep 1895. RtCt 11 Aug 1896. [H:272]

S/A with Gdn J. W. GARRETT: beginning 1 Jan 1896; income from pension, payment to mother, leaving $154.88. RtCt 13 Jul 1897. [H:300]

S/A with Gdn J. W. GARRETT: beginning 1 Jan 1897; paid mother for maintenance, leaving $178.99. RtCt 10 Oct 1898. [H:352]

S/A with Gdn J. W. GARRETT: beginning 4 Mar 1898; income from US pension, payment to mother, leaving $11.10 due to Gdn. RtCt 11 Apr 1900. [H:384]

S/A with Gdn J. W. GARRETT: beginning 4 Mar 1900; income from US pension, payment to mother, leaving $31.80. RtCt 15 Jan 1902. [H:427]

LITTLEJOHN, Forrest C., Paul V & Horace C.

S/A with Gdn Mrs. Julia D. LITTLEJOHN: beginning 1894; $5900 from Admr J. B. McCABE, general expenses, leaving Forrest C. $1340.05, Paul V. $1620.24 & Horace C. $1678.96 [H:275]

Real estate of C. W. LITTLEJOHN dec'd with agent Julia D. LITTLEJOHN: beginning May 1896; income from rent of property, insurance payments, leaving Forrest C. $1627.97, Paul V. $1908.16 & Horace C. $1966.88. RtCt 16 Sep 1896. [H:276]

Real estate of C. W. LITTLEJOHN dec'd with Julia D. LITTLEJOHN: beginning May 1897; income from rents, expenses, leaving Forrest C. $1604.53, Paul V. $1921.04 & Horace C. $2064.85. RtCt 9 Aug 1897. [H:301]

Real estate of C. W. LITTLEJOHN dec'd with Julia D. LITTLEJOHN: beginning 1 May 1898; income from rents, expenses, leaving Julia D. $140.82, $93.99 each to 3 children, leaving Forrest C. $1500.93, Paul V. $1905.37, & Horace C. $2095.76. RtCt 9 Aug 1898. [H:341]

Real estate of C. W. LITTLEJOHN dec'd with Julia D. LITTLEJOHN: beginning 1 May 1899; income from rents, general expenses leaving Forrest C. LITTLEJOHN $1432.89 on 22 Jul 1899 when he reached majority, Paul V. $1729.06 & Horace C. $2176.53. RtCt 15 Aug 1900. [H:391]

Real estate of C. W. LITTLEJOHN dec'd with Julia D. LITTLEJOHN: beginning 1 May 19001; general expenses leaving Paul V. $1463.02 and Horace C. $2179.32. RtCt 15 Jan 1902. [H:425]

Real estate of C. W. LITTLEJOHN dec'd with Julia D. LITTLEJOHN: beginning 1 May 1902; income from rents, general expenses leaving Paul V. $1115.41 on 29 Mar 1902 when he attained his majority and Horace C.$2247.62. RtCt 11 Mar 1902. [H:459]

CHINN, Mary E.

S/A with Gdn F. W. CHINN: beginning 31 Dec 1893; income from rent of house & land, general expenses, totaling $65.15. RtCt 10 Mar 1897. [H:288]

S/A with Gdn F. W. CHINN: beginning Dec 1894; expenses leaving $22.01. RtCt 13 Dec 1898. [H:356]

DONALDSON, Robert B. & Margaret E.

S/A with mother Gdn May C. COPELAND: pension allowance of W. S. to children up to their 16th year of $144/y beginning 15 Dec 1892. Robt's payments ceased 14 Mar 1892. Margaret reached 16y old on 19 May 1896. Gdn inherited larger portion of the real estate of 13 acre lot, wood lot & home tract. RtCt 10 Mar 1897. [H:290]

WILLIAMS, Rebecca J.

S/A with Committee A. W. PHILLIPS: beginning 13 Mar 1893; income from rent in Scotland, crops of Mt. farm, and legacy of R. N. WILLIAMS, general expenses, leaving $647.43. RtCt 10 Mar 1897. [H:292]

S/A with Committee A. W. PHILLIPS: beginning Jul 1896; general expenses leaving $86.79 plus $766 in investments. RtCt 10 Oct 1898. [H:350]

S/A with Committee A. W. PHILLIPS: beginning 12 Aug 1898; general expenses leaving $384.03 plus $3466 in investments. RtCt 13 Feb 1901. [H:411]

S/A with Committee A. W. PHILLIPS: beginning 26 Oct 1900; general expenses leaving $44.74. RtCt 15 Apr 1902. [H:441]

TRITAPOE, William M.

S/A with Gdn H. A. TRITAPOE: beginning 1 Apr 1895; income from pension & interest, fees, leaving $314.98. RtCt 9 Aug 1897. [H:305]

S/A with Gdn H. A. TRITAPOE: beginning 1 Apr 1897; general expenses leaving $390 on 8 Dec 1901 when he reached majority. RtCt 11 Aug 1903. [H:477]

MOORE, Thomas R.

S/A with Gdn W. W. CHAMBLIN: beginning 3 May 1890; payment from estate of J. P. WILLIAMSON, general expenses leaving $6872.68 paid in full as of 22 Jul 1897. RtCt 13 Oct 1897. [H:307]

LOVE, Thomas E.

S/A with father Committee Robert R. LOVE: (of unsound mind) beginning 1 Apr 1891; legacy from estate of Jno. LOVE, totaling $1050.00. Ward now 25y old and confined to his room for past 4-5 years, entirely demented but in good health. RtCt 9 Nov 1897. [H:314]

JENKINS, Joseph R., Ruth H., Sallie & Samuel T.

S/A with Gdn A. J. BRADFIELD: beginning 27 Oct 1896; payment from Admr of Jos. H. JENKINS, Exor of Reuben JENKINS, general expenses, leaving Joseph R. JENKINS $452.37. RtCt 15 Feb 1898. [H:322]

S/A with Gdn A. J. BRADFIELD: beginning 27 Oct 1896; as above, leaving Ruth H. JENKINS $460.22. RtCt 15 Feb 1898. [H:323]

S/A with Gdn A. J. BRADFIELD: beginning 27 Oct 1896; as above, leaving Sallie JENKINS $179.80. RtCt 15 Feb 1898. [H:323]

S/A with Gdn A. J. BRADFIELD: beginning 27 Oct 1896; as above, leaving Samuel T. JENKINS $39.45 at majority on 14 Nov 1897, paid in full. RtCt 15 Feb 1898. [H:324]

S/A with Gdn A. J. BRADFIELD: beginning 14 Nov 1897; general expenses leaving Sallie JENKINS $1188.39. RtCt 12 Feb 1900. [H:377]

S/A with Gdn A. J. BRADFIELD: beginning 14 Nov 1897; general expenses leaving Ruth H. JENKINS $1502.76. RtCt 12 Feb 1900. [H:378]

S/A with Gdn A. J. BRADFIELD: beginning 14 Nov 1897; general expenses leaving Joseph R. JENKINS $1496.79. RtCt 12 Feb 1900. [H:380]

S/A with Gdn A. J. BRADFIELD: beginning 14 Nov 1899; general expenses leaving Sallie $1191.27 on 18 Sep 1900 at majority, paid in full. RtCt 14 Nov 1900. [H:403]

S/A with Gdn A. J. BRADFIELD: beginning 14 Nov 1899; general expenses leaving estate of Ruth H. JENKINS $1384.22, distributed to Craven JENKINS, Sallie JENKINS, Saml. T., JENKINS and minor Jos. R. JENKINS' Gdn. RtCt 14 Mar 1902. [H:433]

S/A with Gdn A. J. BRADFIELD: beginning 14 Nov 1899; general expenses leaving Joseph R. $1861.97 on 14 Nov 1901. RtCt 14 Mar 1902. [H:435]

NUTT, Daniel, James & Carrie
S/A with Gdn J. M. MOUNT: beginning 1 Sep 1888; expenses leaving each $20.54. RtCt 15 Feb 1898. [H:326]

SWANN, Thomas
S/A with Gdn Sherlock SWANN: beginning 8 Jan 1897; $3000 from Royal Arcanum in death certif of Thos. SWANN 3rd, general expenses, leaving $3305.75. RtCt 15 Mar 1898. [H:337]

S/A with Gdn Sherlock SWANN: beginning 8 Jan 1898; general expenses leaving $38.21 plus $1500 US bond. RtCt 14 Mar 1899. [H:362]

S/A with Gdn Sherlock SWANN: beginning 8 Jan 1899; interest on bonds, general expenses, leaving $303.57 plus $800 bond. RtCt 16 May 1900. [H:386]

S/A with Gdn Sherlock SWANN: beginning 8 Jan 1900; general expenses leaving $188.78 plus investments of $400. RtCt 11 Apr 1901. [H:415]

S/A with Gdn Sherlock SWANN: beginning 8 Jan 1901; expenses leaving $96.47. RtCt 14 Mar 1902. [H:438]

S/A with Gdn Sherlock SWANN: beginning 8 Jan 1902; cash from trustee, general expenses, leaving $60.82. RtCt 11 Mar 1903. [H:457]

CHAMBLIN, Clara F.
S/A with Gdn A. G. CHAMBLIN: beginning 29 Jan 1889; $249 from sale of land in Fairfax Co, ward has been living with Gdn since she was 4y old, now abt 15y old, no charges have been made for her expenses. RtCt 15 Jun 1898. [H:338]

HAMPTON, Elwood
S/A with Gdn C. C. GAVER: beginning 17 Sep 1897; income from rent of J. F. HAMPTON, expenses, leaving $43.53 to ward's estate. RtCt 9 Aug 1898. [H:346]

BEAMER, Bessie W.
S/A with Gdn Jno. C. RUST: (of age 3 Mar 1898, now wife of Harry COATES) beginning Mar 1897; $760.38 share of estate of Martha J. BEANS, expenses leaving $647.54 paid in full 2 Apr 1898. RtCt 9 Aug 1898. [H:348]

WARNER, Bessie
S/A with Gdn S. T. HICKMAN: beginning 17 May 1895; expenses leaving $1232.71 on 26 Aug 1898 when she came of age, paid in full. RtCt 13 Dec 1898. [H:353]

DONOHOE, Willie E. & Lee E.
S/A with Gdn Robert L. DONOHOE: beginning 18 Jan 1898; income from sale of realty, general expenses, leaving $1251.92. RtCt 9 May 1899. [H:366]

LENT, Cornelius
Appraisal/Inventory by Committee C. A. ARUNDELL: farm and household items, totaling $232.50. Aprs: M. M. FADLEY, M. J. MORAN, C. T. LAWSON. RtCt 28 Jun 1899. [H:368]

S/A with Committee C. A. ARUNDLE: beginning 18 Apr 1898; general expenses leaving $103.96. RtCt 9 Jul 1900. [H:388]

CHANCELLOR, Helen E. Jr. & Wm. F.
Inventory by Gdn Helen E. CHANCELLOR: $1622.28 each as distributive shares from estate of E. M. CHANCELLOR. RtCt 2 Mar 1900. [H:382]

S/A with Gdn Helen E. CHANCELLOR: both ward of majority, William paid $1622.28 in 1901 and Helen paid $1622.28 in Sep 1902, children of the late R. W. CHANCELLOR, mother Helen E. CHANCELLOR. RtCt 14 Sep 1903. [H:481]

CONARD, Bessie J.
S/A with Shff & Committee H. H. RUSSELL: beginning 28 Mar 1899; general expenses leaving $35.93. Committee's powers revoked due to restoration of Bessie J.'s health. RtCt 16 May 1900. [H:387]

FURR, Walter L., E. S. R. & Minnie
S/A with Gdn Octavia FURR: all have reached majority, their father R. E. FURR dec'd. RtCt 14 Nov 1900. [H:404]

NOLAND, Philip H.
S/A with father & Gdn C. Powell NOLAND: beginning 22 Jul 1897; $969 from life insurance policy loaned on mortgage, general expenses leaving $11.67 plus $1000 investment. RtCt 11 Dec 1900. [H:405]

LITTLETON, S. Campbell
S/A with Gdn R. H. LYNN: beginning 23 Jun 1900; expenses leaving $4006.52 as of 22 Jan 1902, paid in full at majority. RtCt 14 Mar 1902. [H:436]

SANBOWER, Harry H. & Edgar H.
S/A with Gdn F. A. WARNER: beginning 17 Nov 1900; $225.57 from estate of Michael SANBOWER, general expenses, leaving $211.98. RtCt 15 Apr 1902. [H:439]

S/A with Gdn F. A. WARNER: beginning Nov 1901; $107.44 from estate of D. SANBOWER, general expenses, leaving Harry H. SANBOWER $211.41 on 8 Jul 1902 when he attained his majority. RtCt 10 Nov 1902. [H:455]

S/A with Gdn F. A. WARNER: beginning Nov 1901; $107.44 from estate of D. SANDBOWER, general expenses, leaving Edgar H. $257.40 on 19 Apr 1903 when he reached majority. RtCt 14 Jul 1903. [H:472]

FLETCHER, B. J.
S/A with Gdn E. L. FLETCHER: ward is of age and have been paid in full. RtCt 15 Apr 1902. [H:440]

FENTON, Annie L.
Inventory by Committee Chas. NICHOLS: (of unsound mind) numerous bonds, cash in Purcellville & Loudoun Nat. Banks, 1/6 of estate of Enoch FENTON, 1/3 interest in house in Purcellville, 100 acres Enoch FENTON farm nr. Philomont, 1/6 interest in house & lot in Round Hill, 1/6 interest in 2 houses & lots in Round Hill. RtCt 29 Sep 1902. [H:449]

PIGGOTT, Henry
S/A with Committee William T. BROWN: beginning 24 Mar 1897; $137.06 from estate of Mary PIGGOTT, expenses, leaving $187.14. RtCt 10 Nov 1902. [H:453]

SANBOWER, Annie G.
S/A with Gdn J. W. EAMICH: beginning 14 Nov 1900; $112.78 from estate of D. SANBOWER, share of rents, expenses, leaving $210.53. RtCt 10 Nov 1902. [H:456]

SILCOTT, Zula B. & Ella May
S/A with Gdn Sallie A. SILCOTT: beginning 1 Apr 1895; income from rent of house in Hamilton, payments covered by $48 rent, wards live with Gdn. RtCt 11 May 1903. [H:464]

DILLON, William
S/A with Gdn J. D. DILLON: beginning 20 Apr 1902; $3233.33 from Spl Comr of DILLON & DILLON, general expenses, leaving $3426.95 paid at majority of 28 Oct 1902. RtCt 13 Jan 1903. [H:470]

FRY, William H.
S/A with Gdn John S. HICKMAN: beginning 13 Mar 1900; $40 from Hickman estate, general expenses, leaving $34.31 on 22 Jun 1902 when he reached majority. RtCt 11 Aug 1903. [H:476]

ATWELL, Ruth V.
S/A with Gdn W. C. HEFLIN: she attained majority on 27 Jan 1902 and was paid in full, now the wife of C. W. ATWELL. RtCt 11 Aug 1903. [H:479]

RAMY, Walter
S/A with Gdn William TYLER: beginning 20 Oct 1902; expenses leaving $43.19 RtCt 14 Dec 1903. [H:495]

RAMY, Louisa
S/A with Gdn William TYLER: beginning 20 Oct 1902; expenses leaving $43.19. RtCt 14 Dec 1903. [H:497]

KELLY, Elizabeth
Inventory by Gdn C. C. BELL: $343.45 rec'd on 11 Jun 1902 from Joseph H. JENKINS Exor for R. M. CHAMBLIN, rent, 41¾ acres of land. RtCt 13 Jan 1904. [H:500]

PETTITT, William F.
Inventory by Gdn R. M .MORRIS: ½ interest in house & lot. RtCt 25 Jan 1904. [H:500]

LOUDOUN COUNTY, VIRGINIA
GUARDIAN ACCOUNTS
1759-1904

INDEX

ABEL
  George, 5, 23
ACRES
  David, 65
ADAMS
  Francis, 3, 24
  Samuel T., 24
ALDER
  James, 31, 34
ALEXANDER
  John, 2
  John H., 91
ALLEN
  Alexander, 92
  James, 29
  John James, 29
  Julia Teresa, 29
  Mary Elizabeth, 29
  Nathan Reed, 29
  Sarah, 29
  William, 29
AMOS
  Joseph, 56
ANDERSON
  E., 75
  Eleanor, 75
  John, 75
  Lulah, 75
  Martha D., 75
  Nannie D., 75
  Thomas E., 75
ANSEL
  Susan, 43
ARMISTEAD
  Robert, 4
ARMSTRONG
  ___, 50
ARNIS
  Annie R., 93
  Chista V., 93
  Margaret C., 93
  William H., 93
ARNOLD
  Americus S., 66
  Annie E., 66
  Budd, 100
  E., 66
  Elizabeth, 66
  Jacob, 66
  Joseph, 66
  M., 66

  Michael, 66
  Simon, 29, 66
  Thomas Clayton, 66
ARUNDELL
  C. A., 103
ARUNDLE
  C. A., 103
ATHEY
  W. W., 97
ATLEE
  Sally J., 89
ATWELL
  C. W., 104
  Ruth V., 95, 104
AXLINE
  David, 29, 59
  E., 12
  Emanuel, 29, 58
  Eve, 29
BAKER
  George, 77
  John M., 19
  Mary, 17
BALDWIN
  Anna W., 96
  John D., 22
  M. K., 90
  Mary E., 90
  Orion, 90
  Susan H., 22
BALES
  Laney A., 40
BALL
  Burgess, 5
  Elizabeth, 37
  Fayette, 5
  George W., 5
  Margaret, 37
  Martha Dandridge, 5
  Mary A., 37
  Mildred Washington, 5
  Napoleon B., 37
  Washington, 5
BALLENGER
  Edward, 94
BARRETT
  W. F., 85, 93
  Wilson, 77
BARTER
  C. W., 96
BARTLETT

  Ella, 98
  Thomas, 1
  William, 96, 100
BARTON
  C. W., 82, 85, 89
  Sally Ann, 85, 89
  Sarah Amanda, 89
BAUGHMAN
  Charlotte E., 13
  John W., 13
  Margaret, 13
BAYLEY
  J., 14, 15
  John, 62
BEACH
  Martha E., 96
BEALE
  John G., 19
BEALES
  Benjamin C., 63
  Jefferson F., 63
  Margaret, 63
  Norval V., 63
  Rodney D., 63
BEALL
  Avory C., 23
  David, 65
BEAMER
  Bessie W., 103
  Caroline, 85
  Daniel Wine Washington, 85
  George, 80, 85, 93
  George Henry Thomas, 85
  John Samuel, 80
  Joseph Michael
    Bronaugh, 85
  Julia E., 81
  Julietta, 80
  Maggie E., 89
  Maggie Ellen Frances, 85
  Mary Alice Virginia, 85
  Mary Lina May, 85
  Michael, 80, 81, 85
  Michael T., 79
  Rachel, 85
  Samuel Randolph
    William, 85
  William Francis
    Augustus, 85

BEANS
  Aaron, 20
  Absalom, 52, 53
  Amos, 20, 37
  Annie Rachel, 75
  David, 52, 53
  David H., 53, 54
  Elisa Ann, 20
  Eliza J., 20
  Elizabeth H., 20
  Elizabeth Jane, 20
  H. B., 53
  Hannah B., 53
  Josephine, 52, 53, 54
  Lucinda, 20
  Martha J., 103
  Matthew Harrison, 20
  Moses, 20
  Patience, 20
  Rachel A., 52
  Rachel Ann, 53
  Rachel Anna, 53
  U., 60
  Victoria, 52, 53
  Victoria A. L. M., 53
  W. H. H., 53
  William, 20, 53
  William F., 75
  William H. H., 52, 53
BEATTY
  Anna, 66
  Bettie Jane, 95
  Chester M., 95
  Harry W., 95
  John, 77
  John H., 66
  Thomas, 1
  William, 95
BEDINGER
  George R., 58
  Virginia, 58
BEECH
  Lial T., 37
BELL
  C. C., 104
  Theodore, 94
BELT
  Alfred, 11, 12
BENEDUM
  John, 91
BENNET

Charles, 6
BENNETT
   Charles, 3, 4
BENTLEY
   A. C., 79
   Ann C., 79
   Belle, 81
   E. L., 81
   Elizabeth P., 79
   Kate, 81
   Maria W., 79
   Nellie, 81
   R. M., 79
   Robert, 79
BERKELEY
   Benjamen, 3
BERKLEY
   William, 1
BEVERIDGE
   A., 14
BEVERLEY
   R. A., 98
BIRD
   Luke, 3
BIRDSALL
   Benjamin, 40, 41, 73
   Charles W., 73
   David, 40
   David H., 40, 41
   Deborah, 73
   E., 41
   Eliza, 73
   Eliza H., 73
   Elizabeth, 73
   Ellen H., 73
   Hannah, 41
   J. B., 41
   M. E., 41
   Marianna, 73
   Mary, 41
   Mary Ann, 73
   Mary Anna, 73
   Mary Etta, 40, 41
   Rebecca, 73
   Rebecca A., 41
   Rebecca Alice, 41, 73
   Rebecca Ann, 40, 41
   Rebecca K., 73
   Sarah, 41, 73
BISCOE
   James B., 16
BITZER
   C. R., 90
   Conrad, 19, 33, 39, 52, 54
   George, 90
   J., 54
BLACKFORD
   Charles M., 42
   Susan L., 42
BLEAKLEY
   Charles, 39
   Florence L., 39
   Littitia, 39
BLEAKLY
   Eliza P., 39
   Florence L., 39
   Letitia, 39
   William, 39
BLINCOE
   Thomas, 3
BOGER
   Catharine, 73
   Ella Virginia, 76
   Jacob, 76
   John E., 96
   Mary, 76
   Mary Ann, 73
   Mollie J., 76
   Samuel, 73
BOGGESS
   Major, 6
BOLYN
   F. M., 91
   George H., 91
   S., 71, 96
   Summerfield, 71
   T. M., 91
BOND
   Eleanor C., 54
   Sarah F., 54
   Thomas, 54
   Thomas D., 59
BOOTH
   Charlotte, 30, 31
   Charlotte E., 30
   Henry H., 30, 31
   James, 30
   James C., 30, 31
   John, 12
   Matilda, 30, 31
   Robert, 89
BOSS
   S. M., 13, 18
BOUGHMAN
   Ann, 12
   Charlotte Catharine, 12
   James A, 13
   James Andrew, 12
   John William, 12
   Margaret, 12
   Mary Ann, 12
   Sarah Ann, 12, 13
BOYD
   John, 9
BRADEN
   Cecelia D., 96
   Cecelia L., 77
   Cecelia V., 77
   Flavius, 20
   Flavius T., 19
   Florence M., 78
   John, 6, 12
   Joseph, 3
   Noble S., 20, 51
   O. S., 92
   Oscar S., 77, 98
   R., 5
   R. W., 96
   Robert, 3, 4, 6, 9, 77
   Rodney Walter, 77
BRADFIELD
   A. J., 82, 88, 102
   Benjamin, 4
   Hannah, 4
   Hannah L., 4
   James, 4
   James T., 14
   Jonathan, 4
   Joseph, 9
   Julian K., 9
   Rachael, 4
   Rachel, 4
   William, 9
BRADY
   Robert, 100
BRENT
   Hugh, 4
BREWER
   Henry, 1
BRIDGES
   Benjamin, 89
BRONAUGH
   Patrick H. W., 9
BRONLEY
   J. B., 98
BROOKS
   James, 100
BROWN
   Addison, 74
   Albert O., 82
   Arthur, 82
   Benjamin, 74
   Bushrod, 37
   C. E., 39
   Catharine, 39
   Craven, 17
   David, 35, 36
   Edward, 71
   Eliza D., 82
   John, 41
   John N., 74
   Jonathan, 92
   Joseph J., 71
   L. A., 39
   L. P., 39
   Millard, 92
   P. D., 39
   Robert, 12
   Samuel N., 65
   Sarah S., 34
   T., 24
   Thomas, 1, 90
   Thomas J., 67
   W., 41
   William, 35
   William T., 104
BUCK
   W. M., 50
BUCKLEY
   James, 1
BURKE
   Charles W., 36
   Elizabeth, 36
   Mary F., 36
   Virginia E., 36
BUSSARD
   M. W., 79
   Milton M., 13
   O. M., 79
   Perriander L., 13
BUTTS
   William, 89
BYERS
   David, 40
BYRNE
   A. C., 79
   Annie L., 91
   George M., 91
   Henry M., 91
   Sydnor B., 91
   Thomas W., 91
   Uriah E., 91
   Virginia M., 91
BYRNES
   Samuel, 92
CALDWELL

LOUDOUN COUNTY, VIRGINIA
GUARDIAN ACCOUNTS
1759-1904

S. B. T., 26
CAMP
  Isaac, 37
CAMPBELL
  Sarah, 92
CAREY
  Grace A., 47
  H. G., 47
  Henry G., 47
CARNES
  Benjamin, 89
CARR
  D., 63
  John, 19, 75
  John C., 98
  Mary, 6
  Peter H., 83
  W. M., 19
  Washington M., 18, 19
  William, 6
CARRINGTON
  Timothy, 9
CARROLL
  James, 37, 60
CARRS
  John, 19
CARRUTHERS
  James E., 76, 94
  Wesley, 74
CARSON
  Jacob, 100
CARTER, 7
  Alice V., 81
  Catharine, 26
  David, 26
  E., 65
  E. O., 25
  Edward, 26
  Edward D., 26
  Edward David, 26
  Elam, 7
  Eleanor H., 96
  Elizabeth, 7
  F. M., 65, 98
  Francis M., 65, 98
  George, 25
  Francis M., 98
  Jesse G., 26
  John, 7
  John F., 98
  Jonathan, 65
  Landon F., 26
  Landon L., 26
  Landon S., 26

  Landon T., 26
  Leonidas H., 26
  Maria E., 15
  Martha E., 26
  Orra L., 92
  Pattsy W., 98
  Peter, 7
  Presley, 26
  Presley L., 26
  Presly L., 26
  Robert C., 96
  T. H., 94
  William Maulsby, 98
CASEY
  Elisabeth, 6
  Elizabeth, 6
  Grace N., 46
  Henry G., 46
CASSADAY
  Ann C., 26
  Charles B., 26
  Jane, 26
  Mary E., 26
CASSADY
  John H., 18
  William H., 18
CAUFMAN
  E. G., 91, 100
CAVAN
  James, 5
  Patrick, 3
CAYLOR
  James, 23
CHAMBLIN
  A. G., 93, 103
  B. P., 22
  Burr P., 22, 39
  Clara F., 103
  H. C., 93
  J. H., 22
  John, 21
  John R., 93
  Laura, 86
  M., 61
  M. F., 98
  Mason, 39, 86
  Minor F., 92, 96
  Norval, 18
  R. C., 93
  R. M., 104
  Rosa, 86
  W. W., 102
CHANCELLOR
  E. M., 103

  Helen E., 103
  R. W., 103
  S. A., 60
  William F., 103
CHEW
  Elizabeth A., 24
  Elizabeth Ann, 24
  Henry, 24
  James E., 25
  John, 24
  Margaret Jane, 24
  Mary B., 25
  Mary Ellen, 24
  Robert, 24
  Roger, 24, 25
CHICHESTER
  George M., 20
  Sarah E., 20
CHICK
  Charles Edward, 97
  Edward, 94
  George W., 94, 97
CHILTON
  Charles W., 9
CHINN
  Charles, 1
  Christopher, 1
  Elijah, 1
  F. W., 102
  K. C., 95
  Mary E., 102
  R. C., 45
  R. S., 60, 85
  Rawleigh, 1
  Samuel Walter, 45
  Thomas, 1, 2
  W. R., 95
CLAPHAM
  Elizabeth, 98
  J. H., 98
  Saul, 98
CLARKE
  A. H., 5, 58
  Archie M., 58
  Elizabeth J., 58
  Isaac V., 58
  Mary, 58
  Mollie A., 58
CLENDENING
  Samuel, 21, 60, 82, 93
  William, 33
CLEVELAND
  Johnston, 3, 7
CLINE

  A. T., 99
  Beulah, 99
  Corrie V., 99
  Fannie B., 99
  Gracie J., 99
  Mabel R., 99
CLOPPER
  Rachael, 18
CLOWES
  Elizabeth, 16
  Mary Jane, 16
  Thomas, 16
COATES
  Bessie W., 103
  Harry, 103
COCHRAN
  Addison, 23, 33, 35
  Emily, 33
  James, 33
  Mary P., 33
  Nathan, 11, 33
  Samuel G., 33
  Sarah, 23, 33, 35
  Sarah Ann, 33
  Tholemiah T., 33
  Stephen, 33
COCKE
  Amanda, 12
  H., 12
COCKERILL
  Sandford, 1
COCKERILLE
  John, 65
  John W., 65
COE
  Arnelius, 65
  Arulius, 71
  Aurelius, 55
  Cornelius, 19
  David J., 19
  Duane, 71
  Edward M., 19
  Elizabeth, 19, 71
  Henderson, 55
  Jamieson, 19
  Robert, 55
  William, 23
COLBERT
  Samuel, 65
COLEMAN
  J. C., 98
  James, 3
COLLINS
  Christopher, 5

LOUDOUN COUNTY, VIRGINIA
GUARDIAN ACCOUNTS
1759-1904

COLSTON
  Edward, 41, 42
  Elizabeth M., 41
  F. M., 42
  Lucy A., 42
  Nannie F., 41
  Raleigh, 42
  Susan L., 42
  Thomas M., 42
COMBS
  Sally Ann, 26
COMPHER
  Ann E., 54, 55
  J. H. W., 54
  John, 20
  John H. W., 55
  Jonas, 77
  Jonas Curtis, 54, 55
  Marietta, 54
  Peter, 60
  Samuel, 54, 55
  Sarah C., 54
  William, 54, 55
  William F., 54, 55
CONARD
  Abner, 29, 58, 59
  Bessie J., 103
  Ebenezer J., 33
  Henrietta L., 51
  J. M., 51, 64, 84
  Jane A., 33
  John, 51
  John W., 33
  Jonathan, 29, 33
  Jonathan T., 33
  Joseph, 51
  Joseph E., 58
  Joseph Emanuel, 29
  Joseph M., 51, 64, 74
  Louisa Ann, 29
  Mary, 51
  Stephen H., 51
CONNER
  Samuel, 3
COOKE
  Henry S., 19
  John G., 19
  Mary E., 19
  Sarah, 19
  William, 8
  William H., 19
COOMBS
  Sallie A., 86
  Sarah A., 87

COOPER
  Benjamin, 72
  Edgar, 100
  Frederick, 17
  George, 19, 67
  George T., 67
  Hadd, 100
  John, 19, 22, 67
  Margaret, 19
  Margeret E., 84, 92
  Mary, 67
  Sarah R., 67
  Solomon, 67, 80
  Thomas, 72
  William F., 89
COPELAND
  May C., 102
CORDELL
  Adam, 44
  Adam A., 44
  Alexander, 6
  Henrietta, 44
  Jacob, 44
  John F., 44
  Joseph H., 44
  Margaret, 44
  Margaret Jane, 44
  Presley, 9, 11
  Presly, 7
  Susanna, 44
COST
  Ann M., 32
  Jane America, 32
  Thomas J., 32, 33
COSTELLO
  Robert, 95
COTES
  Mollie J., 76
COX
  James, 100
CRAIG
  John A., 92
  Nancy, 14
  Rebecca, 14
  Samuel, 14
  William, 14
  William J., 65
CRANE
  Philo R., 26
CRAVEN
  ___, 6
  Abner, 7
  Ellen, 11
  Euphemia, 11

  G. G., 93
  Giles T., 93
  Harriet, 7
  John H., 7
  Joseph, 7
  Lillie B., 100
  Lucretia, 7
  Sarah, 7
CRIM
  C. F., 60
  John, 60
  John Edward, 81
  S., 60
  Samuel, 37, 60, 81
  T., 60
  W., 60
  William, 60
CRUMBAKER
  Solomon, 37
CUNARD
  Anthony, 5
  Elizabeth, 5
  Jonathan, 29
CUNNINGHAM
  W., 1
DABNEY
  R. Heath, 80
  Virginia, 80
DANIEL
  Hannah, 17
  Hester, 17
  James, 17
  Joshua, 3
  Mary, 17
  Tacey, 17
DANNIEL
  Joshua, 4
DARNE
  Alice, 100
  Maggie, 100
  Mary E., 36
DARR
  Rosa A., 100
DAVIS
  Anna Beall, 85
  Benjamin, 27
  Charles, 1
  Elizabeth, 24
  Howell, 27
  J. H., 85
  Jason, 8
  Joseph, 8
  Mary, 6
  Polly, 8

  S. P., 24
DEAN
  Charles, 92
  Reuben, 92
  Sarah, 56
DEAVER
  Abraham, 11
  Anna, 8
  Basil, 8
  Bazell, 11
  Daniel, 11
  Deborah, 11
  Margaret, 11
DEBELL
  William, 2
DEMORY
  Frank, 92
  Peter, 45
DERRY
  Michael, 23
  Peter, 45
DEVER
  Anna, 8
DIGGENS
  Harriet E., 36
DILLON
  Ann E., 47
  Anne E., 47, 48
  Annie, 47
  Annie E., 47
  Isaac, 47
  J. D., 104
  J. J., 48
  J. W., 91
  John J., 47, 48
  Jonah W., 47
  Jonah William, 47
  Joseph A., 47
  Joseph Abdon, 47
  Lydia, 47
  Lydia Ann, 47
  William, 91, 104
DISHMAN
  Charles E., 101
  Edna E., 101
  Rosa B., 101
DIVINE
  Arthur Fairfax, 98
  Jessie, 98
DODD
  Benjamin, 17
  Bettie, 95
  C. H., 95
  Charles H., 95

LOUDOUN COUNTY, VIRGINIA
GUARDIAN ACCOUNTS
1759-1904

Ethel A., 95
Ida G., 95
J. B., 95
John G., 95
Lilly S., 95
Margaret E., 95
Mary E., 95
Nora J., 95
R. A., 95
Robert A., 95
Ruth V., 95
William, 17
William H., 95
DONALDSON
　Bailey, 3
　Baley, 3
　Margaret E., 102
　Robert B., 102
DONOHOE
　Lee E., 103
　Robert L., 103
　Willie E., 103
DOUGLAS
　Charles, 7
　James E., 83
　Louisa, 7
DOWDELL
　Elizabeth, 13
　Isaac, 13
　Mary, 13
　Moses, 13
　Thomas G., 13
DOWELL
　Albert B., 36, 39
　Ann E., 36
　Archibald P., 45
　C. F., 40
　C. R., 37, 52, 57
　Catharine, 52
　Charles W., 54
　Conrad F., 39
　Conrad R., 33, 36, 39, 54
　Emelia M., 40
　George W., 45
　Isaac, 13
　Jane A., 39
　Julia A., 33
　Jesse, 35
　John F., 39
　John T., 54
　Laura, 57
　Thomas D., 45
　Thomas S., 45
　Virginia E., 57

DOWLING
　Daniel, 45
DOWNEY
　James M., 55
　W. B., 68
DUKE
　R. T. W., 84
DULIN
　E., 7
　Edward, 7
　Harry, 7
　J., 7
　John, 7
　M., 7
　Mary, 7
　William, 5, 7
DUNBAR
　Edward McVeigh, 100
EAMICH
　George F., 96
　J. W., 104
EAMICK
　George F., 98
EATON
　David, 92
ECHHART
　Casper, 10
EDMONDS
　J. S., 15
EDWARDS
　F. M., 30
　M., 9
　Samuel, 7, 8
　Samuel M., 5, 7
　Sanford, 16
ELGIN
　Armistead M., 17
　Charles, 17
　Charles W., 17
　Francis, 6, 18
　Francis W., 17
　Frederick, 6
　G. L., 62
　Gustavus, 17
　Gustavus L., 61, 62
　Ida, 72
　Ida F., 83
　Isabell, 17
　Isabella, 17
　John G., 17
　Margaret, 83
　Margaret E., 72
　Mary A., 29
　R., 61

　Robert, 29, 72, 83
　Robert E., 72
　Rosalie, 72
　Rowena, 17
　Sarah, 6
　Walter, 10, 18
　William, 6
ELGINS
　Gustavus, 17
　Ignatius, 29
ELLIOT
　Henson, 56
ELLIOTT
　David, 6
　S. C., 6
　Sally C., 6
ELLZEY
　L., 8
　William, 1
ERWIN
　Elizabeth, 27
ESKRIDGE
　Charles, 2, 3
EVANS
　Walter, 11
EVERETT
　Elizabeth, 27
　John, 27
　John E., 27
　Sarah, 27
EVERHART
　George, 77, 89
　H., 60
　Henry, 37
　J., 71
　Jacob, 8
　John, 22
　M., 71
　Michael, 13, 14
　Sarah, 11, 13
　Sarah J., 13
　Solomon, 35
EVERHEART
　Anna, 8
　Elizabeth, 13
　J., 13
　Jacob, 8, 11
　John, 8
　Joseph, 8
　Michael, 13
　Sally, 8
　Sarah, 13
EWERS
　Franklin, 59

　James Isaac, 59
　Jonathan, 37
　Laura C., 59
EYRE
　Barclay D., 69
　Emma D., 69
FADELY
　C. F., 39
FADLEY
　M. M., 103
FAWLEY
　Ann E., 40
　Charles, 100
　Charles W., 31
　Ellen C., 40
　George, 40
　George P., 40
　Henry, 31
　James M., 40
　James W., 40
　Jeremiah, 31
　John, 31
　Joseph, 44
　Martha A., 40
　Mary J., 40
　Samuel S., 40
　Sarah E., 31
　William, 40, 77
FENTON
　Annie L., 104
　Charles, 17
　Enoch, 104
FIELDS
　Emily J., 93
　Mary, 93
FILLER
　A. T. M., 67
　Elizabeth, 20
　Frederick, 20
　Jacob, 20
　Jacob A., 26
　John, 60
　Jonathan H., 26
　Joseph H., 26
　Mary, 20
　Samuel, 20
　Sarah, 20, 26
　Sarah Ann, 26
　Sarah J., 81
　Sarah J. M., 89
　William H., 81
FISHER
　Thomas D., 8
FITZHUGH

109

C. E., 25
Dr., 49
E. S., 25
S. S., 25
William, 25
FLEMING
Andrew J., 83
John, 92
FLETCHER
B. J., 104
E. L., 104
John, 100
FLING
George W., 72
W. F., 98
W. H., 100
FOLEY
Benjamin F., 68, 69
Grimes, 92
Margaret J., 92
FONTAINE
Alice Virginia, 11
Lucy M., 11
Lucy Norborne, 11
Mary B., 11
FOSTER
F. H., 79
J. W., 97, 101
James R., 101
Margaret M., 101
Mary Ann, 15
Thomas R., 15
FOUCH
Amos, 1
Thomas, 6
FOX
Amos, 1
B. L., 87
Manly, 100
FRANCIS
Enoch, 27
John, 27, 71
Lewis, 27
Virginia S., 91
W. H., 49
FRANK
Elizabeth, 9, 10
Elizabeth Ann, 9
Hannah, 9, 10
Hannah Ann, 9, 10
Samuel, 9
William, 10
FRASIER
Nancy E., 39

Townsend, 39
FRAZIER
C. A., 61
Catharine, 61
Catharine A., 61
Catharine America, 60
H. T., 38
Margaret, 60
Margaret E., 60
Maria J., 60, 61
Maria Jane, 60
Mary A., 60, 61
Mary J., 61
Mary Jane, 60, 61
S. H., 60
Samuel H., 60
Thomas J., 60, 61
William C., 60, 61
FRITTS
Fred, 91
FRY
Annie, 31
Christena, 44
Christian, 80
Daniel, 77
David E., 59
Emily J., 31
Enos, 31
Isabella, 80
J. W., 96
John, 24
Luther, 100
Margaret, 24
Marietta C. E. C., 59
Mary, 22
Michael, 22, 23, 31
O. J. C. C., 59
Peter, 24
Peter H., 76
Philip, 24
S., 80
Samuel, 43, 44, 55
William H., 104
FURR
E. S. R., 103
Fenton, 30, 91
J. W. T., 30
John L., 96
Joseph, 65
Minnie, 103
Minor, 98
Octavia, 103
R. E., 103
Walter L., 103

GAINES
William, 81, 85, 92
GALLAHER
David, 25
Joseph, 25
Thomas Dorsey, 25
GALLEHER
Marvin, 100
GARDNER
James, 90
GARRETT
J. W., 48, 88
John B., 99
John W., 84, 86, 99, 101
Samuel E., 99
Thomas E., 99
William E., 77
GATTAN
B. F., 37
GAVER
C. C., 49, 93, 97, 99, 101, 103
Henry, 60
GEORGE
Anna Belle, 65
John, 30, 31, 35, 65, 93
Olivia, 65
Rosanna W., 93
S. W., 65, 89
Samuel W., 65, 89
Solomon, 65
William S., 65
GIBSON
(Dr.), 46
A., 7, 8, 9, 14
Ella J., 45, 46, 47
Emsey F., 12
George, 94
Grace A., 47
Grace N., 45, 46
Joseph A., 101
Lillie S., 95
Nelson, 12
Ruth Anna, 12
S. N., 47
S. R., 46
W., 46
W. B., 101
W. E., 101
William, 45
William P., 95
GILL
William H., 33
GILMORE

James, 13
GIST
Harry S., 101
GLASCOCK
Alfred, 93
Fadeley, 93
Fenton F., 93
Hattie B., 93
Lilly, 93
May, 93
Orra M., 93
GOCHNAUER
Charles W., 64, 65
David, 64
E., 64
E. A., 64, 65
Joseph, 64, 65
Pembroke S., 64
Preston B., 64
GOINS
Luke, 17
Susanna, 17
GOODEN
Anne, 15
GOODHART
J. W., 44
Jerome W., 76
Mary C., 95
GOODIN
Martha, 15
Rachel, 15
GORE
Joseph, 11
Rowena, 17
T., 17
Thomas, 65
Tilghman, 17, 27
GOVER
Henry T., 37, 55
S. A., 83
GRADY
Edward B., 9
Frank T., 24, 25
GRAHAM
E., 88
James E., 88
William, 36, 59, 67
GRAY
Albert W., 34
John, 97
Lilias, 80
R. Bentley, 80
Rodney, 94
William H., 55

LOUDOUN COUNTY, VIRGINIA
GUARDIAN ACCOUNTS
1759-1904

GRAYSON
  Ann F., 25
  Benjamin, 1, 25
  Benjamin O., 25
  Col., 1
  G. M., 25
  George M., 25
  Mary S., 25
  Richard O., 25
  Thomas F., 25
  Thomas L., 25
  William, 1
GREEN
  John P. H., 62
  Thomas, 21
GREGG
  Aaron, 10
  Francis, 92
  Guilford G., 35, 61
  H. H., 59
  Harmon, 91
  Henry H., 59
  Jemima, 35
  John, 65
  Martha A., 81
  Martha L., 10
  Mary, 10, 61
  Mary Virginia, 61
  Nathan, 10
  Phebe A., 81
  Rebecca, 10
  Resin, 10
  Ruth, 10
  Samuel, 10
  Sarah Ann, 10
  Stephen, 57
  Thomas, 61
  William, 10
GRIFFITH
  Israel T., 22
  J., 6
GRIGGSBY
  Hannah, 4
GRUBB
  Benjamin H., 26
  Benjamin J., 73
  E., 13
  Ebenezer, 12, 20
  J. T., 91
  John, 36, 91
  Joseph P., 37, 60, 66, 82
  Robert W., 100
  S. M., 96
  Sanford N., 89
  William, 26
  William H., 78
GULICK
  James H., 56
GULLATT
  Eleanor, 56
GUNNELL
  William, 4
HAGUE
  Ann, 1
  John, 1
  Samuel, 1
HAINE
  Addison, 65
HALL
  ___, 80
  Delilah, 10
  John, 1
  Jonathan, 10
  Mary, 10
  Thomas, 10
  Thomas A., 92
  William, 10
HALLEY
  James H., 26
  John H., 26
HALLING
  John Willcoxon, 1
HAMILTON
  Burr W., 60
  Carolina, 63
  Caroline, 63
  Charles B., 15, 16
  Eli W., 63
  Emily, 23
  Harvey, 23
  James, 4
  James W., 29, 63
  John, 3, 4
  John Thomas, 23
  Lydia, 63
  Lydia A., 74
  Maria, 63
  Owen, 23
  P., 88
  Samuel Pugh, 23
  Sarah, 34
  Susan, 63
  William F., 23
HAMMERLY
  J. A., 93
  Mary E., 93
HAMPTON
  Elwood, 103

J. F., 103
James Franklin, 66
Jonah Nichols, 66
Preston, 3
Sallie W., 66
HARDY
  H. W., 60
  William H., 37
HARPER
  Charles E., 88
  James W., 88
  John William, 89
  Margaret, 10
  Robert, 88
  Robert N., 88
  Wells A., 88
HARRIMAN
  Samuel, 2
  Samuel D., 2
HARRIMON
  Francis, 2
HARRISON
  Burr, 1
  Henry T., 58
  M., 74
HARRYMAN
  S. D., 3
  Samuel D., 2
HART
  Sarah, 14
HATCHER
  Addison, 26
  Amanda, 12
  Amanda M., 12
  Anna, 12
  Anna V., 12
  Emsey F., 12
  Fanny, 81
  Gourley R., 12
  Jonah, 12, 17, 21, 35
  Joseph, 12
  Joshua, 26, 86
  Lindig, 81
  Lucy, 81
  M. G., 81
  Mary A., 12
  Nancy L., 81
  Noah, 9
  Rodney G., 81
  Ruth Anna, 12
  Sally Ann, 26
  T. A., 81
  T. E., 53
  Thomas, 10

Thomas E., 53
HAVENER
  Harriet E., 36
  James, 36
  Mary J., 36
  Robert, 36
  William H., 36
HAVENNER
  William A., 89
HAWLING
  Anna, 80
  Cecil, 81
  Eliza, 81
  Elizabeth, 4
  Eugene, 81
  John, 4
  John Wilcoxon, 4
  Joseph L., 80
  Martha, 12, 80
  Mary, 4, 80
  Rose, 80
  Sidney, 80
  William, 4, 12
HAWS
  A. E., 94
  Asker, 93
  Ella, 93
  Ellen, 93
  Oscar, 93
HAZARD
  John, 1
HEAD
  John, 4
HEATON
  Cecelia D., 96
  H., 79
  Henry, 72, 79, 88
  James, 4, 5, 7, 8
  Townsend, 21, 87
HEFFLEBOWER
  Samuel, 60
HEFLIN
  W. C., 95, 104
  W. P., 95
HEFNER
  Carrie, 88
HELLEM
  Mary Ann, 3
  Meredith, 3
HELM
  Lizzie C., 100
  M. C., 100
  Thomas M., 100
HENDERSON

R. H., 17
Richard H., 6
HENDRY
  Elihu E., 28
  Ruth, 28
HEREFORD
  Burr P., 25
  Esther M., 27
  Mary C., 27
  Minerva, 27
  Thomas S., 27
  William S., 27
HERRYMAN
  Francis, 2
HERYFORD
  Henry, 1
HESS
  Elizabeth, 5
  John A., 89
  Sarah Amanda, 89, 96
HESSER
  John, 23
  Martha E., 94
HICKMAN
  Benjamin J., 93
  Catharine, 68
  Catherine, 22
  Eleanor, 93
  Elnora A., 93
  Etchison H., 69
  G. L. Kurtz, 93
  George, 22, 69, 77
  George S., 69
  John, 22, 68
  John E., 93
  John S., 104
  Luther W., 69
  Margaret Susan Mary, 69
  Mary, 22
  Peter, 22, 69
  S. T., 100, 103
  William S., 93
HICKS
  Kimble G., 79
HIGDON
  C. H., 98
HILLEARY
  H. C., 82
HIRST
  Jesse, 4
  Jonathan, 35
  Smith, 65
HIXON
  Bettie, 51
HIXSON
  D., 22, 24, 37
  David, 17, 67
  James, 17
HOBBS
  Hannah, 23
HODGSON
  Julia, 34
  S. L., 34
HODSON
  Caroline O., 34
HOFFMAN
  Peter E., 27
HOGAN
  James W., 100
HOGE
  Anna E., 33
  D., 72
  Elisha H., 33
  Elizabeth, 10
  Elizabeth G., 72
  Hannah, 10
  Henrietta, 72
  Isaac, 12
  J. G., 33
  James M., 88, 94
  Jesse, 72
  Joshua, 12
  Phebe, 10
  Rachel, 10
  William, 10, 65
HOGUE
  Daniel, 65
  Elizabeth, 10
  James, 10, 65
  Joshua, 12
  Phebe, 10
  Rachel, 10
  William, 65
HOLLIDAY
  Anna, 85
  Rosa Lee, 85
HOLLINGSWORTH
  ___, 6
  C. L., 83
HOLMES
  George W., 98
  Joseph F., 67
  Owen, 65
HOOE
  Nancy, 88
  R. T., 1
  Richard, 60
HOOPER
  Fielder, 15
HOSKINSON
  A. W., 101
HOSPITAL
  Andrew, 5
  Lucullus, 26
HOUGH
  Amasa, 22
  Armistead, 17
  Barrett, 4
  Benjamin, 22
  Bernard, 51, 79
  E. P., 93
  E. Stanley, 93
  Edgar, 79
  Elizabeth H., 76
  Ezra, 17
  Isaac, 5
  Isaac S., 63
  Jane, 17
  John, 17
  Joseph, 100
  L. W. S., 96
  Mary, 73, 100
  Mary J., 88
  Samuel, 73
  William, 22
  William H., 17, 63
HOUGHES
  H., 6
HOUSE
  E. C. H., 93
  Mary H., 93, 97
  Samuel M. J., 93
HOUSEHOLDER
  Adam, 72
  Alice M., 63, 72
  Columbus, 63
  Daniel P., 78
  Drucilla, 29
  Drusilla, 63
  Gideon, 17, 18, 29, 62
  Julia, 63
  Kate C., 78
  Martha A., 29, 40, 63
  Susan, 29
HOUSHOLDER
  Adam M., 62
  Alice M., 63
  Columbus, 63
  G., 67
  Gideon, 45, 62, 63
HOWELL
  Amy W., 14
  Eliza, 28
  Reuben, 28
HUFF
  John, 5
HUGHES
  Elias, 65
  Francis, 6
  John, 6, 90
  Mary, 6
  William H., 29
HUMPHREY
  Abner Edward, 72
  Abner G., 72
  Ann Eliza, 72
  Mary C., 72
  Thomas C., 98
  Virginia G., 72
  William D., 98
HUMPHRIES
  Grace, 95
  Henry, 95
HUNT
  Stephen, 3
HUNTER
  George P., 78, 84
  John B., 84
  Margaret E., 84
  Mary M., 84
  Michael L., 84
  Virginia D., 84
HURDELL
  Ann Noland, 14
  Nancy, 14
HURDLE
  Nancy, 14
  Noland, 14
  Pleasant, 14
HURST
  Elizabeth, 1
  Hannah, 27
  James W., 27
  John, 1
  Sarah A., 27
HURSTS
  ___, 6
HUTCHISON
  A. M., 93
  Alexander, 15
  Beverly, 24
  Elijah, 65
  Franklin, 93
  James, 81
  John, 81, 92
  John R., 101

L. E., 92
Ludwell, 92
Maria L., 93
Mary E., 93
Melville, 93
Reuben, 14, 15
Reuben Alexander, 15
S., 15
Sampson, 15, 24
Silas M., 81
William, 1
IRWIN
　Elizabeth, 27
　Frances, 27
　Marcus, 27
ISETTS
　J., 36
ISH
　Edgar, 82
　Robert A., 24
JACKSON
　Benjamin, 19
　Charles H., 101
　Edgar, 97
　Hannie, 101
　John, 19
　William, 19
JACOBS
　___, 7
　Elizabeth, 5
　Price, 18
JAMES
　Alice J., 84
　Asa, 23
　Benton, 39
　Cecelia, 64
　Charles E., 90
　Cravan, 39
　Craven, 35, 39, 63, 64, 94
　Dean, 26
　Elijah, 90
　Eliza, 84
　Fleet, 84
　Florida C., 63, 64
　Joseph, 90
　Mary, 23
　Mary C., 66
　Mary V., 63, 64
　Mason, 84
　Matson, 84
　Mollie, 84
　Richard, 66, 77
　Robert, 23, 35
　Robert M., 63, 64

Sally, 26
Sarah, 23, 35, 90
Sarah C., 63, 64
Thomas, 60
Thomas B., 63, 64
JANNEY
　Abijah, 4
　Amos, 28
　Aquilla, 47
　Asa M., 57
　Cora, 87
　Elisha, 33
　Ella, 87
　Frank, 91
　G. W., 36
　George W., 28, 72, 79, 87
　J. C., 21
　J. R., 91
　James C., 76
　Jesse, 4
　John, 21, 28, 34
　John C., 87
　Jonas, 12
　Joseph, 91
　Mary, 87
　Mary G., 87
　Robert W., 87
　Samuel M., 65
　Stephen, 9
　William, 71
JANUARY
　Ephram, 26
JEFFRIES
　Ann C., 59
　B. B., 58, 59
　Hannah, 59, 60
　Hannah V., 59, 75
　Joseph B., 59
　Joseph D., 59
　Joseph O., 58
　Martha J., 59
　Mary Francis, 58
　Mary T., 59
　Martha J., 59, 60
　Mary T., 59, 60
　Tacey, 58
JENKINS
　Craven, 103
　Joseph H., 102, 104
　Joseph R., 102, 103
　Reuben, 102
　Ruth H., 102
　Sallie, 102
　Samuel T., 102

JENNERS
　Abiel, 6, 7, 9
JENNINGS
　Edmund, 57
JETT
　Catharine, 18
　Peter, 18
JOHNSON
　C. W., 81
　Charles, 100
　Charles W., 65, 81
　Henry J., 22
　Lydia Jane, 22
　Richard, 15
　Robert, 57
JONES
　Arthur Lee, 80
　Henrietta, 80
　James H., 80
　John William, 80
　Lewen T., 77
　M. G., 34
JORDAN
　Bertha, 101
　Catharine, 11
　Claretta, 101
　John L., 63
　Julia, 63
　Katie, 101
　Lizzie, 101
　Robert, 101
KALB
　Benjamin D., 45
　John G. R., 45, 69
　Land, 45
　S. J., 69
　Samuel, 45
　Silas D., 45, 89
　Thomas D., 45
KARN
　Adam, 13
KARNE
　Adam, 20
KEEN
　A., 22
　Lucy, 91
KEENE
　George, 49
　N., 20
　Washington, 90
KEIGHN
　John, 7
KELLY
　Elizabeth, 104

KENWORTHY
　Rebecca, 27
　William, 3
KERCHEVAL
　George E., 92
　Robert H., 49
KERN
　William, 43
KEVAN
　Michael, 5
KEYES
　Philip, 92
KEYS
　Louisa, 101
KING
　Randolph, 94
　William, 17
KLEIN
　Elizabeth, 24
　M. C., 22, 27, 59
　Madison C., 22, 24, 28
KNOTT
　Sarah, 11
KNOX
　T. P., 51
　Thomas, 1
KUGHN
　William, 26
LACEY
　Charles H., 100
　Israel, 4
　Robert A., 8
　Westwood A., 8
LACOCK
　James, 65
LACY
　John, 8
　Robert A., 8
　Westwood A., 8
LAKE
　Martha, 39
　T. S., 38
LANE
　Arthur, 26
　Hardage, 1, 2
　Hellen E., 26
　James W., 26
　P. C., 1
　Presley Carr, 1
　Sally, 1
　William, 1, 3, 4
LARKIN
　T., 8
LAROWE

Isaac, 5
LAUCK
  W. C., 91
LAWRENCE
  Walter B., 83
LAWSON
  C. T., 103
LAYCOCK
  Edward, 86
  Lulu, 86
LEE
  Alexander D., 24
  Bassett, 80
  Bessett, 81
  David, 17
  E. J., 34, 83
  Julietta, 80
  Mary Ann, 27
  Richard E., 27
LEISH
  B. Frank, 100
LEITH
  F. M., 70
  George Ernest, 70
  J. W., 70
  James, 2
  Laurence, 72
  Lawrence, 72
  Louisa, 72
  Nellie E., 70
  Richard D., 70
  Susan V., 70
  Theodore, 70
  Theodorick, 70
  Veturia A., 70
LENHART
  John, 100
LENT
  Cornelius, 103
LESLIE
  Benjamin, 60
  John, 19, 31, 79, 84
  John A., 84
  John B., 84
  John E., 84
LEWIS
  Charles, 3, 7, 14, 15
  James, 3
LICKEY
  Eugenia D., 87
  George, 65
LITTLEJOHN
  C. W., 102
  Forrest C., 102
  Horace C., 102
  John, 4, 5, 8
  Julia D., 102
  Paul V., 102
LITTLETON
  Bushrod, 38
  F., 22, 36
  H., 38
  Hannah, 38
  K., 38
  Richard C., 38
  S. Campbell, 103
  T., 24, 58
  Thomas, 3, 58
LLOYD
  Annie, 80
  Barcklay, 92
  C. E., 80
  Emily E., 80
  George, 80
  H., 80
  Maud, 80
LOCKHART
  Margaret, 18
LODGE
  Joseph, 39
LOGAN
  Anna, 90
  Sarah D., 90
LORENTZ
  J. A., 34
  Jacob, 92
  Laura V., 34
LOVE
  A. D., 62
  Armida E., 94
  C. C., 99
  E. W., 54
  E. Dilley, 94
  Edgar L., 99
  Eli A., 99
  Elizabeth, 21
  Elizabeth L., 28
  F. M., 101
  F. T., 99
  Fenton A., 21
  Henry, 17
  Henry N., 21
  James, 5
  James J., 22, 34
  John, 17, 21, 102
  Lacey R., 99
  Louis N. B., 94
  Lydia, 17
  Maria, 17
  Nathan, 17
  Rebecca, 5, 17, 21
  Richard, 21
  Robert R., 102
  Rufus T., 99
  Samuel, 3, 17, 21
  Samuel H., 66
  Sarah, 17
  Sarah N., 21
  Susan H., 22
  Thomas B., 22
  Thomas E., 102
LOVELESS
  Elizabeth, 88
LOVETT
  Caroline, 90
  Tazwell, 90
  W. Byron, 81
LOWE
  Margaret, 63
  Margaret V., 63
  Moses, 63
LOY
  George H., 44
  Henrietta, 44
LUCIUS
  Charles, 100
  Kate, 100
LUCKETT
  F. W., 25
  Francis W., 9
  Leven, 5
  Ludwell, 17, 25, 27, 49
  Robert F., 14
  Samuel, 5
  Samuel C., 31
LUPTON
  (Dr.), 53
LYNN
  Fanny, 82
  Gertrude, 82
  Hannah, 94
  J. T., 94
  John, 75
  John A., 94
  John F., 94
  John H., 67
  John T., 59, 60, 62, 75
  Pamelia, 30
  Parmelia C., 30
  Permelia C., 30
  R. H., 103
  Sarah G., 30
MACHEN
  J. P., 98
MACKEY
  Thomas, 3
MAFFETT
  Thomas J., 80
MAGILL
  Annie E. T., 55
  Henry D., 55
  Thomas H. M., 55
MAINS
  A., 19
  Archibald, 18
MANKIN
  Charles L., 68
MANN
  Abner W., 64
  Abner Walter, 64
  F. S. L., 84
  Franklin S. L., 64
  George William, 64
  Ida, 64
  Ida S. L., 64
  J. W. C., 74
  John, 89
  John S., 89
  John W., 64
  John W. C., 64
  Joseph W., 64
  Joseph William, 64
  Leanna, 64
  Luther A., 79
  Mary L., 64
  Mary Laura, 64
  Rebecca, 89
MANNING
  Catharine, 52
  Jacob H., 52
MARLOW
  Dr., 7
  George, 10
  Thomas J., 9, 10, 12, 13, 20, 22
  Mary W., 10
MARMADUKE
  Silas A., 14
MARSHALL
  Sarah A., 94
MARVIN
  J. W., 65
MASON
  Armistead T., 7
  Mary A. V. B., 92
  N. Carroll, 55

Temple C., 92
William T. T., 55
MATHEWS
James, 77
MATTHEW
Jonathan, 85, 89
MATTHEWS
Catharine, 51
Jesse, 79
John, 79
Jonathan, 79
Mary C., 79
Rodney, 79
Susan, 79
MATTINGLY
Hattie, 100
MCABEE
M., 81
Nellie, 81
MCARTOR
Thomas, 60
MCCABE
J. B., 102
John H., 6
MCCARTY
Dennis, 56
George B., 97
John, 92
Stephen, 71
MCCRAY
Edgar, 87
William, 26, 35, 81, 86, 87
MCDANIEL
A., 60
Ann, 12
Archibald, 12, 37
Edward, 12
Elizabeth, 12
George W., 27
James, 12
John, 12
Mary Ann, 27
Nancy, 12
Presley, 27
MCFARLAND
A. S., 56
Alcinda, 56
Alcinda S., 56
Alice, 56
Alice S., 56
Edgar, 86
Elizabeth, 56
J. F., 56

Jonathan F., 56
Joseph, 56
Maurice, 56
Maurice W., 56
W. F., 56
W. T., 56
William T., 56
MCGAVACK
Israel, 11
J. T., 100
Mary Pleasant, 11
MCGAVOCK
Henry, 17
James, 17
John, 17
Pamelia, 17
MCGAVVICK
Israel, 11
Mary Pleasant, 11
Patrick, 11
MCILHANY
Cecelia, 6
Elizabeth, 6
James, 6, 7, 21, 22, 37
Louesa, 6, 7
Margaret, 6, 7
Mary, 6
Mortimer, 6, 7, 19
MCINTOSH
J. L., 32
MCIVER
John, 7
MCKENZIE
Ella, 46
MCKIMMA
John, 12
Sarah, 12
MCKIMMEY
Sarah, 11
MCKIMMY
John, 12
MCKNIGHT
Amy W., 14
MCNULTY
Hugh, 55
Mary, 55
Mary T., 55
William T., 55
MCROY
Benjamin, 5
MEAD
Aquilla, 65
John, 65, 83, 87
Joseph, 9

Martha, 9
William, 9
MEGEATH
___, 35
Alfred, 30
Gabriel, 30
James Townsend, 30
Joseph P., 23, 26
MERCHANT
A. W., 95
Landon, 60
Leroy W., 95
MILBOURNE
A. J., 92
Blanche, 92
Orra, 92
MILBURN
Ann E., 96
MILHOLLEN
Albert, 99
E. A., 100
MILLBURN
A. F., 63
David, 63
MILTON
John, 85
MINOR
Ann, 2
Annie M., 97
Benjamin W., 59
Francis, 2
Jackson, 77
John, 2
Nancy, 2
William, 2
MOCK
George W., 54
H. R., 90
Joseph, 37
Mary Ann, 54
MOFFETT
Benjamin, 18
Charles H., 95
Gracie A., 95
J. C., 100
John, 23
John L., 95
Josiah, 4
L. C., 95
Louisa, 59
Mary A., 95
Mary C., 95
Robert, 18, 35
MONEY

Samuel, 77
MONROE
Eugene, 100
Madison, 92
Rosey, 1
MOORE
Asa, 3, 4
C., 88
James, 3, 4, 8
John, 14
L. S., 79
M. E., 88
Mary C., 79
Mary S., 82
Nancy, 85
Sarah A., 82
Thomas R., 102
William, 85, 88, 89
William V., 92
MORAN
John M., 60
M. J., 103
MORGAN
Margaret, 11
MORRIS
George H., 101
Keziah, 23
Lucinda, 23
M., 64, 101
Mahlon, 63, 64
R. M., 104
Sophronia, 23
Thomas, 23
MORRISON
Edward, 79
Joseph, 80
MOSS
Thomas, 6
MOTON
Jesse, 101
MOTT
A. R., 36, 81
MOUNT
C. E., 97
Charles, 67
J. M., 103
MULLEN
Michael, 65
MURPHY
___, 50
MURRAY
Samuel, 3
MURREY
Samuel, 3, 4

LOUDOUN COUNTY, VIRGINIA
GUARDIAN ACCOUNTS
1759-1904

MUSE
  James H., 23
  Walker, 23
MYERS
  Thomas, 65
NEALE
  Elizabeth C., 5
  Presley, 5
  William S., 5
NEER
  Anna, 23
  David, 23
  Elizabeth, 23
  Florence, 81
  George, 23
  Hannah, 23
  Nathan, 45, 72
  Potts, 72
NEGRO
  Aany, 6
  Adam, 2, 5
  Airy, 4
  Alexander, 26
  Alfred, 14, 19
  Allison, 18, 19
  Amanda, 19, 38
  Amelia, 19
  Ann, 17, 25, 60
  Ann Matilda, 79
  Ara, 9
  Armistead, 38
  Arthur, 38
  Austin, 19
  Ben, 15
  Bert?, 2
  Bet, 59
  Betsey, 59
  Bett, 2
  Betty, 51, 59
  Beverly, 19, 40
  Bill, 5, 9, 25, 28
  Billey, 5
  Bob, 15, 17
  Caleb, 18, 19
  Caroline, 11, 42
  Cashus, 34
  Cass, 13
  Catharine, 27, 34
  Cato, 10
  Charity, 13, 60
  Charles, 6, 8, 12, 15, 19, 20, 27, 34, 62
  Charlotte, 14, 18, 19
  Christopher, 31
  Cornelius, 7
  Crab, 4
  Dabas, 1
  Dabbor, 1
  Dabbors, 1
  Daniel, 58
  Delia, 38
  Delpha, 9
  Delphia, 9
  Dennis, 31
  Diadama, 19, 27
  Diadamia, 27
  Dick, 13, 31, 49, 50
  Easter, 9
  Edmund, 38
  Edward, 14, 38, 39, 53
  Eliza, 9, 12
  Ellick, 10
  Elwood, 39
  Emanuel, 6
  Emily, 17, 26, 49, 50
  Enos, 36
  Fan, 11
  Fanney, 2
  Fanny, 2, 11, 12
  Fenton, 15
  Flora, 1
  Frances, 15, 54
  Frank, 54, 60
  Gabe, 42
  Gardner, 5
  George, 5, 6, 14, 15, 17, 60, 61
  George Henry, 60
  Gerard, 18
  Gerrard, 18
  Giles, 18, 19
  Godfrey, 13
  Grace, 7, 11
  Hannah, 1, 2, 5
  Harrell, 19
  Harriet, 18, 19, 28
  Harriett, 17
  Harry, 5, 6, 10, 54
  Henly?, 8
  Henny, 4, 6
  Henrietta, 59
  Henry, 10, 13, 15, 18, 19, 31, 34
  Henry?, 54
  Howard, 14
  Isaac, 1, 17, 42
  Israel, 26
  Jack, 10, 58
  Jack Taylor, 79
  Jacob, 6, 58
  James, 2, 5, 14, 17
  Jane, 15, 59, 65
  Janney, 42
  Jared, 18
  Jean, 2
  Jenny, 50, 79
  Jerrard, 18
  Jerry, 49, 50
  Jim, 2, 14, 79
  Jinny, 2
  Joe, 6, 17, 31
  John, 7, 11, 15, 42, 60, 61
  John Henry, 27
  John Kitt, 60
  John Wesley, 60
  Jordan, 60
  Joseph, 31, 60
  Joshua, 17
  Jude, 2
  Judy, 2, 49
  Julia, 42, 50
  Julia Ann, 50, 79
  Julius, 40
  Ketty, 40
  Kimmico, 5
  Kitty, 60, 61
  Lazett, 8
  Lettice, 79
  Levi, 11
  Levy, 14
  Lewis, 7, 15, 19, 31
  Lizette, 8
  Lloyd, 12
  Lovey, 14
  Luckey, 6
  Lucky, 6
  Lucy, 2, 3
  Maddison, 8
  Madison, 50
  Malinda, 15
  Manuel, 6
  Margaret, 50
  Maria, 6, 14, 27, 38, 54, 60, 61
  Mariah, 38
  Marias, 14
  Marshall, 23
  Martha, 23
  Martha Jane, 19
  Martin, 9
  Mary, 7, 9, 15, 28, 50, 58, 79
  Mary Ann Kitt, 60
  Mary Catharine, 27
  Mary Cross, 50
  Mary Jane, 50
  Matilda, 15
  Melinda, 15
  Milly, 1, 5, 7
  Milton, 60
  Minnie, 38
  Morear, 14
  Moses, 7, 9
  Nace, 17
  Nance, 7
  Nancy, 7, 38
  Nancy Betsy, 15
  Ned, 3
  Nell, 1
  Nelly, 19
  Netly, 5
  Oscar, 38
  Pall, 2
  Patty, 11, 31
  Pegg, 4, 5
  Peter, 3, 4
  Phebe, 5
  Phill, 3, 6
  Poll, 2
  Presly, 27
  Priscilla, 10
  Prisy, 6
  Rachel, 4
  Ruth, 26
  Sale, 2
  Sall, 2, 3
  Sally, 5, 42
  Sam, 7, 10
  Samuel, 10
  Sandford, 15
  Sanford, 15
  Sarah, 15, 17
  Scott, 79
  Silva, 9
  Silvia, 9
  Simon, 5
  Smith, 27
  Solomon, 4
  Stepney, 26
  Susan, 36, 55
  Thomas, 7
  Tim, 7
  Timothy, 3
  Tiner, 7
  Tom, 9, 10, 19
  Townsend, 18

LOUDOUN COUNTY, VIRGINIA
GUARDIAN ACCOUNTS
1759-1904

Townshend, 18
Venue, 26
Vinney, 2
Viny, 2
Violet, 50
Washington, 15
Webster Mitchell, 79
Whaley, 1
Whitely, 1
Whitley, 1
William, 19, 28
Winney, 79
Winny, 2
NELSON
  John H., 98
NERO
  Flora, 56
  Lucy Ann, 56
NEWLON
  C. A., 34
  J. R., 35
NEWMAN
  Mary, 92
NICEWARNER
  Catharine, 40
  Christian, 40
  Christian Thomas, 40
  Emily, 40
  Harriet J., 40
  Jacob R., 40
  John M., 40
  Mary, 40
NICHOL
  J., 26
NICHOLS
  Catharine, 18
  Charles, 104
  Edward, 91
  Eli, 5
  Eli H., 66, 67, 68, 86
  Elizabeth, 18
  George H., 68
  George W., 67, 86, 91
  Henry, 5
  Henry H., 67
  Isaac, 10
  J., 72
  J. W., 66
  Jacob, 18
  John E., 18
  John Ellwood, 18
  Jonah, 17, 18, 66
  Joseph, 65
  L. Ellen, 67, 68

Louisa, 67, 68
Lydia, 5
M. Virginia, 67, 68
Margery, 18
Maria, 67, 68, 91
Mary Ann, 18
Nancy, 18
Nathan, 18
Phebe Louisa, 18
Rebecca, 5
Sallie W., 66
Susan, 18
Swithen, 18
Thomas, 5, 14, 23, 67, 68, 75
Thomas J., 66, 68, 75
Thomas W., 100
Virginia, 66
William, 18, 65
William N., 18
NICKOLS
  Jonah, 21
NISBITT
  James, 3
NISEWARNER
  Catharine, 43
  John, 43
NIXON
  George, 86, 90
  George H., 92
  Hannah E., 61, 62, 94
  J. Ellwood, 94
  Joel, 62
  Joel R., 61, 62
  John, 30
  John E., 61, 62
  Jonah, 86, 89, 90
  Mary A., 90
  Parelia, 94
  Parelia F., 61, 62
  R. J., 62
NOBLES
  George, 27
NOLAND
  B. P., 45
  C. Powell, 103
  Philip H., 103
  William, 5, 11
NOLDAN
  George W., 65
NORRIS
  J. L., 92
  Joseph L., 100
NUTT

Carrie, 103
Daniel, 103
George Whitfield, 57
James, 103
OATYER
  Peter, 23
OBANNON
  Alonzo, 92
OGDON
  ___, 7
ORAM
  Amanda, 56
  Enos, 56
  Henry, 56
  Lucinda Jane, 56
ORR
  J. M., 50, 66, 68
  John, 1
  John M., 49, 50, 51
ORRISON
  Amanda, 63
  America, 63
  Betsey, 63
  David A., 63
  Jonah, 40
  Laney Ellen, 63
  Samuel, 80, 91, 96
  Townshend, 63
OSBORN
  B., 72
  Bushrod, 72
  T. V. B., 72
OSBURN
  ___, 54
  Abner, 7
  Addison, 28
  Alberta M., 80
  Ann, 28
  Balaam, 24
  Bushrod, 73
  Craven, 6, 7, 27
  Decatur, 40
  Emeline M., 40
  Harriet, 7, 8
  Harrison, 40
  Herbert, 97
  Herod, 28
  J. T. M., 40
  Jane, 34, 40
  Joab, 28, 31
  Joel, 37, 51, 80
  Jonah, 25, 34, 40, 94
  Joshua, 17, 28
  Louisa A., 51, 73

Lucinda, 34, 40
Mason, 28
Massey, 7, 8
Maurice, 80, 94
Morris, 80
Octavius, 40
Oscar, 40
Patience, 7, 8
Patsy, 40
Phineas, 28
Priscilla, 28
R., 59
Richard, 40, 59, 62
Sanford J. R., 40
T. V. B., 51, 73
Volney, 28
Walter C., 51, 73
William T., 28
OSBURNE
  Abner, 7
  H., 8
OVERFIELD
  Jessie, 59
  Marshall, 62
  Richard, 59
OXLEY
  Evered, 2
  John, 2
PANCOAST
  Alberta M., 79
  Alice L., 98
  Carrie, 98
  Harry, 98
  Jane A., 39
  John, 48, 80
  Joseph, 36, 39, 54, 79
  Lillias, 79
  Lula, 98
  Rosa Lee, 79
  S. T., 98
  W. P., 91
PANCOST
  Jane A., 80
PARKER
  Deborah, 11
PAXON
  Lillie, 79
PAXSON
  Alice B., 80
  Anna Beall, 85
  Burr W., 90
  C. W., 84, 85, 93
  Charles, 93
  Clara, 79, 91

Cornelius William, 71
Derizo C., 84
Duanna, 17
Fannie H., 93
Hattie A., 93
Kate, 97
Lillie, 79
Louisa E., 93
Rosa, 79
T. M., 41
Townsend M., 37, 41
W. B., 80
Westwood, 79
William, 5
William C. J., 93
PEACOCK
　Lucinda, 20
　N. B., 60, 85, 89
　Noble B., 37
PEERS
　Henry, 8
PEIRPOINT
　Eli, 17
PERRY
　Amelia, 6
　Benjamin, 6
　Benjamin W., 6
　Elisabeth, 6
　Elizabeth, 7
　John, 7
　Margaret, 6
　Mary, 6
　Samuel, 6
PETERS
　Edward W., 93
　Robert J., 93
　Walter G., 93
　William R., 93
PETTITT
　William F., 104
PEYTON
　Cabel Y., 98
　Dr., 5
PHILIPS
　Thomas, 8
PHILLIPS
　A. W., 102
　Arthur W., 75
　Elizabeth J., 75
　J. P., 15
　R. H., 50
　Richard S., 75
　Thomas, 9
PICKETT

W. S., 51
PIERPOINT
　Eli, 17, 21
　Francis, 40
PIGGOTT
　Albert S., 97
　Alberta J., 97, 98
　Burr, 75
　Bushrod, 75
　Henry, 104
　Isaac, 75
　John, 75
　John W., 81
　Mary, 97, 104
　Mary E., 97
　Mary J., 75
　Ruth Hannah, 81
　T. H., 81
　Thomas, 75
　Thomas H., 100
　William, 75
PINKARD
　C. F., 88
PLASTER
　David H., 92
　G. H., 35
　George, 34
　George E., 70
　James H., 34, 35
　John H., 34
　John Henry, 34
　Mary, 34
　Michael, 34, 35
　Michael M., 34, 35
　Sarah Frances, 34, 35
　William A., 34
　William Albert, 34
POLAND
　George, 92
POLLARD
　Braxton, 2
　Thomas, 1
POOL
　William, 91
PORTER
　Jesse, 38
POSTON
　Joseph, 31
POTTERFIELD
　Catharine, 71
　Julius W., 71
　L. H., 71
　Luther H., 71
　Samuel, 71

Silas, 71
POTTS
　David, 9
　E. Fletcher, 67
　Ezekiel, 81, 89
　John L., 72
　John Lewis, 45
　Jonas, 72
　Joseph L., 9
　Mahala, 9
　Thomas W., 45
POWELL
　A. H., 50
　Alfred, 9
　B., 8
　Burr, 4, 7, 9
　C., 7, 8
　Charles L., 25, 26
　Cuthbert, 7, 8, 9
　E. S., 7
　F. W., 14
　George C., 27, 45
　H. B., 45
　Israel G., 72
　John L., 9, 24
　John Leven, 9
　L., 8
　Leven, 1, 7, 9
　Maria, 8
　Maria A., 8
　S. R., 9
　Sally, 8
　Sarah, 27
　W. A., 9, 11
　William A., 9
POWER
　Mary F., 56
PRESGRAVES
　W. W., 90
PRESTON
　George, 60
　Lydia Ann, 47
PRICE
　S. H., 62
PURCEL
　Edgar R., 21
　James H., 21
　Lydia J., 21
　Samuel, 37
　Valentine V., 21
　William Thomas, 21
PURCELL
　E. R., 57
　Edgar R., 21, 22

J. H., 94
James H., 22
Lydia, 22
Lydia J., 21
Thomas W., 22
V. V., 22
William T., 22
William Thomas, 22
PURSEL
　Samuel, 8, 37
PURSELL
　Samuel, 36
　Valentine V., 9
PUSEY
　Joshua, 73, 78
　W. N., 98
　William N., 73
RAMEY
　Sandford, 6
　Sandford J., 26
　Sanford, 6
　Sanford J., 54, 57
RAMSEY
　S. C. E., 60
　Samuel T., 92
RAMY
　Louisa, 104
　Walter, 104
RATTIFF
　Abba, 22
RAWLINGS
　Corrie Lee, 99
　Emma Mary, 99
　Eva V., 99
　John M., 14, 99
　Lucinda, 60
　Mary E. V., 14
　Mary V. E., 14
　Mary Virginia Elizabeth, 14
　S. A., 14
　Samuel A., 14
　Sarah, 14
　Stephen, 14
　William, 14
RECTOR
　Caleb, 12
　Mary A., 12
　Samuel, 12
REDMAN
　W., 85
　Wilfred, 85
REDMON
　Rosa Lee, 85

LOUDOUN COUNTY, VIRGINIA
GUARDIAN ACCOUNTS
1759-1904

REDMOND
  Ann, 62
REECE
  David, 10, 20
REED
  Catharine, 3
  Jesse, 3
  Reuben, 3
  William, 3
REEDER
  Gourley, 12
RHODES
  ___, 88
  George, 19, 101
RICE
  J. E., 96
RICHARD
  Emily Jane, 18
RICHARDS
  David F., 40
  Laney A., 40
  Samuel, 40
  Sarah E., 40
  Thomas, 40
RICHTER
  Charles William, 16
  George, 16
  Henry, 16
  John, 16
RICKARD
  ___, 45
  Dewanna, 17
  Duanna, 17
  Emily Jane, 17
  George, 13, 17
  Jesse L., 97
  John, 17
  Kate, 97
  Mary, 17
  Walter C., 97
  William, 17
  William H., 17
RITICOR
  Joseph, 100
  Joshua L., 100
RIVERS
  Joseph, 89
ROACH
  A., 59
  Jemima, 5
  Nancy, 5
  Richard, 5
  Ruth, 5
  T., 11

ROBERTS
  Mattie E., 78
ROBEY
  Andrew, 60, 76
RODERICK
  Jacob R., 77
ROGERS
  A. H., 56
  Arthur L., 78
  Asa, 45, 46, 47
  Charlotte, 78
  Charlotte R., 78
  Cuthbert B., 57
  Ellen V., 78
  George R., 78
  Henry, 65
  Laura Lee, 78
  Maria C., 78
  S. E., 100
  T., 57
  Thomas, 12, 17
  Walter Thomas, 18
ROLLER
  Aaron, 20
  Priscilla, 20
  Frederick, 20
ROLLINGS
  John M., 16
  Mary Virginia Elizabeth, 16
  Samuel A., 16
  Sarah, 16
  William, 16
  William H., 16
ROLLINS
  Margaret M., 96
  Mary, 91
  V. G. S., 91
  Virginia G. R., 96
ROSE
  John, 5, 7, 9
  Robert, 15
ROWLES
  Edmund J., 57
  Mary C., 98
ROYSTON
  M., 37
ROZZELL
  Kephe E., 6
RUN
  Sarah, 11
RUSE
  Eli T., 40
  Sarah E., 40

  Solomon, 30
RUSSELL
  Emily, 11
  Emily M., 82
  H. H., 77, 96, 97, 98, 100, 103
  Henry, 11
  James, 11, 100
  John, 18
  Louisa, 82, 90
  Mahlon, 11
  Martin W., 90
  Mary, 11
  Matilda, 82
  Nancy, 11
  Polly, 11
  Rachel, 11
  William, 11, 14, 17, 45
RUST
  A. T. M., 78, 83, 90
  Frederick G., 83
  G., 58
  George, 58
  James, 9, 10
  James B., 92
  James Buckannan, 68
  James W., 61, 68
  John C., 68, 103
  M. A. E., 79
  Manley T., 68
  Mandley T., 68
  Margaret Virginia, 68
  Mary Ellen, 68
  R. L. B., 79
  Sallie J., 68
  Sally J., 68
  T. M., 58
RYAN
  John F., 86
SAFFER
  B. F., 92
SANBOWER
  Annie G., 104
  D., 104
  Edgar H., 104
  Harry H., 104
  John, 35
  Julian, 13
  M., 18
  Mary F., 35
  Michael, 104
  Samuel F., 35
  Simon, 79
SANDERS

  Aaron, 4
  Aron, 5
  Barbara, 4
  Bethany, 4, 5
  John, 5
  Nancy, 4, 5
  Parmela, 4
  Parmelia, 5
  Patience, 4, 5
  Presley, 4, 5
  Thomas, 5, 7
  Wilson C., 63
SANDFORD
  Ann, 12
SANGSTER
  Thomas, 2
SAPPINGTON
  John F., 5
SAUNDERS
  A. R., 24
  Aaron, 7
  Aaron R., 25
  Bethany, 5
  E., 23
  Ella, 94
  Everet, 43
  John, 2
  Lee A., 36
  Louis, 94
  Nancy, 5
  Parmelia, 5
  Patience, 5
  Permela, 5
  Presley, 5, 57
  Pressley, 5
  T. R., 16
  Wesley C., 37
SCATTERDAY
  Aaron, 60
SCHOOLEY
  Annette F., 79
  Charles G., 34
  Elizabeth C., 5
  John, 17, 22
  Jonas P., 10, 43, 65
  Kate F., 79
  Mahlon, 34
  Milton, 87
  Sarah Ann, 79
  William H., 54, 59, 77
SCOTT
  Armistead, 60
  Armstead, 37
  Joseph, 3

Robert, 3
Samuel, 3
SEARS
    William Bernard, 1
SEATON
    James W., 49
SEITZ
    Amanda, 32
    Andrew, 32
SELLMAN
    Hy C., 81
SETTLE
    Nelson, 92
SEXTON
    John, 60
SHAFER
    Daniel, 74, 100
    Jacob, 16, 22
    John, 43
    John M., 43, 65
    Joseph H., 43
    Lydia, 43
    Mary Ellen, 43
SHAFFER
    F. W., 56
    Jacob, 13, 15, 16
SHAW
    Rebecca, 10
    Susan Bailey, 10
SHAWEN
    C., 92, 94
    Cornelius, 91, 93
    David, 57
    William C., 78
SHEARMAN
    Thomas, 79
SHEID
    James, 2
    John H., 20
SHEILER
    Elizabeth, 23
SHEPHERD
    Francis C., 29
    Jacob R., 29
    John, 8
    Leven, 8
    Mellville R., 29
    Nancy R., 29
SHOEMAKER
    Elizabeth, 80
    George, 5, 36, 77, 80, 100
    Josiah, 80
    Mary, 80
    Sarah, 80
    William, 80
SHONG
    Peter D., 40
SHORT
    Jacob, 18
SHOVER
    G., 22
    George, 22
    Herod, 22
    M., 13, 20
    Magdalena, 22
    Magdelena, 13
    Sophia, 22
SHOVERS
    M., 12
SHREVE
    Charles, 59
    Daniel, 59
    Daniel S., 77
    Daniel T., 35, 77
    Daniel Trundle, 77
    Francis, 77
    Mary, 77
    Virginia, 77
    William, 77
SHRIVER
    Alice R., 78
    Ann, 78
    Annie Mariah, 78
    Emily Gertrude, 78
    Martha Ellen, 78
    Willie, 78
SHRUEEY
    Sarah, 89
SHUEY
    Mary, 87
SHUMAKER
    Elizabeth, 92
    George J., 92
    Jacob, 76
    James S., 89
    Josiah, 92
    Maggie E., 89
    Mary, 92
    Sarah, 92
    William B., 92
SHUMATE
    Maria, 23
    Murphy C., 23
SILCOTT
    Ella May, 104
    John W., 97
    M., 97
    Mary, 97
    Sallie A., 104
    Zula B., 104
SIMPSON
    Henson, 65
    James R., 55
SINCLAIR
    ___, 7, 35
    Amos, 11
    George, 7
SKILMAN
    Bushrod, 92
SKINNER
    Benjamin F., 56
    Bettie J., 56
    E. W., 96
    Elijah, 4
    Elizabeth, 56
    Gabriel, 56
    Henry W., 56
    James, 56
    Mary C., 96
    Nathaniel, 4
    Nathaniel J., 56
    Phinehas, 4
    Willie H., 96
SLATER
    Ann E., 37
    George, 28
    Jacob, 44
    Jonas, 77
    John M., 29
    Michael, 29
    S., 44
    Samuel, 44
    Samuel W., 37
    William, 28, 29
SLATES
    Adam, 15, 16
    Conrad, 16
    Eliza Ann, 15, 16
    Elizabeth Ann, 16
    Frederick, 15, 16
    Jacob, 16
    Mary, 15, 16
    Savilla, 16
    Solomon, 15, 16
    William, 15, 16
SLAYMAKER
    A. B., 88
    Amos, 88
    Archie C., 88
    Edmund W., 88
    Elizabeth J., 58
    Mary E., 88
    William J., 88
SMALE
    A. J., 89
    Emma S., 89
    G. J., 89
    John, 89
    Mary M., 89
    Olivia J., 89
SMALLWOOD
    James, 47
SMART
    J. P., 58
SMITH
    Alexander, 15
    Alexander M., 14, 15
    Ann, 9
    Catherine, 18
    Charles, 9
    Clater, 3
    Edward J., 65
    Eliza Jane, 52
    Elizabeth, 18
    Eve Virginia, 52
    Fleet, 6
    George, 18, 52
    George D., 10
    Hannah, 7
    Henry H., 49
    Henry W., 49
    Jacob, 7, 24, 28, 52, 66
    Job, 52, 66
    John, 18, 40, 52
    John R., 49
    Jonas, 49
    Joseph, 3
    Joshua, 49
    Lewis M., 14
    Maria, 15
    Maria E., 14, 15
    Mary, 9, 52
    Mary Ann, 14, 15
    Mary J., 52, 81
    Mary W., 10
    Malinda C., 33
    Margaret E., 33
    Phebe, 81
    Ryland G., 33
    Samuel, 66
    Samuel George, 52
    Samuel J., 81
    Sarah Ann, 10
    Seth, 33
    Susan Sophia, 52
    Susannah, 9

LOUDOUN COUNTY, VIRGINIA
GUARDIAN ACCOUNTS
1759-1904

Thomas J., 81
Thomas R., 49
W. M., 66
William, 10, 66, 82
William B., 75
William G., 49
William H., 33
William J., 65
William P., 81
SNOOTS
  George H., 67
  Samuel, 77
  Sarah R., 67
SNOUFFER
  Ashton, 94
  G. A. T., 94
SNOW
  John, 16
  Savilla, 16
  Sevilla, 16
SOUDER
  Catharine E., 28
  Eliza A., 28
  Eliza Ann, 28
  Emeline, 28
  Emily, 28
  George P., 28
  John, 19, 22, 24
  John W., 28
  Margaret, 28
  Mary, 20
  Michael, 28
  Susan, 28
  Susanna, 28
SPRECKERS
  Martha A., 63
  Samuel, 63
SPRING
  William, 77
STANHOPE
  William, 3, 4
STEADMAN
  Carrie H., 81
  Susan F., 81
STEER
  Isaac E., 8
  James M., 83, 87
  William, 17
  William B., 55
  William E., 87
STEERE
  Isaac, 4, 5
STEPHENSON
  James, 49, 50, 51

John, 49, 50
Josephine, 49, 50
Lloyd, 49
Lloyd B., 50, 51
W. A., 50
STEWART
  A. T., 58
  Charles H., 40
STOCKS
  John H., 77
  Mahlon, 77
  Mary E., 77
  William, 77
STONE
  Elizabeth, 10
  Henrietta, 23
  James, 23
  Samuel S., 22
  Sarah Ann, 23
  Thomas, 23
  William, 92
  William J., 84
STONEBURNER
  Catharine, 43, 44
  Daniel, 43, 44
  Elizabeth, 19, 20
  J. C., 44
  Jacob C., 51
  Jacob Curtis, 19, 20
  John Josiah, 19
  Louisa Ann, 19
  Peter, 43, 44
  Sarah, 44
STOUT
  George W., 71
  John L., 71
STOUTSENBERGER
  Albert C., 41
  Ann E., 37
  Clara, 89
  Elevina T., 41
  Elvina T., 41
  Elwina T., 41
  Emanuel W., 37
  Francis A., 37
  Jacob, 29
  Mary C., 41
  Samuel, 29, 37, 41
  Samuel T., 37
STREAM
  George C., 100
  George W., 43
  Mary Ellen, 43
STRIBLING

C. M., 19
Cecelia M., 19
Francis, 8
STRIDER
  Joseph L., 43
STROUD
  William, 91
STUCK
  Elizabeth, 62
  F. F., 62
  Ferdinando F., 13
  Jane C., 62
  Margaret Ann, 62
  Mary Ellen, 62
  Peter, 13
SULLIVAN
  Anna Belle, 56
  Mary F., 56
  Samuel, 56
  Samuel M., 56
SUMMERS
  Edward, 9
  George, 2, 4
  Richard, 92
  Thomas, 92
SURVICK
  Benjamin, 96
  Carrie, 96
  Mary B., 96
  Nora, 96
SWANK
  Samuel, 77, 100
SWANN
  Sherlock, 103
  Thomas, 103
SWART
  William, 76
TALBOTT
  Henry W., 23
TAVENER
  George, 5
  Hannah V., 30
  Jonah, 30
  Joseph, 12
  Noble R., 30
TAVENNER
  J. Wilmer, 99
  Jonathan, 26
  Lot, 65
  R., 60
TAYLOR
  Albert, 65
  B. F., 53
  Benjamin F., 52, 53, 54

Bernard, 4
Elizabeth, 19
Emma D., 69
H. B., 72
Harriet B., 92
Henry S., 10, 26, 35, 36
Joseph, 57
Lewis, 63
Mahlon, 4, 5
Mahlon K., 9
Mary, 9
Mary J., 75
Mary S., 66
Oscar, 94
Samuel, 5
Samuel Townsend, 66
Stacey, 4
Stacy, 4, 5, 6, 7, 9
Thomas E., 69, 72, 75
Timothy, 14, 21, 23
THOMAS
  A. V., 100
  James, 19
  Jefferson C., 90
  Jonah, 31
  Owen, 31, 94
  Ruth, 31
THOMPSON
  Andrew, 37
  Ann Eliza, 80
  Barbara Cornelia, 80
  Edward, 18
  Elizabeth, 37
  George S., 80
  Hugh, 26, 60
  Hugh S., 96
  Irving P., 96
  Israel, 3, 4
  J. A., 96
  James, 33
  J. Harry, 96
  John T., 95
  Joseph, 80
  L. D., 37
  Mary A., 95
  Pleasant, 3, 4
  R. H., 96
  Sally, 3
  Samuel, 80
  Sarah, 3, 4, 80
  W. D., 96
THORNTON
  Anthony, 3
  Benjamin, 3

Benjamin B., 3
Benjamin Berryman, 3
Charles, 11
Mary, 11
Mary Ann, 11
William, 3
THRASHER
　Margaret E., 22
THRESHER
　Luther A., 22
THROCKMORTON
　Annie C., 72
　John A., 31
　Mason, 72
　Richard McC., 31
　Sarah Mc, 31
THROCMORTON
　Hugh William, 31
TILLET
　Giles E., 56
TILLETT
　Anna Bell, 56
　Henrietta, 56
　John L., 65
　Mary F., 56
　Rubanion, 56
　Samuel M., 56
TIPPETT
　Elizabeth, 94
　Henry, 94
　John W., 94
　Sarah, 94
TITUS
　George, 100
　George W., 81, 97
　John, 77
　John H., 80, 92
　Sydnor, 77
　T. Sydney, 88
　Wilbur F., 88
TORRISON
　Lewis, 60
TRAHERN
　Enos, 26
　James, 26
　Martha A., 26
　Thomas, 26
　William C., 26
TRIPLETT
　___, 1
　Frances, 4
TRITAPOE
　George C., 55
　H. A., 102

William M., 102
TRITTAPOE
　H. A., 100
　Walter T., 100
TRITTIPO
　Eliza, 28
　John, 28
TRITTIPOE
　Ann E., 55
　G. C., 55
TRUNDLE
　Esther, 35
TURLEY
　C. W., 56
TURNER
　Lucy, 101
TYLER
　Charles, 1
　John, 4
　William, 104
　William B., 43
UTTERBACK
　John G., 95
VANDERHOFF
　Henry, 91
VANDEVANTER
　Albert, 19, 20
　Cornelius, 27, 37
　D. H., 100
　G., 20
　Gabriel, 19
　Isaac, 19, 27
　James H., 37
　Mary, 19, 20
　Mary E., 20
　T. H., 87
　Washington, 36
VANDEVENTER
　Gabriel, 96
　J. H., 96
VANSICKLER
　Robert, 65
　Rosa Bell, 83
VERTS
　Henry, 12, 20
　John, 20
　Peter, 12
　William, 12
VIAA
　Cochran, 8
VICKERS
　Thomas, 33
VINCEL
　George, 18

VINNEDGE
　___, 72
VIRTS
　America Elizabeth, 75
　Annie Rachel, 75
　Clara Hannah C., 75
　H., 90
　Henry, 20, 75, 77, 81
　Henry J. J., 75
　Jacob, 75
　John, 12, 20
　John W., 82
　Mary L., 75
　Michael, 59
　Orra J., 75
　Rosa A., 82
　Rosella V., 75
　Virginia, 75
　William, 20
VIRTZ
　Daniel, 36
　Delia, 97
　Elizabeth C., 36
　Ella V., 77
　Henry, 97
　Henry T., 97
　Isaiah, 36
　Jane P., 36
　Margaretta, 36
　Michael, 36
　Peter, 36
　Priscilla, 36
WADE
　John E., 26
　Joseph H., 26
　Robert, 26
WAGENER
　Major, 1
WALKER
　James M., 74, 79
　R. L., 92
WALKERS
　John, 1
WALTER
　James M., 73
WALTMAN
　Emanuel, 9, 18
　Jacob, 9, 11, 18
　John, 9
　Margaret, 18
　Milton, 41
　Rachael, 18
　Samuel, 9
　Susan, 18

WARNER
　Bessie, 103
　F. A., 104
　G. V., 78
　Gabriel, 65
　George, 30
　Malinda E., 88
　Mary E., 88
WASHINGTON
　John A., 22
　Lalla, 67
　Lily, 67
　Rosa, 67
　S. E., 67
　Sally B., 67
　Samuel E., 14, 67
　Sarah J., 13
WATERMAN
　Augustus, 34
WATERS
　Jacob, 9, 14
　Sarah, 11, 12
WATSON
　Josiah, 1
　Moses P., 80
WATTERS
　James, 5
WEADON
　David J., 65
　T. William, 88
WEANING
　Eliza A., 28
　J. O., 28
WEEKS
　Burr, 14
WELLS
　Lillie B., 100
WELSH
　F. G., 93
WENNER
　A. A., 61
　Bessie, 100
　C. A., 61
　C. C., 100
　Emanuel, 22
　John, 13
　John W., 89
　Lydia Jane, 22
　S. E., 67, 100
　Sarah, 22, 67
　Sarah J., 13
　W. W., 22
　William, 21
　William W., 22

LOUDOUN COUNTY, VIRGINIA
GUARDIAN ACCOUNTS
1759-1904

WEST
  Cato, 1
  Charles, 1
WETHERALL
  Nancy C., 22
WHALEY
  C. A., 26
  G., 26
  George L., 26
  James, 16, 17
  John, 17
  Levi, 16, 17
  Mary, 16
  William, 16, 17
WHITACRE
  ___, 62
  John, 49
  R., 62
  R. J., 62
  T., 35
  Thornton, 65
WHITE
  Beniah, 24
  Daniel, 27, 89
  E. V., 71
  Edward, 77
  Frances R., 25
  George Anna S., 84
  George W., 24, 25
  John, 8
  John H., 40
  John K., 84
  Josiah T., 24, 25
  Maria, 23
  Mary E., 24, 25
  Mary Louisa, 84
  R. F., 23
  Rachel, 66
  Randolph, 60
  Richard, 63
  Robert, 25
  Robert A., 84
  Robert J., 84
  Thomas, 24, 25
  Thomas W., 60
WHITEHURST
  Lucretia, 7
WHITLOCK
  Henry, 78, 89
  Henry W., 89
  Mattie E., 78
  Robert T., 89
WHITMORE
  M. H., 100
WIGGINTON
  John, 89
  Presley, 23
WIGHTMAN
  Archabald J., 67
  Joseph, 60
  Joseph M. L., 67
WILDMAN
  C. B., 54, 90
  Enos, 9
  J. W., 54
WILEY
  Annie J., 94
  Charles H., 94
  Charlotte E., 63
  Edgar T., 94
  William, 63
  William Decatur, 63
WILLCOXON
  Elizabeth, 1
WILLFORD
  Dr., 3
WILLIAM
  John, 63
WILLIAMS
  Charles, 13
  H. S., 55
  Henry S., 54, 55
  J. C., 14
  James, 77
  John, 4, 6, 8, 77
  Notley C., 4
  R. N., 102
  Rebecca J., 102
  Syddnah, 55
  Sydnah, 55
  William, 83
WILLIAMSON
  J. P., 102
WILSON
  ___, 6
  John, 1
  John H., 83
  John M., 13, 36
  John T., 7
  Sarah, 26
  Stephen, 4
WINE
  John, 17
WINEGARNER
  Henry, 6
WINN
  George, 2
WIRE
  D., 24
  David, 24
  Margaret, 24
  Martha J., 65
  Martha Jane, 24
  Mary A., 24
  Mary Ann, 24, 65
  Mary Catharine, 24
  Mary Louisa Ann, 20
  Peter, 20, 24, 65
  Peter J., 65
  Samuel W., 24
  Sarah E., 24
  Susan F., 24
  Susan R., 24
  Susannah F., 65
WIRTZ
  Jacob, 13, 14
  John, 13
  Loucinda, 13
  Mary Ann, 13
  Susannah, 13
WOLF
  Henry W., 33
WOOD
  Amanda, 17
  Joseph, 57
  Josiah, 57
  Mary F., 17
  William, 4
WOODS
  Blanch, 97
WORKS
  James W., 79
WORNELL
  Thomas, 4
WORSLEY
  Ann Edwards, 57
  Elizabeth, 57
  Thomas L., 57
  Virginia G., 57
WORTHINGTON
  Joseph, 27, 28
WREN
  James, 7
  Mary, 7
  William, 7
WRENN
  Mary, 7
  William, 7
WRIGHT
  A., 3
  B. Oden, 100
  Beverley, 92
  Edward S., 45
  Elizabeth, 65
  Ella, 65
  Henrietta, 56
  John E., 56
  John L., 19
  Joseph, 92
  Joseph E., 100
  Margaret, 88
  Robert L., 65
  Sarah Ann, 45
YAKEY
  Amanda, 32
  Jane, 31
  Jane A., 31, 32
  Jane America, 32
  John, 31, 32
  John W., 31, 32, 91
  Martin, 31, 32
  Mary, 22
  Minnie Belle, 91
  Simon, 32
  Thomas S., 31, 32, 33
YATES
  William, 2
YELLOTT
  Florence, 90
  R. E., 90
  Virginia, 90
  W. R., 90
YOUNG
  Isaac, 88
  Ruth, 27, 28
  Susannah B., 97

Other Heritage Books by Patricia B. Duncan:

1850 Fairfax County and Loudoun County, Virginia Slave Schedule

1850 Fauquier County, Virginia Slave Schedule

1860 Loudoun County, Virginia Slave Schedule

Clarke County, Virginia Death Register, 1853–1896, with Birth Records, 1855–1856, Entered on Death Register

Clarke County, Virginia Marriages, 1836–1886

Clarke County, Virginia Marriages, 1887–1925

Clarke County, Virginia Will Book Abstracts: Books A–I (1836–1904) and 1A–3C (1841–1913)

Fairfax County, Virginia Birth Register, 1853–1879

Fairfax County, Virginia Birth Register, 1880–1896

Fauquier County, Virginia, Birth Register, 1853–1880

Fauquier County, Virginia, Birth Register, 1881–1896

Fauquier County, Virginia, Marriage Register, 1854–1882

Fauquier County, Virginia, Marriage Register, 1883–1906

Fauquier County, Virginia Death Register, 1853–1896

Hunterdon County, New Jersey 1895 State Census, Part I: Alexandria–Junction

Hunterdon County, New Jersey 1895 State Census, Part II: Kingwood–West Amwell

Genealogical Abstracts from The Lambertville Press, *Lambertville, New Jersey: 4 November 1858 (Vol. 1, Number 1) to 30 October 1861 (Vol. 3, Number 155)*

Genealogical Abstracts from The Democratic Mirror *and* The Mirror, *1857–1879, Loudoun County, Virginia*

Genealogical Abstracts from The Mirror, *1880–1890, Loudoun County, Virginia*

Genealogical Abstracts from The Mirror, *1891–1899, Loudoun County, Virginia*

Genealogical Abstracts from The Mirror, *1900–1919, Loudoun County, Virginia*

Genealogical Abstracts from The Telephone, *1881–1888, Loudoun County, Virginia*

Genealogical Abstracts from The Telephone, *1889–1896, Loudoun County, Virginia*

Jefferson County, [West] Virginia Death Register, 1853–1880

Jefferson County, West Virginia Death Register, 1881–1903

Jefferson County, Virginia 1802–1813 Personal Property Tax Lists

Jefferson County, Virginia 1814–1824 Personal Property Tax Lists

Jefferson County, Virginia 1825–1841 Personal Property Tax Lists

1810–1840 Loudoun County, Virginia Federal Population Census Index

1860 Loudoun County, Virginia Federal Population Census Index

1870 Loudoun County, Virginia Federal Population Census Index

Abstracts from Loudoun County, Virginia Guardian Accounts: Books A–H, 1759–1904

Abstracts of Loudoun County, Virginia Register of Free Negroes, 1844–1861

Index to Loudoun County, Virginia Land Deed Books A–Z, 1757–1800

Index to Loudoun County, Virginia Land Deed Books 2A–2M, 1800–1810

Index to Loudoun County, Virginia Land Deed Books 2N–2U, 1811–1817

Index to Loudoun County, Virginia Land Deed Books 2V–3D, 1817–1822

Index to Loudoun County, Virginia Land Deed Books 3E–3M, 1822–1826

Index to Loudoun County, Virginia Land Deed Books 3N–3V, 1826–1831

Index to Loudoun County, Virginia Land Deed Books 3W–4D, 1831–1835

Index to Loudoun County, Virginia Land Deed Books 4E–4N, 1835–1840

Index to Loudoun County, Virginia Land Deed Books 4O–4V, 1840–1846

Loudoun County, Virginia Birth Register, 1853–1879

Loudoun County, Virginia Birth Register, 1880–1896

Loudoun County, Virginia Clerks Probate Records Book 1 (1904–1921) and Book 2 (1922–1938)

Loudoun County, Virginia Marriages after 1850, Volume 1, 1851–1880 (with Elizabeth R. Frain)

Loudoun County, Virginia Partially Proven Deeds

Loudoun County, Virginia 1800–1810 Personal Property Taxes

Loudoun County, Virginia 1826–1834 Personal Property Taxes

Loudoun County, Virginia Will Book Abstracts, Books A–Z, Dec. 1757–Jun. 1841

Loudoun County, Virginia Will Book Abstracts, Books 2A–3C, Jun. 1841–Dec. 1879 and Superior Court Books A and B, 1810–1888

Loudoun County, Virginia Will Book Index, 1757–1946

Genealogical Abstracts from The Brunswick Herald, *Brunswick, Maryland: Mar. 6 1891–Dec. 28 1894*

Genealogical Abstracts from The Brunswick Herald, *Brunswick, Maryland: Jan. 4 1895–Dec. 30 1898*

Genealogical Abstracts from The Brunswick Herald, *Brunswick, Maryland: Jan. 6 1899–Dec. 26 1902*

Genealogical Abstracts from The Brunswick Herald, *Brunswick, Maryland: Jan. 2 1903–June 29 1906*

Genealogical Abstracts from The Brunswick Herald, *Brunswick, Maryland: July 6 1906–Feb. 25 1910*

CD: *Fairfax County, Virginia Personal Property Tax List, 1782–1850*

CD: *Loudoun County, Virginia Order Books: K–W, 1787–1803*

CD: *Loudoun County, Virginia Personal Property Tax List, 1782–1850*

www.ingramcontent.com/pod-product-compliance
Lightning Source LLC
Chambersburg PA
CBHW081133170426
43197CB00017B/2852